comments from Sunday 12/11

add Setiya
  ↓ compare him to Velleman

Velleman

2. The claim in 2 - desires can't be reason for
   acting in evaluative sense

c

identify different objections

separate general thesis: cognitivist
              claims what desire/
              reason for action, no
              evaluation

    in support of general thesis
        - desire not analogous to belief

1. bad way: explicit value judgement
      ⌐ implicit judgment of Dot
                              ↓
                        more plausible
how does Dot support cognitivist

          Stocker, where you don't care

Desire, Practical Reason, and the Good

Raz: just revised version

how Raz allows for perversity

1. Setiya + compare strategies
   + Setiya objections √ does
      not include

2. Does Raz address the objection

should have 3 objections + how
Raz responds.

*Raz worry: not—moved by counter
            examples...? Dubious
            —so narrow is trivial
            —GoG should cover

Desire, Practical Reason, and the Good

EDITED BY SERGIO TENENBAUM

2010

OXFORD
UNIVERSITY PRESS

Oxford University Press, Inc., publishes works that further
Oxford University's objective of excellence
in research, scholarship, and education.

Oxford   New York
Auckland   Cape Town   Dar es Salaam   Hong Kong   Karachi
Kuala Lumpur   Madrid   Melbourne   Mexico City   Nairobi
New Delhi   Shanghai   Taipei   Toronto

With offices in
Argentina   Austria   Brazil   Chile   Czech Republic   France   Greece
Guatemala   Hungary   Italy   Japan   Poland   Portugal   Singapore
South Korea   Switzerland   Thailand   Turkey   Ukraine   Vietnam

Library of Congress Cataloging-in-Publication Data
Desire, practical reason, and the good / Sergio Tenenbaum, ed.
p. cm.
ISBN 978-0-19-538244-0
1. Good and evil. 2. Practical reason. 3. Desire (Philosophy)
I. Tenenbaum, Sergio, 1964—
BJ1401.D46 2009
170—dc22   2009036349

1 3 5 7 9 8 6 4 2
Printed in the United States of America
on acid-free paper

Acknowledgments

I would like to thank the Jackman Humanities Institute at the University of Toronto for sponsoring the workshop "Desire, Practical Reason, and the Good: Classical and Contemporary Perspectives," in which early drafts of most of the papers in the book were presented, and the Centre for Ethics at the University of Toronto for providing additional support and funding for the workshop. I would also like to thank Peter Ohlin for all his advice and encouragement throughout the editorial process.

Contents

Desire, Practical Reason, and the Good

1

Introduction

Sergio Tenenbaum

Questions about the relation between desire, practical reason, and the good lie at the forefront of moral psychology. In their efforts to explain the structure of practical reason and the nature of ordinary action explanations, many philosophers assign a central role either to the notion of desire or to the notion of good. However, philosophers disagree sharply over how we are supposed to understand the notions of 'desire' and 'good,' how these notions relate, and whether *both* play a significant and independent role in practical reason. One central debate concerns the "Guise of the Good" thesis—the view that desire (or perhaps intention, or intentional action) always aims at the good. Are there perverse desires, desires that aim at certain things simply because they are bad? And if it is true that desire does not always aim at the good, or even, at least some times, aim at the bad, does it mean that practical reason, more generally, need not aim at the good?

Not only is there controversy over the notion of desire and its relation to the good, but even after having taken a position on whether a notion of the good plays a central role in motivation and practical reason, philosophers disagree about the relevant notion of good. Is it a purely formal notion, or does it involve a substantive conception of the good? Is the primary notion, the notion of the good for a particular agent, or the notion of good *simpliciter*? Does the relevant notion of good make essential appeal to human nature, or would it in principle extend to all rational beings? While these questions are central in contemporary work in ethics, practical reason, and philosophy of action, they are not new; similar issues were discussed in the ancient period. The book aims to bring together "systematic" and more historically oriented work on these issues.

Matthew Evans looks into the Socratic arguments in defense of the claim that an agent cannot pursue a course of action that he knows to be worse than another course of action available to him. By presenting a careful analysis of the Socratic arguments on this point, and an evaluation of their plausibility, Evans throws light on the central assumptions and argumentative burdens of both the ancient and contemporary debates about the plausibility of the Guise of the Good thesis.

Plato indeed seems to hold at least some version of the Guise of the Good thesis: he often claims that human desire is for the good. However, it is not exactly clear what he means by such claims. In fact, Plato seems to waver between two apparently incompatible versions of the thesis; a view in which desire is for the *apparent* good, and a view in which desire is for the *actual* good. Rachel Barney argues that the Guise of the Good thesis expresses a view of desire according to which all our desires aim to respond to real value we perceive in the world. Both apparently incompatible claims are two facets of the same view; in particular, they express Plato's commitment to a cognitivist or objectivist view of desire, a view in which desire is world-guided and capable of being in error.

Aristotle, like Plato, seems to accept a version of the Guise of the Good thesis; in fact, he seems to accept a particularly strong version of the thesis, a version that extends all the way to nonrational appetites. It seems that any interpretation of such a view will either identify the good with the object of desire (thus making the thesis trivial) or be committed to the view that all appetites, even the appetites of the brutes, include the representation of a certain object as being good, a view that seems clearly false. Jessica Moss defends an interpretation of Aristotle under which he accepts a version of the Guise of the Good thesis that is neither trivial nor obviously false. According to Moss, all desires are based on a "pleasurable perception," a perception of the object of desire as having value. Since these perceptions are a genuine mode of value awareness, the claim that all desires are based on such perceptions is certainly not trivial. At the same time, such a view need not be taken to commit Aristotle to an implausible, overly intellectualist view about the nature of nonrational appetite.

Many contemporary attacks on the Guise of the Good thesis have relied on counterexamples (or purported counterexamples) to the thesis. Kieran Setiya argues against this view not by adding to the list of counterexamples, but by trying to show that the Guise of the Good thesis depends more generally on a false view about reasons for actions. According to Setiya, the thesis is most plausibly understood as a claim about the nature of reasons; in particular, it amounts to a claim that reasons for desires must present their object as good. However, Setiya argues that so understood the thesis is false; a proper understanding of agency leads us to the conclusion that actions can be done for reasons that are not regarded to be good and that we need not show the agent to be in any way approximating an ideal of rationality.

If Setiya tries to criticize the Guise of the Good thesis not through counterexamples but on the strength of more general views about the nature of agency, similarly Joseph Raz and Sebastian Rödl each aim to provide a defense of the thesis based not on the strangeness of valueless pursuits (such as Anscombe's famous case of the desire for a saucer of mud), but on general considerations about the nature of practical rationality and agency. Raz argues that an intention must be constituted in part by a belief of the agent that explains what the agent saw in the action that he undertook. But this is exactly what the Guise of the Good thesis claims; namely, that an agent's intention must include a belief about the value of the action. However, Raz does not ignore putative counterexamples; he tries to show how they lead to important revisions of the Guise of the Good thesis and explains how the thesis can withstand the challenge of various actions that seem to constitute exceptions to the thesis. Rödl tries to understand the role of the representation of the good in intentional action. For Rödl, "good" is not part of the content of a mental state that precedes intentional action, but rather the formal object of the will; it expresses the form of a first-personal productive thought that is the conclusion of practical reason. In other words, the good expresses the form that any act of the will must take as a conclusion of practical reason and the cause of my action.

Matthew Boyle and Douglas Lavin also defend the Guise of the Good thesis on a principled basis, but on their view the original *locus* of the relevant notion of the good is not in rational agency but in *self*-movement, a notion that applies more generally to living things. According to Boyle and Lavin, explanations of self-movement necessarily appeal to a notion of the good of the living being, but in the case of rational beings this general form of teleological explanation can also take the form of an explanation in which a self-conscious animal acts on her conception of her own good.

My own chapter does not try to defend the Guise of the Good thesis per se but aims to show how the thesis can single out one of two seemingly plausible candidates to be that which all desire aims at: what is good *simpliciter* and what is good for the agent. I argue while that the Guise of the Good thesis needs a single "all-out" evaluative notion, both these notions seem plausible candidates to take this role; I also argue against previous attempts to reduce one to the other. What I maintain is that good *simpliciter* is the only genuinely all-out evaluative notion.

All these chapters depend on the assumption that something important hangs on the question of whether we accept or reject the Guise of the Good thesis. Philip Clark argues that this is not true; according to Clark, if we accept the claim that action is made intelligible by relating it to certain guises of the good, to *kinds* of things that are good, we can gain all that there is to be gained from the Guise of the Good thesis without having to settle the question of its correctness.

2

A Partisan's Guide to Socratic Intellectualism

Matthew Evans

I

Most people think that it is possible, if not common, for us to do things that we know are better left undone. But in a celebrated passage of Plato's *Protagoras* (351b–58e) Socrates argues otherwise. His claim, roughly put, is that we are capable of acting incorrectly only if and only when we *fail to recognize that we are* acting incorrectly. If he is right about this, then we could never do anything we knew was better left undone, since our having this knowledge would always be sufficient to prevent us from making any such practical mistakes. So either most people are wrong about the power of knowledge over action, or the argument Socrates gives us in the *Protagoras*—which I will call **the Knowledge Argument**—is unsound.

Of all the counterintuitive arguments in the so-called Socratic dialogues, this one is probably the most famous. Historians have extensively examined its structure, its motivation, and its place within the broader sweep of Socratic and Platonic moral psychology.[1] As a result of this, perhaps, many contemporary philosophers of action now feel compelled to mention it, if not to scrutinize it, when addressing themselves to the general topic of practical irrationality.[2] But in recent years the historians and the philosophers have begun to diverge in their assessments of the argument's intrinsic merit. While most of the philosophers have come to agree that it is implausible, either in whole or in part,[3] many of the historians have defended it against this very charge, and have implied that the argument's detractors are, as a rule, either exegetically misguided or philosophically shallow.[4] Sadly, these two camps seem to have little if any sustained interaction with each other. So it is hardly surprising to find, in the recent literature on the subject, an unresolved and (largely) unengaged dispute between the majority of contemporary philosophers on the one hand and a cadre of devoted historians on the other.

The purpose of this chapter is to get the dispute back on track, by providing both parties with a reliable guide to the issues that continue to divide them. Though I cannot expect to accomplish this task without offering my own (unavoidably controversial) interpretation of the Knowledge Argument, I will not attempt to develop or defend that interpretation in much detail here. Instead I will focus my attention on the various ways in which the Knowledge Argument, as I interpret it, might be challenged, defended, and refined. Often (but not always) I will repress my inclination to take sides in the various confrontations I provoke, since my primary goal here is not to advance the cause of either party, but to give both of them a better sense of the dialectical territory they occupy. If I am successful in this regard, then by the end of the chapter we will have achieved a better understanding of the various ways in which their dispute might be sharpened, advanced, and perhaps even resolved.

II

Parties to the debate over the Knowledge Argument can be assigned to opposing camps based on their responses to the following claim, which Socrates repeatedly attributes to the Many (οἱπολλοί):

Weakness: There is some agent, some act, and some time such that, at that time, the agent
(W1) knows [or believes][5] that forgoing the act is better than doing it;
(W2) is able to forgo it; and yet
(W3) does it.[6]

The two simplest responses to Weakness yield two opposing schools of thought: the view that Weakness is *true* can be called **Emotionalism**, and the view that Weakness is *false* can be called **Intellectualism**.[7] Understood in these terms, then, the Knowledge Argument is designed to support Intellectualism and to undermine Emotionalism.[8] But how exactly is this argument supposed to work?

As Socrates emphasizes at the outset of the discussion, the Emotionalist bears an important explanatory burden that the Intellectualist manages to avoid entirely (352d7–8; cf. 354e5–8). This is because the phenomenon described in Weakness is (at least superficially) quite puzzling: if the agent is able to forgo the act, and if she knows that forgoing it is better than doing it, then why on earth does she do it? Normally the conditions specified in W1 and W2 would suffice to explain why she *forgoes* the act, not why she *does* it. Since this more straightforward explanation obviously does not apply in (purported) cases of Weakness, the Emotionalist needs to provide some alternative explanation—one that manages to show how the conditions specified in W1, W2, and W3 could all be satisfied at the same time.[9] And if the Emotionalist cannot provide any such explanation, then the Intellectualist will secure a major dialectical advantage.[10]

But most Emotionalists are confident that they can provide the required explanation. The Many, for example, are said (by Socrates) to propose something along the following lines:

> **Hedonic Defeat:** In each case of Weakness, the agent does what she does because she is overcome by pleasure.[11]

If this proposal succeeds, then the Many can use it to discharge the Emotionalist's explanatory burden. But Socrates suspects—and then proceeds to argue—that it does not succeed. It fails, in his view, not because agents in general cannot be overcome by pleasure in any way at all, but because agents *who know that forgoing an act is better than doing it and are able to forgo it* cannot be overcome by pleasure *in this particular way*.[12] His conclusion, in other words, is that the explanation embedded in Hedonic Defeat is actually inconsistent with the conjunction of W1 and W2, so that the Many cannot discharge the Emotionalist's explanatory burden after all.

The argument for this conclusion consists of three key premises, the first of which is a rather extreme version of ethical hedonism. This premise, if true, would permit (among other things) the intersubstitution of "more pleasant" and "better" in epistemic contexts such as "she knows that eating chocolate is more pleasant than eating glass" and "she believes that running is better than drinking."[13] It can formulated roughly as follows:

> **Analytic Hedonism:** Knowing that x is better than y is the same as knowing that x is more pleasant than y.[14]

The next premise of the argument is a claim about what happens to agents when they are overcome by pleasure. Socrates thinks that if an agent does an act when she is able to forgo it, then she does it because she "chooses" or "selects" (λαμβάνω) the option of doing it "instead of" or "in exchange for" (ἀντί) the option of forgoing it (355d1–e3).[15] Then he implies that if she chooses the first option instead of the second *because of the pleasure promised by the first*, then it must be that she makes this choice because she believes—on the basis of a (possibly very crude) comparative hedonic assessment—that the first option is more pleasant than the second (356a8–c1). Thus Socrates appears to be proposing something like the following:

> **The Belief Constraint:** If an agent does an act because she is overcome by pleasure, then either she is not able to forgo it or she does it because she believes that doing it is more pleasant than forgoing it.

The third (and final) premise of the argument is best understood as a claim about the *cognitive unity* of the knowledgeable agent. In his fascinating discussion of "the power of appearance" (ἡ τοῦ φαινομένου δύναμις), Socrates strongly suggests that a knowledgeable agent's comparative assessment of practical options is *unified* in the sense that, if she is faced with two different options and assesses the first as more F (for some property F) than the second, then she *does not also* assess the *second* as more F than the *first* (356c5–57b4).[16] So it looks as though Socrates is making an important assumption here, namely:

> **Cognitive Unity**: If an agent knows that x is more F than y, then she does not believe that y is more F than x.

Now these three premises, in conjunction with Hedonic Defeat, do seem to entail that there are no cases of Weakness. To see why, recall that if Hedonic Defeat is true then in purported cases of Weakness the agent does what she does because she is overcome by pleasure. From this and the Belief Constraint it follows that *either* the agent is unable to forgo the act *or* she believes that doing it is more pleasant than forgoing it. Since in purported cases of Weakness the agent is (by definition) *not* unable to forgo the act, it follows that in these cases the agent believes that doing the act is more pleasant than forgoing it. By Cognitive Unity, then, the agent does not *know* that *forgoing* the act is more pleasant than *doing* it. Therefore, by Analytic Hedonism, the agent does not know that forgoing it is *better* than doing it. But in purported cases of Weakness the agent (by definition) *does* know that forgoing the act is better than doing it. Thus there are no cases of Weakness, and Intellectualism is true. Or so at least the Knowledge Argument purports to show.[17]

In order to defeat this argument, the Emotionalist has three different strategies to choose from. The first is to show that one of its three premises—Analytic Hedonism, the Belief Constraint, or Cognitive Unity—is false; the second is to show that these three premises, in conjunction with Hedonic Defeat, do not entail Intellectualism; and the third is to show that Hedonic Defeat can be abandoned in favor of an alternative explanation—one that does not, in conjunction with the argument's three premises, entail Intellectualism. In what follows I will consider the prospects of success for the first two of these strategies, starting with the second.[18]

III

One possible problem with the Knowledge Argument as it stands is that terms like "more pleasant" and "better," which appear repeatedly throughout the argument, are ambiguous enough to inspire bad inferences. There are several potential sources of ambiguity here, in fact, but I want to focus my attention on just one of them.[19] The ambiguity I have in mind emerges most clearly from the distinction Socrates himself draws between (what I will call) the *internal, external,* and *comprehensive* pleasantness (or goodness) of an action (or omission) (353c1–54e2; cf. 351e1). The **internal** pleasantness of an action is how pleasant it is "intrinsically" ($\dot{\epsilon}\nu$ $\alpha\dot{\upsilon}\tau\tilde{\omega}$, 354c8–d1, 354d6), "immediately" ($\dot{\epsilon}\nu$ $\tau\tilde{\omega}$ $\pi\alpha\rho\alpha\chi\rho\tilde{\eta}\mu\alpha$, 353d1, 354b1) or "proximately" ($\dot{\epsilon}\gamma\gamma\dot{\upsilon}\varsigma$, 356a8–b8); the **external** pleasantness of an action is how pleasant it is "in consequence" (ἀποτελευτᾷ/, 353e7, 354b6), "at a later time" (εἰς τὸν ὕστερον, 353d4, 354b2–3), or "remotely" (πόρρω, 356a8–b8); and the **comprehensive** pleasantness of an action is the sum of its internal and external pleasantness (354c5–e2; cf. 356a8–c2).[20] Consider, for instance, the case of invasive dental work: although avoiding it is more *internally* pleasant than receiving it, receiving it is more *externally* pleasant than avoiding it; and, since the external pleasantness of receiving it is greater than the internal pleasantness of avoiding it, receiving it is more *comprehensively* pleasant than avoiding it. This, in crude form, is the framework of hedonic assessment that Socrates himself seems to recommend.

Once this framework is in place, however, an Emotionalist could insist that the Belief Constraint—i.e., the premise that an agent who does something because she is overcome by pleasure *either* is unable to forgo it *or* believes that doing it is more pleasant than forgoing it—is true only if "more pleasant" here is understood to mean "more *internally* pleasant" as opposed to "more *externally* pleasant" or "more *comprehensively* pleasant."[21] (From now on I will call this an *internal* reading of the phrase, as opposed to an *external* or *comprehensive* reading of it.) According to this particular Emotionalist, it is absurd to think that, when you (freely) yield to a habit because you are overcome by pleasure, you believe that yielding to it is more *externally* or *comprehensively* pleasant than fighting it off; on the contrary, what you believe (if anything) is that yielding to it is more *internally* pleasant than fighting it off, and this is the one and only belief that motivates you to yield. On this view, then, the Belief Constraint stands or falls with an internal reading of "more pleasant" as it occurs in that premise.[22]

Can the Intellectualist permit the Belief Constraint to be interpreted in this way? It is tempting to think not. For consider what happens if we follow this suggestion and give "more pleasant" in the Belief Constraint an internal reading. In that case we will want to give "more pleasant" in Analytic Hedonism the same reading, since otherwise the argument will be grossly invalid.[23] But then it looks like we will want to give "better" in Analytic Hedonism an internal reading as well, since otherwise Analytic Hedonism will be manifestly false. (Knowing that x is *more internally pleasant* than y is clearly not the same as knowing that x is *comprehensively better* than y.) Yet if we give "better" in Analytic Hedonism an internal reading, then we will want to give "better" *in Weakness* an internal reading, since otherwise (again) the argument will be invalid. Little by little, then, we will be led to give every occurrence of both "more pleasant" and "better" the same, internal reading.

But now the Intellectualist appears to be in trouble. For it seems obvious that no one—not the Emotionalist, not the Intellectualist, and certainly not Socrates—thinks that in the relevant cases the agent knows that forgoing the act is *internally* better than doing it. Indeed, everyone apparently agrees that, if the agent believes anything at all, she believes that *doing* the act is internally better than *forgoing* it. (For example, you believe that satisfying your thirst is internally better than frustrating it, even if you know that satisfying it will result in your contracting dysentery.) The real disagreement here, as it is normally understood anyway, turns on whether the purportedly weak agent knows that forgoing the act is *comprehensively* better than doing it. So at this stage of the dialectic the Emotionalist might well be entitled to claim that, no matter how "more pleasant" in the Belief Constraint is interpreted, the Knowledge Argument fails. If it is given a comprehensive reading, then the Belief Constraint is false; and if it is given an internal reading, then the argument is either invalid (if "better" in Weakness is given a comprehensive reading) or irrelevant to the underlying debate (if "better" in Weakness is given an internal reading).

The Intellectualist's most obvious line of response at this point would be to maintain that the Belief Constraint is true even if "more pleasant" (as it appears in that premise) is given a comprehensive reading. To take this line is to insist, in effect, that when you (freely) yield to a habit because you are overcome by pleasure, you are motivated to yield to it because you believe that yielding to it is more *comprehensively* pleasant than fighting it off. Socrates himself seems to take this line at 356a8–c3, suggesting that one must always choose whichever of the available options wins out in your comparative assessment of their comprehensive pleasantness.[24] But from what I can tell he has no real argument to back this up.

The closest he gets to an argument is at 356a7–8, where he responds to an objection (from the Many) to the effect that an option's internal pleasantness somehow "far surpasses" (πολὺ διαφέρει) its external pleasantness. His reply to this objection seems to consist of two claims, the first explicit and the second implicit: (C1) an option's internal pleasantness does not count more toward its comprehensive pleasantness than its external pleasantness does; and (C2) if an option's internal pleasantness far surpasses its external pleasantness, then its internal pleasantness counts more toward its comprehensive pleasantness than its external pleasantness does. The problem with this reply is that, even if C1 is true,[25] C2 is either false or question begging. For the Emotionalist can simply respond that the phrase "far surpasses" (as it is used in the objection) does not mean "is more pleasant than" but rather (something like) "is more motivationally effective than." And up to this point Socrates has said nothing to support the idea that, if an option's internal pleasantness *is more motivationally effective than* its external pleasantness, then its internal pleasantness counts more toward its comprehensive pleasantness than its external pleasantness does. So I take it that he gets no genuine purchase on his opponent here.[26]

Perhaps the Intellectualist could maintain that, if an agent knows that some option A is more comprehensively pleasant than some other option B, then her choosing B over A on the basis of B's surpassing pleasantness would be somehow unintelligible or absurd. On a view of this sort, it would make no sense for her to choose B over A, since her choice is based on a comparative assessment of the pleasantness of the two options, and since she knows that A is more comprehensively pleasant than B. But this line of reasoning obviously hinges on the assumption that every motivationally effective assessment of pleasantness is an assessment of *comprehensive* pleasantness. And this assumption strikes me as dubious. Is it really impossible to understand how one's assessment of the internal pleasantness of procrastinating, say, might be more motivationally effective than one's assessment of the comprehensive pleasantness of procrastinating? This particular Intellectualist seems to think so, but I have trouble seeing why. So even if the Emotionalist responds to this whole line of thought with nothing but flat-footed disagreement, my sense is that the result is a stalemate at best.[27]

Does the Intellectualist have any other options here? I believe so. In fact I suspect that the Intellectualist can turn the tables on the Emotionalist in a striking and dramatic fashion. Recall that one of the assumptions underlying the present stalemate is that, in cases of Weakness, the agent does not know that forgoing the act is internally better than doing it, since forgoing the act *is not* internally better than doing it. But what happens if we withdraw this last assumption? In that case we could give "better" in Weakness an internal reading without making the argument irrelevant to the debate, since the terms of the debate have just been changed to accommodate that very reading. On this proposal, then, clause W1 in Weakness should be understood to mean that the agent "knows that forgoing the act is better—*either comprehensively or internally*—than doing it." With this clarification in place, the Intellectualist's prospects are vastly improved. Instead of claiming that your choices cannot be based on your assessments of internal goodness alone, the Intellectualist now claims only that your choices *must* be based *either* on your assessments of comprehensive goodness *or* on your assessments of internal goodness.[28]

It is tempting to assume that the Intellectualist, by making this move, simply changes the subject and obscures the debate. But I think we should resist this temptation. For the Intellectualist's core view is that, if you know which of the available options is best, then you will choose that option (if you choose any). It is not *essential* to this position that "best" be understood as "comprehensively best." Moreover, there are plenty of Emotionalists who will deny Weakness even on this new, expanded reading. These Emotionalists will appeal to cases in which the agent fails to choose what she knows to be the comprehensively better option, even though she *also* knows it to be the *internally* better option. One such agent might be the depressive, who knows that going for a run is both internally and comprehensively better than staying in bed, but stays in bed anyway. Another might be the sadist, who knows that abstaining from torture is both internally and comprehensively better than indulging in it, but indulges in it anyway. Are there really any agents like this? Some Emotionalists, at least, will say yes. Thus the dispute continues. The difference now, though, is that the Intellectualist is in a much better position. For there are many in the audience who will maintain their Emotionalism if "better" is given a rigidly comprehensive reading, but will switch sides otherwise, having been convinced—by philosophers such as Anscombe (1957), Davidson (1980), and de Sousa (1974), perhaps—that even the depressive and the sadist must see *something* good about the options they choose.

What we have discovered, then, is that the Emotionalist has no easy path to victory via the proposed ambiguity of "more pleasant" and "better." If the Intellectualist follows Socrates all the way down the line and demands that these terms be given a comprehensive reading, then the Emotionalist is in good shape; but if the Intellectualist abandons this demand and allows the relevant terms to be given an internal reading as well, then the Emotionalist is put on the defensive. Of course this by itself will provide no immunity against various independent attacks on the Belief Constraint, Analytic Hedonism, or Cognitive Unity. But it will provide a certain limited immunity against the charge that these three premises, in conjunction with Hedonic Defeat, do not entail Intellectualism. So let us assume that the Intellectualist has made the recommended move, and that this particular ambiguity is no longer a significant source of concern for the argument's defenders. Let us also assume, for simplicity's sake, that from now on "more pleasant" and "better" are to be interpreted without qualification, so that no other such ambiguity can be used to harass the argument from a different direction.[29] With these assumptions in place, I believe we are ready to turn our attention to the argument's three premises, starting with Analytic Hedonism.

IV

It is pretty obvious that Analytic Hedonism is false. To see why, consider whether someone, somewhere, might choose a burdensome life of political activism over a luxurious life of political apathy, knowing all along that the former is both better and less pleasant than the latter. If this scenario is so much as *possible*—and it certainly *seems* to be possible—then Analytic Hedonism is false. Of course a stubborn Intellectualist might argue that appearances are deceptive in this case, and that, in fact, this life of luxury is either better or less pleasant than this life of toil. But it is not clear that any such argument could work, since nearly all of us—including Socrates himself in other dialogues—think that goodness and pleasantness can come apart in this way.[30] The closest Socrates gets to an argument in the *Protagoras* is an obscure proposal to the effect that the terms "good" and "pleasant" are synonymous, or that the concepts *good* and *pleasant* are equivalent (e.g., 355b3–c1).[31] Either of these proposals, if true, would probably be sufficient to rule out the relevant scenarios. But it is hard to see why anyone already inclined to accept the possibility of these scenarios would find either proposal any less dubious than Analytic Hedonism itself. So unless the Intellectualist can devise a revolutionary argument to the effect that scenarios of this sort aren't really possible after all, the Emotionalist is entitled to assume that the Knowledge Argument's very first premise is a lost cause.

Can the Intellectualist afford to abandon Analytic Hedonism in favor of something more plausible? Socrates himself seems to think not, since he repeatedly suggests that the case against the Emotionalist stands or falls with this premise (e.g., 354d7–55a5). But if that is what he thinks, then I believe he is mistaken.[32] For it seems clear, on reflection at least, that Analytic Hedonism is much stronger than it needs to be. Its primary function in the argument, remember, is to combine with the other two premises (and Hedonic Defeat) to establish that Weakness is false. But this purpose is served just as well by the following, much less ambitious claim:

> **Hedonic Evaluation**: If an agent does an act because she believes that doing it is more pleasant than forgoing it, then she believes that doing it is *better* than forgoing it *in virtue of being* more pleasant than forgoing it.

According to Hedonic Evaluation, an agent who chooses a particular practical option on grounds of pleasantness must somehow believe *not only* that this option is better than the others *but also* that this option's pleasantness is *what makes it* better than the others. Obviously this is a much weaker claim than Analytic Hedonism. But it still entails—in conjunction with the Belief Constraint—that if an agent does an act because she is overcome by pleasure, then she believes that doing it is better than forgoing it.[33] And this, in conjunction with Cognitive Unity, entails that she does not know that forgoing it is better than doing it. Thus Hedonic Evaluation is just as capable of carrying the argument to its conclusion, but is not nearly as vulnerable to Emotionalist attack. From this I conclude that Socrates is wrong about the relative importance of Analytic Hedonism, and that the clever Intellectualist will gladly abandon it in favor of Hedonic Evaluation.[34] But while Hedonic Evaluation is harder to deny than Analytic Hedonism, it is far from undeniable. Resistance to it runs deep, in fact, and by exploring this resistance we will arrive at what I take to be the first real crux of the Intellectualism debate.

The problem with Hedonic Evaluation, from the standpoint of its critics, is that it cannot accommodate the possibility of an agent whose choices aim at something other than the good. They see it as just one of a family of views, all of which underestimate the power of agents to base their choices on entirely good-independent considerations. Thus the Emotionalist who denies Hedonic Evaluation will almost certainly also deny the claim that gives this premise both its structure and its rationale:

> **The Evaluation Thesis**: If an agent does an act because she believes that doing it is more F than forgoing it, then she believes that doing it is *better* than forgoing it *in virtue of being* more F than forgoing it.[35]

If this claim is correct, then it is impossible for you to commit an action on the basis of considerations that, by your own lights, do not make it something good to do. On this (familiarly Socratic) view, then, deliberate action is always performed under what is sometimes called "the guise of the good."[36] Those who reject this view maintain, on the contrary, that it is possible for you to do something just because you believe that doing it is more cruel, more outrageous, more beautiful, more glamorous, more eccentric, or more *whatever* than forgoing it—even though you are not at all convinced that doing it is any *better* than forgoing it *in virtue of being* any of those things. This disagreement, which turns entirely on whether or not the Evaluation Thesis is true, is what I take to be the first genuine crux of the debate.

Although the Evaluation Thesis is widely endorsed, especially among the ancients, one might wonder whether it really deserves to be so popular. Many philosophers have recently raised doubts about it, and have buttressed these doubts with a wide variety of intuitive counterexamples.[37] One of the most famous of these is the case of Satan, a monomaniacally perverse agent who does an act *only if he does not* believe that doing it is better than forgoing it. Obviously there can be no such agent if the Evaluation Thesis is true, and this alone strikes many philosophers— myself included—as a powerful reason to deny it. But not everyone responds in the same way to cases such as this. Indeed, there are plenty of philosophers who continue to maintain that, when an agent acts on the basis of her beliefs, then she is intelligible as an agent only if she believes that committing the act is somehow better than forgoing it.[38] For otherwise, they argue, the agent's decision to commit the act would make no sense. On this view, then, Satan would be intelligible as an agent only if he saw something good about his actions—their rebelliousness perhaps.

The upshot of all this, I think, is that the Evaluation Thesis is not obviously false. It has attracted many defenders, and there are formidable minds on both sides. So I doubt that the Emotionalist can achieve a clear and decisive victory on this front alone. But actually I suspect that such a victory would have been unsatisfying anyway. To see this, let us introduce some new terminology. Let us call an act **belief-governed** if the agent does it because she believes that doing it is more F than forgoing it; and let us call an act **good-oriented** if the agent does it because she believes that doing it is *better* than forgoing it. With this new terminology in hand we can see that the Intellectualist's most fundamental conviction is not that all unforced acts are *good-oriented*, but that all unforced acts are *belief-governed*. It is this second conviction, not the first, that lies behind the familiar Intellectualist slogan that *knowledge is sufficient to rule a person* (cf. 352c3–4); and it is this second conviction, not the first, that survives (or would survive) the collapse of the Evaluation Thesis. For even if this thesis were decisively refuted, that would have no impact whatsoever on those who insist that all unforced actions are belief-governed, but *do not* insist that all belief-governed actions are good-oriented. According to this hybrid view—which I will call **Disenchanted** Intellectualism—it is possible for an agent (such as Satan) to aim at the bad in his actions, but *what it is* for an agent to aim at the bad in her actions is for *her beliefs about* the bad *to govern* her actions. Thus it is not possible for Satan to act against his knowledge of the bad, unless he is somehow forced to do so. And this is a recognizably Intellectualist conclusion, albeit one that Socrates and many other Intellectualists would not immediately recognize.[39]

It is clear, then, that the Emotionalist cannot secure a fully satisfying victory by attacking only the first premise of the Knowledge Argument. The Intellectualist who accepts a modified version of that premise holds up fairly well under pressure, and the Intellectualist who *denies* this very same version of it escapes completely unscathed. So let us turn our attention now to the argument's other two premises—the Belief Constraint and Cognitive Unity—and see whether the Emotionalist's prospects for a decisive victory improve on either of these fronts.

V

According to the Belief Constraint, an agent who does something because she is overcome by pleasure either has no choice in the matter, or is acting on the basis of her beliefs about the pleasantness of what she is doing. Like Hedonic Evaluation, this claim seems to derive both its structure and its power from a more general thesis—one that does not rely on any particular claims about pleasure or pleasantness. This thesis can be formulated roughly as follows:

> **The Belief Thesis**: If an agent does an act because she is overcome by something, then either she is not able to forgo it or she does it because she believes that doing it is more F than forgoing it.[40]

To accept this thesis is, in effect, to accept that all unforced acts are belief-governed. And, as we have seen, it is this claim above all that unites every Intellectualist, Disenchanted or not, in the conviction that one's practical knowledge is always sufficient to determine one's practical choices.

Many Emotionalists will reject the Belief Thesis on the grounds that being overcome by something—pleasure, perhaps, but also pain, anger, love, fear, or whatever (352b7–8)—is neither a matter of *believing* something, nor a matter of *being forced by* something. Rather it is a matter of basing one's choices (and hence one's unforced actions) on impulses, inclinations, or feelings—motivationally effective mental states that are not themselves beliefs.[41] If the Intellectualist demands to be told what these mental states are, then the Emotionalist will presumably respond that they are *desires*.[42] In that case we can say that an act is **desire-governed** if the agent does it because she desires to do it more than she desires to forgo it. According to the Emotionalist, an agent who is overcome by something can commit an act that is *neither* forced *nor* belief-governed, as long as it is *desire*-governed. This proposal clearly threatens the Intellectualist, since it yields a reasonable alternative explanation of what happens to agents in cases of Weakness—an explanation that does not depend in any way on the truth of the Belief Thesis.[43] So unless the Intellectualist can find a way to block this proposal, it looks as though the Emotionalist will win the exchange, and probably also the debate.

The Intellectualist's only workable strategy at this point, as far as I can tell, is to show by some argument or other that the desire-based explanation on offer here actually *does* depend on the truth of the Belief Thesis. Evidence from other dialogues suggests that this is a strategy Socrates himself would be inclined to pursue. In the *Meno*, for example, he proposes an account of desire that closely resembles the following:

> **Doxastic Desire**: If an agent desires x more than y, then that is because she believes that x is more F than y.[44]

If the Intellectualist could somehow establish Doxastic Desire, then that would be enough to eliminate the Emotionalist's advantage.[45] For if Doxastic Desire is true, then the Emotionalist cannot appeal to desires *rather than* beliefs in order to explain why agents do what they do when they are overcome by something.

But could the Intellectualist give the Emotionalist any reason to believe that Doxastic Desire—or something near enough—is true? We can see fairly easily how such an argument would go: it would hinge on the idea that an agent who commits an act simply because she desires to do it would be unable to forgo that act unless *desiring* something is, at bottom, just a matter of *believing* something. On a view of this sort, desiring something—in the absence of the relevant belief—would not be significantly different from *being shoved*, and being shoved is a way of being moved that deprives the agent of her power to resist.[46] In order to make this point more precise, let us call a desire **brute** if it does not allow the agent to forgo whatever action it prompts her to commit, and let us call a desire **smart** if it does; likewise, let us call a desire **belief-based** if it is grounded in some belief, and let us call a desire **belief-independent** if it is not. Then the Intellectualist's claim here will be that *only belief-based desires are smart*. Of course this does not entail that *all desires are belief-based*, as Doxastic Desire does, but it gets the job done anyway. For if it is true, then the Emotionalist still cannot appeal to desires *rather than* beliefs in order to explain why agents do what they do when they are overcome by something.

To surmount this resistance in a decisive fashion, the Emotionalist needs to find a plausible way to characterize states of desire such that at least some of them turn out to be both belief-independent and smart.[47] And here again—as in section II—Socrates provides his opponent with some surprisingly useful resources. For in the "power of appearance" passage he suggests that there are certain states of *being appeared to* that are closely linked to states of desire, but that are clearly belief-independent (356c4–e4). According to the view he spells out here, any two equally pleasant events—if placed at different temporal "distances" from a given agent—will appear to her to be unequally pleasant, and will appear this way to her whether or not she knows (or believes) that they are *not* unequally pleasant (356c4–8).[48] If we follow this suggestion and suppose that states of appearance (rather than states of belief) ground at least some states of desire,[49] then an interesting alternative to Doxastic Desire suddenly comes into view:

> **Phenomenal Desire**: If an agent desires x more than y, then that is *either* because she believes that x is more F than y *or* because it appears to her that x is more F than y.

Since Phenomenal Desire leaves room for the existence of belief-independent, *appearance*-based desires, the only task left for the Emotionalist at this point—that is, once Phenomenal Desire is in place—is to show that some appearance-based desires are smart. (Recall that a desire is smart if it allows the agent to forgo whatever action it prompts her to commit.) And this burden seems extremely easy to bear, since agents who act on the basis of appearances do not *for that reason alone* seem incapable of forgoing the actions they commit. So the Emotionalist's original line of attack on the Belief Thesis looks even more promising than before.

Could the Intellectualist develop a radically concessive response here, as in section II? This would involve accepting not only that there are some smart, appearance-based desires but also that the Belief Thesis as it stands cannot accommodate their existence. The task then would be to show that the Belief Thesis, and the Knowledge Argument as a whole, can be salvaged by modification. The first step, I assume, would be to replace the Belief Thesis with:

> **The Appearance Thesis**: If an agent does an act because she is overcome by something, then *either* she is not able to forgo it *or* she does it because she believes that doing it is more F than forgoing it *or* she does it because it appears to her that doing it is more F than forgoing it.

So far so good. But once the Belief Thesis is replaced with the Appearance Thesis, the argument will be invalid unless Cognitive Unity is replaced with:

> **Cognitive Dominance**: If an agent knows that x is more F than y, then she does not believe that y is more F than x *and* it does not appear to her that y is more F than x.

Yet Cognitive Dominance is almost certainly false. For as Socrates himself suggests, this premise cannot accommodate familiar cases of perceptual illusion—cases in which knowledge conspicuously fails to silence the appearances (356c5–8).[50] Consider, for example, the familiar case of the Müller-Lyer lines, which stubbornly appear to you not to be equal in length, even though you know, on the basis of careful measurement, that they are.[51] From this and similar cases I think we must conclude that Cognitive Dominance is a dead end, and that the Intellectualist cannot afford to develop a radically concessive response to this particular line of attack.[52] Instead, the Intellectualist must claim either (B1) that there are no smart, appearance-based desires, or (B2) that the Belief Thesis as it stands can accommodate the existence of such desires. Let us consider each of these options in turn.

In order to defend B1, the Intellectualist would need to hold either that no desires are appearance-based, or that all appearance-based desires are brute. Both views strike me as extremely unattractive. The first requires an ad hoc rejection of Phenomenal Desire, which looks like the most plausible account of desire to be found anywhere in the Socratic neighborhood;[53] and the second carries with it the utterly implausible consequence that appearance-based desires cannot be responsible for any unforced actions.

Would the Intellectualist fare any better by defending B2? I believe so. Let us assume that there are some smart, appearance-based desires, and that what makes an appearance-based desire smart is its power to generate an action-causing belief with the same content as the appearance. Then let us call a desire **belief-generating** if it generates an action-causing belief with the same content as the appearance, and let us call a desire **belief-neutral** if is not belief-generating. Now suppose that (i) it appears to you that drinking a certain glass of water is healthier than not drinking it, where (ii) this appearance constitutes a desire, and (iii) you drink the water because you have that desire. According to the view at issue, then, this desire is *smart* only insofar as (iv) it generates a belief in you to the effect that drinking the water is healthier than not drinking it, and (v) you drink the water because you have that belief.[54] So, if this view is correct, then the Belief Thesis is true *even though there are* smart, appearance-based desires.[55] For it is a consequence of this view that appearance-based desires are smart only insofar as they are belief-generating.

At this point the Emotionalist will presumably try to show that some appearance-based desires are both smart and belief-neutral. And the most obvious way to do this, I take it, would be to find a case in which an agent does an act simply because it appears to her that doing it is more F than forgoing it, even though she does not believe that doing it is more F than forgoing it, and even though she is able to forgo it. Consider, for instance, the case of a mildly agoraphobic agent who decides to stay inside one day simply because it appears to her that staying inside is safer than going out, even though she has no belief one way or another about whether staying inside really is safer than going out, and even though she is able to go out. Could there really be such an agent? The Emotionalist here says yes, and the Intellectualist says no. This disagreement, which turns entirely on the question of whether any appearance-based desires are both smart and belief-neutral, forms what I take to be the *second* genuine crux of the Intellectualism debate.

Though this second disagreement is not easy to resolve, I suspect that it is easier to resolve than the first. One indication of this is that most contemporary philosophers—especially those who entertain various fictionalist approaches to ethical, mathematical, or semantic discourse—would be strongly inclined to side with the Emotionalist on this point.[56] For in their view there is an important distinction to be drawn between *accepting* an appearance *as a basis for action* and *believing* an appearance *to be true*. Sometimes they illustrate this distinction with cases of make-believe, familiar from childhood, in which we seem to commit a wide variety of unforced actions on the basis of appearances that we know to be false.[57] Consider a case in which two agents interact with each other on the basis of a fiction to the effect that one is a cop and the other is a robber. It seems wrong to think that neither of these agents is able to forgo any of the acts they commit within this fiction—a staged footrace, say—simply because neither of them believes this fiction to be true. An Intellectualist might object that these actions are (or seem to be) unforced only because the agents who commit them (typically) have some clear rationale for engaging in the relevant type of make-believe. But at first glance this objection seems unconvincing. For even if an agent has no clear rationale for engaging in a certain type of make-believe, it does not seem to follow from this that she is forced to engage in it, or that she is forced to do whatever she does while she is engaged in it. Actions freely committed under these conditions may be to some extent irrational, but they do not *for that reason alone* seem to be impossible.

Perhaps the Intellectualist could reply at this point that what makes appearance-based, belief-neutral desires brute in the first place is precisely their failure to rationalize the actions they generate. Then the idea would be that an agent can forgo what her desire prompts her to do only if this desire not only *causes her to do* what she does but also *rationalizes* or (in other words) *makes it reasonable for her to do* what she does; otherwise being subject to this desire is not significantly different from being pushed or dragged. Though many Emotionalists would no doubt reject this idea, let us suppose for the sake of discussion that it is correct. Then all the Intellectualist would need to establish is that appearance-based, belief-neutral desires systematically fail to rationalize the actions they cause.

But can the Intellectualist establish this? I doubt it. Recall that at this point in the dialectic the Intellectualist has conceded that at least some appearance-based desires have the power to generate action-causing beliefs with the same content as the appearances. The trouble now, from the Intellectualist's perspective, is that these desires pretty clearly have the power to rationalize the beliefs they generate. To see why, suppose that you have an appearance-based desire with the content that drinking a certain glass of water is healthier than not drinking it, and suppose that this appearance-based desire generates a belief in you with that same content. Surely this desire *rationalizes* this belief, in the sense that your having that particular desire makes it reasonable (all else equal) for you to have that particular belief.[58] And from this it seems to follow that appearance-based desires have the power to rationalize at least some of the things they *immediately* cause—that is, the things they cause in the absence of any mediating belief. But now it becomes very difficult to see what justification the Intellectualist could have for thinking that these appearance-based desires *do not* have the power to rationalize any of the *actions* they immediately cause.

The Intellectualist might try to respond by simply denying that appearance-based desires have the power to rationalize the beliefs they generate.[59] But this strikes me as a very dangerous path to take, epistemically speaking. For it seems to lead more or less directly to a rejection of the view that it is reasonable (all else equal) to treat the appearances of things as reliable indicators of the way things are. And only a skeptic would be tempted to reject that view.[60] Since there is no way for us to acquire (perceptual) knowledge of the things around us unless we are warranted in trusting how they appear to us, at least to some extent, the epistemic cost of denying our defeasible entitlement to believe that things are as they appear to us is high indeed. So if the Intellectualist is forced to deny this, then so much the worse for Intellectualism.

At this point I am inclined to conclude, albeit tentatively, that the Emotionalist's line of attack on the Belief Thesis is likely to succeed. Of course this is not to say that the Intellectualist's position is hopeless. It is only to suggest that the defenders of the Belief Thesis are at a significant dialectical disadvantage, and that they have a much heavier burden to bear than their opponents do. But even if this is so, let us suppose for the sake of inquiry that the burden can be borne, and that the Intellectualist will ultimately be in a position to show why one cannot act freely on the basis of belief-neutral desires. Could an Emotionalist still derail the Knowledge Argument by giving us a conclusive reason to think that Cognitive Unity—the third and final premise of the argument—is false?

VI

Though Cognitive Unity is clearly the strongest of the argument's three premises, some Emotionalists—particularly those who are sympathetic to various modular accounts of the mind—might be inclined to take issue with it.[61] Close readers of the Socratic dialogues, for example, might think it possible (and perhaps even common) for a cognitively confused person to hold two contradictory beliefs about the nature of virtue, say, and for one of these beliefs to be more justified than the other.[62] As a result they might also think it possible for the more justified of these two beliefs to be both true and warranted, and therefore to count as knowledge. If a scenario of this sort really is possible, then counterexamples to Cognitive Unity will be easy to come by. Lots of people will turn out to believe the opposite of what they know. But is a scenario of this sort really possible?

In order to answer this question properly, we need to get a clearer sense of what it would be for one and the same agent to hold two contradictory beliefs. In most of the cases familiar from the Socratic dialogues, we find agents who reveal themselves—under elenctic examination—to believe things the logical consequences of which contradict each other. If this is all it takes for an agent to hold contradictory beliefs, however, then something like the following thesis must be true: *If it follows from p that q, then, if an agent believes that p, then she believes that q.* And this thesis is almost certainly false. For it entails (among other implausible things) that each of us has an infinite number of beliefs, most of which are so complex that no mortal creature could ever succeed in expressing them. Surely, then, there is a substantive distinction to be drawn between *what you believe,* on the one hand, and *the logical consequences of what you believe,* on the other. So even if we assume that an agent is somehow rationally committed to the logical consequences of what she believes, it would be wrong for us to assume that she holds contradictory beliefs simply because she believes things the logical consequences of which contradict each other. Evidently the Emotionalist needs to find some other account of what it is to believe something.

Perhaps the best way to proceed at this point would be to figure out why an Emotionalist would expect the falsehood of Cognitive Unity to help explain cases of Weakness in the first place. For if the falsehood of that premise were to help explain such cases, then there would have to be some clear sense in which the agent who acts contrary to her knowledge also *believes* contrary to her knowledge. What sense would that be? Presumably the belief in question would have to be both *motivationally effective,* since it serves as the basis for the agent's action, and *consciously occurrent,* since—in the standard cases, at least—the agent is aware *not only* of her knowledge that what she is doing is better left undone *but also* of her motivation for doing what she is doing.[63] So it looks as though the Emotionalist must assume that in cases of Weakness the agent acts on one of two consciously occurrent but contradictory beliefs, the other one of which is both true and warranted. Is this assumption at all plausible?

There are some powerful reasons to think not. For even if it is psychologically possible for a single person to hold two consciously occurrent, contradictory beliefs—which I am inclined to doubt[64]—it seems fairly clear that neither of these beliefs could be warranted. To see this, consider a person who consciously disbelieves something that she also consciously believes, and suppose that what she believes is not only true but also well supported by her evidence. Would it really be appropriate to claim that her belief constitutes knowledge, even though she herself is consciously convinced that what she believes is false? This strikes me as outlandish. Surely the fact of her conscious disbelief would be sufficient to defeat whatever warrant her true belief might otherwise have had, if only because one's knowing that p is incompatible with one's contradicting oneself about whether it is the case that p. Thus it seems unlikely that the Emotionalist will be able to overturn Cognitive Unity in this fashion.

Maybe the Emotionalist could dispel the air of paradox here by exploiting Plato's famous suggestion in *Republic* IV that every agent is composed of at least two potentially conflicting subagents. Adopting a view of this sort might allow the Emotionalist to deny that, in cases of Weakness, the agent contradicts herself in a way that is sufficient to defeat whatever warrant her true belief might otherwise have had. For cases of Weakness could be understood as cases in which the agent is composed of two *actually* conflicting subagents—the believer and the disbeliever—neither of whom is implicated in any self-contradiction. In that case it is not obvious that the believing subagent's true belief would lose its warrant, since the believing subagent and the disbelieving subagent are cognitively distinct.

But now notice that the Emotionalist, in order to bring *the agent* back into the picture, will need to defend a principle of roughly the following form:

> **Belief Inheritance**: If one of an agent's constituent subagents has the (warranted) belief that p, then *that agent also* has the (warranted) belief that p.

And it is hard to see how the Emotionalist could use this principle to fend off a determined Intellectualist attack. For at this point the Intellectualist is free to challenge any of the following four claims, each of which is integral to the Emotionalist's current position, and each of which is at least somewhat dubious: (1) it is reasonable to divide every agent into distinct subagents; (2) agents believe whatever their subagents believe; (3) it is possible for one of an agent's subagents to have the warranted belief that p even though another of that agent's subagents has the belief that not-p; and (4) if one of an agent's subagents has the warranted belief that p, then, even if another of the agent's subagents has the belief that not-p, the agent nonetheless still has the warranted belief that p. It seems extremely unlikely to me that these four claims could all be successfully defended at once. But let us suppose for the sake of argument that they could. Would this be enough to guarantee an Emotionalist victory?

My suspicion is that it would not. For even if the Emotionalist manages to convince the Intellectualist that agents have warranted beliefs insofar as their subagents do, the Intellectualist may still respond that, on a view of this sort, the *real* agents here are not the (so-called) agents but rather the (so-called) subagents. This is because the subagents have now turned out to be the primary bearers of the motivating attitudes, and the Intellectualist's assumption all along has been that the primary bearers of the motivating attitudes are (by definition) *the agents*. On this view, then, the Emotionalist position has the strange consequence that people like you and me, because of our fundamentally corporate structure, are not the agents in cases of Weakness. That role is reserved for our parts. Yet if the agents in these cases are not us, but *parts of* us, then Cognitive Unity remains untouched. For the Emotionalist is not claiming that an agent— understood now as a constituent part of some corporate person—could both know and disbelieve the same thing at the same time.

It is worth pausing for a moment to appreciate what an odd effect this last move would have on the underlying debate. Up to this point the governing assumption has been that the agents in (purported) cases of Weakness are people like you and me. But now the Intellectualist, in an effort to save Cognitive Unity from the implications of a quasi-Platonic division of the agent, has rescinded that assumption. According to this Intellectualist, the proposed division would establish that the agents in cases of Weakness are not people like you and me but *parts of* people like you and me. On this view, cases of Weakness are not cases in which *a person* does something that *she* knows is better left undone, but cases in which *some part of* a person does something that *this part* knows is better left undone. And since the Emotionalist has not shown that this could ever happen, the Intellectualist position remains unscathed. The Intellec- tualist can gladly accept that one part of a corporate person could commit an act even though *another* part of *that same* person knows that this act would be better left undone. What we would have in that case is not an Emotionalist explanation of genuine Weakness, but an *Intellectualist* explanation of *apparent* Weakness.[65]

Of course the Emotionalist need not go along with any of this, and remains free in particular to claim that corporate people are no less agents for being corporate. On a view of that sort, the agents in cases of Weak- ness could just as easily be people like you and me, whose parts are busy pulling them in different directions. But this does not tell against the main point here, which is that establishing Belief Inheritance would not be sufficient, by itself, to win the day for the Emotionalist. More argument would be required. And since the task of establishing Belief Inheritance is extremely difficult to begin with, this provides even greater evidence that Cognitive Unity, while perhaps not invulnerable, is the Knowledge Argu- ment's strongest premise. The prospects for overturning it—in a way that matters to the Intellectualist, at least—are bleak indeed.

VII

All things considered, the case against the Knowledge Argument is strong, and its defenders have a lot of work to do. But their work is not obviously doomed. Of the various tasks they face, two in particular stand out. The most urgent (to my mind) is the task of explaining why *one cannot act freely on the basis of appearances alone*. If I am right about the structure of the argument, then this thought—which strikes many of us as dubious at best—constitutes the innermost core of the Intellectualist's position. Without a robust justification of it on hand, the Intellectualist will remain highly vulnerable to attack. The second crucial task is that of explaining why *one cannot act on the basis of entirely good-independent considerations*. As we have seen, this is an important component of the classical account of agency, on which the Knowledge Argument at least partially depends. Any defense of the argument that would be acceptable to someone like Socrates himself would need to find some way to support this claim. As I see it, then, progress in the Intellectualism debate will be marked by various decisive successes or failures in the (partial) performance of these two tasks. Whether (and if so, how) the debate will finally be resolved I leave to the reader to decide.[66]

Notes

1. Detailed accounts of the argument can be found in Santas (1966), Vlastos (1969), Dyson (1976), Taylor (1976: 161–212), Klosko (1980), Zeyl (1980), Kahn (1998: 234–247), and Wolfsdorf (2006).

2. See Watson (1977), Mele (1987: 8–9; 2004: 241), Kennett (2001: 11), Stroud and Tappolet (2003: 2), and Tenenbaum (2007: 257–58).

3. For a useful overview of the contemporary consensus, see Stroud and Tappolet (2003: 1–9).

4. See Penner (1990, 1996, 1997), Segvic (2000), Reshotko (2006), and Shields (2007: 67–70).

5. Socrates introduces this "knows or believes" disjunction very late in the game, at 358b6–c1, but he uses it there to convey what he takes to be the overall upshot of the argument. This suggests that, as far as he is concerned, the argument will go through even on the assumption that the agent *believes but does not know* that forgoing the act is better than doing it. Useful discussions of this feature of the argument can be found in Vlastos (1969: 72–73), Penner (1996, 1997), and Carone (2001: 109–16). But the more fundamental issue here, and the one I will confine my attention to in this chapter, is whether the argument will go through on the stronger assumption that the agent *does* know that forgoing the act is better than doing it. This version of the argument is less ambitious, to be sure, but it is more than ambitious enough. So from now on I will bracket out the second disjunct.

6. Socrates gives this proposal its clearest and fullest articulation at 352c2–53a6, but he revisits and rehearses various parts of it throughout the argument. In his formulations of clause W1 he typically uses the verb γιγνώσκω or the noun ἐπιστήμη (cf. 355a7–d2 and 357a1–e1, excepting 352c6, 358b7, and 358c3); and in his formulations of clause W2 he typically uses a participle of ἔξεστι (e.g., ἐξὸν τὰ βελτίω at 358c1 and ἐξὸν μὴ πράττειν at 355a8); see also his use of ἐθέλω at 355b2 and 358d2, αἱρέομαι at 358d3, and ἑκών at 358c7.

7. Let us also assume that, according to both the Emotionalist and the Intellectualist, each of the conditions mentioned in W1, W2, and W3 is

sometimes satisfied. That way we can avoid having to assign oddballs like
evaluative skeptics and hard determinists to the Intellectualist camp.

8. As my formulation of Weakness indicates, I am deliberately restricting my
attention here to what Terry Penner calls **synchronic** knowledge *akrasia* (SKA)
rather than (what he calls) **diachronic** knowledge *akrasia* (DKA). In cases of
SKA, the agent knows at the time of action that it would be better to forgo the
act; but in cases of DKA, the agent knows *at some time during the process of
deliberation* that it would be better to forgo the act, but for some reason *does not
know at the time of action* that it would be better to forgo the act. According to
Penner (1971, 1990, 1996, 1997), the full argument that Socrates gives us in this
part of the *Protagoras* is designed to show *not only* that there are no cases of SKA
but also that there are no cases of DKA. Compare Devereux (1995: 390–96),
Segvic (2000: 22–24), Carone (2001: 109–16), Reshotko (2006: 74–91), and
Brickhouse and Smith (2006: 269–71). Probably Penner and the others are right.
But for my purposes here it does not really matter. All I am concerned with in
this paper is Socrates' argument to the effect that there are no cases of SKA, and
everyone agrees that there is such an argument to be found in the *Protagoras*.

9. Of course the Intellectualist also has some explaining to do, as Socrates
acknowledges at 357c6–d1. One fact that is especially difficult for the
Intellectualist to handle is that many (if not most) of us sincerely claim to have
had first-personal experience of doing something we knew at the time of action
to be wrong. So the Intellectualist must explain how it is possible for so many of
us to be so mistaken about our own states of mind. But I take it that the
Intellectualist who fails to explain how we could be so ignorant of ourselves is
still dialectically better off than the Emotionalist who fails to explain how we
could have done what we claim to have done in the first place. For excellent
discussions of this issue, see Segvic (2000: 27–34) and Bobonich (2007).

10. Compare Santas (1966: 4–8).

11. In his formulations of this proposal, Socrates typically uses the phrase ὑπὸ
ἡδονῆς with ἡττάομαι or with the passive of a verb like κρατέω or ἄγω (cf.
355a8–b1, 355e7–56a1, and 357c7). Sometimes he calls the condition of "being
overcome" a πάθος (e.g., 352e6) or a πάθημα (e.g., 353a5); and once, when
emphasizing its explanatory role, he calls it αἴτιον ai[tion (352d8). He also suggests
at 352b3–c2 that the explanation on offer in Hedonic Defeat could be expanded
to include other potentially overwhelming psychological forces, such as anger, pain,
love, and fear. But he never explicitly considers whether (and if so, how) the
Knowledge Argument might be augmented to show that these other forces are just
as powerless against knowledge as pleasure is. For an attempt to spell out how the
argument might be augmented in this way, see Santas (1966: 20–22).

12. It is worth emphasizing here that the Knowledge Argument, as I read it,
does not purport to show that there are no cases of *akrasia*, if "*akrasia*" is taken
to refer to any and all lapses in practical self-control. As many commentators
have pointed out, the argument leaves plenty of room for—and the text itself
even suggests—an account of *akrasia* according to which the akratic agent does
what she does because of a sudden and unjustified change of belief, possibly in
response to misleading evidence. And this account of *akrasia* is entirely consistent with Intellectualism. Cf. Penner (1971, 1996, 1997), Devereux (1995:
387–89; 2008: 144–50), Carone (2001: 109–16), Reshotko (2006: 74–91),

Singpurwalla (2006), Brickhouse and Smith (2007: 6), and Shields (2007: 67–70).

13. See 355b3–56a5, and note especially the parallel constructions at 355d1–3 (γιγνώσκων ὅτι κακά ἐστιν) and 355e4–56a1 (γιγνώσκων ὅτι ἀνιαρά ἐστιν).

14. It seems fairly clear from the text that this is not the only version of ethical hedonism that Socrates either entertains or endorses in the course of the argument. By my count he manages to propose *no fewer than five* different versions, only the last of which is as strong as he thinks he needs it to be: (H1) x is better than y insofar as (καθ' ὅσόν) x is more pleasant than y (351b3–e7); (H2) x is better than y insofar as, and only insofar as, x is more pleasant than y (353e5–54d3); (H3) for x to be better than y is for x to be more pleasant than y (354e8–55a2; cf. 355b6); (H4) saying that x is better than y is the same as saying that x is more pleasant than y (355b3–c1); and (H5) knowing that x is better than y is the same as knowing that x is more pleasant than y (355c1–56a5). It is possible that Socrates assumes, incorrectly in my view, that H5—the position I am calling Analytic Hedonism—somehow follows from (some combination of) H1, H2, H3, or H4. But I cannot hope to settle that issue here. For an especially penetrating general discussion of hedonism in the *Protagoras*, see Irwin (1995: 81–92).

15. As Gallop (1964: 122–24) has shown, my formulation here actually violates the letter of the text. Strictly speaking, what the agent (allegedly) "chooses" or "selects" is not some particular course of action in exchange for another, but *the bad things to be had from* some particular course of action in exchange for *the good things to be had from* that very same course of action. But I take it that my formulation does not violate the *spirit* of the text, since in this case it is obvious that the agent *also* (and for the same reason) chooses the option of doing the action over the option of forgoing it. On the sense of λαμβάνω here, see Santas (1966: 16–20).

16. See Morris (2006: 199–205).

17. Of course I do not claim that this is the actual structure of the argument as it appears in the text. All I claim is that this is *a reliable reconstruction of the reasoning expressed by* the argument as it appears in the text.

18. I will not be discussing the third strategy, mostly for reasons of space. But in any case I suspect that it is the least interesting of the three. For, as we shall see, the argument's premises are quite malleable and can most likely be adjusted to whatever alternative explanation the Emotionalist might propose.

19. For some other potential sources of ambiguity, see below, note 29.

20. For the sake of simplicity I am bracketing Socrates' talk of pain and painfulness here and in what follows.

21. Socrates himself seems to anticipate a response of this sort at 355a5–b3 and 356a5–7.

22. See Rudebusch (1999: 23–24) for a roughly similar line of objection.

23. Eric Brown (in conversation) has convinced me that more needs to be said here. For we could give Cognitive Unity a *mixed* reading and end up with something like this: If the agent knows that x is more *comprehensively* pleasant than y, then she does not believe that y is more *internally* pleasant than x. And in that case the argument's validity would *not* depend on giving "more pleasant" as it

appears in Analytic Hedonism an internal reading. But I take it that the argument's soundness would still be in jeopardy, since on this mixed reading Cognitive Unity is pretty obviously false. (Surely it is possible for you *both* to know that receiving invasive dental work is more *comprehensively* pleasant than avoiding it, *and* to believe that avoiding it is more *internally* pleasant than receiving it.)

24. Santas (1966: 18–20), Irwin (1995: 83–84), Price (1995: 20–21), and Klosko (1980).

25. Perhaps C1 is true by definition. But if it is not, then it is probably false. For as anyone with an economist's cast of mind will point out, it would be unreasonable of an agent not to apply some sort of variable discount rate to an option's external pleasantness prior to calculating that option's comprehensive pleasantness—assuming of course that an option's comprehensive pleasantness can be calculated in this way. And in that case C1 is false.

26. Compare Weiss (2006: 56–57), who amusingly describes the entire line of reasoning in this passage as "verbal hocus-pocus."

27. In fact, I doubt that the Intellectualist can avoid losing this exchange, if only because common sense so clearly supports the other side. But I do not wish to insist on this point here. Suffice it to say that the Intellectualist who gives "more pleasant" in the Belief Constraint a comprehensive reading cannot reasonably expect anything better than a draw.

28. Obviously this is not how Socrates himself (or any of his most prominent and loyal supporters) would be inclined to proceed. But I am assuming here that the defenders of the Socratic legacy are not required to follow their leader at every dialectical turn, especially if it becomes clear that doing so will result in either a loss or a draw.

29. The purpose of this second assumption is to exclude in advance any objection that would involve drawing a distinction between two or more *respects in which* an option might be (viewed as) pleasant or good, and then alleging that some inference in the argument is insensitive to the distinction. Various objections along these lines can be found in Davidson (1980: 21–42), Taylor (1976: 194–99), Irwin (1977: 106–7), Nussbaum (2001: 113–17), and Price (1995: 23–26). On the legitimacy of excluding objections of this sort for the purpose of assessing Intellectualist arguments in general, see Mele (2004: 241).

30. See, in particular, *Gorgias* 497d8–99b3.

31. But see Irwin (1977: 104n10).

32. Compare Vlastos (1969: 85–88) and Morris (2006: 204).

33. Strictly speaking, the conjunction of Analytic Hedonism and the Belief Constraint entails that, if an agent does an act because she is overcome by pleasure, then *either* she is not able to forgo it *or* she does it because she believes that doing it is better than forgoing it. I have omitted the first disjunct because we already know that, in purported cases of Weakness, this first disjunct is false.

34. It is at least somewhat surprising to discover that Analytic Hedonism is a red herring in the Intellectualism debate, since so many scholars have spent so much time attacking it, defending it, or contrasting it with positions that Socrates appears to endorse elsewhere. For useful, compact overviews of the vast literature on this subject, see Annas (1999: 167–72) and Weiss (2006: 48n32).

35. I am taking it for granted that, in cases where an agent does something simply because she believes that doing it is better than forgoing it, the consequent of the Evaluation Thesis would not thereby be falsified. Strictly speaking, however, it would. For the agent obviously does not believe that doing the act is better than forgoing it *in virtue of being* better than forgoing it, since the "in virtue of" relation is irreflexive. If I were trying to be as precise as possible, I would replace the phrase "then she believes that . . ." with the phrase "then *either* F = good *or* she believes that . . . ."

36. The terminology here is due to Velleman (2000: 99–112). For an especially penetrating discussion of the role this thesis plays in the version of Intellectualism that Socrates himself insists on, see Segvic (2000).

37. See Stocker (1979), Velleman (2000: 99–122), and Setiya (2007: 59–67, 86–99).

38. See Anscombe (1957: 70–78), Davidson (1980: 83–102), Pears (1984: 198), and Stampe (1987).

39. To locate this position within the quasi-formal framework I have developed here, take whatever property F the relevant agent is aiming at in her actions, and then replace "better" in Weakness with "more F." The Disenchanted Intellectualist holds that Weakness is false on this new interpretation, but true on the previous one.

40. Obviously, the property in question here—that is, the property of *being F*—would need to be connected somehow to whatever the agent is overcome by. If the agent is overcome by fear, for example, then presumably it would be the property of *being fearful*.

41. Compare Irwin (1977: 107).

42. Santas (1966: 14).

43. For an excellent discussion of the standards any such explanation would have to meet, see Santas (1966: 23–29).

44. See 77b2–78b6. The account Socrates actually proposes here is both stronger and less complex than Doxastic Desire: *if an agent desires x, then she believes that x is good*. Some such thesis has long been thought to be a centerpiece of the Socratic theory of motivation. See Frede (1992: xxix–xxx), Irwin (1977: 78; 1995: 75–76), Nehamas (1999: 27–58), and Segvic (2000). But in recent years several commentators have argued, mostly on the basis of passages from other dialogues, that Socrates fully accepts the possibility of knowingly desiring bad things. See Devereux (1995, 2008), Singpurwalla (2006), and Brickhouse and Smith (2006, 2007).

45. Another option would be to follow Socrates' lead at *Gorgias* 466a–68e, where he seems to suggest that, although we do whatever we do because we believe that doing it is better than forgoing it (468b1–6), we *desire* to do whatever we do *if and only if* doing it *really is* better than forgoing it (468c2–7). Like Doxastic Desire, this view would leave no room for our desires to play any belief-free role in determining what we do. But I take it that this view is far less plausible than Doxastic Desire, and that the Emotionalist remains perfectly free to deny it. On this issue, see Penner (1991), Segvic (2000: 5–11), Kamtekar (2006), Reshotko (2006: 21–56), and Devereux (2008: 150–54).

46. For arguments to this effect, see Santas (1966: 29–32) and Watson (1977). For dissent, see Smith (2003).

47. Of course, many Emotionalists would simply assert that *all* desires are smart, whether they are belief-based or not. But I take it that these Emotionalists would be less dialectically effective than those who accept that *some* desires are *not* smart.

48. But if the agent *knows* that they are not unequally pleasant, then (according to Socrates) this appearance will have lost its "power" to make her *believe* that they *are* unequally pleasant (356d4–e4). Compare Bobonich (2007: 54–55).

49. Not everyone agrees with this way of seeing the suggested relation between states of appearance and states of desire. According to Devereux (1995: 390–96) and Brickhouse and Smith (2006: 271–72; 2007), for example, the idea is not that states of appearance can ground states of desire, but rather that states of desire can ground states of appearance. Their interpretation is controversial, however. For some contrasting views, see Reshotko (2006: 83–88) and Singpurwalla (2006: 249–54).

50. In other words, Socrates wants to deny that if you know that p, then *it will not appear to you* that *not*-p. This is the sense in which he thinks that knowledge does not silence the appearances. But he also wants to insist that if you know that p, then its appearing to you that not-p *will not make you believe* that not-p. In this second sense, at least, he thinks that knowledge *does* silence the appearances.

51. For useful discussion, see Penner (1971: 97–103), Moss (2006: 505–10; 2008: 50–57), and Morris (2006: 202–3).

52. Although Rudebusch (1999: 25–27) concedes that Cognitive Dominance fails when the objects of appearance are "concrete quantities" such as those of gold or sand, he insists that it *does not* fail when the objects of appearance are "abstract quantities" such as those of money or pleasure. This strikes me as dubious. Cognitive Dominance seems to fail even when the objects of appearance are abstract quantities. Consider, for example, persistent illusions in mathematical reasoning, such as the appearance that $4^5 < 1019$, or the striking phenomenon of compound interest, or the equinumerosity of the set of even numbers and the set of natural numbers. To my mind, at least, these examples suggest that abstract quantities are not without "the power of appearance" either.

53. As a number of commentators have argued, it is certainly more plausible than Doxastic Desire, which strikes nearly everyone as phenomenologically obtuse. For even if we assume that Intellectualism is true, we must admit that there are cases of mental conflict, and in these cases the desires that assail us certainly do not *seem* to be belief-based. On this point, see Devereux (1995: 387–89; 2008: 147–50), Brickhouse and Smith (2006: 264–72), and Singpurwalla (2006: 245–49). For dissent, see Segvic (2000).

54. Notice that conditions (iii) and (v) can be jointly satisfied, since the "because" relation is transitive: you drink because you have the belief, and you have the belief because you have the desire; so you drink because you have the desire.

55. Many of the recent commentators want to tell a story of this general sort, although they differ on the details. See, for example, Devereux (1995: 390–96; 2008: 147–50), Brickhouse and Smith (2006: 271–72; 2007), and Singpurwalla (2006: 249–54).

56. See Kalderon (2007) and the essays compiled in Kalderon (2005).

57. Velleman (2000: 244–81).

58. At the very least, your having that particular desire makes it reasonable for you to have that particular belief *as opposed to some other one*—such as the belief that whales are mammals, or that the pope is infallible.

59. Some of the recent commentators use language that suggests as much. Devereux (1995: 390–96), for example, describes belief-generation as a case in which any belief that contradicts the generating appearance is "pushed aside and replaced" (393) by the belief that is generated by it, and this is a process that merely "*happens to*" the agent (392). So it is hard to see how, on this account, the agent's change of mind has been rationalized.

60. Of course it is possible that Socrates himself, in the "power of appearance" passage, *does* reject that view. When he repeatedly opposes the (reliable) "art of measurement" ($\dot{\eta}\mu\epsilon\tau\rho\eta\tau\iota\kappa\grave{\eta}$ $\tau\acute{\epsilon}\chi\nu\eta$) to the (unreliable) "power of appearance" (e.g., 356d3–e2), he seems to imply at times that the way things appear to us is somehow systematically misleading. But I am not quite convinced that this is what he means. For he never explicitly denies that it is precisely by measuring the appearances of things that the expert measurer measures the things themselves. And if this is his view, then he would be in no position to claim that we are making some kind of mistake when we treat the appearances of things as, at bottom, reliable indicators of the way things are.

61. See Davidson (1982) and Pears (1984). For an interesting discussion of this sort of strategy, particularly as it bears on Plato's account of *akrasia*, see Penner (1990).

62. See, especially, *Gorgias* 474b2–c1 together with 475e3–6.

63. Some Emotionalists might deny that, in cases of Weakness, the agent is aware of her motivation for doing what she is doing. Instead they might attempt to model such cases on a certain kind of self-deception, in which agents reveal themselves—through their overt behavior—to believe things that they sincerely deny. If cases of Weakness are really like that, then the agent's motivationally potent belief is *not* consciously occurrent. But is it reasonable to think that cases of Weakness are really like that? I am skeptical. Consider the previously discussed cases of the lapsing addict and the mild agoraphobe. Surely the agents in these cases are aware of what it is that motivates them to do what they are doing. If so, then the Emotionalists in question will be forced to agree with the Intellectualist that these are not genuine cases of Weakness after all—a miserable concession for any self-respecting Emotionalist to make. Compare Irwin (1995: 84n22).

64. But see Singpurwalla (2006: 252–54).

65. For an interesting discussion and development of a slightly different version of this idea, see Penner (1971).

66. For discussion, criticism, and encouragement I am grateful to Rachel Barney, Eric Brown, Mitch Miller, Phillip Mitsis, Jessica Moss, David Owens, Casey Perin, Jim Pryor, Nishi Shah, Matt Smith, Sharon Street, Sergio

Tenenbaum, Iakovos Vasiliou, and audiences at the University of Toronto and the
CUNY Graduate Center.

Bibliography

Annas, J. (1999). *Platonic Ethics, Old and New*. Ithaca, N.Y.: Cornell University
    Press.
Anscombe, E. (1957). *Intention*. Oxford: Blackwell.
Bobonich, C. (2007). "Plato on Akrasia and Knowing Your Own Mind," in C. Bobonich
    and P. Destrée (eds.), Akrasia *in Greek Philosophy*. Leiden: Brill, 41–60.
Brickhouse, T. C., and Smith, N. D. (2006). "The Socratic Paradoxes," in H. Benson
    (ed.), *A Companion to Plato*. Oxford: Blackwell, 263–77.
———. (2007). "Socrates on Akrasia, Knowledge, and the Power of Appearance,"
    in C. Bobonich and P. Destrée (eds.), Akrasia *in Greek Philosophy*. Leiden: Brill,
    1–17.
Carone, G. R. (2001). "*Akrasia* in the *Republic*: Does Plato Change His Mind?"
    Oxford Studies in Ancient Philosophy 20:107–48.
Davidson, D. (1980). *Essays on Actions and Events*. Oxford: Oxford University
    Press.
———. (1982). "Paradoxes of Irrationality," in R. A. Wollheim and J. Hopkins
    (eds.), *Philosophical Essays on Freud*. Oxford: Clarendon, 289–305.
de Sousa, R. (1974). "The Good and the True," *Mind* 83:534–51.
Devereux, D. (1995). "Socrates' Kantian Conception of Virtue," *Journal of the
    History of Philosophy* 33:381–408.
———. (2008). "Socratic Ethics and Moral Psychology," in G. Fine (ed.), *The
    Oxford Handbook of Plato*. Oxford: Oxford University Press, 139–64.
Dyson, M. (1976). "Knowledge and Hedonism in Plato's *Protagoras*," *The Journal
    of Hellenic Studies* 96:32–45.
Frede, M. (1992). "Introduction," in S. Lombardo and K. Bell (trans.), *Plato:
    Protagoras*. Indianapolis: Hackett.
Gallop, D. (1964). "The Socratic Paradox in the 'Protagoras,'" *Phronesis* 9:117–29.
Irwin, T. (1977). *Plato's Moral Theory*. Oxford: Clarendon.
———. (1995). *Plato's Ethics*. Oxford: Oxford University Press.
Kahn, C. (1998). *Plato and the Socratic Dialogue*. Cambridge: Cambridge University
    Press.
Kalderon, M. E. (ed.) (2005). *Fictionalism in Metaphysics*. Oxford: Clarendon.
———. (2007). *Moral Fictionalism*. Oxford: Oxford University Press.
Kamtekar, R. (2006). "Plato on the Attribution of Conative Attitudes," *Archiv für
    Geschichte der Philosophie* 88:127–62.
Kennett, J. (2001). *Agency and Responsibility*. Oxford: Clarendon.
Klosko, G. (1980). "On the Analysis of *Protagoras* 351b–360e," *Phoenix* 34:307–22.
Mele, A. (1987). *Irrationality*. Oxford: Oxford University Press.
———. (2004). "Motivated Irrationality," in A. Mele and P. Rawling (eds.), *The
    Oxford Handbook of Rationality*. Oxford: Oxford University Press, 240–56.
Morris, M. (2006). "*Akrasia* in the *Protagoras* and the *Republic*," *Phronesis* 51:
    195–229.
Moss, J. (2006). "Pleasure and Illusion in Plato," *Philosophy and Phenomenological
    Research* 72:503–35.
———. (2008). "Appearances and Calculations: Plato's Division of the Soul,"
    Oxford Studies in Ancient Philosophy 34:35–68.

Nehamas, A. (1999). *Virtues of Authenticity*. Princeton, N.J.: Princeton University Press.

Nussbaum, M. (2001). *The Fragility of Goodness*, rev. ed. Cambridge: Cambridge University Press.

Pears, D. (1984). *Motivated Irrationality*. Oxford: Clarendon.

Penner, T. (1971). "Thought and Desire in Plato," in G. Vlastos (ed.), *Plato II*. New York: Doubleday, 96–118.

———. (1990). "Plato and Davidson: Parts of the Soul and Weakness of Will," in D. Copp (ed.), *Canadian Philosophers*. Calgary: University of Calgary Press, 35–74.

———. (1991). "Desire and Power in Socrates," *Apeiron* 24:147–201.

———. (1996). "Knowledge vs. True Belief in the Socratic Psychology of Action," *Apeiron* 29:200–29.

———. (1997). "Socrates on the Strength of Knowledge," *Archiv für Geschichte der Philosophie* 79:117–49.

Price, A. W. (1995). *Mental Conflict*. London: Routledge.

Reshotko, N. (2006). *Socratic Virtue*. Oxford: Oxford University Press.

Rudebusch, G. (1999). *Socrates, Pleasure, and Value*. Oxford: Oxford University Press.

Santas, G. (1966). "Plato's *Protagoras* and Explanations of Weakness," *The Philosophical Review* 75:3–33.

Segvic, H. (2000). "No One Errs Willingly: The Meaning of Socratic Intellectualism," *Oxford Studies in Ancient Philosophy* 19:1–45.

Setiya, K. (2007). *Reasons without Rationalism*. Princeton, N.J.: Princeton University Press.

Shields, C. (2007). "Unified Agency and *Akrasia* in Plato's *Republic*," in C. Bobonich and P. Destrée (eds.), *Akrasia in Greek Philosophy*. Leiden: Brill, 61–86.

Singpurwalla, R. (2006). "Reasoning with the Irrational: Moral Psychology in the *Protagoras*," *Ancient Philosophy* 26:243–58.

Smith, M. (2003). "Rational Capacities, or: How to Distinguish Recklessness, Weakness, and Compulsion," in S. Stroud and C. Tappolet (eds.), *Weakness of Will and Practical Irrationality*. Oxford: Clarendon, 17–38.

Stampe, D. (1987). "The Authority of Desire," *The Philosophical Review* 96:335–81.

Stocker, M. (1979). "Desiring the Bad," *The Journal of Philosophy* 76:738–53.

Stroud, S., and Tappolet, C. (2003). "Introduction," in S. Stroud and C. Tappolet (eds.), *Weakness of Will and Practical Irrationality*. Oxford: Clarendon, 1–16.

Taylor, C. C. W. (1976). *Plato:* Protagoras. Oxford: Clarendon.

Tenenbaum, S. (2007). *Appearances of the Good*. Cambridge: Cambridge University Press.

Velleman, D. (2000). *The Possibility of Practical Reason*. Oxford: Oxford University Press.

Vlastos, G. (1969). "Socrates on Acrasia," *Phoenix* 23:71–88.

Watson, G. (1977). "Skepticism about Weakness of Will," *The Philosophical Review* 86:316–39.

Weiss, R. (2006). *The Socratic Paradox and Its Enemies*. Chicago: University of Chicago Press.

Wolfsdorf, D. (2006). "The Ridiculousness of Being Overcome by Pleasure: *Protagoras* 352b1–358d4," *Oxford Studies in Ancient Philosophy* 31:113–36.

Zeyl, D. J. (1980). "Socrates and Hedonism: 'Protagoras' 351b–358d," *Phronesis* 25:250–69.

3

Plato on the Desire for the Good

Rachel Barney

In a number of dialogues, Plato affirms in various ways that human desire is for the good. In the *Protagoras*, Socrates proposes that "no one who knows or believes there is something else better than what he is doing, something possible, will go on doing what he had been doing when he could be doing what is better" (358b7–c1).[1] Likewise, "No one goes willingly toward the bad or what he believes to be bad; neither is it in human nature, so it seems, to want to go toward what one believes to be bad instead of to the good" (358c6–d2). In the *Meno*, Socrates argues that no one really desires or wants [*epithumein, boulesthai*] what is bad (77a–78c). In the *Gorgias*, he claims that when we act, what we want [*boulesthai*] is some beneficial outcome; if it does not ensue, then the agent does what seems good to him, or as he sees fit [*dokei autô*], but not what he *wants* [*bouletai*] (466a–468e). Diotima and Socrates agree in the *Symposium* that the desire [*epithumia*] for happiness or good things is the supreme love or longing [*erôs*] in everyone (205d); in fact, "What everyone loves [*erôsin*] is really nothing other than the good" (205e7–206a1).

This *Desire thesis*, as I will call it, forms a key part of the so-called 'Socratic intellectualism' of the early dialogues, along with several other paradoxical claims: that the virtues consist in a kind of knowledge, and thus form a unity; that *akrasia* or weakness of will is impossible; and that all wrongdoing is involuntary [*akôn*]. The Desire thesis seems to be foundational for the others, for it (arguably) precludes *akrasia*, and, in conjunction with the fact that what is really good for us is virtue, entails both that moral knowledge suffices for virtuous action and that wrongdoing can only be caused by ignorance. It is often claimed that in Book IV of the *Republic*, Plato rejects the Desire thesis, and with it this whole package of Socratic moral theory.[2] Recognizing—rather late in life, one might think—that some desires are not directed toward the good at all, Plato introduces the lower parts of the tripartite soul to house these "good-independent" desires, thus repudiating the Desire thesis and its intellectualist implications. Yet in Book VI of the *Republic*, Socrates goes on to say that the good is "what all soul [*hapasa psuchê*] pursues [*diôkei*] and does everything for the sake of" (505e1–2). And in the late *Philebus*, Socrates says of the good that "everything that has any notion of it hunts for it and, desiring [*boulomenon*], reaches out [*ephietai*] to get hold of it and secure it for its very own, caring nothing for anything else except for what is connected with the acquisition of some good" (20d7–10). The corollary that wrongdoing is involuntary is also repeated emphatically in the very late *Timaeus* (86b–87b).

So we have reason to suspect that the Desire thesis is a sustained and foundational principle of *Platonic* moral psychology. But whether the various statements I have quoted really do boil down to a single, consistently held thesis is far from certain. And indeed there seem to be two distinct versions of the thesis in play. One, which I'll call the *Appearance thesis*, is that all desire is for the apparent good—that is, for an object the desiring agent *takes* to be good. It is this claim, that desire is *sub specie boni*, which recurs in later philosophers such as Aquinas and Spinoza, and remains a live and controversial option today. The other, the *Reality thesis*, looks odder and more distinctively Platonic: it is that human desire can only be for *what, in fact, is good*. It is the latter that in the *Gorgias* leads to the shocking corollary that wrongdoing is involuntary [*akôn*]—specifically, that Archelaus, the brutal yet glamorous tyrant cited by Polus as a paradigm of flourishing injustice, does not do what he wants.[3]

It's some measure of the sheer confusingness of the issues here that, depending on how they are presented, the Reality thesis can seem either to follow trivially from the Appearance thesis or to contradict it. On the one hand, it seems natural to say that if some desire is perspicuously described as being for *x*, then it is for what really, genuinely is *x*. After all, if I say that I want to eat an apple, you probably do assume, without further inquiry, that I want to eat a real apple—as J. L. Austin noted, in the absence of some particular puzzle or contrast, the term 'real' doesn't seem to add anything in everyday contexts.[4] And when Plato (or for that matter Aristotle) says that wealth is desired as an apparent good, what he means is that the desiring agent takes it to be a *real* good—'apparent goods' aren't some natural kind that we might prefer to real ones, but are just the class of things thought to be genuinely so. So the Reality thesis can be read as essentially a gloss on the Appearance one—and indeed I will eventually argue that this is the right way to take it. On the other hand, consider again the desires of Archelaus the tyrant. Suppose that Archelaus avows a desire to be the most powerful man in Macedonia. The Appearance thesis diagnoses that desire as a desire for an apparent good; power without wisdom is not really a good, Socrates argues, but Archelaus desires it because he thinks it is. But the Reality thesis simply rejects Archelaus' self-description: given that power without wisdom is not a genuine good, it can't be the object of his desire *at all*. So the two theses give directly conflicting results, and the Reality thesis seems to preclude precisely that fallibility in selecting objects of desire that the Appearance thesis attributes to us.

In rough outline, it is clear what Socrates wants to say about Archelaus. Given that it, in fact, frustrates his desire to obtain the good, Archelaus' wrongdoing must be understood as *misguided* action, based on a faulty evaluation of the object that motivates it. As Santas explains in a classic discussion, the agent who pursues what is not really good is like one who, desiring pepper (the 'intended object' of his action), reaches out for what is actually the salt shaker (the 'actual object').[5] In such a case, if we grasp what is going on, we may feel licensed to warn the agent: 'You don't really want that!' Given Plato's relentless objectivism about the good, such trivial misidentifications represent one end of a whole spectrum of 'miswanting,' with the ostensibly satisfied tyrant at the other. There will of course be important differences between the tyrant and the confused condiment-seeker, for the tyrant's false beliefs are not merely ad hoc perceptual errors. They may comprise a whole network of mistakes about value, involving deep conceptual confusions and failures of self-knowledge; and attempts to correct them are likely to meet with enormous psychological resistance. But all these complex psychological ramifications have their origin in what is nonetheless the same *kind* of cognitive mistake. The question that remains is whether the 'actual object' fixed on by that mistake is properly counted as an object of desire at all. If it is, then the Reality thesis and the corollary that wrongdoing is involuntary seem to be given up; if not, then desire no longer seems to occupy its standard functional role in the motivation of Archelaus' behavior.

This chapter attempts to work out what each of these two versions of the Desire thesis means, as well as the puzzling relation between them. Ideally, such a reading of the Desire thesis should meet a number of desiderata. First, it should take both theses seriously and literally as presented—that is, as psychological laws, not as eristic gambits, disguised normative claims, or exaggerated generalizations. Second, it should respect the fact that both theses are presented as global claims about conation in general, not just desire in some special restricted sense—in contrast, for instance, to Aristotle's account of *boulêsis*, rational desire, in *Nicomachean Ethics* III.4. Though some interpreters detect a distinction between *epithumein* and *boulesthai* here (as I will discuss in section I), Plato himself seems to vary his terminology in order to emphasize its indifference: as we saw in the first paragraph above, he speaks not only of wanting [*boulesthai*] and desiring [*epithumein*] the good but also of loving [*erân*], pursuing [*diôkein, Rep.* 505e1], choosing [*haireisthai, Prot.* 358d2–3], hunting for, aiming at [*thêreuein, ephiesthai, Phil.* 20d8], and "being willing to go toward" [*ethelein ienai epi, Prot.* 358c6–d2] it. This gratuitous variation is a strong signal that we should understand the Desire thesis as one about motivation across the board: thus, following Plato, I will, for the most part, use 'want,' 'desire,' and so forth interchangeably.

An ideal interpretation of the Desire thesis would also show how Plato might reasonably take the Appearance version to be an intuitively plausible principle, so that it may in some contexts be proposed without argument (*Rep.* 505e1–2, *Prot.* 358d), while in others Plato supports it with what looks more like dialectical clarification than demonstration (*Gorg.* 467c–68c; *Symp.* 205e). It would show how the Reality thesis warrants the scandalous inference that Socrates draws from it in the *Gorgias:* that actions that obtain the bad—e.g., the unjust decrees of the tyrant Archelaus—are involuntary [*akôn*] (509e). And it would explain how, in both the *Meno* and the *Gorgias* (as we will see), the Appearance and Reality theses are not only treated as compatible: the Reality thesis is introduced by being *added on* to the Appearance one, as if it were a trivial variant or a snappy corollary.[6] Thus a fully satisfactory reading would depict the two theses forming a coherent unity, with the Reality thesis being easily derived from the Appearance one. Finally, an optimal reading would explain how Plato could continue to hold some version of the Desire thesis even after writing *Republic* IV.[7]

So far as I can see, not all of these desiderata can be met; and most recent interpretations have given up on at least one of them. Thus both Rachana Kamtekar and Heda Segvic have recently argued for taking Plato's talk of 'wanting' [*boulesthai*] as sharply distinct from ordinary desire [*epithumein*]. On Kamtekar's reading, which relies heavily on an analogy with our real latent beliefs as revealed by the Socratic elenchus, the thesis holds that while all people desire [*epithumein*] good things, vicious people desire bad ones as well; but wanting [*boulesthai*] is oriented to the good alone.[8] This 'wanting' is a real if mysterious psychological phenomenon, a kind of latent teleological orientation to the good revealed less in our avowed desires than other conative behavior (for instance, our being *satisfied* or not by the attainment of some perceived good). Heda Segvic has also developed an account of the Reality thesis as expressing a special Socratic conception of 'wanting' [*boulesthai*]. Like perception, wanting is a kind of successful interaction with the world:[9] to want something in this sense involves *knowing* that its object is good, and that one cannot want the bad is simply part of the concept. Both of these readings are carefully argued and illuminating on many points; but neither is easily reconciled with Plato's own statements of the Desire thesis, which certainly sound like naturalistic, lawlike claims about the causality of conation in general as normally understood. The leading representative of a more literalist reading of the Desire thesis is Terry Penner, and this chapter is greatly indebted to his work.[10] However, Penner's reading (or evolving family of readings) takes Plato's views on desire to be enmeshed with a complex set of commitments regarding reference and psychological states; it is hard to see the theses so read as intuitively graspable and widely accepted ones, which again is what Plato's own presentation of them seems to call for. Penner's reading also involves doing away with the Appearance thesis altogether—a heavy cost since it is, on the face of it, better attested than the other version.

My own solution, briefly, will be to take the Appearance thesis *au pied de la lettre*, while opting for a deflationary reading of the Reality thesis. The latter, I will suggest, is not intended as an independent thesis at all but rather as an *interpretation and clarification* of the Appearance thesis: It is *not* to be taken in the strong and literal sense that would render Plato's argument self-defeating, by in the end denying that we are fallible in our desiring. Rather, taken together, the two versions of the Desire thesis express a position I will term *cognitivism* about desire. As the Appearance thesis says, I always desire what seems good to me. But, as the Reality thesis clarifies, that does *not* mean that I desire objects *under the description* 'what seems good to me,' taking my subjective responses to be constitutive of value. Rather, in desiring I do my best to track what is antecedently valuable, insofar as I can detect it. Properly understood, the Desire thesis is really a claim about the priority of cognition to motivation, and depicts the latter as world-guided in just the same way as the former.

In section I, I begin with detailed analysis of the *locus classicus* of the Appearance thesis, the rather tricky argument at *Meno* 77–78. Section II tries to explain what 'good' means in the Appearance thesis, and introduces this 'cognitivist' reading. Section III turns to the *Gorgias* and the Reality thesis, and considers the thorny question of how the Appearance and Reality theses are related. Section IV then places the Desire thesis as a whole in the broader context of Plato's realism: its real force, I will argue, is to claim that there is a certain commitment to objectivity built into our ordinary ways of believing and desiring.

I

The starting point of Socrates' argument in the *Meno* is Meno's proposal to define virtue, *aretê*, as "to desire [*epithumein*] fine things [*ta kala*] and have the power to acquire them" (77b), a suggestion that Socrates reformulates in terms of desiring good things [*agatha*]. (The sort of good things a virtuous person wants to secure are specified in Meno's later remarks: health and wealth, gold and silver, honors and offices in the city [78c].) Socrates then rejects the first part of the definition as idle. Desiring good things is not a perspicuous criterion for virtue, for no one ever does otherwise.[11]

Socrates begins by distinguishing two putative groups who might be described as desiring what is bad: those who do so believing the bad things to be good (call these group A), and those who do so knowing them to be bad (group B). Meno affirms the existence of both (77c2–5). Socrates then divides the latter group into those who desire bad things believing that those things *benefit* their possessors (group B1), and those who recognize that they are harmful (group B2) (77d1–4). He gets Meno to agree that those who believe that the bad things will benefit them do not really know that they are bad: in effect, group B1 really must be subsumed under group A (77d4–7). In a somewhat mysterious move to which I will return, Socrates adds that those who desire what they believe to be good *desire good things;* that is, there is really no group A either (77d7–e4). Finally, Socrates turns to deal with group B2. Those who believe that the bad things they desire harm their possessors must know that they will be harmed by possessing them, that they will be miserable to the extent they are harmed, and that they will thereby be made unhappy (77e5–78a4). But nobody wants [*boulesthai*] to be unhappy (78a4–5). So nobody wants to possess bad things: there is no group B2. Given that B1 and A have already been shown to be empty, there is therefore no one at all who wants what is bad (78a5–b2).

My switch from 'desire' to 'want' above reflects a shift in Socrates' usage from *epithumein* to *boulesthai*, which raises a basic question as to whether the same attitude is under discussion throughout this passage. The two terms certainly have different connotations, and, in some contexts, different senses.[12] Thus a number of interpreters, including Kamtekar and Weiss, take Socrates to here distinguish two distinct attitudes with different objects, with *boulesthai* restricted to the genuinely good.[13] But any such reading comes at a high price, making the argument as a whole a matter of deliberate fallacy. For when Meno finally grants that "no one wants [*boulesthai*] bad things" (78b1–2), it is clearly an admission that his opening thesis has been refuted. Socrates even presses the point in a way that rephrases Meno's earlier claim: "Were you not saying just now that virtue is to want [*boulesthai*] good things and be able to get them?" (77b3–4). Their shared conclusion, that the first part of Meno's definition of virtue should be dropped, follows from these steps. But if the two terms are not legitimately interchangeable, then none of this genuinely follows.

So it is better to take the difference between *boulesthai* and *epithumein* here as one merely of connotation.[14] The final steps of the argument are, after all, structured just as we would expect them to be if *epithumein* had been used throughout (which is not, of course, to deny that Socrates aims to exploit the differing connotations of the terms in order to maximize the plausibility of his argument to Meno);[15] and as I noted earlier, such terminological vacillation is, in fact, characteristic of Plato's presentation of the Desire thesis. In a passage of the *Symposium* that echoes this one in many respects (204d–6b),[16] there is again a switch from *epithumein* to *boulesthai* (205a2ff.) when the object is happiness in general; but Diotima also mixes and matches the terms *en passant*, speaking of a *boulêsis* and *erôs* to have good things forever (205a5) and of an *epithumia* for good things and to be happy (205d1–3). And Plato's affirmations of the Desire thesis often bypass attitude terms altogether in favor of more behavioral talk about what we 'go toward' or 'pursue,' casting the good as object of *all* the motivations that cause intentional action (*Protagoras* 358c6–d2; *Republic* 505e1; *Gorgias* 468b1; *Philebus* 20d8).[17]

So read, the *Meno* argument proceeds by a reasonably straightforward exhaustion of alternatives.[18] The key eliminative moves come as the groups B1, A, and B2 are successively redescribed and excluded from the ultimately empty set of those who desire the bad. The most transparent of these moves is the first, at 77d4–7. No one can be correctly described as 'desiring the bad believing it will benefit him,' presumably because to think of something as beneficial *just is* to think of it as good. As this reveals, the argument is structured around a framework of conceptual connections embedded in everyday Greek usage, which are presented as uncontroversial here and in other similar contexts.[19] Most of Socrates' moves here function primarily as reaffirmations and clarifications of this framework, which Meno is happy enough to accept. As it eventually emerges, good things [*ta agatha*] are as such beneficial [*ôphelima*] while bad ones [*ta kaka*] are harmful [*blabera*]; and the beneficial and harmful as such contribute to our happiness [*eudaimonia*] and unhappiness [*kakodaimonia*], respectively. Desire, meanwhile, is what I'll term an *appropriative* attitude, an impulse to *obtain* some object (or a standing disposition to have such an impulse): when we desire, as Socrates says, what we want is for the object of desire to become ours (77c7–8; see also *Symp.* 204e3–4, 206a6–8; *Philebus* 20d9). Of course, none of this tells us anything about what objects *are* good and bad to obtain. Rather, all these connections are conceptual or formal, and can be shared by interlocutors with radically different substantive conceptions of what the good and happiness consist in. (*A fortiori*, 'good' here, as in Plato's other expressions of the Desire thesis, clearly does not mean *morally* good—though Socrates does also hold that, as a matter of fact, the life of virtue is what our good consists in. Hence 'evil' is a very misleading translation for *kakon*, despite the awkwardness of 'bad' in plural uses.)

This framework is also in play in Socrates' second move of exclusion, when he rejects the possibility of desiring the bad while recognizing it as harmful. This seems to presuppose that, if I do not want the effect, I cannot want the cause; and it might be objected that this is (if anything) a normative rather than a descriptive principle. For surely desire does not always respect causal relations in a rationally coherent way: I can recognize that something will cause me unhappiness and, irrationally, want it nonetheless—not want the unhappiness, perhaps, but want the very thing that causes it.

This objection could be blocked if we could assume that all our particular desires trickle down, so to speak, from One Big Desire, our desire for happiness—that is, that whatever I want, I want strictly as an instrumental *means* to happiness.[20] The difficulty is that, despite the conceptual relations between goods and happiness I have just sketched above, this does not appear to be what Plato has in mind. Rather, the thesis seems to be concerned with immediate, piecemeal responses to things found attractive in their own right—bright shiny objects like health and wealth, honor and high office (see *Meno* 78c–d, 87e; *Euthyd.* 278eff.). Perhaps we could see these as (on Meno's view) constituent or ingredient means to happiness, or even as a rather crass 'objective list' account of what happiness is. But since it is generally accepted that such goods can fail to benefit (*Euthyd.* 280b–81e), their relation to happiness is presumably mediated by the experiential benefits they are intended to secure, such as pleasure, satisfaction, freedom, the beautiful [*kalon*], etc. I will refer to these general kinds of value as 'mid-level' goods.[21] And in any case, neither Meno nor Socrates seems to suppose that any thought about my happiness—that is, my overall long-term welfare or flourishing—must play a causal role in my desire either for particular goods *or* the mid-level benefits they secure. In most of the relevant texts, Socrates does not even seem to be discussing comparative or 'all things considered' desires.[22] For the purposes of the Desire thesis, desire is evidently conceived as a simple, direct, two-place relation between an agent and a perceived good such as power or fame. And this gives us an important clue for interpreting the Appearance thesis. Plato is *not* claiming that every desire must be mediated by some thought about our own long-term welfare, in a way that would exclude self-destructive or wanton desires; his claim is only that our appropriative impulses proceed from cognition of their objects *as* valuable in some way.

So these two exclusionary moves, eliminating groups B1 and B2, really work the same way. Their point is to nail down Meno's assent, in the face of his initial wavering, to the identity of the good, the beneficial, and the happiness-inducing, as interchangeable descriptions of the object of desire. Meno's initial inclination is to see the three as capable of coming apart to some extent, presumably because reflective thoughts about what is beneficial and about happiness might generate desires in conflict with others not so mediated. But under just a little conceptual pressure from Socrates, Meno is prepared to join him in treating the three as equivalent.

The remaining turning point in the argument is its most mysterious and controversial step: namely the exclusion of group A, immediately following its subsumption of B1, when Socrates disqualifies from 'desiring the bad' those who desire objects they *think* are good:[23]

> It is clear then that those who do not know things [that is, the things they desire] to be bad do not desire what is bad, but they desire those things that they believe to be good but that are in fact bad. So that those who have no knowledge of these things and believe them to be good clearly desire good things.

Despite its breezily inferential air, that crucial second sentence doesn't really follow in any obvious way. Plato seems to be engaging in legislation about the ascription of desires, to the effect that they are to be ascribed using a description of the object that the desiring agent would avow (viz., 'good'). In terms of the distinction introduced by Santas,[24] where there is a gap between the 'intended object' of a desire (the description the agent would avow) and the 'actual object' (what we observe him going for), we should identify desires in terms of their intended objects only. But no argument has been given, or even hinted at, for us to accept that stipulation. As McTighe and Vlastos have pointed out, we might consider the case of Oedipus.[25] Oedipus wants to marry Queen Jocasta (under that description); he doesn't want to marry his mother (under that description); unfortunately for him, he cannot marry a description and they are, in fact, the same person. If we accept the Socratic stipulation, it is simply wrong to say that Oedipus desires to marry his mother. But there are contexts in which it might seem correct and informative to say exactly that, and Socrates has given us no reason not to.

This question is complicated by another, related puzzle raised by the same passage. Whether the Reality thesis, as well as the Appearance thesis, is in play anywhere in the present argument is a matter of interpretive controversy.[26] It *should* be: Meno, like Callicles and Thrasymachus, is an advocate for the political life, with wealth and power as his canonical 'good things' (78c), and it seems most unlikely that he would endorse as happy anyone who manages to get whatever odds and ends *he* happens to think good. More explicitly, at 77c5 Meno affirms that he includes among those who want bad things people who do so thinking that those things are good. So for Socrates really to exclude all of Meno's proposed ways of desiring the bad, as he must do to warrant dropping the first part of his definition of virtue, the Reality thesis *must* be in view. Now the most plausible point at which to locate an assertion of the Reality thesis in the *Meno* argument is in this same mysterious elimination of group (A). For we may read it as affirming that everyone who wants what he *thinks* good is, *ipso facto*, properly described as wanting what *is* good—and not what is bad, even if the 'actual object' he pursues is bad. In that case, Socrates' claim that group A should count as desiring the good (full stop) is not best read as a stipulation about the priority of descriptions the desiring agent would avow (not, at any rate, unless we also stipulate that nothing is properly desired under any description *other* than 'good'). For the Reality thesis claims that a desire for the tyrant's license to do injustice, say, should *not* be ascribed to the person who avows it. Like everyone else, he *really* desires only what really is good. Admittedly, much more would need to be said to spell out a viable view here. In particular, we would need a characterization of the difference between avowed 'desire' and *really* desiring that renders the distinction intelligible, a problem I will turn to in the next section. Be that as it may, Socrates' inference here at 77e2–3 seems to amount to a kind of slippery-slope transition from the Appearance thesis to the Reality one. To desire what seems good to us is to desire it *qua* good, and this is *really* to desire what really is good.

To sum up the story so far: Plato in the *Meno* intends to assert both the Appearance thesis and the Reality thesis, and both are intended as theses about human conation across the board. He presents the former as more or less intuitively obvious, by showing that just a little conceptual clarification induces Meno's assent to it; and he seems to think, for reasons that are so far mysterious, that the Reality thesis follows unproblematically from the Appearance one.

II

To see what Plato is driving at here we need to begin by taking a closer look at his understanding both of desire and of goodness. As I noted earlier, desire is here conceived as an appropriative impulse, a cause of actions intended to obtain the desired object for the agent. We might be tempted to construe the Appearance thesis as *identifying* this appropriative attitude with a cognitive state.[27] But the *Meno* passage consistently presents thinking good and desiring as two distinct psychological operations, one of which is causally prior to the other. And this seems right given Plato's other commitments. For one thing, it is an important principle for Plato, made explicit in relevant passages of the *Symposium* (204a) and *Philebus* (34d–35d), that we can only desire what we *lack*.[28] But since the belief that something is good can be held just as easily about an object one already possesses, the desire for a thing cannot be identical with that belief.

So the Appearance thesis is not a direct ancestor (at least not a legitimate one) of those views that explain desire as *itself* an evaluative belief or a perception-like experience of value.[29] Nor is it a claim about the conditions required for us to interpret something as a desire in the first place; nor a set of necessary and sufficient conditions for desiring.[30] In fact, it does not seem to me an attempt to analyze desire itself at all. Rather, it is a simple *causal* claim about the mechanics of human motivation, to the effect that we cannot desire something without first finding it good. This is a claim about the limits of human nature (*Protagoras* 358c6–d2, cited in the opening paragraph above), for which the ultimate explanation presumably lies in the providential teleology of the *Timaeus*.

As to what desire itself consists in, Plato has little to say beyond characterizing it as an appropriative attitude. But in the *Republic*, he explains that a soul experiencing a desire 'takes aim at it' or 'draws it to himself'; or again 'nods assent to it as if in answer to a question' (437b1–c6). In the opposite states, the soul 'pushes and drives things away' (437c6–d1). So desire seems to be quite literally a psychological inclination, an inner impulse or lunging toward an object at some remove—a kind of internal rehearsal for the motion of the body in voluntary action. The Appearance thesis thus amounts to the claim that an inner, action-causing inclination of this kind is causally dependent on a certain kind of cognitive state, specifically the belief that its object (that is, the object to be obtained by the corresponding external movement) is good.

We can now turn to consider more closely what that belief amounts to. This can best be clarified by considering two familiar lines of objection to the Appearance thesis. First, we might think that some desires are too *primitive* to count as dependent on a belief about the goodness of their objects. Second, it seems that a desiring agent might have a conception of the good but, perhaps quite deliberately, not desire what fits it—that is, a desire might be deliberately bad-seeking or *perverse*.

Whether any version of the Desire thesis can account for the desires of perverse and primitive agents remains a matter of deep philosophical controversy. As G. E. M. Anscombe noted, even Milton's Satan, with his resounding cry "Evil be thou my Good,"[31] may reasonably be asked:

'What's the good of its being bad?' And some perfectly intelligible, even familiar answers can be supplied: "condemnation of good as impotent, slavish, and inglorious . . . the good of making evil my good is my intact liberty in the unsubmissiveness of my will."[32] This points toward a strategy well suited to the Platonic version of the Desire thesis, namely the explanation of perverse desires as only superficially deviant instances of desire for intelligible and even familiar 'mid-level' values. Satan desires what is *liberating*; other ostensibly bad-oriented agents might be found to desire the objects they do under the generic description 'pleasant,' say, or 'vindicating' or 'surprising.' And this prospect can help us to understand the role and content of the 'good' in the Desire thesis. Goodness here operates as a formal concept—the highest genus uniting such mid-level values, the positive evaluative valence they all have in common.

So read, the Appearance thesis presents human desire as a response to two in principle distinct cognitive operations. One is the taking of some object to have a certain property—or, better, a set of properties, nested at different levels of generality and culminating in one or more 'mid-level' values: this is salty-and-thereby-delicious-and-thereby-pleasant, for instance. The other is the taking of this hierarchy of properties as *good*. There may or may not be an explicit or propositional judgment involved in these acts of cognition; but they are both acts of *classification*, and thus imply the possibility of universal judgments. *This* has *this* feature, and *this* feature is good: implicitly, *any* relevantly similar object would count as having this feature, and *anything* with this feature would count for us as to that extent good. And Plato's point seems to be that in principle, this provides an explanatory schema for the explanation of *all* human desire, which cannot take place without these cognitive acts.

If this is right, we should not see Plato as insisting that the belief that precedes desire must be *explicitly* about the good (let alone about the morally good, the good all things considered, or happiness). It need only be an evaluative belief of positive valence, picking out *as* valuable some property possessed by the object in view. Something is good by virtue of its participation in some mid-level value: by being pleasant, honorable, virtuous, liberating, sacred, and so forth. And to say that *these* values are good is not (or not only, and not exactly) to say that they contribute to our happiness; rather, it is to say that they carry a positive evaluative charge—a location on a table of values—that triggers pursuit as the appropriate response. The residual puzzle, of course, is whether this is a sufficiently robust conception of 'good' for the Appearance thesis to have any real force. What, if anything, constrains our selection of mid-level values? And what exactly does it mean for us to classify them *as good*, if this is to be something distinct from and causally prior to desiring them— *and* also distinct from thinking of them as part of our happiness (as I insisted in rejecting the One Big Desire hypothesis)? Absent an account of what the positive evaluative valence here amounts to, 'good' threatens to collapse into 'desirable,' and from there into the merely desired.

We can reach the same point from the other direction, through consideration of primitive desires. That our most basic physical appetites are good-independent seems to be a point raised and treated as an objection to the Desire thesis by Plato himself in *Republic* IV. Socrates here goes out of his way to argue that the appetite of thirst is not for good drink but for drink simpliciter: "Thirst itself isn't for much or little, good or bad, or, in a word, for drink of a particular sort . . . thirst itself is in its nature only for drink itself" (439a4–7). This stipulation provides a crucial step in Plato's argument, since it secures the claim that when a thirsty person decides not to drink, it must be because of a *second*, distinct part of his soul, which rejects the drink as a result of rational calculation. Still, exactly what Socrates means to claim is not so obvious.[33] For he here explicitly excludes the possibility of thirst being for hot or cold drink, or much or little drink; yet he also allows that "where heat is present as well as thirst, it causes the appetite to be for something cold as well, and where cold for something hot" (437d8–e2). In other words, he recognizes perfectly well that the actual appetites we experience often *are* qualified, insisting only on the abstract point that those qualifications form no part of *thirst as such*. This seems a point of metaphysics rather than psychology, amounting to an application of the general principle that correlatives are either both unqualified or both qualified. In this, it is akin to a number of other Academic-looking quasi-digressions in the central books of the *Republic*, such as the analysis of *dunameis* in Book V (477c–e). Indeed, it looks rather like a precursor of that analysis, defining a particular kind of *dunamis*, thirst, strictly in terms of what it is 'set over,' namely drink.

So it is not clear that Plato's discussion of thirst really intends to reject the Desire thesis. A further reason to doubt that it does so is that (as I noted earlier and will discuss in section III) Book VI of the *Republic* presents what looks very much like a restatement of the Appearance thesis. Obviously it would be preferable to find a reading on which the two passages are compatible. One possible solution is to say that just as a city may take wealth or freedom as its good (*Rep.* 562b–c), thirst is the appetitive drive that constitutively *takes drink as its* good. This involves attributing to the appetitive part of the soul a certain amount of cognitive equipment, sufficient for performing the two operations I sketched above; but then there is strong independent evidence in the *Republic* for doing so.[34]

Now at this point we seem to have come around again to the problem raised by my discussion of perverse desires, the problem of what exactly it *means* to say that some desire depends on taking its object *as* good. For it sounds like little more than saying that, for instance, the appetitive soul takes pleasures to be desirable, or just that it does constitutively desire them. So the Desire thesis seems to be threatened by a dilemma, or a Scylla and Charybdis. If 'good' is construed in wholly formal and nonrestrictive terms, so that perverse and primitive desires are no counterexample, then the thesis risks collapse into the tautological-sounding claim that desire is for the desirable or the desired. In that case empirical adequacy comes at the cost of vacuity. The framework of mid-level values may still be useful, for it applies to primitive and perverse agents as easily as any others, and indeed provides a way of defining them. We may say that a perverse agent is one guided by a bizarre, irrational or incoherent set of mid-level values, while a primitive agent is one governed by a narrow and inflexible set of them (e.g., 'drink' and nothing else), and incapable of rational reflection thereon. But that does not yet tell us what work the concept *good* is doing here.

It will help at this point to compare the Desire thesis to a similar-sounding view that Plato clearly does *not* intend. According to Thomas Hobbes, "Whatsoever is the object of any mans Appetite or Desire; that is it, which he for his part calleth Good: And the object of his Hate, and Aversion, Evill . . . . For these words of Good, Evill, and Contemptible, are ever used with relation to the person that useth them: There being nothing simply and absolutely so" (*Leviathan*, Part I, ch. 6). In other words: "The common name for all things that are desired, insofar as they are desired, is good; and for all things we shun, evil" (*De Homine* I.xi.4).[35]

Now this subjectivist account of Good and Evil is, I take it, exactly what Plato is *denying* when he says that desire is for the good.[36] For though he and Hobbes agree in identifying the good with the desired in extension, they differ on the all-important question of explanatory direction. Plato insists that we only desire what we antecedently believe to be good; Hobbes, that the description 'good' doesn't correspond to any real or even projected property of things, but is simply attached by fiat to whatever we happen to desire. On the Desire thesis, contra Hobbes, desiring is a teleological business governed by intrinsic norms of success. When we desire *there is something we are trying to get right*, and we get it right when we desire what is really valuable. To anticipate a bit, this will be the key to understanding how the Reality thesis can be not only compatible with but derivative from the Appearance thesis. The force of the Reality thesis is simply to make this claim about world-guidedness explicit, clarifying that in pursuing what *seems* good to me I aim at what really *is* good. Together, the two versions of the thesis present a position I will refer to as *cognitivism* about desire: the claim that our desires are causally contingent on positive evaluative beliefs about the objectively real, antecedently valuable properties of their objects.[37]

So read, the Appearance thesis is neither implausibly restrictive nor vacuous. It cannot be restrictive, since it sets no limit to the *range* of objects on which desire may fall. At the same time, the merely formal role of 'good' here does not render the thesis vacuous. For it is used by Plato to make the substantive and highly controversial claim that desiring is an activity structured by norms, in which we undertake to be properly guided by the way the world is. Put in other terms, his claim is that reasons, in the form of evaluative perceptions and cognitions, govern and explain our desires, and not vice versa.[38]

It is not hard to see why Plato might present the Appearance thesis so understood as intuitively intelligible and widely acceptable, as he does in the *Protagoras* (358b–c), *Republic* (505d–e), and *Philebus* (20d). (I have also argued that the argument for it in the *Meno* is really just a matter of conceptual clarification.) Long before Plato's time it had been taken as obvious that we naturally pursue what seems beneficial, so that self-harming actions require special diagnosis as involuntary or abnormal. In the *Iliad*, when the warrior Glaucus exchanges his gold armor for bronze, Homer explains: "The gods took away his wits" (VI.234–36). In Gorgias's *Defense of Palamedes*, Palamedes declares: "All people perform all actions for the sake of these two things: either to gain some profit or escape a loss" (19).[39] Gorgias's *Encomium of Helen*, the most intriguing pre-Platonic work on moral responsibility, is a very enigmatic and controversial work, but it can be read as an extended exploration of the same principle, arguing that any manifestly self-destructive action, such as Helen's flight to Troy, must have been caused in such a way as to count as involuntary. Strikingly, when Socrates first proposes the Appearance thesis in the *Protagoras*, it is as an uncontroversial starting point for argument, in less need of defense than the hedonism that accompanies it; and it is accepted without demur by the circle of sophists gathered round—otherwise a rather contentious group (358c; see also 335d–338b, 351b–e). So we might plausibly tell a story according to which a commonsensical, traditional presumption that voluntary action aims at the good of the agent came to be made explicit by the sophists (a group including Socrates, in the eyes of his contemporaries), and adopted as an exceptionless first principle for the philosophical explanation of action. In that case, what is distinctively Platonic here is not, after all, the Appearance thesis as such, but rather his use of it *as a vehicle for cognitivism*—his faith that, properly understood, this commonsensical view commits us to an objectivist conception of the good as object of desire. To see how he thinks it does so, we first need to look closely at the Reality thesis.

III

Though I have argued for its fleeting presence in the *Meno*, the *locus classicus* for the Reality thesis is *Gorgias* 466a–68e. Here Socrates insists to an outraged Polus that orators and tyrants have no real power, at least if power is presumed to be a good thing; for to do as one sees fit without intelligence is a bad thing (466e–67a). That orators and tyrants act without intelligence is made out a bit later on when Socrates argues that injustice in one's soul is the worst condition anyone can experience (474c–81b), which implies that anyone who seeks out the power to do injustice with impunity is acting unintelligently. But before then Socrates argues for the even stronger claim, not strictly necessary for his broader argument, that the unjust tyrant or orator does not even do what he *wants*. Socrates starts from noting cases in which it would sound wrong to say that someone wants [*boulesthai*, used consistently throughout the argument] to do the action he performs, and right to say that he wants some distinct end to which it is a means: taking prescribed medicine in order to become healthy, for instance, or undertaking a dangerous sea voyage to make money. Socrates then gets Polus to agree to the general principle that when we act for an end, what we want in acting is that end, which is always some good (467d6–e1).

Socrates initially flip-flops on the question of whether I should be said to derivatively want an action I perform as a means to some end, or *only* the end itself (467d6–e1; cf. 468b8–c1). The appropriative conception of desire suggests the latter, since the objects of desires are properly speaking the 'things' to be 'acquired' by our actions, not the actions themselves. Still, Socrates soon allows that "we want to do these things if they are beneficial, but if they're harmful we don't" (468c). Evidently actions can inherit derivative standing as objects of desire, from the goods for the sake of which we perform them. What is important for Socrates' argument is that there is always a conceptual *gap* of some kind between an action and the prospective benefit in virtue of which we perform it, so that an action can always fail to attain its end and thus fail to have value. This seems fair enough as a characterization of teleological action—that is, action per-formed 'for' a distinct end, no matter how narrow the distinction between the two. Even if I play basketball simply for the joy of playing basketball, the result I desire is something distinct from the action I can perform, and the two can come apart: This fallibility seems to be part of what it means for an action to have an end. (Of course, whether all voluntary actions *are* teleological in this sense is another question.) The questionable move is the further inference that when the performance of an action fails to obtain the value desired, the action itself fails to count as desired. Exactly how Socrates reaches this inference is controversial,[40] but, schematized, the key moves of his argument seem to run as follows (468b–e):

A. 'It's for the sake of what's good that those who do all these things do them': Archelaus wants to kill his enemies if it is better for himself to do so. [*Appearance thesis*] (468b7–8)

B. If it is better for himself, Archelaus wants to kill his enemies; if it is not better for himself, Archelaus does not want to kill his enemies. (468c3–5)

C. If Archelaus kills his enemies, and it is not better for himself to do so, Archelaus does not do what he wants [*Reality thesis*]. (468d1–7)

Socrates' argument here appears to turn on an equivocation at (B),[41] the dangerous ambiguity of which is signaled by Polus' marked reluctance to assent at 468c6–7. For claim (A) presents *anticipated* benefit as a *cause* of present desire, as per the Appearance thesis; claim (C) presents *real* future benefit as a *criterion* for ascriptions of present desire; and (B) seems to pivot between the two.[42] Archelaus might well assent to (B), or more

simply to the conditional: 'If it doesn't benefit me, I don't want to do it.'
But in doing so he would mean to endorse what is really a future-oriented
subjective principle equivalent to (A): if I don't *think* it will benefit me, I
won't form the desire to do it. Socrates instead infers a present-tense claim
about the status of the desires that Archelaus in fact avows. So, though the
presentation is not quite so elliptical as in the *Meno*, the *Gorgias* too seems
to illegitimately infer the Reality thesis from the Appearance one by
equivocation.

Worse, (A) and (C) seem to give conflicting diagnoses of Archelaus'
condition. The Appearance thesis (A) implies that Archelaus' unjust actions are caused by his desire for wealth, which he takes to be good. That
seems plausible enough; but how then does he *not* do what he desires in
so acting? Moreover, if we are to accept the Reality thesis as Plato's final
diagnosis here, it needs to be supplemented by two things that are difficult to supply. The first is an account of what *does* cause Archelaus' action.
What is this 'seeing fit' that motivates misguided action, and how does it
motivate us? It seems that an attitude of 'seeing fit' performs all the functional roles of a desire without being a desire—a rather fishy status given
that, as we saw, the Desire thesis is supposed to be about conation across
the board. The other is some account of how these mysterious real desires
for the real good actually contribute to our psychological economy. Without explanations on these two points, Plato seems just to be feebly stipulating that motivations of which he disapproves should not be counted as
real desires; and that we all really do desire whatever he thinks we ought
to. It would be hard to see this as anything other than a confusion of the
descriptive and the normative.[43]

I will return in a moment to consider our interpretive options here, but
it is worth noting first that this is far from the end of Socrates' argument.
At this point it remains an open question what the good that we desire
consists in. Socrates' conclusions at 468c–e are scrupulously conditional,
viz that the unjust tyrant does not do as he wishes *if* those unjust actions
are bad for him; and this shows only that *it is possible* to hold political
power yet not do what one wishes. His later, scandalous conclusions that
the tyrant Archelaus is miserable, and that the unjust act involuntarily,
depend on two further tranches of argument that are soon provided: the
empirical claim that Archelaus is in fact unjust, established by Polus's
recounting of his story at 470c–73d, and the argument at 473d–77e by
which Socrates establishes that injustice in the soul (if one escapes punishment for it) is the worst evil one can possess. The conclusion that
Archelaus is miserable then follows (479a–e); and only later, in a somewhat inaccurate moment of retrospect to Callicles, does Socrates throw in
the corollary about involuntariness:

> Do you think Polus and I were or were not correct in being compelled to agree
> in our previous discussion when we agreed that no one does what's unjust
> because he wants to, but that all who do so do it involuntarily [*akôn*]? (509e)

In fact, at no earlier stage of the argument had Socrates said anything about the voluntary: but the equation of the not-wanted and the involuntary is apparently supposed to be unproblematic.[44]

For our purposes the crucial phase of the argument is Socrates' fancy footwork at (A)–(C) above, with (C) understood as a negative formulation of the Reality thesis. I will briefly note what seem to me some of the more promising interpretive options here: most are owed to or inspired by Terry Penner, but I will not here engage with the complexities of his accounts of them, and will just skim the surface of considerations for and against each. One such option would be to construe the relation of a desire to its object as *referential*, and as constituted by successful relation to that object.[45] Given the reading of the Appearance thesis that I offered earlier, on which a desire depends on our taking its object to have some positively valued property, we might think that the object of a desire is properly *the goodness of the value instantiated by that object*. For instance, strictly speaking, what Archelaus desires is 'the benefit of the pleasures of tyranny.' Since that object does not exist (tyranny does not have pleasures, or if it does they are not beneficial), the desire is null and void; it fails to be a desire, just as a would-be sentence with a nonreferring subject term fails to be a sentence (*Sophist* 262e). We can perhaps make this more plausible, or at least intelligible, by thinking of a desire as a 'power,' a *dunamis*, and thus by nature fixed on its correlative object (*Rep.* 477a–d). (Perhaps we can no more desire the bad than we can see the audible or hear colors.) However, though these potential connections to other Platonic principles are intriguing, it is hard to see how this reading can meet the twin desiderata noted above. If desires for the bad fail to be desires at all, what does cause Archelaus's action when he does injustice? (Of course, if his unjust action is *involuntary*, one might argue that there is really *no* action here and thus no causally efficacious motivation either: but I will soon argue that this is too strong a sense to give to Plato's 'involuntary.') And what role does his alleged desire for the good ever actually play in his agency?

Alternatively, and more straightforwardly, we might insist that desire for the good—the real good—is directly in play in causing *every* action. For the *only* desire we have is a general standing desire for 'the good, *whatever it may turn out to be*.'[46] When I 'see fit' to φ, the cause of my action is simply the conjunction of that standing desire with, as a sort of minor premise, a belief that φing will satisfy it. This does fairly well at satisfying our two desiderata, for it gives desire for the real good a genuine psychological role, and gives an account of 'seeing fit' without introducing good-independent conation. On the other hand, this option involves attributing to Plato the One Big Desire picture that I rejected earlier—and that in an especially strong form, with no genuine conative 'trickle-down' to any desiderata more specific than happiness. Besides sounding un-Platonic, this is hardly an intuitively plausible picture of human desire. We are all familiar with desires having the form 'I want x, whatever x may turn out

to be'—to go to the best restaurant in Chinatown, say, quite independently of any beliefs one might have about which restaurant that is. And,
as this reading helps to bring out, the Desire thesis implies that we all
have a general, unspecified desire of this kind for 'the good, whatever it
may turn out to be.' Still, we experience these unspecified desires as distinctive in *kind* [47]—it is hard to accept that *all* our desires are structured in
this way, still less that all really amount to a *single* desire having this form.
Moreover, on this reading as on the first, there is *nothing* of which the
Appearance thesis is true—we have, properly speaking, *no* conative attitude toward the apparent-but-not-real goods that we mistakenly pursue.
Yet it is hard to see how the Appearance thesis is dispensable. It figures,
after all, as premise (A) in the argument above, and seems to be the basis
for the Reality thesis in the *Meno* as well.

Another alternative would be to say that whatever desire Archelaus
acts on when he commits injustice is *trumped* by a stronger or deeper
desire that conflicts with it. This possibility is suggested by the parallel
case of belief as disclosed by the Socratic *elenchus*.[48] It is no accident that
the *Gorgias* argument for the Reality thesis leads into a methodological
debate in which Socrates comes as close as he ever does to explaining his
dialectical method, using as a case study his plan to elicit from Polus an
affirmation that (contrary to his initial avowals) it is worse to do injustice than to suffer it (468e—74b). Plato thus frames the Reality thesis
and the elenctic display as twin exercises in depth psychology. We may
well *neither* avow what we really believe *nor* pursue what we really
desire, and either lack of self-knowledge will lead us to self-frustrating
behavior. And there is more than a parallel here. Socrates' two claims are
meshed together, for the evaluative beliefs about doing and suffering
injustice that he scrutinizes in the *elenchus* are actually phrased in motivational terms: Socrates and Polus are arguing about which course of
action the other would *really* 'prefer,' 'want,' 'welcome,' and 'take'
(474c), and who is really to be envied. And it is, of course, the Desire
thesis that licenses this taking of conative attitudes as proxies for beliefs
about better and worse.

Now in the discussion about the *elenchus*, Socrates presents his en-
deavor as one of showing his interlocutor what he really believes, deep
down: "For I do believe that you and I and everybody else consider doing
what's unjust worse than suffering it, and not paying what is due worse
than paying it" (474b). That is, here as always, the *elenchus* is supposed to
result in the interlocutor giving up on his initial mistaken avowal rather
than its latent contrary, which is to be accepted as in some sense his true
position all along (476a, 480a). But Socrates will go on to insist, against
the equally misguided and refutable Callicles, that the price of his false
avowed moral beliefs is a kind of *disharmony*—a lifelong mental conflict
and psychological incoherence (481e–82c). And it is hard to see how that
can be the case unless his *false* beliefs are psychologically real as well, even
if the latent ones are somehow deeper or more truly representative. There

is obviously scope for a parallel claim in the case of desire. For our standing desire for happiness could both conflict with and be reasonably assumed to trump all our more specialized desires, without the reality of either coming into question. (Nothing in the Desire thesis, as I understand it, precludes conflicting desires; it only insists that they must be based on conflicting evaluative beliefs.)

I think there must be a grain of truth to this interpretation (and will shortly spell out what it seems to me to consist in). At any rate, Plato's intertwining of the cases of desire and belief here cannot be accidental. However, Socrates does not explicitly diagnose Polus as having conflicting desires. (Perhaps Plato does not yet see how such conflicts are possible: in Book IV of the *Republic*, conflicting desires will be the basis for the individuation of psychological parts, and there is no account of such parts in the *Gorgias*, though there may be hints in their direction.) It might also be objected that if Archelaus has a real (albeit trumpable) desire to exile his enemies, it is hard to see how Socrates can claim, as he later will, that his action is *involuntary*. That it does not represent what he *most* wants, and indeed conflicts with it, may make his action less than fully endorsed and autonomous, perhaps even akratic. But it is not obvious that we should understand Socrates' claim of involuntariness as meaning no more than that (though I will argue shortly that this is probably right).

In short, it is hard to come up with a fully satisfactory explanation of how the Reality thesis is to be understood. As I have already suggested, the best solution seems to be to understand the Reality thesis in somewhat deflationary terms, as a clarification. It specifies that 'good' in the Desire thesis is to be understood in objective rather than subjective terms, and thus makes explicit the cognitivist conception of desire that I offered as a reading of the Appearance thesis in section II. This is why it is introduced so casually in the wake of the Appearance thesis in the *Meno* and the *Gorgias* alike: not because it is being fallaciously inferred, but because it is to Plato's mind merely a disambiguation. And an intuitively reasonable one at that—after all, in garden-variety contexts we assume that someone whose desire is appropriately described as a desire for an *x* desires a *real x*, not a merely apparent one.

A passage in *Republic* VI provides support for this reading. In leading up to the analogy of the Sun, Socrates explains that knowledge of the good must belong to the Guardians. Socrates goes on to explain the special status of the good as follows:

> In the case of just and beautiful things, many people are content with what are believed to be so, even if they aren't really so, and they act, acquire, and form their own beliefs on that basis. Nobody is satisfied to acquire things that are merely believed to be good, however, but everyone wants the things that really *are* good and disdains mere belief here.
> —That's right.

> All soul [*hapasa psuchê*] pursues the good and does everything [*panta prattei*] for its sake. It divines that the good is something but it is perplexed and cannot adequately grasp what it is or acquire the sort of stable beliefs it has about other things, and so it misses the benefit, if any, that even those other things may give. (505d5–e5)

Socrates initially presents it as a distinctive feature of desires for the good that they are for the real thing, as if desires for justice or beauty might be for their merely apparent instantiations. But this is immediately followed by the affirmation that the soul does *everything* it does for the sake of the good.[49] So, in fact, *all* our desires have this orientation to reality. There is no contradiction here, since as Plato brings out there *is* still a sense in which someone might fairly be said to desire 'apparent justice.' This would be a true if potentially misleading way of describing a desire—not a distinctive kind of desire for justice, nor a desire for some defective species of justice, but a desire for the real goods to be obtained by possessing 'apparent justice'—i.e., by possessing a *reputation* for justice. Such goods would include security from punishment, presumably, and the esteem of one's neighbors;[50] and these are things that, unlike justice, the agent takes to be *really* good. No desire is *most* perspicuously described as a desire for an apparent x, and if I avow a desire for x *simpliciter* you are licensed to assume that I want the real thing. But in some cases it may still be useful to describe a desire as one for an apparent x, where apparent x's are reliable means to, or proxies for, real (and really valued) y's.[51]

The *Republic* passage thus makes explicit the connection between the Appearance and Reality theses. The Appearance thesis claims that we always pursue what we think good: 'good' is always a perspicuous (if somewhat underspecified) description of the object of desire. *Republic* VI tells us that if 'x' is a perspicuous description of the object of my desire, then my desire is for a *real* x. And that means that my desire—always—is for the real good. What *that* means in turn is that the Appearance thesis cannot be reduced to the subjectivist claim that I call whatever I happen to pursue good. Rather, I pursue what seems good *as an attempt* to obtain what really is so. None of this requires Plato to deny the psychological reality of the desires we avow and are moved by, including those oriented to bad objects; his claim is just that there is something we are *trying to do* when we desire, at which we fail when we desire the bad. (That is why Socrates can casually allow, at the end of the *Meno* argument, that wretchedness is a matter of wanting [really] bad things and getting them. This is not a lapse from the Desire thesis properly understood, but a corollary to it [78a7–8].)

The obvious objection to this interpretation of the Reality thesis is that it is insufficiently radical. For so read, the thesis does not properly entail that Archelaus does not do what he wants, at least not in such a way as to render his actions involuntary. As Santas pointed out regarding the person who confuses the salt and pepper shakers, *in a sense* he is not doing what he wants to do; but Vlastos remains equally right that in a different sense or respect an Oedipus, say, also *does* want to perform the misguided action. Whether a desire is best described in terms of the 'intended' or the 'actual' object seems to be, as I noted in section I, somewhat context-dependent. And if desires may at least sometimes be usefully ascribed in terms of a mistaken actual object, Socrates is surely not licensed to state without qualification that Archelaus acts unwillingly [*akôn*].

How far Plato can be defended from a charge of fallacy or confusion on this point is a delicate question. But my deflationary reading of the Reality thesis suggests that we might also take the corollary about involuntariness in a weakened sense. And there are some independent grounds for doing so. For it is important that we not retroject on Plato Aristotle's very restrictive account of involuntariness in *Nicomachean Ethics* Book III, which seems deliberately designed to clamp down on a broader and more flexible earlier usage. The very fact that Archelaus 'does as he sees fit' would be sufficient to class his actions as voluntary by Aristotle's standards; but in a way Plato can agree. For in denying that the tyrant does what he wants, Plato clearly does *not* mean that his action is not attributable to him, in the manner of a reflexive physical movement or some completely inadvertent behaviour. On the contrary—it is crucial to Plato's argument in the *Gorgias* that the 'involuntary' wrongdoer is morally responsible for his actions, for which he will be punished in the afterlife. The function of the involuntariness claim is to bring out that there is *a further threshold* of free agency, one higher than mere 'doing as one sees fit,' which the wrongdoer fails to meet.[52] He fails to meet it because he makes a mistake in forming the more determinate desires by which he aims at the good, and thereby fails to do what he *most deeply* wants to do. He thus deserves pity and reeducation as well as punishment and condemnation.[53] This is, I take it, the important truth brought out by the reading of the Reality thesis on which the tyrant's unjust desires are 'trumped' by other, deeper ones in conflict with them—in particular, by the underspecified standing desire we all have for 'the good, whatever it may really be.'

For Plato, at least part of the point of the Reality thesis is to warrant the positing of this higher threshold for agency. The idea is that we can measure the proximate, behaviorally manifest desires of the wrongdoer against his standing desire for the genuinely good; insofar as they veer off target we can diagnose him as failed by his own lights. The tyrant may in a sense do what he wants, but *he does not want as he wants to want.* To that extent his action is inadvertent, self-frustrating, and unfree, and the desire itself is inauthentic, false to his own aims in desiring.[54] We would be more likely to call this higher threshold *autonomy,* and at least some philosophers today would explain it in terms of efficacious second-order desires: Plato calls it acting willingly, or doing what one wants.[55]

IV

I have argued for a reading of the two formulations of the Desire thesis as together expressing a cognitivist conception of desire. On this reading, the thesis belongs to a group of Platonic positions and arguments that might all be loosely described as giving an objectivist or realist account of central features of human agency. In the *Cratylus*, for instance, Socrates argues that naming is an activity that can be performed correctly or incorrectly, by arguing that this is true of agency in general:

> So an action's performance accords with the action's own nature, and not with what we believe. Suppose, for example, that we undertake to cut something. If we make the cut in whatever way *we* choose and with whatever tool *we* choose, we will not succeed in cutting. But if in each case we choose to cut in accord with the nature of cutting and being cut and with the natural tool for cutting, we'll succeed and cut correctly. (386e–87a)

This argument takes as its explicit starting point the rejection of Protagorean relativism; but it can also function as an independent argument for that rejection.[56] For it is criterial for agency that not everything can count as success: I must aim at some determinate outcome that my performance may or may not bring about. There is a parallel here with Socrates' arguments against Protagoras in the *Theaetetus*. The famous *peritropê* argument claims that Protagoras is committed to endorsing as true the claims of those who reject his theory (170a–71c); the precise flow of the argument is notoriously difficult to spell out, but Myles Burnyeat has argued plausibly that it aims to show that some commitment to objectivity is built into the act of assertion itself.[57] And a parallel point is made in more restricted terms by Socrates' final argument against Protagoras, which turns on the possibility of predicting wrongly (177c–79b). I *cannot* make a prediction about some matter of which my current state stands as truth-maker. A prediction can only count as such if it incorporates some risk of falsification by the future. Both asserting and predicting are only intelligible as *fallible* practices, and Plato's claim is that this fallibility implies at least a limited realism; that is, commitment to a truth understood to outrun our capacity to shape it.

What the Desire thesis claims is that, as with naming, acting, predicting, and asserting, so too with desiring. I have already noted the parallels between desire and the assertion of belief in the context of the elenchus; desire is even more closely akin to action and prediction, for it is inherently forward-looking. Recall that Socrates in the relevant passages identifies the good with the beneficial, so that the claim that something is good is really a kind of prediction about its effects if acquired. Like all these other activities, desiring is purposeful and world-guided, for when I desire there is something I am trying to do. Thus desiring too is an activity that can go well or badly for us; and we can expect it to go no better than our thinking.

On all these fronts Plato is exploring the idea that a certain commitment to an objective reality is built into our ordinary understanding of cognition and action as fallible. And it is natural to see cognitivism about desire as fundamental here, for if what we want is the real good, this had better be what our thought is about and what our actions aim at. At the same time, cognitivism itself stops short of offering any purchase against an enlightened subjectivism or hedonism. Archelaus can agree that in pursuing the apparent good, what he desires is *really* to be benefited; he can still insist that, as a matter of objective fact, his good is to be found in subjective states about which, in the long run, he cannot be mistaken. But this is already a long way from the infallible subjectivity of Hobbesian desire. If Plato is right about the structure of acting and desiring, some possible accounts of value are excluded: and the way lies open to a fully realist conception of the good.[58]

Notes

1. Quotations from Plato are as translated by the various hands in the Hackett *Complete Works*, in some cases with revisions (John Cooper with D. S. Hutchinson, eds., *Plato: Complete Works*. Indianapolis: Hackett, 1997).

2. See, for instance, Irwin 1995: 223–43.

3. A further wrinkle is that, strictly speaking, both theses can be presented in either a positive version (all desire is for the good; everyone desires the good) or a negative one (no desire is for the bad; nobody wants what is bad). Plato seems to treat these formulations as interchangeable, and I will do the same. In some contexts he also, more dangerously, seems to conflate not wanting to φ with wanting *not* to φ, as if there were no difference for his purposes between the absence of a desire and an aversion as possible responses to what is not good.

4. Austin 1979: 86–89.

5. Santas 1964: 149–57; and 1979: 185–89.

6. The *Protagoras* even seems to flop back and forth between the Appearance and Reality theses (my emphases): "No one who *knows or believes* there is something else better than what he is doing, something possible, will go on doing what he had been doing when he could be doing *what is better*" (358b7–c1); "no one goes willingly toward the bad or what he believes to be bad; neither is it in human nature, so it seems, to want to go toward what one believes to be bad instead of to the good" (see 358c6–d2). But these passages are probably better read as expressions of the Appearance thesis, with reference to beliefs occasionally omitted for the sake of concision.

7. As do Carone 2001 and Moss 2008.

8. Kamtekar 2006: 150.

9. Segvic 2000: 9–11. For some objections, cf. Kamtekar 2006: 138. Terry Penner's objections to 'special sense' readings also seem applicable (1991: 149).

10. See Penner 1987, 1988, and esp. 1991; Penner and Rowe 1994 and 2005; also Reshotko 2006; and Rowe 2007. Penner's arguments are so complex and detailed that it is virtually impossible to do them justice *en passant*; I fear I

cannot properly engage with them here, but only draw on them as useful for developing my own view.

11. How exactly the argument is supposed to work has been much debated. For differing analyses, see Santas 1964: 150–57; Penner and Rowe 1994; Kamtekar 2006: 150–53; Weiss 2001: 32–38; and Scott 2006: 46–53. Penner and Rowe seem to me importantly right in insisting that the Reality thesis must be in play here if Meno's position is really to be engaged (16 with n. 21). But what Meno affirms at 77c5 is that people desire bad things *both* under that description *and* believing them good. So if he is to be refuted, *both* options must be eliminated, i.e., the Appearance and Reality theses must both be made out. Penner and Rowe (18–22) rely on what seems to me a very strained reading of 77d7–e2 in order to eliminate reference to people who desire bad things thinking them good (see Kamtekar 2006: 152–53).

12. For Aristotle, *boulêsis* and *epithumia* are technical terms for rational desire and nonrational appetite, respectively, and there are precursors for such a distinction in Plato (*Charm.* 167d–e; *Prot.* 340b). In the *Gorgias*, *boulesthai* is consistently used in relation to the Desire thesis at 466eff., while later on Socrates and Callicles discuss appetites, *epithumiai*, without any apparent regard for the earlier thesis (though see Carone 2004). Their discussion also seems to look forward to the *Republic* in taking those appetitive desires to have a distinctive 'location' in the soul (493bff.). Still, these contexts are all casual or *ad hominem*. It is certainly plausible that Plato's deployment of *boulesthai* and *epithumein*, in the *Meno* and elsewhere, reflects a division of labor in contemporary usage, and that Socrates gets some persuasive mileage from their differing connotations. It is much harder to believe that the early dialogues operate with a theoretical typology of human desires that Plato at no point articulates or defends.

13. Kamtekar 2006: 127, 150–51; Weiss 2001: 35–39. See also Santas 1964: 152n15; Segvic 2000: 14–15.

14. Even in the *Republic*, every part of the soul, reason included, has its own *epithumia* (580d7), and *boulesthai* is used of the lower parts (439b1)—as if to challenge any quick assumptions we might make that the motivations of the different parts are different kinds of thing. As Lorenz (2006: 45–46) notes, even in the *Republic*, *epithumia* does not *mean* 'low appetite,' but something more like '(intense) desire' (see Carone 2001: 122n30).

15. The only possible exception is one that Kamtekar emphasizes, Socrates' rhetorical question at 78a7–8: "For what else is being miserable but to desire [*epithumein*] bad things and to possess them?" She takes this to imply that the results of Socrates' argument must be compatible with the claim that some people *do epithumein* what is bad, and that therefore *boulesthai* must be something different (150n44, 153). I take him rather to be emphasizing that, on reflection, Meno's own definition of happiness at 77b2–5, to which this line clearly alludes, supports the conclusion that no one could (lucidly) want bad things.

16. Features common to the two passages include the following: (1) a preliminary replacement of *kala* by *agatha* as the object of desire (*Symp.* 201c, 204c–d; cf. 202c10–d5; *Meno* 77b6–7; cf. also *Lysis* 216c); (2) the specification of desire as desire to secure for oneself (*genesthai hautô*; *Symp.* 204e4, 206a6–8; *genesthai autô*, *Meno* 77c7–8); (3) the assumption that we become happy by

acquiring good things (*Symp.* 205a1, d2; implicitly, *Meno* 77e–78b); (4) the claim that all desire is alike in being for the good (205a–b, d–e; *Meno* 78b4–6); and (5) as noted above, the treatment of *epithumein* and *boulesthai* as interchangeable (*Meno* 77e–78a)—and *erân* as well, at certain points in the *Symposium.*

17. *Philein* is rather different, since its paradigmatic usage is for a non-appropriative, (ideally) reciprocal attitude of affection toward another person. So, despite its overlap on many points with the dialogues discussed here, I will avoid making use of the *Lysis*, which offers a discussion (one that is in any case perplexing and apparently aporetic) of the object of *philia.*

18. As Scott (2006: 48n4) notes, the structure of argument, by elimination of alternatives, is Gorgianic.

19. See, for instance, *Euthyd.* 278e–82d; *Symp.* 204e–5a. In the *Republic,* when Thrasymachus challenges Socrates to say what he thinks justice is, he adds a preemptive attack: "And don't tell me that it's the right, the beneficial, the profitable, the gainful, or the advantageous, but tell me clearly and exactly what you mean; for I won't accept such nonsense from you" (336c–d). The implicit accusation has little basis in the *Republic* so far. Presumably we are to understand that Socrates habitually builds arguments around such formal conceptual connections, in a way that strikes others as evasive on the substantive questions.

20. See Vlastos 1991: 203–9 on the 'Eudaemonist Axiom.' As Vlastos notes, for Plato (and more explicitly for Aristotle), intrinsic goods seem to be those that are valued both as ends in themselves (i.e., severally and independently) *and* as constituents of happiness. (Vlastos compares enjoying a movement of a symphony both in itself and as part of the whole composition.) There is thus a conceptual difference between thinking of and valuing some object as a part of happiness and simply as good: Presumably each description has motivational force.

21. Properly speaking, as Socrates argues (to general assent) at *Meno* 87d–88d and *Euthydemus* 280c–81e, we are happy not by *possessing* good things but by being *benefited,* which involves using good things correctly. To do so requires intelligence—which, in turn, suggests that intelligence is the real source of the benefit and, therefore, the only unconditionally good thing. However, Plato never brings this argument to bear on his account of desire itself, which continues to be presented in strictly appropriative terms.

22. There is no doubt a slippery slope between thinking something good, thinking it better than some alternative, and thinking it best, especially in the context of occurrent desires in particular deliberative contexts. However, it seems to me significant that Plato usually prefers non-comparative locutions. (The exceptions would be *Protagoras* 358b7–d4 and arguably some moments of the *Gorgias* [466e2; but the 'better' at 468b2, b6, and d3 is in comparison to not doing the action in question, not to a less beneficial alternative].)

23. See Kamtekar 2006: 151–52.

24. Santas 1964: 154–56.

25. See McTighe (1984: 205–6) and Vlastos (1991: 148–54). Vlastos sees this move—and with it the whole of the Desire thesis—as a tragic mistake on Socrates' part, derived from a failure to distinguish between the actual and

intended objects of desire. He adds that, had Socrates properly grasped the import of his own views, he would realize that (emphasis in original) "*he has no reason to deny that those wicked tyrants and their ilk do desire* those horrible things—assassination, etc.—which 'seem best' to them: under their misdescriptions of those actions as 'good' they most certainly do desire them" (153); thus "his famous doctrine that all wrongdoing is involuntary would dissolve" (154).

26. See Penner and Rowe 1994: 16n21; and Kamtekar 2006.

27. See Moss 2008 for the argument that, for Plato, nonrational desires are perceptions of value. See also Segvic 2000: 35.

28. This principle does important ethical work for Plato. In the *Philebus*, it shows that desire presupposes memory (since the desiring creature must have some awareness of the opposite of its current state), and thus that desire belongs to the soul, not the body (33c–35d). In the *Symposium*, it shows that the gods are not lovers of wisdom, and neither are those who mistakenly think they are wise already (204a). See also *Lysis* 215e, 217e–18b, 221e on desire as directed toward an opposite or what one is deficient in.

29. Such views would include conceptions of desires as cognitive but not doxastic: i.e., as identical with cognitive states, perhaps perceptual or perception-like ones, which fall short of full-blown belief. I have argued elsewhere on independent grounds that for Plato, to be 'appeared to' or to 'have an impression' just *is* for some part of the soul to adopt a belief, however preliminary and unreflective it might be (Barney 1992: 286–87). So the 'non-doxastic' option is not really available to him—though one might still see his view as akin to modern ones that, lacking the apparatus of the partitioned soul, parse desire in non-doxastic terms.

30. So far as I can tell, no Platonic text claims that we *always* desire what we believe to be good, still less that the strength of our desire for something always perfectly tracks the *degree* to which we believe it good. This seems a matter of common sense, at least in the case of general beliefs and occurrent desires for particular objects. I may believe that fish delicacies are very good indeed, yet feel no desire for them by the time the tyrant's banquet gets to the fifteenth course.

31. *Paradise Lost* IV.110.

32. Anscombe 1963: 75.

33. See Carone 2001: 116–21 and Moss 2008. On the broader question of whether the *Republic* repudiates the Socratic moral psychology of the earlier dialogues, see also Rowe (2007: 18): "Plato remains throughout essentially a *Socratic.*"

34. Of course, it is an open philosophical question just what cognitive resources are required for beliefs, concepts, and so forth; but it has been widely accepted since Moline 1978 that the lower parts of the soul in the *Republic*, which regularly communicate and politick with the rational part, must be seen as having significant independent cognitive resources. For the depiction of the lower parts as having beliefs, see *Rep.* 442c–d, 574d–e, 605c (see also Barney 1992: 286–87; Lorenz 2006; Carone 2001: 117–21; Moss 2008). This is not to deny that the psychology of the *Republic* is in part driven by the problem of how to understand desires *we experience as* independent of, and resilient against, our considered beliefs about the good. I cannot discuss this question in detail here,

but it seems to me that the psychology of the *Republic* should be understood as Plato's solution to some of the puzzles raised by the Desire thesis in earlier works, including the *Gorgias* (the status of the *epithumiai*, 492d–95a) and the *Protagoras* (the denial of *akrasia*, 352b–58c). Far from being a renunciation of the Desire thesis, the theory of the tripartite soul rescues it by showing that, *if conjoined with a suitably complex and psychologically realistic account of the agent who desires*, it can account for all the diverse phenomena involved in nonrational desire and motivational conflict.

35. Hobbes evidently intends this subjectivist Desire thesis as one about conation in general, since he holds that "of the voluntary acts of every man, the object is some Good to himselfe" (I.14). And Hobbes's claim that "Aristotle, and other Heathen Philosophers define Good, and Evill, by the Appetite of men" (IV.46) suggests that he believes (or wants the reader to believe) that this version of the thesis has a respectable ancient ancestry (presumably *N.E.* III.4).

36. This way of putting it raises the question of whether Plato might have had some view along Hobbesian lines already in his sights. In section IV I will say a bit about the Desire thesis as part of Plato's broader realism, which certainly was in part a response to the subjectivism of Protagoras and others. But whether Protagoras himself might have intended something like the Hobbesian view as part of his 'Man is the measure' thesis seems to me unclear from Plato's own account of it in the *Theaetetus*. Rudebusch (1999: 27ff.) takes Polus's initial position in the *Gorgias* to be a kind of 'ethical Protagoreanism.'

37. Of course, there are other positions that might be appropriately called 'cognitivism,' including those on which desires just *are* evaluative beliefs; and these would contrast with Hobbes' view in much the same way. But, as I noted earlier, there is no reason to saddle Plato with this problematic conception of desire; his consistent practice of referring to thinking good and desiring as separate operations, one of which is the cause of the other, tells strongly against it.

38. This cognitivist conception of desire is brought out by Plato in a series of etymologies in the *Cratylus* that link desire and belief. Like *doxa*, 'opinion,' *boulê*, 'planning' has to do with trying to hit (*bolê*) some target, and '*boulesthai*' ('wanting') and '*bouleuesthai*' ('deliberating') signify aiming at something (*ephiesthai*). "All these names seem to go along with '*doxa*' in that they're all like '*bolê*,' like trying to hit some target" (420c5–6). Kamtekar (2006: 146–47) has a good discussion of the significance of this passage. As I argued earlier, for Plato a desire is not a belief; but at a sufficiently high level of generality, desiring *resembles* believing, as a different *kind* of attempt to 'grasp' or 'latch on to' the world as it is.

39. Unfortunately, the following sentence, which seems to be a diagnosis of self-harming actions, is apparently textually corrupt.

40. See, for instance, Penner 1991: 173–88.

41. See McTighe 1984: 206–7. Segvic 2000 defends the argument, on the grounds that Socrates has all along been speaking of 'good things' as the ends of action, rather than things thought to be good. But she admits that in that case Polus's assents depend on his misunderstanding the argument (44n39). Penner 1991 (149) argues that it is "an entirely successful refutation."

42. To put the problem in different but perhaps equivalent terms, there seems to be something dubious in the way that the condition embedded in the content of Archelaus' desire in (A) is extracted from its scope in (B) and (C). This has been pointed out to me by John MacFarlane, whose work with Niko Kolodny on conditionals may well be relevant to a full understanding of the logical difficulties here; I hope to pursue these issues elsewhere. A further complication is that, as Sergio Tenenbaum points out to me, Socrates' conclusion should be that Archelaus wants *not* to do what will not benefit him—which is compatible with his *also* having a conflicting desire to do it, perhaps under a different description. I do not think that Plato means here to illicitly rule out the possibility of conflicting desires. Rather, he is for simplicity's sake conflating not wanting to φ with wanting not to φ, to avoid having to continually distinguish the three categories harmful-beneficial-neutral and the corresponding attitudes desire-aversion (i.e., desiring *not*)-neither.

43. Or perhaps a flight to a fanciful metaphysics of postulated 'real selves'; see Kamtekar 2006: 137 and McTighe 1984: 195ff. on the 'neoplatonic' reading.

44. The reference to a previous agreement with Polus is often taken (for instance, by Dodds 1959 and Zeyl 1986 *ad loc.*) as referring to 467c–68e; but this is at best an oversimplification, since the result there is still conditional (that is, injustice has not yet been shown to be bad).

45. This is influenced by, but not quite the same as, the proposal of Penner 1991, according to which actions should be individuated, for Plato's purposes, as incorporating *all* their consequences. See Kamtekar 2006: 141–43 for some serious difficulties with this reading: notwithstanding these, the account is suggestive and, I think, Platonic in spirit in that it vividly depicts the vicious person as a prisoner of *fantasy*, deluded by various cultural clichés about the sources of happiness (see Penner 1991: 188–89 on the 'Private Benjamin' problem).

46. See the fuller and more complex version in Penner and Rowe 1994: 3–10.

47. Moreover, an important group of texts suggest that Plato not only recognizes such desires as having a distinctive structure, but assigns them a distinctive role. The texts I have in mind relate to prayer. In the *Laws*, the Athenian observes that we all pray that our desires will be satisfied, but this is mistaken. We should pray not that all things follow our desire, but that our desire follows our rational judgment (687e). Socrates' prayer at the close of the *Phaedrus* leaves up to gods the determination of what external goods are appropriate to him (279b–c). Xenophon's Socrates prays the same way, "since the gods know best what things are good" (*Mem.* I.3.2; see *Cyr.* I.6.5). The (inauthentic) *Alcibiades* II teases out a Socratic argument for the claim that we should all pray in just this way. It is clear why such prayers are ethically appropriate for a Socratic. To pray is to officially register a desire; and to desire in this deliberately underspecified way expresses an epistemic humility appropriate to our human limitations. So what Penner 1991 takes as the essential structure of human desire according to Plato seems rather to represent a Socratic ethical *norm*.

48. The parallel is emphasized by Kamtekar (2006: 143–48), who concludes that "as people latently believe truths, so they latently want good things" (148).

49. All this is controversial: for contrasting interpretations, see Kamtekar 2006, esp. 154n52; Irwin 1977: 336n45; and Segvic 2000. Interpreters who take Book IV to assert the existence of good-independent desires must take the present passage as weaker in at least one of two ways. First, the crucial phrase *pasa psuchê* can be taken as referring not to *all* soul but to *every* human soul, and thus as referring to the desires of the rational part only. Second, the 'does everything for' [*panta prattein*] can be taken nonliterally, as an idiom loosely meaning 'goes to great lengths for.' Both readings are possible, but seem less natural than those I offer here.

50. This argument in *Republic* VI recalls a passage from Glaucon's earlier speech against justice in Book II. With a paradoxical rhetorical flourish, Glaucon imagines the defenders of injustice casting it as a kind of pursuit of truth: "A really unjust person, having a way of life based on the truth about things and not living in accordance with opinion, doesn't want simply to be believed to be unjust but actually to be so" (362a4–6). In the Book VI passage, Socrates recalls and reaffirms this point in earnest. The unjust man is indeed a seeker of the real thing—the real thing that he values, which is, of course, his own good.

51. This is different from the sense in which Plato or Aristotle may speak of a desire for wealth, for instance, as one for an apparent good; here the sense is that the agent *himself* takes wealth to be a real good, whereas 'apparent justice' in *Republic* VI is what will look like justice to other people. Granted this asymmetry, in both cases the point stands that a desire for an apparent x can always be redescribed more perspicuously as a desire for a real something—the real good in the case of desire for the apparent good, real security and esteem in the case of apparent justice, and so forth.

52. It is also worth noting that in later dialogues Plato defends the view that wrongdoing is involuntary by a somewhat different route. In the *Timaeus* and *Laws*, he is primarily concerned to describe bad states of *character* as involuntary, rather than wrong actions, on the grounds that no one would deliberately receive into his soul the evil of vice (*Laws* 731c–e, 860d–61d; *Timaeus* 86d–e). In these later dialogues, Plato's position seems to be the one attacked by Aristotle in *Nicomachean Ethics* III.5, that people only act wrongly on the basis of bad character, and bad character is itself involuntary.

53. In the *Protagoras*, Socrates insinuates the thesis that wrongdoing is involuntary into his exegesis of a poem by Simonides. He comments: "I am pretty sure that none of the wise men thinks that any human being willingly makes a mistake or willingly does anything wrong or bad. They know very well that anyone who does anything wrong or bad does so involuntarily" (345e). Here too, the idea of *mistakenness* is central.

54. See Plato's (notoriously difficult and controversial) account of false pleasures in the *Philebus*. Here too Plato insists that an affective or motivational state, in this case pleasure, can *directly* incorporate cognitive error. (At 38a–40c he explicitly acknowledges that this will strike most people as a category mistake, and bites the bullet.)

55. This way of looking at the Desire thesis is presumably unavailable to Plato since, at *Charmides* 167e, he seems to hold that second-order desires are impossible. Plato's reasoning there is dubious, but it is also not clear that the apparatus of higher-order desires would really be helpful to him here. As I will

try to bring out in section IV, Plato's point is really one about the teleological, and thus fallible, character of desire at *any* level; to attempt to capture this formal feature of all desire through the relation of higher-order desires to lower-order ones seems misleading, and would invite an infinite regress.

56. For further discussion, see Barney 2001: 42–44.

57. Burnyeat 1990: 30–31.

58. This chapter began life as a paper for a seminar taught by Alexander Nehamas at Princeton University in 1991, and has been changing continually ever since. I am indebted for improvements to audiences at the Texas Workshop in Ancient Philosophy, the University of Chicago, the University of Toronto, the University of Pittsburgh, Lehigh University, Universität Köln, and the Townsend Working Group in Ancient Philosophy at the University of California, Berkeley; I fear I have lost track of all the individuals who have helped me to shed various mistakes, but they certainly include Tad Brennan, Matt Evans, Michael Green, Rachana Kamtekar, Jessica Moss, Alexander Nehamas, Terry Penner, Kieran Setiya, and Roslyn Weiss. More recently, John MacFarlane, Gurpreet Rattan, and Sergio Tenenbaum have all raised puzzles about which I need to think more, and hope to address in the future.

References

Anscombe, G. E. M. 1963: *Intention;* 2nd ed. Ithaca, N.Y.: Cornell University Press.
Austin, J. L. 1979: Other minds, reprinted in *Philosophical Papers;* 3rd ed. Oxford: Clarendon.
Barney, R. 1992: Appearances and impressions, *Phronesis* 37: 283–313.
————. 2001: *Names and Natures in Plato's* Cratylus. London: Routledge.
Burnyeat, M. 1990: Introduction, *The Theaetetus of Plato.* Indianapolis: Hackett.
Carone, G. 2001: Akrasia in the *Republic:* Does Plato change his mind? *Oxford Studies in Ancient Philosophy* 20: 107–48.
————. 2004: Calculating machines or leaky jars?: The moral psychology of Plato's *Gorgias, Oxford Studies in Ancient Philosophy* 26: 55–96.
Dodds, E. R. 1959: *Gorgias.* Oxford: Oxford University Press.
Hobbes, T. 1934: *Leviathan.* London: Dent.
————. 1972: *De Homine.* Garden City, N.Y.: Anchor.
Irwin, T. 1977: *Plato's Moral Theory.* Oxford: Clarendon.
————. 1979: *Gorgias.* Oxford: Clarendon.
————. 1995: *Plato's Ethics.* New York: Oxford University Press.
Kamtekar, R. 2006: Plato on the attribution of conative attitudes, *Archiv für Geschichte der Philosophie* 88: 127–62.
Lorenz, H. 2006: *The Brute Within: Appetitive Desire in Plato and Aristotle.* Oxford: Clarendon.
McTighe, K. 1984: Socrates on desire for the good and involuntariness of wrongdoing: *Gorgias* 466a–468e, *Phronesis* 29: 193–236.
Moline, J. 1978: Plato on the complexity of the psyche, *Archiv für Geschichte der Philosophie* 60: 1–26.
Moss, J. 2008: Appearances and calculations: Plato's division of the soul, *Oxford Studies in Ancient Philosophy* 34: 35–68.
Penner, T. 1987: *The Ascent from Nominalism: Some Existence Arguments in Plato's Middle Dialogues.* Dordrecht: Reidel.

———. 1988: Socrates on the impossibility of belief-relative sciences, *Proceedings of the Boston Area Colloquium in Ancient Philosophy* 3: 263–325.

———. 1991: Desire and power in Socrates: The argument of *Gorgias* 466A–468E that orators and tyrants have no power in the city, *Apeiron* 24, no. 3: 147–202.

Penner, T., and Rowe, C. 1994: The desire for good: Is the *Meno* inconsistent with the *Gorgias? Phronesis* 39: 1–25.

———. 2005: *Plato's Lysis*. Cambridge: Cambridge University Press.

Plato. 1997: *Complete Works*. Edited by John Cooper and D. S. Hutchinson. Indianapolis: Hackett.

Reshotko, N., 2006: *Socratic Virtue: Making the Best of the Neither-Good-nor-Bad*. Cambridge: Cambridge University Press.

Rowe, C. 2007: *Plato and the Art of Philosophical Writing*. Cambridge: Cambridge University Press.

Rudebusch, G. 1999: *Socrates, Pleasure, and Value*. New York: Oxford University Press.

Santas, G. 1964: The Socratic paradoxes, *Philosophical Review* 73: 147–64.

———. 1979: *Socrates: Philosophy in Plato's Early Dialogues*. London: Routledge & Kegan Paul.

Scott, D. 2006: *Plato's* Meno. Cambridge: Cambridge University Press.

Segvic, H. 2000: No one errs willingly: The meaning of Socratic intellectualism, *Oxford Studies in Ancient Philosophy* 19: 1–45, reprinted in Segvic, H. 2009: *From Protagoras to Aristotle: Essays in Ancient Moral Philosophy*. Princeton, N.J.: Princeton University Press.

Vlastos, G. 1991: *Socrates: Ironist and Moral Philosopher*. Ithaca, N.Y.: Cornell University Press.

Weiss, R. 2001: *Virtue in the Cave: Moral Inquiry in Plato's Meno*. Oxford: Oxford University Press.

Zeyl, D. J. 1986: *Gorgias*. Indianapolis: Hackett.

4

Aristotle's Non-Trivial, Non-Insane View that Everyone Always Desires Things under the Guise of the Good

Jessica Moss

I. TROUBLE

Aristotle evidently holds the most extreme possible version of the view that we desire things under the guise of the good. Famously, he holds it in the case of the desires he marks as distinctively rational, wish (*boulêsis*) and decision (*prohairesis*):[1]

> (1) . . . every decision seems to aim at some good . . . (*Nicomachean Ethics* [*EN*] 1094a1–2)

> (2) The object of wish without qualification and in truth is the good, but for each person the apparent (*phainomenon*) [good]. (*EN* 1113a23–31)[2]

Less famously—and more problematically—he extends the view to cover *every* desire (*orexis*), including appetite (*epithumia*) for the pleasant, the paradigmatically nonrational kind of desire:

> (3) The object of desire (*orekton*) always moves, but this is either the good or the apparent good (*phainomenon agathon*). (*de Anima* [*de An.*] 433a26–29)

> (4) The object of desire (*orekton*) and the object of wish (*boulêton*) is either the good or the apparent good. And this is why (*dio*) the pleasant is desired, for (*gar*) it is an apparent good . . . (*Eudemian Ethics* [*EE*] 1235b26–27)

> (5) What causes movement in the first place is the object of desire (*orekton*) and the object of thought . . . . And we must suppose that the apparent good also holds the place of a good, and also the pleasant, for it is an apparent good. (*de Motu Animalium* [*MA*] 700b23–29)

> (6) The apparent fine (*kalon*) is the object of appetite, the really fine the primary object of wish. (*Metaphysics* XII.7 1072a27–28)[3]

> (7) Appetite [moves one] on account of the now, for (*gar*) the presently pleasant appears both absolutely pleasant and absolutely good, on account of not looking to the future. (*de An.* 433b8–10)

Appetite is for what appears good; indeed, we have appetites for things just *because* they appear good to us (most explicit in [4] and [7]).[4]

I take these passages to demonstrate that this is indeed Aristotle's view. The trouble is that it looks very strange. So far as rational desires go, it may raise few eyebrows: Many hold that rational desire is simply to be equated with desire for things *qua* good, both as a matter of Aristotle exegesis and as a matter of fact.[5] The claim that nonrational appetites are for things *qua* good, on the other hand, might—especially given Aristotle's other commitments—sound either misleading and trivial, or patently insane.

Let us take the insanity horn of the dilemma first. Desiring under the guise of the good seems to presuppose having thoughts and beliefs about what is good—one consideration that has led people to think that such desire must be distinctively rational. How then can Aristotle maintain that animals—nonrational creatures who lack beliefs of any kind (*de An.* 428a19–24)—desire things *qua* good? What about babies? Things look worse still when we come to akratics (incontinent or weak-willed people). Aristotle himself avows that they choose the pleasant "instead of the things they themselves believe (*dokounta*) good" (*EN* 1166a15)—that the desires they act on are in direct conflict with their judgments about what is good. In fact, he explicitly distinguishes between appetite (*epithumia*), defined as desire for the pleasant, and wish (*boulêsis*), defined as desire for the good (*EN* 1111b17; cf. *de An.* 414b5–6; *Topics* VI.8). Not only does it seem bizarre to insist that babies, animals, and akratics desire their objects as good, then, but Aristotle himself evidently introduces the category of appetite in part to show that this is not so: Some desires are for things *qua* pleasant instead of *qua* good.

If Aristotle nonetheless insists that appetites are for the apparent good, we seem to be driven to the second horn of the dilemma: triviality. Anyone who maintains the extreme guise of the good thesis must be defining 'appears good' in such a way as to make the thesis analytic: 'X appears good to S' can mean nothing more than 'S desires x,' or at very best 'x attracts S in some way.' Such a view is not only boring, in that it makes no substantive philosophical claim about desire or action, but also misleading. Take (2)–(6) above. Each seems to make an interesting claim about the objects of desire: They all either are good or appear so. That is, there is some one property, goodness, such that all objects of desire either have this property or appear to have it. This property is the proper or natural (formal) object of desire, and an agent will desire an object just in case she takes the object to have it. (Compare: There is some one property, being red, that all the handkerchiefs in this field either have or appear to have. This property is the proper object of bull anger, and a bull will charge at a hankie just in case he takes the hankie to have it.) If 'appears good' turns out to mean 'is desired,' this interesting claim dissolves. Apparent goodness bears no closer relation to genuine goodness than it bears to, say, genuine leather. Or at least there is no straightforward connection between the two of the kind indicated by the 'apparent.'

Of course we can escape the dilemma entirely if we abandon the face value reading of Aristotle's claims, and simply deny that he thinks animals and babies and akratics desire things under the guise of the good. Aristotle sounds much saner on the deflationary reading we find, for example, in Irwin:

> . . . 'apparent good' need not refer to something's appearing *as* good, but may instead refer to the good that appears, even if it appears as something other than good—as pleasant, for instance. . . . When the animal acts to get what appears to it, the appearance must be in general an appearance of its good—an appearance of something that is in fact good for the animal, though not necessarily an appearance of it *as* good. (T. Irwin, *Aristotle's First Principles*, 331–32)[6]

Thus a hungry slug pursues a leaf not because the leaf appears good to it, but because the leaf appears to be a leaf, or appears pleasant.

As reasonable as this sounds on its own terms, as an interpretation of Aristotle it is problematic. First, when Aristotle says the pleasant is desired *because* it appears good (see [4] and especially [7]), he evidently means to be saying something more explanatory than that the pleasant is desired because it appears pleasant. Second, the strategy cannot help us with the akratic: To say that the akratic goes for "an appearance of something that is in fact good" for him—a mirage of vegetables, perhaps—would be to deny the distinctive and problematic feature of *akrasia*, namely that the akratic goes for something he himself thinks *not* good, and rightly so.[7] Third (as Irwin acknowledges), the strategy forces an awkwardly hybrid account of "apparent good." Passage (2) shows that when Aristotle says that rational desires are for the apparent good he means that they are for what the agent herself considers good; it would be very misleading of him to use the same words to apply to the object of nonrational desires without meaning to suggest that in this case too the agent in some way finds the desired object good.

The aim of this chapter is to save the appearance that Aristotle does indeed embrace the guise of the good view even for appetites, while showing that, on his version of it, the view is substantive, tolerably sane, and philosophically compelling. I base my solution on a fairly widespread interpretation of Aristotle's view of pleasure: that to feel pleasure in something is to perceive it as good. What I want to show is that we can take this much more literally than one might suppose. Pleasurable perception, even in nonrational animals who lack value-concepts or beliefs, is a genuine cognitive state: a full-blooded awareness of value. (This is not to say, of course, that it is always veridical; the point is that it is a genuine mode of cognition, even if a highly fallible one.)

By 'cognition,' I mean to capture a notion that Aristotle introduces in the *de Anima* and *de Motu Animalium* with the claim that there is an important similarity between the faculties of perception, *phantasia* ('imagination'), and thought. What these faculties have in common—and what allows them each to combine with desire to produce action—is that they are all *kritika*, faculties by which we *krinein:* discern, distinguish, or judge.[8] They are all ways of registering information about objects, and of doing so in a way that can, in principle, make those objects the focus of desire. I will use 'cognitive' to stand in for Aristotle's *kritikon*. Thus on my use the word carries no implications of anything conceptual, rational, propositional, or doxastic: Even the simplest animals who have only the sense of touch and no higher faculties at all count as cognizers.

If we can show that Aristotle treats pleasure as genuine cognition of value, we can attribute to him a theory of apparent goodness on which:

(i) things can appear good to creatures entirely independently of any beliefs about goodness, and yet

(ii) experiencing an appearance of something as good is a genuinely cognitive state

where (i) frees Aristotle from the insanity charge, while (ii) frees him from the triviality charge.

I will not, by the way, have much to say about whether or not Aristotle's guise of the good view is *true*. I suspect, alas, that it is not, on the grounds that we sometimes voluntarily do things we in no way find pleasurable.[9] What I want to show is that the view is worth taking seriously. It is my own opinion that by freeing the guise of the good from its bonds to rationality, Aristotle gives it its very best chance.

II. PLEASURE AS VALUE-PERCEPTION

When people attribute to Aristotle the idea of pleasure as value-perception they generally have in mind his discussion of pleasure in the *Nicomachean Ethics*. I will have something brief to say about that discussion below, but the main evidence for my interpretation comes from a single passage on perceptual pleasure from the *de Anima:*

> (8) (a) Perception, then, is analogous to simply stating or thinking. But whenever the perceptible thing is pleasant or painful, the soul, as if affirming or negating, pursues or avoids it. (b) In fact, to feel pleasure or pain (*to hêdesthai kai lupeisthai*) is precisely to be active (*energein*) with the perceptual mean toward the good or bad as such. (c) And actual avoidance and actual desire are this/are the same,[10] (d) and the faculty of desire and the faculty of avoidance are not different either from each other nor from the perceptive faculty; but they are different in being. (*de An.* III.7 431a8–12, based on Hicks's translation)

The central claim for our purposes is (b). 'The perceptual mean' (*têi aisthêtikêi mesotêti*) must refer either to the faculty of perception itself or to an organ of perception;[11] and I take the 'as such' to pick up the nearest and most obvious antecedent, the good or bad.[12] Thus (b) says that to feel pleasure in something is to be perceptually active toward it *as good*. But what does that mean?

We can begin by considering what it means be to "be active toward something as good" in general, bracketing for the moment the role of perception. Here we are helped by the fact that throughout the corpus Aristotle links the notion of the good with another notion, that of the end (*telos*), so much so that he often equates the two. (See, e.g., *Physics* 194a32–33, 195a23–25; *Politics* 1252b34–35; *EE* I.8 1218b9–11; *Metaphysics* 1.3 9833102; *de Partibus Animalium* 639b19–20; and the opening lines of the *EN*.) The function argument of *EN* I.7 is a good example: For everything that has a good, "its good seems to be in its function" (1097b26–7), where a thing's function (*ergon*) is identical with or closely linked to its *telos* (*EE* 1219a8). Thus the good in general for a thing is the attaining of its *telos*, and whatever contributes to that is instrumentally good. In the biological works, as Gotthelf shows, "the good" for an animal always refers to what contributes to and promotes its life: what is *oikeion*, familiar or proper to it, what benefits it in the sense of contributing to the actualization of its innate potentials, the realization of its form.[13] There is a debate among scholars as to which is metaphysically basic: Gotthelf argues that good is defined in terms of *telos*, while Cooper and others argue that *telos* is defined in terms of good.[14] Whichever way the metaphysical reduction works, however (if either), the near equation between goods and ends suggests that we can understand what sounds like a mysterious psychological state, being active toward something as good, in terms of one more readily understandable: being active toward something as an end. This, surely, means aiming at the thing, striving for it, pursuing it or being disposed to do so.

Thus we can say that when a sapling draws water up through its roots, it is "being active toward the water as good." The water is good for it—contributes to its actualization and flourishing—and in drawing up the water the sapling is acting in the appropriate way toward the water, acting toward it *as* good. It is doing so with its only psychic faculty, its *threptikon*, faculty of nutrition and growth.

Living things endowed with perception have a more complex way to be active toward something as good. They can become aware of something as good, not only having it as an end in the way that a plant can have an end (on Aristotle's view), but being aware of it as an end, discerning it as an end through perception. That is, there is a special state a perceptive agent can be in, a special kind of awareness such an agent can have of an object, in which the object impacts her not simply as, e.g., blue or sweet or in motion, but as to-be-pursued. I take (b) to be telling us that this state is precisely the one we call feeling pleasure.

Of course sometimes what seems to be value-awareness is delusive: A creature can be perceptually active toward something as good even if it is, in fact, bad.[15] In fact, it is a crucial claim of Aristotle's ethical theory that many human beings systematically take pleasure in things not genuinely good: people with bad ethical characters take pleasure in base, harmful things (like overeating and adultery) that would not please the virtuous (*EN* 1119a12, 1176a13–22).

It is notable, however, that Aristotle views taking pleasure in the bad not merely as a regrettable tendency, but as a kind of malfunctioning of the pleasure-taking apparatus, akin to ordinary perceptual error:

> (9) The pleasures that bring reproach . . . are not pleasant: that they are pleasant for those in a bad condition does not mean that we should think them to *be* pleasant, except for this sort of person, any more than we should think things healthy or sweet or bitter that are so to people who are ill, or again think things to be white that appear so to those suffering from eye disease. (*EN* 1173b20–25)[16]

Why does Aristotle say that base people are making some kind of factual error in feeling pleasure in base things?[17] The explanation, I suggest, lies in his view that a thing's nature is defined by its *telos* (see especially *Physics* II.7: "What a thing is and what it is for are one and the same"). The essence of perceptual pleasure, like the essence of anything else, is revealed not by defective cases but by the cases in which things go well—in which it achieves its *telos* and serves its function. And the function of perceptual pleasure, as a look at the psychological works will show, is precisely to direct the perceiver toward its good.

To see this we must begin by noting that Aristotle's theory of perception is thoroughly teleological. He asks himself why certain creatures should be endowed with perception, where this means asking in what way perception serves their good.[18] He is perfectly explicit that a main purpose of perception is to further the survival of the perceiver (*de Sensu* 436b15–437a1; *de An.* III.12 434b22–27). Nature, who does nothing in vain, equips animals and people with a special faculty that increases their opportunities for survival, by allowing them to discriminate (*krinein*) objects that would benefit them and ones that would harm them.

This is, however, a very unsophisticated faculty: It cannot reason that something is beneficial; on some interpretations, it cannot even recognize things as, e.g., leaves or lions, having access only to "proper" perceptible qualities (color, sound, etc.) and "common" perceptibles (size, shape, motion, number).[19] Aristotle scholars have wondered how such a limited faculty can possibly serve its teleological function in animals that lack the power of reasoning: How can it enable them to recognize things as food, or as threats? Some argue that Aristotle simply has no answer to this worry.[20] Others try to solve the problem by bringing in *phantasia*, ascribing to it powers or roles nowhere explicit in Aristotle's texts, on the grounds that some such filling-in is needed to make sense of his account.[21]

Our passage (8), however, suggests a simple explanation: The perceptual faculty is designed so that when it comes in contact with beneficial and harmful objects, it responds with special feelings—pleasure and pain—and it is these feelings that guide the animal toward the beneficial and away from the harmful.[22] We get strong confirmation of this view from the *de Sensu*:

(10) Taste [must belong to all animals] on account of nutrition, for by it one distinguishes the pleasant and the painful in food, in order to flee the one and pursue the other . . . When we are hungry the smells of [foods] are pleasant, but not pleasant to those who have been filled and need no more. (*de Sensu* 436b16–18, 443b24–26).[23]

Creatures are so designed that, when all goes well, when and only when food will benefit them does its taste or smell please them; given the essential connection between pleasure and appetite (which we will consider below), this is enough to ensure that they pursue foods that benefit them and avoid those that would harm them. An animal pursues her food not because she judges "This is food," or "This is a banana," and then reasons or intuits that she needs to eat such things in order to survive, but because when she smells or eats it, she gets a special feeling: pleasure.[24]

For the teleological account to work pleasure must be closely linked to desire. Earlier in the *de Anima* Aristotle has asserted that it is:

(11) Wherever there is perception there is also pain and pleasure, and wherever these are there is of necessity appetite too . . . ; Whatever has the perceptive faculty also has the desiderative, for . . . whatever has perception also has pleasure and pain and the pleasant and painful, and whatever has these also has appetite. For appetite is desire for the pleasant. (*de An.* II.3 413b23–24; 414b1–6)

(8c–d) may simply reiterate the claim that pleasurable perception necessarily entails desire; it is often taken to imply the much stronger claim that pleasurable perception *is* desire.[25] The lines are difficult and contentious, however, and for our purposes there is no need to take sides. We set out to show that Aristotle holds that appetite is for the apparent good in the robust sense of being for something the agent is in some way aware of as good. Aristotle defines appetite as desire for the pleasant (see [11]). Thus—whether or not the desiring is distinct from the pleasure taken or anticipated in its object—*if* feeling perceptual pleasure in something is literally cognizing it as good, we have shown what we needed to show.

Before we turn to consider that 'if,' I should note that while the arguments I have given in this section go beyond what others have said, this general interpretation of the *de Anima* passage is supported by commentators ancient and modern:

To experience pleasure or distress . . . is nothing else but to perceive something as commensurate or incommensurate with the perceiver. (*Philoponus*, commentary on Aristotle's *de Anima*, ad loc.)

In being pleased perception cleaves to its proper (*oikeia*) activity as good, while in being pained it rejects it as bad. (Simplicius, commentary on Aristotle's *de Anima*, ad loc.)

[Aristotle] defines pleasure and pain to consist in 'the consciousness, by means of the discriminating faculty (*tê aisthêtikê mesotêti*) of the senses, of coming into contact with good or evil. (A. Grant, *The Ethics of Aristotle*, vol. 1, 256)

Finally, a very brief comment on Aristotle's more famous discussion of pleasure in the ethical works. Here the focus is not mainly on the pleasure involved in appetitive desire, but it is notable that Aristotle's more general theory of pleasure is, according to an established interpretation, very close to the account of perceptual pleasure we derived above. Pleasure is "a way in which the goodness of the activity is experienced through its effects on our subjectivity in general, or our sensibility in particular";[26] "something's being pleasant is a prereflective way of its seeming to be good."[27]

III. NON-TRIVIAL, NON-INSANE

I wanted to show that Aristotle construes perceptual pleasure as literal cognition of value, and thus that his view that appetites are for the apparent good is both substantive and sane. So far as the insanity charge goes, we are doing well. If feeling perceptual pleasure in something counts as a way of finding it good then one requires almost no cognitive sophistication whatever to desire something as good; hence the claim that animals and babies desire things *qua* good loses its absurdity. Akratics might seem still to pose a worry, but here we must distinguish between different modes of value-cognition. On Aristotle's account there can be cognitive dissonance between the perceiving part of the soul (the source of appetites) and the reasoning part (the source of the rational *prohaireseis*, deliberated desires, which conflict with appetites in cases of *akrasia*):

> (4) [expanded] The desired and the wished for is either the good or the apparent good (*phainomenon agathon*). And this is why the pleasant is desired, for it is an apparent good; for some believe it is, and to some it appears [good] although they do not believe it so. For *phantasia* [quasi-perceptual appearance] and *doxa* [rational belief] do not reside in the same part of the soul. (*EE* 1235b26–29)[28]

The akratic agent rationally judges some tempting object bad, and thus forms a deliberated desire to avoid it, but the object appears good to her perceptive soul, and so she appetitively desires it.[29] Her appetite, just as much as her rational desire, is for something she finds good.

On the triviality front, however, things might look bad. What I have said so far, instead of diminishing the worry set out in section I, may only strengthen it. For it might seem that we can cash out the notion of value-perception I have attributed to Aristotle entirely without reference to cognition.

When a creature comes into perceptual contact with something in fact good for it, and all is functioning smoothly, it registers the presence of the object with a feeling of pleasure; I want to say that on Aristotle's view this feeling *is* its cognizing (*krinein*) the goodness of the object. The deflationist will object that perceptual pleasure is not itself a way of perceiving the qualities of external objects, but rather a purely affective state, a feeling that arises from perception as a separable result. The slug discerns, through its sense of taste, some perceptible properties of the leaf, and as a consequence gets a special tingle, just as it might as another consequence get a nasty rash. The slug is designed to get this special tingle when and only when it tastes something good for it (although the system fails in the case of poisoned leaves and the like), but what it is actually perceiving is only the taste of the leaf, not the leaf's goodness. Thus talk of value-perception turns out to be mere metaphor: When Aristotle says that the pleasant appears good he means no more than that it is pleasurable, and when he says that appetites are for the apparent good, he means no more than that they are for the pleasant. Appetite directs us, when all goes well, toward what is, in fact, good for us, without depending on any awareness of that good *as* good.

There are, however, three important reasons for rejecting this deflationist view—three reasons for maintaining that pleasurable perception is genuine cognition of value. Two of them emerge from our account of the *de Anima* passage, as follows.

The main reason to count perceptual pleasure as a literally cognitive state concerns its function. Recall that I am using 'cognitive' to stand in for Aristotle's *kritikon*, i.e., to denote the property that thought, perception and *phantasia* have in common. A state is cognitive, on this use, just in case it is a creature's way of discerning or discriminating some property. That something is beneficial or harmful to a creature—that it contributes to or detracts from her flourishing—is on Aristotle's view an objective, although of course agent-relative, fact about that thing: Being beneficial is a property of external objects out there to be discovered. More specifically, it is what the *Categories* would classify as a relation (*pros ti*): for some food to be good for an animal (e.g.) is for that food to stand in a certain relation to the animal—the relation, as we saw above, of contributing to her *telos*.

If feeling pleasure is, as I have argued, an agent's way of becoming aware that a perceived object is beneficial, then pleasure registers a fact about an external object: that the object stands in this particular relation to the agent.[30] It is thus fully cognitive in the relevant sense. That it does not require possession of the concept of goodness, nor the ability literally to predicate 'good' (or even 'pleasant') of an object, in no way impugns its status as genuine awareness: In feeling pleasure a creature's perceptual system need not perceive *that* the object is good, but it does discriminate (is aware of, *kritikon* of) the object's goodness. Just as in tasting a leaf the slug's perceptual system discriminates the leaf's dryness, so in pleasurably tasting the leaf it discriminates the leaf's goodness.

None of this is meant to downplay the aspects of Aristotle's account of value-perception that make it sound at times noncognitivist. Perceiving something as good is inseparable from having "pro-attitudes" toward it, affective and conative: being in favor of it, being disposed to pursue it, being

pleased by it. My claim is just that finding something good does not reduce
to these noncognitive states. Even though it is an affective state (and on
some interpretations of [8c–d] a conative one as well), it is at the same
time a genuinely cognitive state: perceptual discrimination of a perceptible
feature of an external object.[31] Thus we have in *de An.* III.7's description
of perceptual pleasure an account of a kind of finding-good that one can
attribute to nonrational agents without triviality as well as without insanity.

Our *de Anima* passage also suggests a second important reason for con-
struing pleasure as genuine cognition: In calling pleasure an activity of the
"perceptive mean," Aristotle implies that it is literally an exercise of the
perceptual faculty, the *aisthêtikon*.

The simplest way to understand this is saying that pleasure is itself a
form of perception, and there is some evidence for this being precisely
Aristotle's view:

> (12) The movements (*kinêseis*) of pleasures and pains and in general
> (*holôs*) of every perception appear to begin from [the heart] and terminate
> there.[32] (*PA* 666a11–13, emphasis mine)

Aristotle nowhere else says that pleasures and pains are perceptions;
at one point—*EN* 1175b34–35, discussed below—he outright denies it.
But throughout the corpus he treats pleasures and pain as affections or
states of the perceptual system, physiologically very similar to ordinary
perception. In the *de Anima* he defines perception in general as a "kind
of alteration" of the *aisthêtikon* (415b24); in the *Physics*, he defines pleasures and pains in just the same way, as "alterations of the *aisthêtikon*"
(*Phys.* 247a16–17). Some argue that this line from the *Physics* must
represent an Academic view that Aristotle later rejected, because it
seems incompatible with the *Ethics*' argument that pleasure is an activity (*energeia*) rather than process (*kinêsis*). If Aristotle changed his mind
about whether pleasure is an activity or process, however, he remained
constant about the system to which it belongs: As we have just recalled,
(8b) from the *de Anima* calls being pleased an activity (a way of *ener-
gein*) of the "perceptive mean." Moreover, just after *EN* X denies that
pleasures are identical with perceptions it argues that the two are so
intimately related as to be "inseparable" (1175b34–35); this makes its
view in principle compatible with the *Physics*' and *de Anima*'s claims
that the pleasures of perception are themselves activities or affections of
the perceptual system. (*EN* VII, meanwhile, arguably confirms the identity thesis: Pleasures are unimpeded activities, so when perception is
unimpeded, it *is* pleasure.) Let us consider how one might reconcile
these views of pleasure with Aristotle's general account of perception.

According to the *de Motu Animalium*, when an agent perceives (or
otherwise cognizes) an object of pursuit or avoidance, the bodily parts
around her heart are altered in a special way (see *MA* 702b15–25): They
are heated or chilled. (This, in turn, leads to other bodily changes, including expansions and contractions of these and adjacent parts, and thereby

to large-scale locomotion.) This phenomenon particularly—perhaps uniquely—occurs with pleasant and painful objects:

> (13) . . . for the painful is to-be-avoided, the pleasant to-be-pursued. . ..
> And nearly all painful and pleasant things are accompanied by some
> chilling or heating. (*MA* 701b36–702a1)

Although the *MA* does not spell out the connection between physical states and psychological states as clearly as we would like, it suggests that when an animal perceives some pleasant or painful taste or other quality, that quality further affects it by heating or chilling the area around its heart, this being the physical aspect of its experiencing pleasure or pain.

This means that the process is similar to that whereby, on a plausible interpretation of Aristotle's theory, we perceive "common" perceptibles like being square or in motion.[33] In perception of commons, some proper perceptible (e.g., taste or color) strikes a peripheral sensory organ, and from there impacts the central organ of perception, the heart, thereby effecting perception of the common perceptible.[34] Just as with pleasurable or painful perception as described in the *MA*'s account, in the course of perceiving some proper perceptible quality of an object the perceiver undergoes alterations in the region around her heart.

If pleasure is literally a species of perception (as arguably implied by [12] from the *PA* and *EN* VII), then it is just like perception of commons in that these alterations around the heart constitute perception of some further property of the external object. The main difference is that when what we are perceiving is (e.g.) the squareness of a blue object, the changes around the heart involve no temperature changes, while when what we are perceiving is (e.g.) the goodness of a sweet object or the badness of a bitter one, they include heating or chilling—and thus the experience is pleasurable or painful rather than affectively neutral.

This view allows us to take the idea that pleasure and pain are *kritika* of value very straightforwardly. What about the *EN* X view of pleasure as an "inseparable" effect of perception? Here the analogy with perception of commons is looser, but still holds. If pleasure is an inseparable effect of activities, "a supervening perfection like the bloom of youth on those in their prime" (1174b33), then the pleasure proper to each activity is so closely bound up with the activity that the activity could not occur without it, would not be that very activity. (To put it another way, if pleasure is what "completes" activities, then there can be no complete activity without pleasure.[35]) And thus there is an intrinsic difference between the perceptual system and its activities on occasions when there is no pleasure and on occasions when there is; pleasurable perceptions are different, *qua* perceptions, from nonpleasurable ones. If we are to reconcile this view with the *MA*, the idea would be that heatings and chillings, although effects of perception rather than actual perceptions, are effects on the perceptual system itself—consistent with both *Phys.* 247a16–17 and (8b) from the *de Anima*.

Thus on either view of pleasure, when one feels pleasure in, e.g., a sweet taste, one's perceptual system is functioning differently from how it functions when one feels no pleasure in the taste. And since, as we have already seen, this psychophysical difference makes for a cognitive difference as well—in the former case the perceptual system is discriminating not merely the leaf's taste, but also its value—it is a difference in the perceptual system *qua* perceptual (rather than a difference that is merely incidental to that system's nature and function). Here then is a second reason to count perceptual pleasure as genuine value-cognition: It is an exercise of the perceptual system *qua* perceptive.

Parallels between Aristotle's theoretical epistemology and his view of moral education suggest a third reason. To develop and defend this claim is too big a project to undertake here; I will leave it as a suggestion that, if accepted, strongly bolsters the conclusions of this chapter.[36]

The claim is that on Aristotle's view, perceptual pleasure forms the basis for our thoughts about goodness. Just as ordinary perception is at the basis of all theoretical cognition, so practical perception, i.e., pleasurable or painful perception, is at the basis of all practical cognition, i.e., finding-good. We can call this Aristotle's practical empiricism: Just as one gets to grasp the universal squareness by having perceived particular squares (see e.g., *Posterior Analytics* I.18), one gets to grasp the universal goodness by having perceived particular things as good—i.e., by having felt perceptual pleasure in them.[37]

Given an epistemology like Aristotle's, the perceptual state one is in when all is going well and one looks at something square deserves to be called "perceiving as square" both because it is caused by squareness in an external object and because it is on the basis of such perceptions that one comes to have a concept of squareness. If pleasurable perception provides the inductive basis for the concept of goodness, then it deserves to be called "perceiving as good" for the same kinds of reasons.[38]

Notes

1. *Prohairesis* is rational in the straightforward sense of being the product of rational deliberation (see *EN* III.2–3); it is more difficult to say in what sense *boulêsis* is rational (Aristotle declares that it is at *de An.* 433a22–25, *Topics* 126a13, and *Rhetoric* 1369a3), but at the least it occurs only in rational animals (*EN* 1111b12–13).

2. Compare "All men strive for the apparent good (*phainomenon agathon*), but no one is in control of the appearance (*phantasia*): the way the end appears to someone depends on what sort of a man he is" (*EN* 1114a32–b1). Translations throughout are mine unless otherwise noted.

3. Aristotle uses 'fine' in this context as interchangeable with 'good': cf. *MA* 700b25–26.

4. The discussion surrounding (2) reveals that 'apparent' is ambiguous: Some desires are for things that are in fact good, and others for things *merely*

apparently good, but every desired object appears good to the one who desires it. Thus, although Aristotle never draws attention to the ambiguity, "Desire is for the good or the apparent good" should be read as "Desire is for what appears good to the desirer, where this is either genuinely good—in the case of correct rational desire—or merely apparently so."

5. This is not to say that the view that rational desires are for the good needs no defense. On my view—which I will not have room to present here—Aristotle thinks rational desires are good-dependent because he thinks they are ultimately based on pleasurable perception. [For a brief indication of how this will work, see the final section of this chapter; for much fuller defense, see my *Aristotle on the Apparent Good* (work in progress)]. In saying that all desire is for the apparent good, then, Aristotle is not bizarrely extending a feature distinctive of rational desire to appetitive desire; instead, he is extending a feature of appetitive desire—that it is for what one finds pleasant, and thus, as I shall argue here, for what one finds good—to rational desire.

6. Irwin offers this as a response to what I have called the insanity charge.

7. Irwin does not mean to apply his analysis to akratic appetites, but only to those of lower animals; in the texts that characterize the object of appetite as the apparent good, however—see especially *MA* 6 and *de An.* III.10—Aristotle seems unconcerned to draw any distinctions between human and animal appetites.

8. "We see that the things which move the animal are thinking (*dianoia*) and *phantasia* and decision (*prohairesis*) and wish (*boulêsis*) and appetite (*epithumia*). And all these can be reduced to thought (*nous*) and desire (*orexis*). For both *phantasia* and perception hold the same place as thought, for they are all *kritika*" (*MA* 700b17–20); cf. *de An.* 432a16.

9. Aristotle outright denies this possibility at *EN* 1110b10–15: Voluntary action is always pleasurable.

10. The manuscripts are divided between *touto* and *tauton* or *tauto* at 431a12. See discussion below.

11. See Hamlyn's note *ad loc* (D. W. Hamlyn, *Aristotle, De Anima Books II and III* (Oxford: Oxford University Press, 1968).

12. This is a common interpretation, but some take the "as such" to mean "as perceptible," or even "as pleasant or painful." I take my reading to be supported by the arguments I give in what follows.

13. A. Gotthelf, "The Place of the Good in Aristotle's Natural Teleology," *Proceedings of the Boston Area Colloquium in Ancient Philosophy* 4 (1989): 113–39.

14. See Gotthelf, op. cit., and J.M. Cooper, "Aristotle on Natural Teleology," in M. Schofield and M. C. Nussbaum, eds., *Language and Logos* (Cambridge: Cambridge University Press, 1982), 197–222

15. For that matter, there can be mistakes in the nutritive case too: just as a slug might take pleasure in the taste of a poisonous leaf, a tree's roots might soak up acid rain.

16. Translation by C. Rowe, in S. Broadie and C. Rowe, *Aristotle, Nicomachean Ethics: Translation, Introduction, and Commentary* (Oxford: Oxford, 2002). Compare Aristotle's claims that the things that please the base are not pleasant "without qualification" (*haplôs*), or not pleasant "by nature" (see, e.g., *EN* 1153a5–6; compare 1176a13–22).

17. This is a version of the question that arises in Plato's *Philebus:* Why does Socrates say that bad pleasures are false, rather than merely bad? For accounts of the *Philebus*'s answer that accord with what I say here about value-perception, see V. Harte, "The *Philebus* on Pleasure: The Good, the Bad and the False," *Proceedings of the Aristotelian Society* 104, no. 2 (2004): 113–30; and M. Evans, "Plato on the Possibility of Hedonic Mistakes," *Oxford Studies in Ancient Philosophy* 35 (2008): 89–124.

18. This is ground well covered in the literature; see, e.g., Irwin, *Aristotle's First Principles*, 303–5.

19. That is, "incidental" perceptibles can only be recognized by perception in combination with the higher cognitive faculties that nonhuman animals lack: see, e.g., J. I. Beare, *Greek Theories of Elementary Cognition* (Oxford: Clarendon, 1906), 286ff.; and C. Kahn, "Aristotle on Thinking," in M. Nussbaum and A. Rorty, eds., *Essays on Aristotle's* De Anima (Oxford: Clarendon, 1992), 359–79.

20. "[There is] a major problem for the interpretation of animal perception. Clearly animals need to 'make sense' of their perceptions. Do they have something corresponding to sortal classifications like *man, dog* [which in humans are the work of *nous*]? Aristotle has apparently nothing to say on this question except that, lacking *logos*, animals cannot have *our* way of understanding what they perceive" ["Aristotle on Thinking," in M. Nussbaum and A. Rorty, eds., *Essays on Aristotle's* De Anima (Oxford: Clarendon, 1992), 359–79., 369 note].

21. M. Nussbaum, *Aristotle's* De Motu Animalium (Princeton, N.J.: Princeton University Press, 1978), Essay V; H. Lorenz, *The Brute Within: Appetitive Desire in Plato and Aristotle* (Oxford: Oxford University Press, 2006), chapter 9. On Nussbaum's influential account, *phantasia* must be present along with perception to interpret sounds, colors, and shapes *as* bananas and lions and the like. Lorenz argues that through *phantasia* animals envisage complex scenarios, and associate them with present perceptions, so that they are motivated to pursue goals.

22. Many have recognized that pleasure plays some crucial role here: see, e.g., C. Freeland, "Aristotle on Perception, Appetition, and Self-Motion," in M. L. Gill and J. G. Lennox, eds. *Self-Motion* (Princeton, N.J.: Princeton University Press, 1994), 49; D. Modrak, "*Phantasia* Reconsidered," *Archiv fur Geschichte der Philosophie* 68 (1986): 47–69, at 60; and J. Whiting, "Locomotive Soul: The Parts of Soul in Aristotle's Scientific Works," *Oxford Studies in Ancient Philosophy* 22 (2002): 141–200, at 173. My interpretation differs from Modrak's and Freeland's by making the link between pleasure and perception more direct (not requiring the mediation of *phantasia*); it is in many ways close to Whiting's.

23. Compare *de Partibus Animalium* (= *PA*) 661a6–8: "All animals have appetite for food because they have (*hôs echonta*) perception of the pleasure that arises from food."

24. There will still be important questions as to how the animal associates the pleasant taste of her food with the mere sight of it, or what motivates her to set off in search of food when none is in view. Here *phantasia* must indeed play a crucial role, conjuring up a memory or anticipation of the pleasant taste. I would argue, however, that *phantasia*'s efficacy depends on its reproducing the pleasurable quality of perceptions, so that perceptual pleasure remains the basic mechanism of motivation.

25. "That which is appetitive, then, is not different as a subject from the power to perceive but differs only in account, since sense is simple cognition of the sensible as such, whereas appetition is cognition of the sensible as destructive or preservative of the animal" (Philoponus, commentary on Aristotle's *de Anima*). For extensive defense and discussion of the view, see D. Charles, "Aristotle's Desire," in V. Hirnoven, T. Holpainen, and M. Tuominen, eds., *Mind and Modality: Studies in the History of Philosophy in Honour of Simo Knuuttila* (Leiden: Brill, 2006)

26. J. M. Cooper, "Reason, Moral Virtue and Moral Value," 270, on *EN* X.4 in M. Frede and G. Striker, eds., *Rationality in Greek Thought* (Oxford: Clarendon, 1996), 81–114; reprinted in Cooper, *Knowledge, Nature, and the Good: Essays on Ancient Philosophy* (Princeton, N.J.: Princeton University Press, 2004), 107–29.

27. S. Broadie, *Ethics with Aristotle* (Oxford: Oxford University Press, 1991), 329. There is one passage in *EN* X.5 that may seem to contradict this interpretation directly: here Aristotle says that while pleasure is closely related to, indeed inseparable from, perception (and thought), it would be "absurd" (*atopon*) to hold that pleasure is itself perception (or thought) (1175b34–35). I discuss this passage below.

28. Compare the parallel explanation of perceptual illusions: "The cause of these is that the faculty in virtue of which the ruling part judges is not identical with that in virtue of which *phantasmata* [quasi-perceptual appearances] come before the mind. A proof of this is that the sun appears only a foot in diameter, though often something else contradicts the *phantasia*" (*de Insomniis* 460b16–20).

29. For this interpretation, see my "Aristotle on *Akrasia* and Perceptual Illusion," *Archiv fur Geschichte der Philosophie*, 91 (2009): 119–56

30. For a detailed account along these lines, see D. Achtenberg, *Cognition of Value in Aristotle's Ethics: Promise of Enrichment, Threat of Destruction* (Albany: State University of New York Press, 2002. She argues that "perception of value is . . . perception of a certain kind of relatedness, namely, the internal relation [Aristotle] calls '*entelecheia*' or '*energeia*' and that we might call 'development,' 'completion,' 'or 'fulfillment'"; "Since good means *telos* or its variants, when we see something as good, then, we are seeing it as a *telos* or as *teleion* [complete/ perfect] or a *teleiôsis* [completion/perfection], and so forth" (*Cognition of Value in Aristotle's Ethics*, 44 and 65).

31. For a similar view of perceptual pleasure, see D. Charles, "Aristotle's Desire" ; for a parallel view about *prohairesis* (that it is at once a cognitive, affective, and conative state), see R. Demos, "Some Remarks on Aristotle's Doctrine of Practical Reason," *Philosophy and Phenomenological Research* 22 (1961–62): 153–62.

32. Aristotle often uses 'x, y and in general (*holôs*) z' when x and y are species of z: Compare, e.g., *de Sensu* 436a9: "spirit and appetite and in general desire," and *EN* 1105b21–23: "I mean by passions appetite, anger, fear . . . pity, in general those things which pleasure and pain attend."

33. Indeed this is what we should expect: Pleasures and pains are more similar to perception of common perceptibles than to perception of "proper" perceptibles—color, sound, smell, and the like—for we can experience them through any of the five senses. Another way to state the point is that being beneficial or harmful, like being in motion but unlike being blue, can be perceived (granting that it can be perceived at all) through more than one sense.

For different arguments for a similar view of pleasure—that it is an analogue of perception of common perceptibles, with the object perceived being goodness— see T. Tuozzo, "Conceptualized and Unconceptualized Desire in Aristotle," *Journal for the History of Philosophy* 32 (1994): 525–49, at 535–36.

34. Suggested by Aristotle's claim that the heart is the organ of the common sense, as at, e.g., *de Somno* 2 and *de Juventate* 469a5–18, in conjunction with his claim that it is the common sense that directly grasps the common perceptibles (e.g., *de Memoria* 450a9–14). For one version of the view that common perceptibles are grasped by the common sense, see Hicks, *Aristotle, De Anima*, 427. Gregoric refers to it as "the standard view" (and rejects it: Gregoric, *Aristotle on the Common Sense*, 71ff.).

35. *Contra* G. E. L. Owen, "Aristotelian Pleasures," *Proceedings of the Aristotelian Society* (1971/2): 135–52. For an interpretation on which pleasure is even more closely linked with perception than I have proposed, see J. C. B. Gosling and C. C. W. Taylor, *The Greeks on Pleasure*, 209–13. As I understand their argument, pleasure is what actualizes the faculty of perception in certain circumstances, and thus there are not two separate things, the activity of perceiving and the pleasure arising from it, but only one thing, the perfect, i.e., pleasurable, activity; on this view, Book X is compatible with Book VII (Gosling and Taylor, *The Greeks on Pleasure*, 207–8).

36. I develop the view in my manuscript *Aristotle on the Apparent Good*. For a compelling defense of the main claim, on different grounds, see T. Tuozzo, "Conceptualized and Unconceptualized Desire in Aristotle"; a view similar to mine is strongly implied by J. Burnet (*The Ethics of Aristotle* (London: Methuen, 1900), 76).

37. I find my evidence for the view in the *EN*. The idea, very briefly, is this: Habituation leads us to take pleasure in (to perceive as good) a certain kind of activity, virtuous or vicious (*EN* II); this forms our moral characters, where part of this formation is giving us a certain general *phantasia* of the good (*EN* III.4–5); on the basis of this *phantasia* we reach our rational judgments about what is good. For a related view, see D. Achtenberg, *Aristotle on the Cognition of Value*.

38. I am extremely grateful to Sergio Tenenbaum, and to the other participants in the conference he organized on desire and practical reason. Many thanks also to an extremely helpful audience at USC, and for comments and discussion from Klaus Corcilius, Cian Dorr, Simon Keller, and Wolfgang Mann.

Works Cited

Achtenberg, D. *Aristotle on the Cognition of Value: Promise of Enrichment, Threat of Destruction* (Albany: State University of New York Press, 2002).
Beare, J. I. *Greek Theories of Elementary Cognition* (Oxford: Clarendon, 1906).
Broadie, S. *Ethics with Aristotle* (Oxford: Oxford University Press, 1991).
Broadie, S. and Rowe, C. *Aristotle, Nicomachean Ethics: Translation, Introduction, and Commentary* (Oxford: Oxford, 2002).
Burnet, J. *The Ethics of Aristotle* (London: Methuen, 1900).
Charles, D. "Aristotle's Desire," in V. Hirnoven, T. Holpainen, and M. Tuominen, eds., *Mind and Modality: Studies in the History of Philosophy in Honour of Simo Knuuttila* (Leiden: Brill, 2006).

Cooper, J. M. "Aristotle on Natural Teleology," in M. Schofield and M. C. Nussbaum, eds., *Language and Logos* (Cambridge: Cambridge University Press, 1982), 197–222.

———. "Reason, Moral Virtue and Moral Value," in M. Frede and G. Striker, eds., *Rationality in Greek Thought* (Oxford: Clarendon, 1996), 81–114; reprinted in Cooper, *Knowledge, Nature, and the Good: Essays on Ancient Philosophy* (Princeton, N.J.: Princeton University Press, 2004), 107–29.

Demos, R. "Some Remarks on Aristotle's Doctrine of Practical Reason," *Philosophy and Phenomenological Research* 22 (1961–62): 153–62.

Evans, M. "Plato on the Possibility of Hedonic Mistakes," *Oxford Studies in Ancient Philosophy* 35 (2008): 89–124.

Freeland, C. "Aristotle on Perception, Appetition, and Self-Motion," in M. L. Gill and J. G. Lennox, eds. *Self-Motion* (Princeton, N.J.: Princeton University Press, 1994).

Gosling J. C. B. and Taylor, C. C. W. *The Greeks on Pleasure* (Oxford: Oxford, 1982).

Gotthelf, A. "The Place of the Good in Aristotle's Natural Teleology," *Proceedings of the Boston Area Colloquium in Ancient Philosophy* 4 (1989): 113–39.

Grant, A. *The Ethics of Aristotle* (London: Longmans and Company, 1874).

Gregoric, P. *Aristotle on the Common Sense* (New York: Oxford, 2007).

Hamlyn, D. W. *Aristotle, De Anima Books II and III* (Oxford: Oxford University Press, 1968

Hicks, R. D. ed., *Aristotle, De Anima* (Cambridge: Cambridge University Press, 1907).

Harte, V. "The *Philebus* on Pleasure: The Good, the Bad and the False," *Proceedings of the Aristotelian Society* 104, no. 2 (2004): 113–30.

Irwin, T. *Aristotle's First Principles* (Oxford: Oxford University Press, 2008).

Kahn, C. "Aristotle on Thinking," in M. Nussbaum and A. Rorty, eds., *Essays on Aristotle's De Anima* (Oxford: Clarendon, 1992), 359–79.

Lorenz, H. The Brute Within: Appetitive Desire in Plato and Aristotle (Oxford Oxford University Press, 2006).

Modrak, D. "*Phantasia* Reconsidered," *Archiv fur Geschichte der Philosophie* 68 (1986): 47–69.

Moss, J. "Aristotle on *Akrasia* and Perceptual Illusion," *Archiv fur Geschichte der Philosophie* 91 (2009): 119–56.

Nussbaum, M. *Aristotle's De Motu Animalium* (Princeton, N.J.: Princeton University Press, 1978).

Owen, G. E. L. "Aristotelian Pleasures," *Proceedings of the Aristotelian Society* (1971/2): 135–52.

Philoponus, "Commentary on Aristotle's *de Anima*," ed. M. Hayduck, *Commentaria in Aristotelem Graeca* 15 (Berlin: Reimer, 1897).

Simplicius, "Commentary on Aristotle's *de Anima*," ed. M. Hayduck, *Commentaria in Aristotelem Graeca* 11 (Berlin: Reimer, 1882).

Tuozzo, T. "Conceptualized and Unconceptualized Desire in Aristotle," *Journal for the History of Philosophy* 32 (1994): 525–49.

Whiting, J. "Locomotive Soul: The Parts of Soul in Aristotle's Scientific Works," *Oxford Studies in Ancient Philosophy* 22 (2002): 141–200.

Evaluation – not essential to intentional action → so evaluation not part of reasons for acting

5

Sympathy for the Devil

Kieran Setiya

We tend to want what we perceive as being in some way good, to choose what seems worthy of choice, and to act in ways we think we can justify, at least to some extent.[1] The question for action theory is not whether to accept or deny these platitudes about human agency, but how to interpret and explain them. Are they contingent generalizations, principles of human nature, or something more? Does a connection between agency and evaluation belong to the essence of intentional action, and thus to any adequate account of the capacity to act for reasons?

In what follows, I will argue that it does not. What I say expands upon, and qualifies, a previous discussion of the topic, the gist of which appears in section 2.[2] My aim, however, is not to respond to objections or to resume a polemic. Much of the argument below is devoted to understanding the different ways in which the exercise of rational agency might depend on judgments or appearances of the good, the logical relations among such claims, and the scope for views that concede some truth in what might seem to be their opposites. This approach will tend to blur some contrasts and bring into relief the ones that matter most.

Begin with a distinction and a first concession. There are two contrasting directions of dependence that might be thought to hold between desire, or intentional action, and the good. On the one hand, there are forms of "motivational internalism" whose shape is roughly this:

> If A believes that x is good, or perceives it as being good, then she desires it.

On the other hand, there is the doctrine that we act intentionally "under the guise of the good":

> If A is doing ϕ for reasons, or doing it intentionally, she sees some good in doing it.

These formulations are deliberately crude. The point of introducing them is to set aside the question of motivational internalism, and to focus on the guise of the good. Let it be a necessary truth that judgments or appearances of the good have some defeasible influence on action. It

Rejects that GoG belongs to rational agency.

Sympathy for the Devil   83

Positive evaluation not a part of intentional action

would be a further claim that attitudes of this kind are involved whenever we exercise the capacity to act for reasons. One can accept motivational internalism, even in the most unguarded form, while denying that we act intentionally under the guise of the good.

Our topic can be further refined. It is the guise of the good, understood as a claim about rational agents, as such: about what it is to act for reasons or to act intentionally. It is not sufficient for the truth of this claim that, as it happens, we tend to act in ways we see as being in some way good, plausible though that is. Nor would it be sufficient if this were a fact of human nature, of the sort to be described in section 4. My conjecture is that part of the appeal of the guise of the good, in its action-theoretic form, derives from being conflated with doctrines of this other kind. At any rate, what I reject is the claim that it belongs to rational agency, in the abstract, to be exercised under the guise of the good, so that the need for a positive evaluation of action can be derived from the bare idea of its being intentional or being done for reasons.

Objections to the guise of the good often take the form of examples, cases of perversity or depression in which it is argued that someone acts in a way that she regards as bad without qualification, or simply finds indifferent.[3] Without elaboration, however, this strategy is bound to fail. The description of the examples is controversial, and advocates of the guise of the good will find ingenious ways in which to make sense of them.[4] What is more, taken by themselves, the examples leave untouched the *grounds* for accepting the guise of the good. How does our reflection on agency push us toward it? And where does it go wrong? Without answers to these questions, the examination of cases, however subtle and psychologically perceptive, will be unsatisfying.[5] The point cuts both ways. If descriptions of spiteful action do not refute the guise of the good, it is not established by Anscombe's (1963: 70–71) well-known remarks about wanting a saucer of mud. She doubts that anyone could have this desire unless he can say what makes its object desirable. But the example is inconclusive. To begin with, there is a problem of indeterminacy: It is not clear what the object of the man's desire is meant to be. When we have a desire, what we want is to act in a certain way or for something to be the case; desire is for an action or an outcome. The ascription of desire for an object is always elliptical. As soon as we fill this gap, Anscombe's desire begins to seem possible. Someone may want to own a saucer of mud, to have one in his hand even for a moment, for one to exist, without seeing any good in any of these things. Apart from a more theoretical investigation of rational agency, we won't know how seriously to take such appearances—that Anscombe's example is possible, or that it isn't. For the most part, then, my arguments will turn on rather abstract principles of reasons-explanation. (Even when they do rely on examples of acting for reasons, as in section 3, the examples will be used to make a systematic point.) Despite my title, nothing will rest on thoughts about the proper interpretation of Milton's Satan.[6]

The structure of the chapter is as follows. In section 1, I argue that the guise of the good is fundamentally a claim about *reasons*, not about *desires*. In section 2, I argue against a simple version of the guise of the good. It may be true that, in acting for reasons, one must know one's reason for acting, but what one knows is a reason that explains what one is doing, not a reason that purports to justify it. In the remaining sections, I examine more sophisticated versions of the guise of the good. It might be held, for instance, that the kind of explanation one gives of what one is doing, in doing it for a reason, has normative or evaluative content, and thus involves a qualified but positive evaluation of one's action. That proposal is the target of section 3. Finally, it might be held that the preceding arguments mistake the kind of generality the guise of the good is meant to have, wrongly treating it as a claim about every instance of intentional action. A different sort of generality can be employed in specifying the nature of something, as when we say that cats have four legs or human beings have thirty-two teeth, allowing for car accidents and British dentistry.[7] Once we have such "generic" essentialism in view, the guise of the good may seem to be revived. I end by considering this move in section 4, arguing that, while the guise of the good may be a principle of human nature, an account of rational agency cannot be given in generic terms. This result sheds incidental light on the foundations of practical reason.

1. DESIRING THE GOOD

On the face of it, there are two quite different ways in which the guise of the good could turn out to be true, one resting on the concept of a reason, the other on the concept of desire:

> (R) If someone acts intentionally in doing ϕ, she is doing it for a reason, and reasons must be seen as good.
> (D) If someone acts intentionally in doing ϕ, she is acting on a desire, and desires represent their objects as good.

Many hold views in the vicinity of (R). They follow Davidson (1963: 6) in "defining an intentional action as one done for a reason" and think of acting for a reason as acting on a ground one takes to *be* a reason—that is, at least a partial or *pro tanto* justification—for what one is doing.[8]

> The basic case [of acting for a reason] must be that in which A ϕ's, not because he believes only that there is some reason or other for him to ϕ, because he believes of some determinate consideration that it constitutes a reason for him to ϕ. (Williams 1979: 107)

> I cannot act for reasons if I do not care about doing what's justified or (as I would prefer to put it) what makes sense. (Velleman 1992a: 121)

> Both choice and decision are subject to rules of rational constraint, the most important of which is that one can only choose or decide for a reason, i.e. for what one takes to be a good reason for the option chosen. (Raz 1997: 8)

It is perhaps less common these days to find echoes of (D). But it seems more or less trivial to say that people want to do whatever it is they do intentionally, and desires have been conceived as appearances of the good.

> Desire is a kind of perception. One who wants it to be the case that *p* perceives something that makes it seem to that person as if it would be good were it to be the case that *p*, and seem so in a way that is characteristic of perception. (Stampe 1987: 359)

> Desiring is, in my view, simply *identified* with conceiving something to be good from a certain perspective. (Tenenbaum 2007: 14)

It is a picture of desire that forms the classical source of the guise of the good, in Plato's *Republic*—"Every soul pursues the good and does whatever it does for its sake" (505e)[9]—and in the moral psychology of Aristotle's *De Anima:* "It is always the object of desire which produces movement, [and] this is either good or the apparent good" (433a27–29).[10] These formulations became a dogma of scholastic philosophy, cited with approval by Kant in the *Critique of Practical Reason:* We desire only what we conceive to be good; we avoid only what we conceive to be bad.[11]

Despite these precedents, the guise of the good is best understood as a claim about reasons, and only derivatively a claim about desire. The argument for this turns on some modest connections among desire, reasons, and the good. First: When the object of desire, an action or outcome, is good, there is always some respect in which it is good, which is a reason to perform or to pursue it. This need not be heard as a reductive claim, an analysis of "good" for actions and outcomes on which a good thing for A to do just is something there is reason for her to do, and a good state of affairs is one there is reason to bring about.[12] What we need is something weaker, that there are "good-making" features of good actions and outcomes that count as reasons of the appropriate kinds, whatever the constitutive story turns out to be.

Second: If desires represent their objects as good, they represent them as being good in some respect—say, in being *F*—and the fact that the object is *F* is a reason why the agent wants to perform or pursue it. This proposition has two parts. To begin with, it excludes the conception of desire on which it depicts its object as being good but leaves us wholly in the dark when we ask what is good about it, as though this were a matter for guesswork or speculation. That seems absurd. Once we accept that desiring something is conceiving it as good, we should think of desires as presenting the specific appeal of their objects, what it is about them that seems to make them good.[13] This is reflected in the first quotation about desire, above: "One who wants it to be the case that *p* perceives *something that makes it seem* to that person as if it would be good were it to be the case that *p*" (Stampe 1987: 359, my emphasis). The proposition further implies that the respects in which desire represents its object as being good are reasons why the agent wants it. If sleeping late seems good to me in being restful, and this constitutes a desire to sleep late, my reason for wanting to sleep late is that it will be restful. If learning history seems good to me as a source of knowledge, and this constitutes a desire, my reason for wanting to learn history is that it is a source of knowledge. In the limiting case, what I want may be something that seems good for its own sake.[14] Why do I want to know things? What seems good about that? Perhaps no more than its being knowledge that I'll have: That is what makes the state of affairs good in which I know things, and my reason for wanting to bring it about. Once we allow for reasons of this kind, we can see that whenever a desire presents its object as being good in being F, its being F is an answer to the question "Why do you want it?"

The upshot is that, if desires represent their objects as good, they must be had for reasons that are seen as good, at least in being seen as respects in which the *object* of desire is good. In principle, one could concede this point, insist that desires represent their objects as good, and still reject the guise of the good as a general constraint on reasons for wanting. One would have to claim that, while we can want things for reasons that we do not see as good, it is a necessary truth that every desire is had for some reason that *is* conceived as good. But that position is unstable. If some of my reasons for wanting to be famous are not respects in which being famous seems like a good thing to me, why must I have some other reason through which it does? And if I do, what is to prevent me from realizing that this other reason is misconceived or false without relinquishing the desire for fame, something I now want only for reasons that are not respects in which fame seems good? Only if reasons for desire *must* be seen as good, in the corresponding sense, can we explain what blocks such possibilities. It follows that, if desires represent their objects as good, the following principle holds:

> When someone wants to ϕ, or wants it to be the case that p, they want it for a reason, and reasons for desire must be respects in which the object of desire is seen as good.[15]

Although this is not a claim about the evaluation of reasons, as such, it involves a version of the guise of the good applied to reasons for desire. They need not be seen as good reasons for wanting, perhaps, but they must be seen as respects in which it would be good to ϕ or for it to be the case that p. Thus, even when it rests on an evaluative conception of desire, the guise of the good for intentional action can be addressed by investigating the nature of reasons. We lose nothing of substance and gain something in generality if we adopt that focus throughout.[16]

2. REASONS

In order to do so, we have to be much more careful about the logic of propositions that use concepts of reason, making explicit a distinction that has been tacitly presupposed so far. Switching from desire to action, there is a contrast between claims of the following two kinds:

The fact that p is a reason for A to ϕ.

A is doing ϕ on the ground that p; that is his reason for doing it.

To say that there is a reason for A to ϕ is to say that A would be *pro tanto* justified in doing it. The justification may not be decisive; it may be outweighed by other reasons. But there is something to be said for doing ϕ, a consideration that counts in favor. Claims of this kind are normative or evaluative; they belong to ethics, broadly conceived. When the fact that p is a reason for A to ϕ, we can just as well report that it is a *good* reason for A to ϕ. In this sense, "bad reasons" are not reasons at all.

To say that A is doing ϕ for a certain reason, on the other hand, is to give a distinctive kind of explanation. It is to state a ground on which he is acting and thus to account for that action, at least in part. There is disagreement about the connection between explanations of this sort and ones that appeal to psychological states like belief, intention, and desire—"motivating reasons" in the technical sense employed by Michael Smith (1987, 1994), or Davidson's (1963: 3–4) *"primary reason[s]."* For the most part, I will try to be agnostic about that.[17] But we can say, at least, that it is not sufficient for the truth of our second proposition that A is doing ϕ because he believes that p and has some relevant desire. This comes out in Davidson's (1973: 79) well-known examples of "causal deviance," as when a nervous climber wants to be rid of his companion's weight and knows that he can manage this by dropping the rope. These attitudes make him anxious, with the result that he inadvertently drops the rope. He does not act for a reason in doing so, despite the causal role of his belief. Giving someone's reason for acting is not just citing a belief that is a cause of action; it implies that he is acting *on* that reason, which bears on what he is doing in a more intimate way.

Our topic is not the problem of causal deviance but the connection between explanations that give our reasons for doing things and reasons that justify doing them. Or, to return to section 1, it is the connection between agent's reasons for wanting things and reasons that would justify those desires by showing their objects to be good. What we can note at once is this: The propositions distinguished above differ in that the first is factive and the second is not; and neither of them entails the other. In *Practical Reality*, Jonathan Dancy gives examples in which someone acts for a reason that turns out to be false:

His reason for doing it was that it would increase his pension, but in fact he was quite wrong about that.

The ground on which he acted was that she had lied to him, though actually she had done nothing of the sort. (Dancy 2000: 132)

These descriptions are sometimes questioned, though they seem innocent enough to me. Accepting them as true is far less contentious than accepting

Dancy's further claim that they are instances of irreducibly non-factive explanation. As remarked above, we can afford to be agnostic about the reduction of such claims to propositions about the causality of psychological states. More importantly, even explanatory claims that use "because" to give an agent's reason—"He is doing it because *p*"—which arguably do entail the truth of that proposition, and perhaps that the agent knows it to be true, are consistent with its being no reason at all in the justifying sense.[18] We can fail to act for reasons that count in favor of doing something, as when we are ignorant of them, and we can act for reasons that don't. That the house is on fire may be no reason for me to flee when my wife and child are sleeping upstairs; still I can run outside because of it. And it is a notorious fact that wicked pleasures do not provide us with reasons to act; but we can act in pursuit of them nonetheless.

None of this conflicts with the simplest version of the guise of the good for reasons:

> If A is doing ϕ because *p*, or on the ground that *p*, he *believes* that the fact that *p* is a reason for him to ϕ.

According to this principle, agents' reasons reveal the positive light in which an agent saw his action by giving a consideration that he took to justify it, perhaps not consciously, perhaps not adequately or sufficiently, but to some extent. This is the sort of claim endorsed by the authorities cited at the beginning of section 1. It could be adapted to reasons for desire, which are believed to be respects in which the object of desire is good: worth doing or worth pursuing. And each claim could be weakened by replacing beliefs with appearances or facts about how things seem.

The crucial argument against the guise of the good for reasons, in this simple form, turns on the nature of intentional action and thus of action done for reasons. What it requires is not a tendentious theory of action-explanation, but some observations about the subject matter of action theory that appear at the beginning of Anscombe's *Intention*.[19]

> What distinguishes actions which are intentional from those which are not? The answer that I shall suggest is that they are actions to which a certain sense of the question 'Why?' is given application; the sense is of course that in which the answer, if positive, gives a reason for acting. (Anscombe 1963: 9)

Apart from its deliberately conditional note—the question "Why?" is "not refused application because the answer to it says that there is *no* reason" (Anscombe 1963: 25)—this seems hard to deny. When someone acts for a reason, in the explanatory sense, the question "Why?" has application to what they are doing, and they count as doing it intentionally. But Anscombe has a stronger premise in mind, not just that the question *has* application, but that the agent *gives* it application in being able to answer it. She imagines the question "Why?" being put to the person who is doing ϕ and the answer as constituted by his response. Hence her otherwise puzzling doubts about whether we can count on agents to be honest.[20] We can avoid one source of difficulty here by crossing the gap between belief and its linguistic expression. The pivotal claim is that the answer to the question "Why?" understood as a request for reasons has to be something that the agent who is acting for that reason *believes*.

This picture of what is involved in acting for a reason is not innocuous, but it is, so far, relatively weak.[21] In the present context, any doubts can be set aside. Our topic is the guise of the good for reasons, and this doctrine is best conceived as an interpretation of, and therefore as committed to, the requirement of belief on answers to the question "Why?" It is the view that when this question is given application, the answer, if positive, is contained in the agent's beliefs about the reasons for acting as he is: If A is doing ϕ on the ground that p, he believes that the fact that p is a reason for him to ϕ.

The problem is that, in illuminating the source and structure of the guise of the good for reasons, this perspective casts it in a negative light. The answer to Anscombe's question is an *explanation* of what one is doing and why one is doing it, not—or not explicitly—a justification. Its form is:

explanation not justification

I am doing ϕ because p,

or,

I am doing ϕ on the ground that p; that is my reason for doing it,

not:

The fact that p is a reason for me to ϕ.

That answering the question "Why?" is, in the first instance, giving an explanation comes out in Anscombe's (1963: 11) further observation that this question "is refused application by the answer: 'I was not aware I was doing that.'"

> "Why do you humiliate him by telling that awful story?"
>
> "Does he mind? I thought he'd be amused. I didn't mean to humiliate him—I wasn't doing that intentionally."

Switching again from the linguistic to the psychological mode, we can say that knowing *why* I am doing something—having an answer to Anscombe's question—is a way of knowing *that* I am doing it. Again, the belief that corresponds to the question is the belief that I am doing ϕ because p or on the ground that p, the truth of which entails that I am doing it, not that the fact that p is a reason for me to ϕ, which implies nothing of the sort. Knowing that a fact is a reason to ϕ is not a way of knowing what one is doing. If there is a connection between answering the question "Why?" and believing that one's answer describes a normative reason for one's action, this connection is indirect.

The assumption that in doing ϕ intentionally one must believe that one is doing it may have to be qualified. There are cases in which that condition appears to fail, as when I am doing ϕ by doing something else intentionally as a means to it, and I am not sure that it is getting done.[22] But the present argument survives. What it requires is a claim about sufficiency, not necessity. Whether or not one must have an answer to the question "Why?" in order to be doing ϕ intentionally, it is sufficient to answer this question that one has a belief of the form, "I am doing ϕ because p," in the sense of "because" on which this entails that I am doing ϕ on the ground that p and therefore acting for a reason. The object of belief here is a proposition about the explanation of action. That it is cast in the first person cannot alter its logical powers. It does not follow from the fact that I am doing ϕ because p that the fact that p is a reason for me to ϕ, any more than it follows when those propositions are about someone else. The truth of my answer to the question "Why?" is thus consistent with the absence of any justification for what I am doing, and so I can give that answer without believing, or being required in consistency to believe, that I have such justification. Having a story about what justifies one's action goes beyond what is involved in having an answer to the question "Why?" More generally:

> (1) It is sufficient to answer the question "Why?" that one has a belief of the form, "I am doing ϕ because p," in the sense of "because" that gives an agent's reason.
>
> (2) That I am doing ϕ because p, in this sense, is consistent with the fact that p not being a reason for me to ϕ.
>
> (3) If one proposition is consistent with the negation of another, it is possible to believe the first without believing the second.

So:

> (4) It is possible to believe that I am doing ϕ because p, and thus to answer the question "Why?" without believing that the fact that p is a reason for me to ϕ.

We can illustrate this in cases of "silencing," where a consideration that would otherwise be a reason to act has no force whatsoever.[23] McDowell (1979: 56) may be wrong to say, in general, that when courage calls for action, "the risk to life and limb [should not be] seen as any reason for removing [oneself]." But there are surely occasions on which that is right, as for instance the one hinted at before, in which I discover that the house is on fire while my wife and child are sleeping upstairs.

> "Why are you running outside in your underwear?"
>
> "Because the house is on fire!"
>
> "What about your family? Won't they be trapped by the flames? In a circumstance like this, the fact that the house is on fire is a reason to rush upstairs and rescue them, not to look after your own safety while they burn!"
>
> "You're right. I can't justify my action at all: the danger is not a reason for me to flee; but it is the reason for which I am doing so."

The point of this example is not to carry the weight of the argument, but to clarify its conclusion. Insofar as it is motivated by the idea that in acting for a reason one can answer the question "Why?" the guise of the good is misconceived. The answer to that question is not a proposition about what justifies one's action, but about its explanation.

What else could be the source of the guise of the good for reasons? What could account for the alleged necessity that, in doing ϕ because p one must believe that the fact that p is a reason to ϕ? Once we admit the possibility of someone who meets Anscombe's condition on acting for a reason without conforming to this demand, it is hard to see why any further belief should be required. So long as he is doing ϕ and believes that he is doing ϕ because p, where this is an explanation that purports to cite his reason, and so long as there is the right sort of connection between the two, a person is acting on the ground that p. The last resort for the defender of the guise of the good, in application to reasons, is to insist that the right sort of connection must be one that invokes the relevant evaluative belief. Perhaps the problem of causal deviance is solved, in part, by the belief that one's reason does something to justify one's action. But this is hopeless. If there can be the wrong sort of connection between the belief that one is doing ϕ because p and one's doing it, there can be the wrong sort of connection between doing ϕ and a belief about its justification. Problems about the right connection between attitude and action, as in cases of causal deviance, cannot be solved by adding more beliefs, whose relationship to what one is doing will be equally problematic.

It follows that, although we have not tried to find sufficient conditions of acting for a reason that define it in other terms, we have found sufficient *cognitive* conditions for acting on the ground that p. One need only believe that one is doing ϕ because p, so long as there is the right sort of connection between one's action in doing ϕ and this belief. (Doing ϕ *because* p may require, in addition, that one's belief amount to knowledge.) Since the right connection need not involve the belief that one's reason for doing ϕ is a good reason for doing it, one need not have that further belief. There is nothing in the cognitive conditions of acting because p, or on the ground that p, that could account for its necessary presence. The guise of the good for reasons, at least in the simple form considered so far, is false.[24]

Given the argument of section 1, the same point holds against evaluative conceptions of desire. Recall that, in order to represent their objects as good, desires must be had for reasons, and reasons for desire must be respects in which the object of desire is seen as good. The problem is that, if I am running outside because the house is on fire without believing that this fact provides a reason for flight, I also *want* to run outside for just that reason. No further evaluative belief need be involved. In finding sufficient cognitive conditions for *acting* on the ground that p, we have also found sufficient cognitive conditions for *desiring* on the ground that p. Since these conditions do not involve the belief that there is good reason to flee, or that it would be good to do so, we have found an instance of nonevaluative desire.

Nor would it help the proponent of the guise of the good for intentional action to deny that these are real desires, or to restrict the evaluative conception to a special kind of affective state.[25] For it is crucial to his view that, in acting intentionally, one always acts on a desire. In any case, why should things be different for desires that do not issue in action? Here, too, we can answer the question "Why?" by giving an explanation of our desire that purports to cite our reason"I want to ϕ because p"—and it is sufficient to count as wanting for a reason that this belief has the right sort of connection with that desire.

> "Why do you want to run outside?"
>
> "Because the house is on fire!"
>
> "What about your family? Won't they be trapped by the flames?"
>
> "You're right. The danger is not a reason for me to flee, though it is my reason for wanting to. I should resist temptation and attempt a rescue. I'm going upstairs."

No doubt we sometimes believe that an action would be right or good, or that an outcome is worth pursuing, and want it for the corresponding reasons. But that is not a condition of having a reason for one's desire.

Finally, although the argument so far has focused on evaluative beliefs, nothing changes when we allow for versions of the guise of the good that deal in appearances or how things seem. There are sufficient cognitive conditions for acting or desiring on the ground that p that do not include beliefs about justifying reasons or about respects in which the object of desire is good; nor do they involve appearances to that effect. Such presentations are not required for us to answer the question "Why?" and they would not help to explain the right connection between beliefs that answer that question and intentional action or desire: If beliefs can figure in the wrong sort of connection, or contribute to causal deviance, so can psychological states in which things seem to be a certain way.

Where do these conclusions leave the guise of the good? They show that one can act for a reason without believing that there is a reason that counts in favor of what one is doing, or any respect in which it is a good thing to do, and without either of these propositions seeming to be true.[26] It does not follow that "reason" is implausibly ambiguous or that there is no connection between the capacity to act for reasons and the capacity to govern one's action by one's conception of what the reasons are. For one thing, the senses of "reason"—justifying and explanatory—are very closely related. A justifying or *good* reason is, roughly speaking, a good thing to have as one's reason for acting; it sets a standard for what one's reasons ought to be.[27] For another, the capacity for evaluative control of one's action depends upon the capacity to know what one is doing and why. If I have no idea what my reasons are, I am no position to stop myself from acting on considerations that are not, as I believe, good reasons to act. In fact, if I am to put my conception of reasons into practice, I had better know what my reasons are *spontaneously*, without observation or inference. Otherwise, the best I can manage is to aim at acting for good reasons, attend to whether I am doing so, and try to correct them afterward if I am not: a bizarre form of *post hoc* self-management. A line of dependence therefore runs from the capacity for rational self-governance to the kind of self-knowledge that Anscombe associates with acting for reasons.[28] It is even consistent with the failure of the guise of the good as a claim about the answer to the question "Why?" that the capacity to act for reasons depends on the capacity to evaluate them as good or bad, and so to entertain thoughts about the justification of action. We would need a story about why this dependence holds, but there is no principled obstacle to giving one, at least so far.

Nor is there, as yet, a decisive refutation of the guise of the good for intentional action, as opposed to some of the grounds on which it might be held. It may still be true that in acting for reasons one must see one's action in a positive light. What we have is pressure to interpret and defend this doctrine in another way. The skeptical argument of this section can therefore be regarded ecumenically. It helps to indicate the proper *form* of the guise of the good, as a putative constraint on rational agents. The mistake is to think that seeing one's action as good involves a belief—or an appearance; the nature of the attitude is immaterial—whose content goes beyond the proposition that one is acting on the ground that *p*. If the guise of the good is to apply to rational agency, as such, it must apply because beliefs of this kind are essential to its exercise, and because the proposition one thus believes already contains the positive light in which one's action is cast, even though it does not entail that the reason for which one is acting is a reason to act in that way, or that it is good to do so, in fact. Explanations of action in terms of reasons must involve some weaker affirmation, so that believing an explanation of that kind amounts to seeing one's action in a positive light. Only if this condition is met will the beliefs about one's action involved in doing it intentionally, or in doing it for reasons, vindicate the spirit of the guise of the good.

3. INTELLIGIBILITY

Taken critically, the conclusion of section 2 is that reasons for action and desire need not be seen as good. Taken constructively, its conclusion is that the guise of the good for intentional action must rest, in the end, on a claim about the normative or evaluative character of explanations that appeal to agents' reasons. It must take the following shape:

(a) In doing ϕ on the ground that p, one believes that one is acting for that reason, if not in doing ϕ itself, then in taking further means.

(b) Although the explanation, "A is doing ϕ on the ground that p," does not imply that the fact that p is a reason for A to ϕ, it casts that action

explanation entails value, even if minimal

in a positive light. To explain an action in this way is to accept some weaker proposition about the justification for doing ϕ in the circumstance that A is in.

(c) Thus, in acting on the ground that p, one accepts a weak proposition about the justification for one's action, or for taking the relevant means. In this modest sense, one sees some good in what one is doing.

(d) Since acting intentionally is acting for a reason, it follows that we act intentionally under the guise of the good.

Although this argument could be disputed in several ways, it captures the most compelling source of the guise of the good. Some will balk at its initial premise, which is inspired by the passages from Anscombe already discussed. There are difficult questions there, but since I accept the premise, I am willing to set them aside.[29] Others will suggest, with Anscombe (1963: 25) or Hursthouse (1991), that we can act intentionally for no particular reason, rejecting (d). That objection leaves untouched the core idea that, when we do have reasons for acting, we see what we are doing as in some way good. Our principal focus should thus be on explaining action by giving reasons, the sort of explanation of what one is doing that answers the question "Why?" Do explanations of this kind involve a positive assessment of action, albeit one that is weaker than the claim that there is good reason to perform it?

The conception on which they do is sometimes expressed in terms of intelligibility:

[The] concepts of the propositional attitudes have their proper home in explanations of a special sort: explanations in which things are made intelligible by being revealed to be, or to approximate to being, as they rationally ought to be. This is to be contrasted with a style of explanation in which one makes things intelligible by representing their coming into being as a particular instance of how things generally tend to happen. (McDowell 1985: 328)[30]

If someone's reason for acting makes what he is doing intelligible by showing it to be *approximately* rational, it need not, in fact, be a reason for what he is doing, even when it is true. Still, the explanation casts his action in a positive light. To believe such an explanation is to believe a suitably weak proposition about the justification of action, in the circumstance its agent occupies. In explaining one's action in this way, one would conform to a modest version of the guise of the good.

Although it is offered by McDowell as an interpretation of Davidson on the "constitutive ideal of rationality," the claim that reasons-explanation is in this way normative goes beyond the existence of limits on the degree of irrationality consistent with thought. According to Davidson:

The semantic contents of attitudes and beliefs determine their relations to one another and to the world in ways that meet at least rough standards of consistency and correctness. Unless such standards are met to an adequate degree, nothing can count as being a belief, a pro-attitude, or an intention. (Davidson 1987: 114)

What this passage demands is rough conformity to standards of reason across the whole array of one's psychological states. It does not follow that, in each particular case, the explanation of belief by belief, or the motivation of intentional action, approximates to rationality. Within a profile of beliefs, desires and dispositions that is more or less rational, there may be room for individual episodes of thought that are thoroughly defective or confused. We can consistently hold that thought is subject to the constitutive ideal of rationality and that explanations that appeal to agents' reasons rely on dispositions that approximate to reason only in general, not in every case. This weak constraint does nothing to support the picture of explanation required for the guise of the good.

Should we then accept the further claim that explanation by reasons makes action intelligible by revealing it to be at least approximately rational? The reasons for which we act may not be reasons for acting in that way, not only because they can be false, but because it can be a failure of practical reason to be moved by them at all. Still, the suggestion runs, to explain what someone is doing by giving their reasons is to bring out the sense in their behavior by showing how it resembles or comes close to being an exercise of practical rationality, understood not as the mere capacity to act for reasons—the claim is not trivial—but as the excellence of that capacity. In acting for reasons, one's practical reasoning or practical thought must be approximately good.

Talk of "approximation" is unhelpfully vague, but even so, it is possible to frame an argument against the present account of reasons-explanation. The difficulties come out in the common understanding of acting from a trait of character as a matter of acting for distinctive sorts of reasons. As Rosalind Hursthouse (1999: 128) notes, the courageous person is moved by such thoughts as "I could probably save him if I climb up there," "No-one else will volunteer," "If we give in now, it will be hard to stand firm later"; the temperate person is moved by such thoughts as "I'm driving," "You need it more than I do," "The cheaper one will do the job"; and so on.[31] The question is: In explaining one's action in terms like these, how does one show it to be approximately rational?

The answer is not, or not always, by relating it as causal or constitutive means to an end supplied by a further desire, and thus to instrumental reason.[32] Take, for instance, generosity. Someone who is generous may be acting in character when she helps a stranger because he needs help. And then it will be correct to say that she *wants* to help him, and to explain the particular things she does for him by citing that desire. What need not fit the instrumental pattern is her account of why she wants to help the stranger in the first place, and thus why she is doing so. She is helping him because he needs help, of course, but how does her belief that he needs help present the act of helping him as the means by which to satisfy a prior desire? It would do so if she had a completely general desire to bring aid to those in need. But that is not what generosity implies. A generous person need not be in the business of helping just anyone who needs help or want to do so in every case. Suppose she comes upon a thief who needs help making off with stolen goods?[33] Even if we are wary of the view that virtues can be expressed only in acting well, so that one displays no generosity in providing help when it is unjust to do so, one does not show a *lack* of generosity in refusing it: "Do we not think that someone not ready to act unjustly may yet be perfect in charity, the virtue having done its whole work in prompting him to do that the acts that are permissible?" (Foot 1978: 15).[34] If the generous person is also just, there will be a nuanced web of conditions in which she will not want to offer aid; if she is also temperate, the web becomes more intricate; if she is honest, loyal, brave, even more so. Acting from generosity need not be acting from an unqualified or unconditional desire to help.

This does not by itself prevent us from treating the potential complexity of generous motivation on the model of means to ends. In helping the stranger because he needs help, the generous person may be acting in a way that satisfies a highly qualified conditional desire, in light of her beliefs—a desire to help those in need *if* certain conditions are met and others are not. But since we are looking for an explanation that the generous person herself would give, her own account of what she is doing and why, this is not enough. For she need not be able to articulate the conditions under which she wants to help others and so explain her own behavior in helping the stranger as a way of satisfying a prior desire: "I want to help those in need if and only if *x, y,* and *z.* Those conditions were met in the present case. So I'm going to help." This is the truth in the moral-psychological doctrine of "uncodifiability" (McDowell 1979: 57–58): It is not a condition of virtue that one have the power to formulate one's practical reasoning as the deductive application of a general principle to the case at hand. It does not follow that there is no finite codification of practical reason, only that it need not figure as the explicit object of one's propositional attitudes in acting from a virtue of character. Instead, the character of a virtuous person partly consists in being disposed to act and desire for just these reasons in just these ways, and to know that she is doing so when she does, whether or not she is able to specify, in advance, how she will react to every case.

At this point, several moves could be made on behalf of the instrumental model, of which I consider three. First, if the generous person takes herself to be doing ϕ on the ground that p and q and . . ., in this particular case, and so to be moved by the corresponding beliefs, won't she also accept a means-end account of her action, on which it is explained in part by the desire to ϕ *if p* and q and . . .? This account reveals her as approximating instrumental rationality. Reply: If being moved to ϕ by the beliefs that p and q and . . . is in this way sufficient for desiring to ϕ *if p* and q and . . ., the requirement of intelligibility as approximate rationality is trivialized. Whenever someone acts on *any* belief, they count as having a desire in light of which their motivation shows some degree of means-end rationality, and is therefore made intelligible. Approximate rationality no longer

constrains or limits the grounds on which we can act.[35] Second, can it be
said that our generous person understands her motivation as instrumental
by referring to a less determinate desire, like the desire to help those in
need, other things being equal? Not necessarily. If conditions are sufficiently bad and it is rare for those in need to deserve help, justice may
sharply circumscribe her desire. She wants to help sometimes, not always,
not even for the most part. Nor could the proposal in question work for
every virtue: What general desire would characterize the courageous person, or the temperate? It is a special feature of generosity that it can be
roughly specified in terms of an end or goal. Finally, can we supplement
the generous person's understanding of herself with the desire to do whatever it is generous to do and assume that she would explain her action in
helping the stranger by appeal to this desire? Again, the answer is no. For
she need not conceive what she is doing in just those terms. The point
applies to other virtues, too: "A courageous person does not typically
choose acts as being courageous, and it is a notorious truth that a modest
person does not act under the title of modesty" (Williams 1985: 10).

    If the last three paragraphs are right, explanations that answer the
question "Why?"—"I am showing him the way home because he needs
help"—do not always make action intelligible by depicting it as the means
to a prior end in light of the reason supplied. They need not show its motivation as approximating instrumental rationality. How else might they
bring out the practical rationality of what someone is doing? In the case
of acting from virtue, the answer may seem obvious. For it is plausible
that the properly generous person sees what she is doing as the thing to
do, and therefore acts under the guise of the good in the sense rejected (as
a requirement on acting for reasons, as such) in section 2.[36] Her answer to
the question "Why?" presents her as conforming to the principle of acting
as one thinks one should. But this merely defers the search for intelligibility. We do not capture what is rational in someone's acting for a given
reason merely by noting that she believes it to be a reason. The following
dialogue is futile:

"She is drinking coffee because she loves Sophocles."[37]

"What? That makes no sense at all."

"Oh yes it does! She thinks it is a *reason* to drink coffee."

That she sees this consideration as a reason needs to be made intelligible,
as approximately rational, no less than her being moved by it. In any case,
we have already seen that it is not a general condition on acting for a reason that one regard it as a reason for what one is doing, let alone that one
regard it as sufficient to establish that action as the thing to do. Even if the
perfectly virtuous conceive their actions under the guise of sufficient reason, the partly or imperfectly virtuous need not; but they act for reasons
nonetheless. On the view we are discussing, the explanations that give
those reasons, which are in substance the same as those of the perfectly

virtuous person, must reveal approximate rationality even when they cannot be assimilated to the instrumental pattern and do not invoke beliefs about what there is reason to do.

There is, I think, only one way to vindicate this demand. If the reasons-explanations of the imperfectly generous person make her out to be approximately rational, even when she cannot cite a corresponding background desire or the belief that her reasons are good, they must do so "directly": simply because the disposition to be moved by these considerations, in the circumstance she takes herself to be in, is or approximates to being an expression of practical rationality. When we tried to assimilate such explanations to the instrumental pattern, we treated them as shorthand for more complete accounts of action that cite desires along with facts about what would satisfy them. These more complete accounts reveal approximate rationality because means-end efficiency is, or approximates to being, practically rational. The proposal at hand is that we can omit the reference to desire and take the relevant explanations to show approximate rationality because the disposition to be moved by the considerations they cite is, or approximates to being, a good disposition of practical thought. Practical rationality is at least partly constituted by dispositions that resemble those of the imperfectly virtuous person and in terms of which she explains what she is doing.

This conclusion is close to one McDowell explicitly accepts:

> To explain an action we regard as virtuous, we typically formulate a more or less complex characterization of the action's circumstances as we take the agent to have conceived them. Why should it not be the case [. . .] that the agent's conception of the situation, properly understood, suffices to show us the favourable light in which his action appeared to him? (McDowell 1978: 80)

I have argued that this *must* suffice, all on its own, if reasons-explanation is to make action intelligible as approximately rational. It does not follow that, as McDowell also claims, we must "[take] a special view of the virtuous person's conception of the circumstances, according to which it cannot be shared by someone who sees no reason to act as the virtuous person does" (McDowell 1978: 80).[38] The sense in which his conception casts a positive light on what he is doing is not that it is impossible to accept it without concluding that there is reason to act as he does, but in depicting his motivation as more or less rational.

There are the makings of an argument here, from the possibility of explaining action by giving the sorts of reasons a generous or courageous or just person would give, and from the premise that reasons-explanations demonstrate at least approximate rationality, to conclusions about the content of practical reason that connect it with ethical virtue. The scope of that argument is unclear, and it is not my principal focus. For even if it is true that acting from a virtue of character is acting in a way that therefore counts as (approximately) rational, nothing similar can plausibly be said about *vice*. The pursuit of interpretations on which we turn out always to be acting for something like good reasons tends to obscure the varieties of corruption and deformity to which our second natures are susceptible.

Some vices merely involve the unfettered pursuit of intelligible goals, as when one acts unjustly to benefit oneself. Here the explanation of what one is doing and why shows it to approximate to instrumental rationality. Like generosity, however, a defect of character need not work this way. It may issue in desires for particular actions so selectively and with such sensitivity to the details of the circumstance that they cannot be explained by the agent as directed at the means to an end. Nor does she have to regard her reasons as even *pro tanto* justifications for her action, given the argument of section 2. If not in displaying her conformity to the means-end pattern, then, or being offered as justification, how do the reasons of someone who acts in this way bring out her approximate rationality? Can we say, as we did with the virtues of character, that they do so "directly": by drawing on dispositions that are in their own right, or approximate to being, good dispositions of practical thought? That is hard to accept. Some defects of character are recognizable distortions of virtue, and their reasons mimic those of a decent person: "It's not my responsibility"; "I'll enjoy it more than he will"; "But they deserved it." Here, despite its obscurity, the claim of approximation gets some grip. In giving such reasons, one shows oneself to be in touch with the sorts of considerations that do provide reasons, if not in just this case. One's motivation can be seen as the flawed or imperfect exercise of a capacity to get things right. But other vices are more severe. As well as bitterness and spite ("It will ruin things for me" as a reason for doing it), there are pessimism and despair ("It's hard to achieve much in this world" as a reason for not even trying), bigotry and prejudice ("He's not one of us" or "It's a job for a woman" as reasons for disdain). The disposition to be moved by these considerations, in the situation one takes oneself to occupy, is not well conceived as a good disposition of practical thought in its own right, or even as resembling one. These are not the sorts of considerations that ordinarily help to justify action, and that merely fail to do so because the conditions are wrong. As reasons for acting, they are not just bad; they are awful. They do not even come close.

We can make this vivid by imagining an all-too-credible scenario. A certain community is viciously xenophobic, although their hatred of foreigners interacts with other putative virtues in complicated ways. They do not simply desire to harm others, but react to them with a nuanced array of violence, indifference, and contempt, depending on the circumstance of interaction. Perhaps the reflective members of the community have a story to tell about the value of all this. It helps to preserve their distinctive traditions and way of life. They see their xenophobic practice under the guise of the good, at least to some degree. The unreflective, however, do not. What they have is little more than an acquired tendency to act in

certain ways, on certain grounds. "He's not one of us," they say to themselves as they refuse to help or actively hurt an apparent outsider. The
ways in which they do this are too complex for them to articulate for
themselves as means to the satisfaction of a multiply conditional desire.
Nor do they believe that their reasons for acting justify what they are
doing. (The argument of section 2 ensures this possibility.) "Who cares
whether it is right or wrong?" they ask. "This is what we do." That human
nature is malleable enough to permit such corruption is surely plausible.
What I need is something less: That deformations of this kind are consistent with rational agency. There is nothing in the nature of reasons to
prevent the xenophobes from harming a stranger on grounds like these.
When they do so, they can explain their action ("because he is not one of
us") without reference to a further desire, to justifying reasons, or to dispositions that resemble those of good practical thought. Nor do things
change when we drop the stage setting of reflective participants. That
helps to give the story life, but it is not essential. Let the whole community be unreflective, at least in their prejudice, passed on by the contagion
of habit. In this department, at least, they do not act under the guise of
approximate rationality or the approximate good.

The argument of the last two paragraphs relies on claims about what is
and is not a reason for acting, and about the sorts of dispositions that help
to make up practical rationality. It would not be persuasive to someone
who believes that xenophobia is or approximates to being good practical
thought, even when it is thoroughly unreflective. But the principal claim
is quite abstract: To hold that our account of what we are doing in acting
for reasons must show it to be approximately rational, even when it does
not conform to the instrumental pattern or involve the belief that we are
acting for good reasons, is to lose the contrast between incomplete or
imperfect possession of practical reason and habituation into forms of
practical responsiveness that are simply misguided or wrong. This echoes
the contrast, which belongs to common sense, between the failure to be
virtuous and possession of a positive vice. Second nature can be shaped to
incorporate dispositions that are not mere perversions of rationality, but
actively depraved: basic tendencies to act and desire on irrelevant or unjustified grounds. In exercising dispositions of that kind, the vicious person
need not conceive herself as acting for good reasons, or as aiming at the
satisfaction of a general desire; she may explain what she is doing as the
exercise of an acquired disposition that does not even approximate to
practical rationality.

The demand for such approximation is sometimes expressed by saying
that reasons-explanations "rationalize" action or desire, adding immediately
that the term "rationalization" is being used in a technical not a colloquial
sense. The contrast between imperfection and positive vice suggests that
this is wrong on both counts. The doctrine of approximate rationality por-
trays the depraved and ill habituated as compulsive rationalizers,
excusing their bad behavior with the semblance of good reasons. The truth

is less comforting. One can act for reasons that are wholly and irredeemably bad, and thus with knowledge of what one is doing and why that does not present it under the guise of the approximately good. Even in its modest from, which rests on the alleged normativity of reasons-explanation and its role in answering the question "Why?" the guise of the good for intentional action is false.

4. HUMAN NATURE

It is an assumption of the preceding arguments that the guise of the good takes the form of, or entails, a universal generalization:

> Any possible instance of acting for a reason is an instance of acting under the guise of the good.

The task of section 2 was to show that it is not a condition of acting on the ground that p that one take it to be a reason for what one is doing or to indicate some respect in which one's action is a good one to perform. The task of section 3 was to show that, even if it is a condition of acting for a reason that one be able to supply an explanation of what one is doing that gives one's reason, this explanation may fail to cast one's action in the positive light of approximate rationality. It is possible to act for a reason in doing ϕ without acting under the guise of the good.

This way of putting things prompts a final objection, which turns on the logical weakness of possibility claims. For there are forms of generality that permit exceptions, even as they seem to describe the essence or nature of what they generalize about. If the doctrine that we act under the guise of the good is intended as a nonuniversal generalization, the arguments above may seem to miss the point. Does the present discussion go wrong by presupposing an unduly simple view of the generality involved in the relevant essentialist claims?

Our question is inspired by a revived Aristotelianism about living things that finds its fullest expression in Michael Thompson's essay "The Representation of Life."[39] He draws attention to the way in which we state how a certain species of living things goes on:

> Let us call the thoughts expressed in the field guide and in the nature documentary *natural-historical judgments*. We may take as their canonical expression sentences of the form 'The S is (or has, or does) F—'The domestic cat has four legs, two eyes, two ears, and guts in its belly,' 'The Texas blue-bonnet harbors nitrogen-fixing microbes in certain nodes on its roots,' 'The yellow finch breeds in spring, attracting its mate with such and such song,' whatever. Such *sentences* I will call 'Aristotelian categoricals.' But our language of course permits the same judgments to be expressed in a number of other ways, for example, by 'S's are/have/do F,' or 'It belongs to an S to be/have/do F,' or 'S's characteristically (or typically) are/have/do F,' and a hundred others. (Thompson 1995: 281)

What is involved here is a form of generality that is expressed by what linguists call "generic" sentences. Not all generics purport to capture the nature of a kind or species, but some do, and their doing so is consistent with their failing short of universal generality. That wolves hunt in packs is some sort of insight into what they are, even though this one or that one may go it alone.

No doubt more needs to be said about the metaphysics of this generic essentialism, about the prospects for its reductive treatment—which Thompson (1995: 284–88) contests—and about the scope of its application. Our interest is confined to its interaction with the guise of the good. Nothing in the argument so far conflicts with the truth of natural-historical judgments, or nature-expressing generics, that connect human action and desire with appearances of the good:

> Human beings want what seems good to them; and they act for reasons they regard as good.

If generic essentialism makes sense, these propositions could be necessary truths of human nature even though some of us want to own saucers of mud and others act from spite or vanity or despair. It has been proposed, if only in passing, that this is the intended form of the guise of the good for desire. It is "an assertion about the 'essence' of desire, rather like the assertion that fish are vertebrates: either is consistent with the occurrence of freaks" (Stampe 1987: 366). Michael Stocker (2004: 319) considers, without endorsing, the related claim that it is "natural for any being to seek its good." For all I have said, then, it may be a natural-historical fact about us, a necessary truth of human nature, that we act under the guise of the good.

What I have argued against is the rather different view that it belongs to rational agency, as such, to be exercised under the guise of the good. As at the end of section 2, the point can be stated ecumenically. There are two different ways to understand the doctrine that we act under the guise of the good: as a fragment of the natural history of human beings, limited to our particular way of acting for reasons and consistent with exceptions; and as a partial account of the abstract capacity to act for reasons. The first claim is perhaps defensible. At any rate, I don't object to it. That human beings act under the guise of the good would help to justify the sense of aberration, though not impossibility, in cases where we don't. What I have argued is that the guise of the good is not contained in the bare idea of intentional action or acting for a reason. To claim otherwise is to fall into misconceptions in action theory: of the kind of proposition that answers the question "Why?"—which gives an explanatory not a justifying reason—or of the nature and normativity of the explanation involved. Rejecting these misconceptions is not as radical as it may seem, since we can do so while accepting the analogous generic claims about humanity: We tend to want what we perceive as being in some way good, to choose what seems worthy of choice, and to act in ways we think we can justify, at least to some extent.

This is a substantive concession, but a limited one. It allows for generic essentialism in application to human nature, but not the nature of rational agency, as such. It thus invites a further question. Why can't we propose, in the mode of nonuniversal but nature-expressing generality, that rational agents, those capable of acting for reasons, act and desire for reasons they perceive as good? That would make the arguments of sections 2 and 3 irrelevant, directed at the wrong sort of proposition even about their abstract topic. What prevents this is a restriction on the kinds of things whose nature or essence is properly captured in generic terms. "Those capable of acting for reasons" do not form an appropriate target for the sort of generalization that permits exceptions even as it tells us what its subjects are. We say that the cat has four legs, and the human being thirty-two teeth, but not that "the rational agent" decides what to do in this way or that—unless we mean to imply that every one of them does so, of necessity, or to be reporting a merely accidental fact.

This seems evident to me, but it can also be supported by argument. When Fs are by nature G, in the generic sense, but their being G depends on the circumstance in which they find themselves, there is a distinction to be drawn among such circumstances, between those that do and those that do not fit with the nature of the F. The conditions in which an F is not G are ones that prevent it from realizing its nature; they are excluded from its natural circumstance, which is itself to be specified with nonuniversal generalizations. Thompson illustrates this point with an example:

> Now suppose I say, 'Bobcats breed in spring': it is again obvious that this isn't going to happen in any particular case unless certain conditions are satisfied. Perhaps a special hormone must be released in late winter. And perhaps the hormone will not be released if the bobcat is too close to sea-level, or if it fails to pass through the shade of a certain sort of tall pine. But, now, to articulate *these* conditions is to advance one's teaching about bobcats. It is not a reflection on the limited significance of one's teaching. The thought that *certain hormones are released*, or that *they live at such and such altitudes and amid such and such vegetation*, is a thought of the same kind as the thought that *they breed in spring*. The field guide and the nature documentary assign an external environment to the intended life-form, after all, and in the same 'voice' they elsewhere employ in describing its bearers' inner structure and operations. These conditions are thus 'presupposed' by the life-form itself, and not by the poor observing subject with his low-resolution lens. (Thompson 1995: 287)

All of this applies to the generalizations about human nature above, assuming that they are true. Human beings want what seems good to them; and they act for reasons they perceive as good. Still, some do not, as perhaps in conditions of bad upbringing or severe deprivation. But then it belongs to human nature not to be brought up in those ways or deprived of those things. Our natural environments are ones that foster the tendency to act and desire under the guise of the good. Or if they are not, the guise of the good is not an essential truth about human nature; it is, at best, a contingent fact about humans hereabouts. The central point is this: When Fs are by nature G, but it is possible for an F not to be G, there are further truths about the nature of the F that describe its natural circumstance, and this circumstance excludes the conditions that prevent an F from being G. Thus, if rational agents by nature act under the guise of the good, but some do not, it must be natural for them to inhabit conditions in which they are not prevented from coming to act under the guise of the good—as we may be prevented by corrupt habituation. But this is nonsense. There is no such thing as the natural environment of a rational agent, abstractly conceived, only for particular kinds of living thing. It follows that we cannot capture the essence of rational agency in generic terms. If it belongs to rational agents, as such, to act under the guise of the good, there cannot be exceptions.

Where does this leave our guiding question, about agency and evaluation? I have argued for the following principal claims:

> If desires represent their objects as good, they must be had for reasons, and reasons for desire must be respects in which the object of desire is seen as good.

> One can act and desire for reasons without regarding them as reasons for what one is doing, or as respects in which it is a good thing to do; thus one can act for reasons without regarding one's action as *pro tanto* justified.

> Explanations of what one is doing in terms of reasons, of the kind one must accept in answering the question "Why?" need not reveal even approximate rationality.

> It follows that the guise of the good does not apply to intentional action, as such; nor can it be rescued by generic essentialism.

It is consistent with these claims that the tendency to act and desire for reasons we regard as good is a natural-historical necessity of human life. The source of the guise of the good in action theory may be a familiar and tempting parochialism: the mistake of thinking that our characteristic form of agency shows us what agency essentially is.

There is a further moral to be drawn, in closing, from our brief examination of generic essentialism. When the nature of a kind can be specified in generic terms, as seems possible with species of living things, it is tempting to regard this specification as normative: It defines the good or healthy or well-functioning individual. As Thompson remarks:

> We may implicitly define a certain very abstract category of 'natural defect' with the following simple-minded principle of inference: *From* 'The S is F *and* 'This S is not F' *to infer* 'This S is defective in that it is not F.' (Thompson 1995: 295)

This is probably *too* abstract; it needs refinement.[40] But it is enough to encourage the hope that, at least sometimes and to some extent, generic essentialism provides a model for the derivation of norms from natures. One form of ethical rationalism applies this hope to the standards of practical reason, which it purports to derive from the nature of rational agency, generically described.[41] If the argument above is right, however, this strategy cannot succeed. The nature of rational agency is not the sort of thing that can be stated in generic terms.

It does not follow from this alone that ethical rationalism is false. After all, it may take a different form, resting on essentialist claims that imply universal generalizations. But even here, our arguments support a provisional skepticism.[42] The ethical rationalist cannot rely on the doctrine that agency is exercised under the guise of the good or that it must conform to approximate rationality. The second restriction, in particular, is severe. If the form of explanation characteristic of rational agency does not invoke or draw upon the standards of practical reason, how could those standards be implicitly contained within it?

Notes

1. For helpful discussion of this material, I am grateful to Robert Audi, Rachel Barney, Matt Boyle, Doug Lavin, Jessica Moss, Evgenia Mylonaki, Joseph Raz, Sebastian Rödl, Geoff Sayre-McCord, Michael Smith, Sergio Tenenbaum, Jennifer Whiting, to participants at conferences held in Toronto and Syracuse in the summer of 2007, and to Michael Smith's Seminar in Systematic Ethics at Princeton, fall 2008.

2. Setiya 2007, part 1.

3. A classic source is Stocker 1979. See also Stocker 2004: 324; Frankfurt 2004: 122ff.; Frankfurt's replies in *Contours of Agency*, ed. Buss and Overton, 2002: 87, 89, 160, 187, 223; and Setiya 2007: 36–38.

4. As, for instance, in Tenenbaum 2007.

5. The accusation is perhaps unfair to Stocker. His essay "Desiring the Bad" ends with a more general account of the connection between evaluations and motives on which "the controverting cases are not exceptions, aberrations, mere anomalies or mere counterexamples"; even in the positive case, where we do act in ways that we regard as good, or for reasons we take to justify what we are doing, the "connections between motivation and evaluation are mediated by arrays of structures of mood, interest, energy and the like" (Stocker 1979: 750–51).

> When I consider people who see no hope for themselves or those they care for, who lack physical and spiritual energy, I am not at all surprised that—as political and anthropological data suggest—they may not seek even what little good they do perceive. Life may be too much for them. We, on the contrary, see the world as open to us, and more important, open for us. We can progress. We can make it. We see ourselves out there to be won. We have self-confidence and hope. Indeed, we have more than this: We have an optimistic certainty. We have energy. We know we are worthy. We know that, barring bad luck, our enterprise will be rewarded. And so on. Such an array of structures of mood, interest, energy, . . . makes it natural, almost inevitable, that we seek the (believed) good for ourselves or others. And it seems at least arguable that such an array must be posited to give an adequate account of how, at least according to our cultural ideal, motivation and evaluation are related in us. (Stocker 1979: 752)

6. Compare Anscombe 1963: 75; and Velleman 1992a: 118–19.

7. See Anscombe 1958: 38; and, more extensively, Moravcsik 1994, Thompson 1995, and Foot 2001.

8. Along with the authors quoted in the text, see Darwall 1983: 205; Bond 1983: 30–31; Velleman 1992b: 140–42; Korsgaard 1997: 221; Broome 1997; Wallace 1999; Dancy 2000: 97; Moran 2001: 124–28; and many others.

9. The translation is by G. A. Grube and C. D. C. Reeve (Cooper 1997: 1126).

10. Quoted from Hamlyn 1968: 69–70.

11. Kant 1788, Ak. 5:58–59. Kant's attitude to the "old formula of the schools" is, however, complicated. In saying that he cites it with approval, I do not mean that he would accept it in just its original sense.

12. For such accounts, see Thomson 1992: 107–13; and Scanlon 1998: 95–100.

13. For this point, see Johnston 2001.

14. What is it for something to be good "for its own sake"? The basic notion here is "for the sake of": x is valuable for the sake of y just in case the value of x is partly explained by its relation to the value of y. Perhaps x is a means to y, or approximates y, or bears some symbolic connection with y. For x to be valuable for its own sake is for it to have value that is not wholly explained by its relation to the value of other things. This is to be distinguished from having value as an end, not wholly as a means to other valuable things, which is a logically weaker property, and from being intrinsically valuable or valuable in virtue of one's intrinsic nature. If the value of x is explained by its relation to y though not through the value of y, then x is valuable for its own sake, but not intrinsically. And while value for the sake of something else is typically not intrinsic, it can be. Suppose, for instance, that x is valuable for the sake of one of its parts.

15. This conception of desire is found in Raz 1999b: 52–56.

16. The argument so far neither supports nor refutes the idea that desires represent their objects as good. It does suggest, however, that desires are not "appearances" of the good, except perhaps in the modest sense that would distinguish them from *beliefs*, so as to allow for illusions of value that we do not accept. In particular, we should be wary of the claim that desires are perceptual states (as in Stampe 1987). The fact that desires are typically had for reasons speaks against this. Although there are reasons why we perceive things as we do, and why they appear that way to us, we don't have reasons for perceiving that things are thus-and-so or for being appeared to as we are. Perceiving is not something we do for reasons, as we act and desire for reasons. Desires are in this respect quite unlike perceptual states.

17. I give a causal-psychological account of acting for a reason in Setiya 2007: 28–59.

18. This is apparently denied by Raz (1999a: 23), when he writes that "intentional action is action done for a reason; and [. . .] reasons are facts in virtue of which those actions are good in some respect and to some degree," and by Dancy (2000: 9): "to explain an action is [. . .] to show that it would have been [what there was most reason to do] if the agent's beliefs had been true." These claims are surely too strong, just as they stand: They are best read as exaggerations of the theory criticized in section 3.

19. The argument in the following text is a version of one I have proposed elsewhere—in part 1 of *Reasons without Rationalism*—stripped of its constructive ambitions. The objection to the guise of the good does not depend on giving a causal-psychological account of action, and the attempt to do so would be a distraction here.

20. See, for instance, Anscombe 1963: 11, 42–44, 48.

21. For similar claims about knowledge of reasons, see Milligan 1974: 187–88; Audi 1986: 82–85; Wallace 1999: 241; and Searle 2001: 16.

22. "A man may be making ten carbon copies as he writes, and this may be intentional; yet he may not know that he is; all he knows is that he is trying" (Davidson 1971: 50; see also Davidson 1978: 91–94). For further discussion, see *Reasons without Rationalism* (Setiya 2007: 25–26) and section I of "Practical Knowledge" (Setiya 2008).

23. See also Stocker 2004: 326–29 on "conditional or circumstantial goodness."

24. In making this argument, I ignore the suggestion that "practical knowledge"—the fact that we typically *know* and do not merely *believe* that we are doing ϕ in doing it for reasons—is explained by the guise of the good. On the kind of account proposed by Wilson (2000: 12–16) and Moran (2001: 124–28), knowledge of what one is doing intentionally derives from practical judgment, a verdict about the reasons that bear on what to do. But this is the problematic, in two ways. First, what it explains is at most how the agent is "in a position to know" what she is doing, if she takes her action to be determined by the balance of reasons, not why she must believe that she is doing it. Second, accounts of this kind struggle to accommodate knowledge of intentional action against one's evaluative beliefs, or when one has sufficient reason for doing more than one thing. In "Practical Knowledge" (Setiya 2008), I give an account of knowing what one is doing that avoids these difficulties.

25. As, for instance, in Johnston 2001.

26. A difficult question can be raised about the scope of this result. Does it apply to reasons for belief, where we can equally distinguish propositions about justification and evidence from propositions about the grounds on which a given belief is held? That I believe that p on the ground that q is consistent with there being no evidence at all for the truth of my belief. Is it sufficient to answer the question, "Why do you believe that p?" that I can cite a proposition of the former kind? In my view, the answer is no: Reasons attach to actions and beliefs in quite different ways. For instance, it is sufficient for believing that p partly on the ground that q that one believe that p and believe that the fact that q is evidence that p. There is no need for a causal relation between these beliefs, and no analogue of Davidson's argument in "Actions, Reasons and Causes" (1963: 9). Believing for a reason is independent of causality in a way that acting for a reason is not. This claim is no doubt controversial, and the issues are too complicated to examine here. I hope to address them more adequately in future work.

27. I try to articulate this connection precisely, through the idea of good practical thought, in the introduction to *Reasons without Rationalism* (Setiya 2007).

28. For a similar claim about reason and volition, see Frankfurt 2004: 120–21, esp. n. 2.

29. Again, see *Reasons without Rationalism* (Setiya 2007: 25–26) and section I of "Practical Knowledge" (Setiya 2008).

30. For related claims about the normative character of reasons-explanation, see Nagel 1970: 33–34; Korsgaard 1997: 221–22; Raz 1999a: 22–24; Dancy 2000: 9–10, 95–97, 106; Wedgwood 2006: 662; and Tenenbaum 2007: 9–17.

31. See also Williams 1995; Foot 2001: 12; and Setiya 2007: 71–74.

32. In the present context, we need not distinguish different versions of instrumental reason or the instrumental principle, some of which appeal to our intentions, others to mere desires. The argument relies on the general concept of being a means to an end.

33. The example is adapted from Herman 1981: 364–65.

34. For the claim that "a genuine virtue [must] produce nothing but right conduct," see McDowell 1979: 52–53. This doctrine tends to support the unity of the virtues, though not without some further argument. The issues here are critically discussed in Watson 1984: 59–62, 67–69.

35. For related discussion, see *Reasons without Rationalism* (Setiya 2007: 101–6).

36. This seems to be accepted by McDowell (1978: 90; 1979: 51) in contexts where he rejects the assimilation of acting from virtue to acting from desire.

37. For this example, see Raz 1997: 8.

38. Unless, trivially, the conception is taken to include the fact that there is reason to act in that way, as, for instance, at McDowell 1978: 90; and in McDowell 1979; the more restrictive understanding in the text seems to operate at McDowell 1978: 87.

39. He is drawing on brief remarks by Anscombe (1958: 38); see also Moravcsik 1994 and Foot 2001.

40. As in Foot 2001: 29ff.

41. See Lavin 2004: 456n56 on "constitutive" accounts of practical reason:

[We] lack a correct conception of the logical form of [. . .] claims describing the essence or nature of agency, the claims in virtue of which we are supposed to understand the force of "oughts" applying to particular agents. [. . .] A promising direction for the constitutivist to go, I think, is to resist the urge to assimilate [descriptions of essences] to universal generalizations and instead look toward generics to describe "the what it is" which is to serve to underwrite standards of assessment.

42. For more decisive resistance, see part 2 of *Reasons without Rationalism* (Setiya 2007).

References

Anscombe, G. E. M. 1958: Modern moral philosophy, repr. in G. E. M. Anscombe, *Ethics, Religion and Politics*. Oxford: Basil Blackwell, 1981: 26–42.
———. 1963: *Intention*, 2nd ed. Oxford: Basil Blackwell.
Audi, R. 1986: Acting for reasons, repr. in A. Mele, ed., *The Philosophy of Action*. Oxford: Oxford University Press, 1997: 75–105.
Bond, E. J. 1983: *Reason and Value*. Cambridge: Cambridge University Press.

Broome, J. 1997: Reason and motivation, *Proceedings of the Aristotelian Society, Supplementary Volume* (71): 131–46.

Buss, S., and Overton, L., eds. 2002: *Contours of Agency: Essays on Themes from Harry Frankfurt*. Cambridge, Mass.: MIT Press.

Cooper, J. M., ed. 1997: *Plato: Complete Works*. Indianapolis: Hackett.

Dancy, J. 2000: *Practical Reality*. Oxford: Oxford University Press.

Darwall, S. 1983: *Impartial Reason*. Ithaca, N.Y.: Cornell University Press.

Davidson, D. 1963: Actions, reasons and causes, repr. in D. Davidson, *Essays on Actions and Events*. Oxford: Oxford University Press, 1980: 3–19.

———. 1971: Agency, repr. in D. Davidson, *Essays on Actions and Events*. Oxford: Oxford University Press, 1980: 43–61.

———. 1978: Intending, repr. in D. Davidson, *Essays on Actions and Events*. Oxford: Oxford University Press, 1980: 83–102.

———. 1987: Problems in the explanation of action, repr. in D. Davidson, *Problems of Rationality*. Oxford: Oxford University Press, 2004: 101–16.

Foot, P. 1978: Virtues and vices, in P. Foot, *Virtues and Vices*. Oxford: Basil Blackwell, 1978: 1–18.

———. 2001: *Natural Goodness*. Oxford: Oxford University Press.

Frankfurt, H. 2004: Disengaging reason, in R. J. Wallace, P. Pettit, S. Scheffler, M. Smith, eds., *Reason and Value: Themes from the Moral Philosophy of Joseph Raz*. Oxford: Oxford University Press, 2004: 119–28.

Hamlyn, D. W. 1968: *Aristotle: De Anima, Books II and III*. Oxford: Oxford University Press.

Herman, B. 1981: On the value of acting from the motive of duty, *Philosophical Review* 90: 359–82.

Hursthouse, R. 1991: Arational actions, *Journal of Philosophy* 91: 57–68.

———. 1999: *On Virtue Ethics*. Oxford: Oxford University Press.

Johnston, M. 2001: The authority of affect, *Philosophy and Phenomenological Research* 63: 181–214.

Kant, I. 1788: *Critique of Practical Reason*, M. Gregor, trans., Cambridge: Cambridge University Press, 1997.

Korsgaard, C. 1997: The normativity of instrumental reason, in G. Cullity and B. Gaut, eds., *Ethics and Practical Reason*. Oxford: Oxford University Press, 1997: 215–54.

Lavin, D. 2004: Practical reason and the possibility of error. *Ethics* 114: 424–57.

McDowell, J. 1978: Are moral requirements hypothetical imperatives? repr. in J. McDowell, *Mind, Value and* Reality. Cambridge, Mass.: Harvard University Press, 1998: 77–94.

———. 1979: Virtue and reason, repr. in J. McDowell, *Mind, Value and Reality*. Cambridge, Mass.: Harvard University Press, 1998: 50–73.

———. 1985: Functionalism and anomalous monism, repr. in J. McDowell, *Mind, Value and Reality*. Cambridge, Mass.: Harvard University Press, 1998: 325–40.

Milligan, D. E. 1974: Reasons as explanation, *Mind* 83: 180–93.

Moran, R. 2001: *Authority and Estrangement*. Princeton, N.J.: Princeton University Press.

Moravcsik, J. 1994: Essences, powers and generic propositions, in T. Scaltsas, D. Charles, and M. L. Gill, eds., *Unity, Identity and Explanation in Aristotle's Metaphysics*. Oxford: Oxford University Press, 1994: 229–44.

Nagel, T. 1970: *The Possibility of Altruism*. Princeton, N.J.: Princeton University Press.

Raz, J. 1997: When we are ourselves: The active and the passive, repr. in J. Raz, *Engaging Reason*. Oxford: Oxford University Press, 1999: 5–21.

———. 1999a: Agency, reason and the good, in J. Raz, *Engaging Reason*. Oxford: Oxford University Press, 1999: 22–45.

———. 1999b: Incommensurability and agency, in J. Raz, *Engaging Reason*. Oxford: Oxford University Press, 1999: 46–66.

Scanlon, T. M. 1998: *What We Owe to Each Other*. Cambridge, Mass.: Harvard University Press.

Searle, J. 2001: *Rationality in Action*. Cambridge, Mass.: MIT Press.

Setiya, K. 2007: *Reasons without Rationalism*. Princeton, N.J.: Princeton University Press.

———. 2008: Practical knowledge. *Ethics* 118: 388–409.

Smith, M. 1987: The Humean theory of motivation. *Mind* 96: 36–61.

———. 1994: *The Moral Problem*. Cambridge: Cambridge University Press.

Stampe, D. 1987: The authority of desire. *Philosophical Review* (96): 335–81.

Stocker, M. 1979: Desiring the Bad. *Journal of Philosophy* 76: 738–53.

———. 2004: Raz on the intelligibility of bad acts, in R. J. Wallace, P. Pettit, S. Scheffler, M. Smith, eds., *Reason and Value: Themes from the Moral Philosophy of Joseph Raz*. Oxford: Oxford University Press, 2004: 303–32.

Tenenbaum, S. 2007: *Appearances of the Good: An Essay on the Nature of Practical Reason*. Cambridge: Cambridge University Press.

Thompson, M. 1995: The representation of life, in R. Hursthouse, G. Lawrence, and W. Quinn, eds., *Virtues and Reasons: Philippa Foot and Moral Theory*. Oxford: Oxford University Press, 1995: 247–96.

Thomson, J. J. 1992: On some ways in which a thing can be good. *Social Philosophy and Policy* 9, no. 2: 96–117.

Velleman, J. D. 1992a: The guise of the good, repr. in J. D. Velleman, *The Possibility of Practical Reason*. Oxford: Oxford University Press, 2000: 99–122.

———. 1992b: What happens when someone acts? repr. in J. D. Velleman, *The Possibility of Practical Reason*. Oxford: Oxford University Press, 2000: 123–43.

Wallace, R. J. 1999: Three conceptions of rational agency. *Ethical Theory and Moral Practice* 2: 217–42.

Watson, G. 1984: Virtues in excess. *Philosophical Studies* 46: 57–74.

Wedgwood, R. 2006: The normative force of reasoning. *Noûs* 40: 660–86.

Williams, B. 1979: Internal and external reasons, repr. in B. Williams, *Moral Luck*. Cambridge: Cambridge University Press, 1981: 101–13.

———. 1985: *Ethics and the Limits of Philosophy*. Cambridge, Mass.: Harvard University Press.

———. 1995: Acting as the virtuous person acts, in R. Heinaman, ed., *Aristotle and Moral Realism*. London: University College London Press, 1995: 13–23.

Wilson, G. 2000: Proximal practical foresight. *Philosophical Studies* 99: 3–19.

6

On the Guise of the Good

Joseph Raz

Every action and pursuit is thought to aim at some good.

—Aristotle

I don't care what's right or wrong.
—Kris Kristofferson, "Help Me
   Make It Through the Night"

In an article that established this phrase[1] as the standard name by which this ancient thesis is referred to these days Velleman rhetorically challenges its adherents:

> The agent portrayed in much philosophy of action is, let us face it, a square. He does nothing intentionally unless he regards it or its consequences as desirable. . . . Surely, so general a capacity as agency cannot entail so narrow a cast of mind. Our moral psychology has characterised, not the generic agent, but a particular species of agent, and a particularly bland species at that.[2]

To launch us on our way I will provisionally take the Guise of the Good Thesis to consist of three propositions:

(1) Intentional actions are actions performed for reasons, as those are seen by the agents.
(2) Specifying the intention which makes an action intentional identifies central features of the reason(s) for which the action is performed.
(3) Reasons for action are such reasons by being facts that establish that the action has some value.[3]

From these it is said to follow that

(4) Intentional actions are actions taken in, and because of, a belief that there is some good in them.

For most purposes we can ignore the second proposition, which is often assumed but rarely considered when discussing the Thesis. There are other ways in which the Thesis was understood and formulated. Velleman, for

111

example, assumes a relation between intentions and desires. Explaining
the rationale for the Thesis he writes:

> The reason is that he acts intentionally only when he acts out of a desire for
> some anticipated outcome, and in desiring that outcome he must regard it as
> having some value.[4]

I will remain noncommittal about the relations of intentions and
desires, and will therefore not discuss desires in this chapter.[5] The above
statement of the Thesis presupposes cognitivism about discourse on
reasons and values. Trying to state and discuss the Thesis in a way that
is neutral between cognitivism and non-cognitivism would unreason-
ably complicate matters. There should be little difficulty in applying
the considerations below to non-cognitivist or other versions of the
Thesis.

On the face of it Velleman is blaming supporters of the Thesis for a
factual mistake, a mistake about human psychology. Perhaps because they
are bland and square they think that all people are. But it is more likely
that he is merely teasing his fellow philosophers. After all, the Thesis fits
Hitler and religious fanatics more straightforwardly than it does your
neighborhood grocer (as the examples below will illustrate), and they are
hardly your common or garden square and bland types. Besides, if it is
wrong the Guise of the Good is more likely to be wrong about all people
some of the time than about only some people all of the time. Commonly
alleged counterexamples to the Guise of the Good (for example, touch-
ing a dark spot on the wall or passing one's fingers through one's hair
'for no reason at all') are hardly actions unknown to the square or bland
among us.

The Guise of the Good is best understood as a conceptual thesis; the
three propositions constituting the Thesis are taken to be conceptual
truths. Section 2 considers the case for the first leg of the Thesis. It will
lead to the formulation and defense of a revised version of the first part of
the Thesis in section 3. Sections 4 and 5 will then tackle objections to the
third part of the Thesis. But first, in section 1, some different ways of
understanding the Thesis are considered, and a *prima facie* argument for it
is offered. In the final section I will raise the issue of the significance of the
Thesis as it emerges from these discussions. Does it still fulfil the aspira-
tions of its traditional supporters?

1. INITIAL OBJECTIONS, CLARIFICATIONS, AND A
PRIMA FACIE CASE

What could support the Guise of the Good, given the many apparent
counterexamples? Here are two such counterexamples:

> *A: The miner:* The management proposes to close the colliery. The miners
> vote on whether to accept the proposal and the redundancy pay that goes

with it or to oppose it. You talk to one of the miners: 'You are voting to stay put.' 'Sure,' he says. 'So you must have some hope [of keeping the mine open].' 'No hope. Just principles.'

  B: The fish: Sitting in the bath, Johnny, and it does not matter whether he is a child or an adult acting like a child, says, 'I am a fish' and beats the water with his open palm (presumably pretending to flap it with his tail). 'Why did you do that, Johnny?' 'That's what fish do.'

We can readily imagine how in cases like these it may be difficult to get the miner or Johnny to acknowledge that there was value in the action. The miner may insist that his vote does no good. He just had to vote that way. Perhaps, we may say, it is a matter of integrity for him. Johnny may be altogether puzzled by the thought that there was some value in the action. He was just playing at being a fish. → Vellemans account

We know how the argument develops, or one way in which it may develop. When thinking about their intentional actions agents do not necessarily think of them under the Guise of the Good, and they may not even be disposed to think of them in that way. That is, there may be no ready way, no readily available evidence or argument that would lead them to acknowledge that their intentions express, imply, or presuppose belief in the value of the intended actions. So the Thesis assumes that when such acknowledgment is not forthcoming people nevertheless believe that there is something good about their intentions, or intentional actions (which therefore conform to the Guise of the Good), and are start somehow mistaken if they deny that.

But perhaps, contrary to (4) above, the Guise of the Good does not presuppose that agents believe that there is value in their actions. Let us allow, for the sake of argument, that reasons are facts that endow the action with some value. Is action for a reason action taken in the belief that there is value in the action? There may be an alternative. It is difficult to deny that actions are intentional only if and because the agents are aware of some of their characteristics. But need they believe that the characteristics constitute reasons for actions? One alternative suggestion is that action for a reason is action performed in the belief that it has certain characteristics that the agent treats as reasons, that is as good-making. He need not believe that they are good-making, just as someone who believes a proposition treats it as true, though he need not believe ✱ that it is true. The analogy is Velleman's. He thinks that that is the most that can be claimed by supporters of the Guise of the Good. But, he contends, this claim is true only if 'take it as good-making' means that one treats the characteristic in the same way one would if one thought that it is good-making, which can be the case even though one may believe that it is not good-making. Velleman's point is that supporters of the Guise of the Good must resist this interpretation. They must understand 'take it as good-making' to mean take it to be good-making, which—according to this suggestion—describes their attitude to the fact so taken.

✱agrees with Velleman

A terminological convention may help. Let's say of people that they think that something is the case only when they believe so, and the belief is in their mind at the time. People have many beliefs that are not present to their mind. They believe much more than what they currently think about. Many such beliefs are remote from their thoughts, except on rare occasions. I believe that my mother was thirty when I was born. But it must have been some twenty years or more since I last had that thought. Applying this to the matter in hand I think that taking a feature of an action to make that action good in some respect is tantamount to believing that the feature is good-making. We say that the agents take the feature to be good-making rather than that they believe it to be good-making to intimate that they do not necessarily think of that at the time, but their conduct implies having that belief, it shows it to be one of their beliefs. It is not merely that they have the belief that the action has some value and that they take that action, but that the belief is part of what leads them to take the action, and that it guides the action. It is not in their mind, but it is part of the explanation of what they do. There is of course the alternative understanding of what is meant by treating a feature as good-making, but as Velleman points out, that alternative does not support the Guise of the Good. So I conclude that to defend the Guise of the Good one has to accept proposition (4) above, that is that intentional action is action performed because of a belief that the action has some value.

Supporters of the Guise of the Good must, therefore, attribute to the miner and to Johnny, in the examples above, mistakes about their own beliefs; at the very least they must be held mistaken in rejecting certain characterizations of their beliefs. What could explain such a mistake? Two responses help to explain what is at issue. First, the notion of 'the good' or 'value' used in expressing the Thesis is not to be confused with the concepts that are normally expressed by ordinary use of these terms. This is evident from the fact that in discussions of the Guise of the Good Thesis 'value' and 'good' are used interchangeably, even though they are neither synonymous nor does their normal use express the same concept. In arguing for and applying the Guise of the Good Thesis philosophers rely on a concept with broader applications than those associated with the normal use of those words. There is no point in trying to describe this concept here. It is familiar from the writings on the subject, and on value theory generally. And of course, one familiar aspect of it is the absence of agreement about its nature.

The second response, made necessary by the first, as well as by other considerations, is that the Thesis does not assume that agents capable of intentional action must have the concepts used in stating the Thesis (the concepts of the good, intention, reason for action), nor does it claim that they believe that these concepts apply to each of their intentional actions. It assumes that they have a belief about their action that can be truly characterized as a belief that the action has a good-making property, one that constitutes a reason for the action, and that reason or their belief in it, explains why they perform the action.[6]

In attributing to the miner, in the example above, the belief that the action is good because, for example, it is required by principles, we are not distorting his views. We neither attribute to him a concept of value according to which being required by sound principles endows an action with value, nor do we ignore or pervert his distinction between actions that are good because they promote good ends and actions that are required by principles. We are simply describing his views using a broader concept of value, one that allows that an action can have value either because it advances the realization of good ends or because it is required by a valid principle, as well as in other ways.

More, however, is required to deal with Johnny. First, we need to distinguish Johnny the child from Johnny the adult playing at being a child playing at being a fish. We—their parents and others—attribute to children beliefs they do not altogether have, and concepts they do not altogether possess, and our doing so is a vital part of their learning process.[7] Others may also have a defective grasp of concepts, and therefore a defective grasp of the beliefs that they use those concepts to express. Such cases are not counterexamples to this, any more than they are to other conceptual theses.

How about Johnny the adult? Even when prompted he does not endorse the thought that there is something good in acting as a fish would. Possibly he would assent to it if subjected to a lengthy explanation and argument. But that is not the point. The Guise of the Good Thesis claims that he has the belief when he acts like a fish, not that he can be brought to adopt that belief. To maintain the Thesis, to show that it applies to people like Johnny, one has to establish that his pretending to be a fish discloses a belief that there is some good in acting like a fish, perhaps because he believes that imaginative playacting is good, or for some other reason.

There may be other positive indicators that Johnny does indeed have such a belief. But perhaps there are none. In that case defenders of the Guise of the Good will say that the fact that Johnny's playacting is intentional shows that he believes that there is some good in his action. They will, in other words, take the Thesis to be at least to some extent self-verifying. This may look like a refutation of the Thesis, but it is not. For example, we would not hesitate to attribute to Johnny belief that his brother is unmarried, on the sole ground that he believes that his brother is a bachelor, given that it is a conceptual truth that bachelors are unmarried (and that Johnny is a competent user of the language, or of some relevant segment of it).[8] We do not require an independent ground for the attribution of the belief.[9]

The difference, some will say, is that the Guise of the Good cannot be relied upon until it is established. True. My point was merely that it is no refutation of it, no argument against it that on occasion the Thesis itself is the main ground for the attribution of the appropriate belief. I will return to cases like Johnny's once the case for the Thesis is examined.

But what is the case for the Thesis? It starts from a crucial point, made by Anscombe, and recently emphasized by Setiya,[10] namely that those who act intentionally know what they do (know it under the description under which the action is intentional, as some will add). In itself mere knowledge is consistent with the actions being done unintentionally. Agents may be mere witnesses to what is happening to them, or to what they do accidentally. What marks intentional actions is that they are done because of what their agents believe the action is (including what it may bring about). That means that what the agents believe about the action leads them to do it, and guides their doing of it, all the way to its conclusion, and that suggests that they approve of the action, given what they believe about it. They so act because they approve of the action, and that in turn means that they think that it has some value, since value is what we approve of.

Human beings being what they are, their attitude to their intentional actions is often too ambivalent to say that they approve of what they do. They may retain doubts about the wisdom of their actions. They may believe that it would be better to avoid what they are (intentionally) doing. They may even do what they do because it is not the best thing to do, do it in order to hurt themselves, or someone else, or for other (explanatory) reasons. The Guise of the Good is meant to accommodate such ambivalent and akratic conduct by claiming merely that agents see some good in what they do, which they may do even when they are ambivalent or convinced that they are acting for the lesser good (or the greater evil).

The Thesis does not express optimism about human nature. It is meant to accommodate not only mistakes, even gross mistakes about what is of value, but also anomic conduct in defiance of value.[11] Its point is that intentional actions are actions we perform because we endorse them in light of what we believe about them, and that means that we must believe that they have features that make them attractive, or as we say, features that give them value. The thought is that endorsement presupposes an appropriate object. It does not presuppose that the action has endorsable properties, but it does presuppose that it is taken by the agent to have such properties.

Talking of agents endorsing their intentional actions is metaphorical. It is meant to point out a feature of intentional action of which the Guise of the Good is meant to be an account. It assumes that intentions are partly constituted by associated beliefs about the intended action, rather than merely by their felt quality, or by their direction of fit. The thought is familiar: Fear is what it is partly because those afraid think that they are in danger. Envy is what it is partly because the envious believe that the object of their envy is superior in some desirable respect (success, reputation, happiness, possession of some advantages, etc.). Neither can be identified by their 'felt' qualities alone. The Guise of the Good takes a similar view of intentions. They differ from other mental attitudes or states that

[handwritten: Independent Intentions: have the intention before acting / have the intention at any time]

accompany some of our actions, the Thesis claims, by being constituted in part by a belief about the action and by its role in the acting. The belief has to explain why the agents took the action, that is, it must figure in an explanation of their action that relates to the way they saw the action, and aspects of themselves and the world, and how that led them to take the action. Hence the Guise of the Good's claim that intentions must include a belief that there is something attractive about the action, that it has some value.

The preceding four paragraphs present a case for the Guise of the Good, which is good enough unless there are considerations militating against it. That is what we must examine next.

2. ARE INTENTIONAL ACTIONS ACTIONS FOR REASONS?

[handwritten: beliefs that the object has some value must be most of the explanation of why acted]

The Guise of the Good is, whatever else it is, a thesis about intentions. How does it relate to intentional actions? There are independent intentions, as I will call them, that are ones one can have at a time one is not doing what the intention is an intention to do. My intention to fly to New York next week is an independent intention, as is my intention to complete this chapter. I have the second intention while doing what I intend to do, that is while being engaged in the activity of bringing the chapter to completion, but I can have it while I am eating, sleeping, or gossiping with friends. It is not an intention that I can have only when doing what it is an intention to do.

[handwritten: not all intentional actions have intent]

On the other hand, when I (intentionally) drink some water the intentionality manifest in my action is an aspect of the action, an aspect of the way the action is performed. It could be that I am drinking the water because I have an (independent) intention to drink the water, but it could be otherwise. I may just distractedly pick up the glass of water and sip from it, while thinking about the implications of a flaw in my argument. My action is intentional, but there is no intention with which I perform it. At other times, while there is an independent intention with which I perform an intentional action, it is not an intention to perform that action. When talking about my friend's holiday I uttered the word 'went' and did so intentionally, but I was hardly aware that I used that word at that moment. I did it intentionally because I intended (had the independent intention) to describe his holiday experience, and saying 'went' was part of that activity. I did not have an independent intention to say 'went,' but I said the word in the course of acting for an independent intention that I did have.

[handwritten: embedded intentions are intentions that all ICs have]

Embedded intentions, the intentions present in all our intentional actions, are aspects of, manners of acting, and thus distinct from independent intentions even when we act intentionally because we have an independent intention. They consist in facts such as that our actions are guided by beliefs about what we are in the process of doing (what we do if our action is to be intentional), so that at the sub-personal level our movements

[handwritten: II = embedded action intention you have while completing it]

Guise of good about embedded intentions?

are continuously monitored and adjusted to fit those beliefs, and in other facts playing a similar role in the performance of the actions.

Given this distinction between independent intentions and embedded intentions, which is the Guise of the Good about? The first part of the Thesis, as stated, is about embedded intentionality, as that is the feature that makes all intentional actions intentional. There can, of course, be a sister thesis to the effect that independent intentions to perform an action involve a belief that there is some good in the action. It may well be thought that this sister thesis is less vulnerable to objections than the Guise of the Good in the provisional form given it at the beginning of the chapter. I will return to this possibility. For the time being let us take 'intentions' in the discussion of the Thesis to refer to embedded intentionality. Right now I consed intentions as embedded

Consider Ignatius who placed a bomb on a regular commercial flight in order to destroy incriminating documents being transported on it, knowing with complete certainty that if the documents are destroyed everyone on board will be killed. The bomb explodes, destroys the documents, and kills everyone. I think that Ignatius has murdered the people on the airplane, and that he did that by intentionally killing them.

It is sometimes said that one Φs intentionally if and only if one Φs with the intention of Φing. In the preceding paragraphs I suggested that some intentional actions are not performed with an independent intention, and it is natural to say that they are not performed with an intention. They are intentional because of their embedded intentionality, as I called it, that is, because of the manner in which they were performed. But there is no need to make an issue out of a point of linguistic propriety. We can accept that whenever one Φs intentionally one Φs with the intention to Φ, provided it is understood that the intention need not be an independent intention. It may be merely an embedded intention, that is, nothing other than the intentionality embedded in the action.

Ignatius did not have an independent intention to kill the passengers and crew. He would have been just as happy, or even happier, had the documents been on a pilotless plane with no passengers, or if through a freak chain of events the documents were destroyed, but the passengers and crew left uninjured. But given how things were he did kill them intentionally. Therefore—by our terminological stipulation—he had an embedded intention to kill when acting to carry out his independent intention of destroying the evidence. His embedded intention to kill, his intentionality in killing the people, derived from his independent intention to destroy the evidence. More generally:

Derived embedded intentions (definition): whenever one intentionally performs one action by performing a second action, if one has an independent intention to perform the second action, but no independent intention to perform the first, then one's embedded intention to perform the first derives from one's embedded intention to perform the second. Putting it semi-formally: (x) (Φ) (ψ) [If x intentionally Φs by intentionally ψ-ing, and if x has an independent

Positive account: first proposition of Guise of Good must be changed/re-formulated

intention to ψ, but no independent intention to Φ, then x's embedded intention to Φ derives from x's embedded intention to ψ.]

Does Ignatius's case constitute a counterexample to the Thesis? After all, Ignatius intentionally killed people without believing that there was reason to kill them. This is familiar territory, and the responses to the alleged objection are numerous and well known. Some of them are more controversial than others, and there is no point in rehearsing them all. Think of one possible response to the objection, that is that Ignatius has a reason to kill the people, namely, that the killing is a by-product of the destruction of the evidence, and Ignatius thinks that he has reason to destroy the evidence. This reply is unhappy as it stands. It does not even purport to show that Ignatius believes that he has reason to kill the people onboard the plane. Rather, it claims that because he believes that he has reason to destroy the evidence he has reason to perform those actions that he will be performing by destroying the evidence. This cannot be right. One's belief (possibly mistaken) that one has a reason to do one thing cannot, in this way, generate reasons to do other things.[12]

Possibly if Ignatius has a reason to destroy the evidence he has a reason (obviously not necessarily undefeated) to kill the people on the plane, though even this is far from clear. After all, killing them is not a means to the end of destroying the evidence. Be that as it may, it is irrelevant to the assessment of the Guise of the Good, which is, as it must be, about people's beliefs about their actions. That there was (possibly unbeknown to the agent) a reason to perform an action is no ground at all to think that it was performed intentionally.

So, does Ignatius believe that he has reason to kill the people? He may well not believe that, and if so he would not be mistaken. He believes that he has reason to destroy the evidence. But that, in itself, does not show that he believes that he has reason to do anything else, not even if he does believe that destroying the evidence will also constitute doing those other things.

Nevertheless, the objection fails to undermine the Thesis. Ignatius intentionally killed the people because he killed the people by intentionally destroying the evidence, and he knew it (knew that that was what he was doing while doing it). All that the objection shows is that the first proposition of the Guise of the Good, which says

(1) Intentional actions are actions performed for reasons, as those are seen by the agents

should be augmented to clarify its meaning:

(1') Φ-ing is intentional only if, in the belief of its agent, there is either a reason to Φ or a reason to perform another action such that by performing it he will, as he knows, be Φ-ing.

start

The question we face is whether the argument for the Thesis, namely that it contributes a vital element to the explanation of intentions, applies to the Thesis in this amplified form. We can reply by considering again the example: Had the embedded intention to kill the people not been derived from the embedded intention to destroy the evidence, one might have felt that (1') defeats the promise the Guise of the Good holds of contributing to the explanation of intentions. Had the intention not supported by belief in a reason, not been derived from the other intention, which is supported by such a belief, it would have appeared that the Thesis applies to some intentions only. Therefore it is not part of an explanation of intentions generally. But given that the objection relies on derivative intentions, that problem is avoided.

The Guise of the Good explains nonderivative embedded intentions, and the derivative ones are explained by being derivative. There is nothing more to them. That is, it is not as if Ignatius has two separate (embedded) intentions. Rather, in the circumstances his (embedded) intention to destroy the evidence is extended, as it were, and counts also as an (embedded) intention to kill. As mentioned above, the intentionality of an action consists largely in its performance being responsive to a belief about what the action is to be. Ignatius's action of killing the people on board is responsive to the belief that the action is to be a destruction of the evidence, and to no other. There is no independent existence to the derivative-embedded intention to kill (beyond his knowledge that in destroying the evidence he will be killing the people).

It is instructive to compare cases like Ignatius's with some activities consisting of a sequence of actions,[13] activities such as giving a lecture, singing a song, driving a car, or walking to the door. Here too each of the actions, which in combination constitute the activity, is intentional. But while every one of them could be an action we attend to and think about, our attention to them is intermittent, and of varying degrees of intensity. Typically, agents are not aware of many of the individual actions that constitute such activities (saying 'and then' in the middle of the lecture, or singing an A-flat note, or using turn signals when driving, or slightly adjusting one's direction when walking to the door, and so on). Consequently, agents are guided by knowledge of how to produce the sequence, and not by beliefs about the reasons for many of the individual actions constituting the activities.[14]

Yet these cases differ from Ignatius's. While here too the performance of one action depends on performing the others, the dependence is very different. It is not a case of each of them being performed by performing another of them (though the activity as a whole occurs by performing all of them). Each requires different movements, or their absence, and each is governed and controlled by us separately. Their dependence expresses itself by the fact that later actions are modified in light of earlier ones, so that all are governed (to various degrees of success) by the overall purpose of the activity as a whole. (If in driving I stray slightly to the left at one point I will compensate by turning slightly to the right and so on.)

This suggests that the embedded intentions of each of the actions that constitute such activities are governed by one or more independent intentions that determine the content of the embedded intentions, thus making the activity as a whole intentional: an intention to give that lecture, sing that song, drive home, and the like. It is tempting to go further and to claim that

(5) Every intentional action or activity is governed by some independent intention, which determines the content of its embedded intention(s).

If so, then the relationship of the governing independent intention to the embedded intentionality of the action merits careful exploration, which it cannot receive here. Roughly understood, if intentional actions are not only performed because of their agents' belief in reasons for them, but are also controlled and guided by the agents in light of those beliefs, then the independent intention that involves belief in a reason for the action determines the content of the embedded intentionality that guides the performance of the action, to make it what it must be to conform to the believed reason. Proposition (5) can be supplemented by

(6) Every independent intention involves belief in a reason for the action intended.

and together (5) and (6) can replace (1') in a new version of the Guise of the Good Thesis. Is this new version immune to criticism? (6) seems plausible. I will consider it later on. The weakness is in (5).

We can accept that in the case of many intentional actions their intentionality (their embedded intentions) is governed by independent intentions. Some such relationship between independent and embedded intentions is needed to explain how independent intentions lead to intentional actions. The question is whether all our intentional actions are governed in this way by independent intentions.

We have already seen examples that show this not to be the case. Acts such as passing one's hand through one's hair while thinking or talking, or of idly scratching the surface of the table, and many others, are intentional, but normally the people performing them do not have independent intentions to perform them. This is not because they do not plan or decide on them in advance. Independent intentions, just like embedded ones, can be formed in the acting. They need not precede the action. Nor are they counterexamples merely because the agents are disposed to say that they performed these actions for no reason (or for no special reason). Such utterances can be reconciled with the Thesis by claiming that people mean that there is no reason worth mentioning, that the reasons are too insignificant to mention. It is just that while all the counterexamples of this kind are actions that can be performed with an independent intention, typically they are not. Normally they are on the periphery of their agents' attention, and are genuinely performed idly, for no reason or purpose. But it is at the core of (6) that independent intentions are constituted in part by belief in reasons or purposes. It is therefore impossible to endorse both (5) and (6). Since (6) seems plausible, we must take the examples to refute (5), and with it the new version Guise of the Good.

3. REVISING THE GUISE OF THE GOOD

Without (5) the Thesis of the Guise of the Good must be weakened to apply only to actions that are done with an independent intention. (1) now becomes

> (1") Actions performed with an independent intention are actions performed for reasons, as those are seen by the agents.

The rest of the Thesis is unaffected:

> (2) Specifying the (independent) intention that makes an action intentional identifies central features of the reason(s) for which the action is performed.
> (3) Reasons for action are facts that establish that the action has some value.

The problem is that this revised version appears not to be supported by the argument adduced at the end of section 1 in support of the Guise of the Good. The argument for the Thesis was that it explains what it is to act intentionally, and how intentional actions differ from others. The counterexamples establish that there are intentional actions to which the Thesis does not apply, and that undermines its claim to explain the nature of intentional actions. But without this argument what is there to support the Thesis?

One is tempted to dismiss the counterexamples as dealing with insignificant actions. I have sympathy with this response, but it cannot consist simply of dismissing the counterexamples. To sustain the Guise of the Good we cannot rely on the insignificance of those examples. On the contrary, we need to establish their significance, their role in our life as persons, and to show how this is consistent with the claim that the Guise of the Good explains the nature of intentional actions, once the Thesis is adjusted to allow for the counterexamples.

Nor is the task of explaining the significance of the examples likely to be simple. There are other counterexamples, which are very different from the ones mentioned so far. One well-known class of counterexamples is expressive actions, such as kicking whatever is nearby in anger, or uttering swear words in exasperation. Nor do these two classes exhaust the counterexamples. I doubt that there is an informative way of drawing up a comprehensive list of types of counterexamples. But here are two others:

> *Hypnosis:* Acting under the influence of posthypnotic suggestion, Jane goes to her wardrobe, puts on a dress, then takes it off and returns it to the wardrobe.
> *Kleptomania:* Rachel, a kleptomaniac, picks up a tin of pickled gherkins in the supermarket, and leaves the shop without paying.

Both Jane and Rachel knew what they were doing, and by all normal tests both acted intentionally. Both acted in a controlled way, tending to

These are embattled(?)

ensure that the actions would be successful (namely, that they accomplish what they intended to do). But both deny that they saw any reason to do what they did.

In considering these cases it is useful to return to the case of Johnny playing at being a fish, and of course his example stands for many. There I have suggested he did believe both that there was reason to playact, and that there was some good in his playacting. He is, I wrote, mistaken in denying these facts. It would, however, be implausible to think that this is true in the types of cases we are now considering. The intentions manifested in them do not, in the actual circumstances of these cases, reveal a possible reason for their actions in which they might believe. It is not like the case of someone who plays at being a fish, where the obvious reason is that it is fun. Second, we have an alternative explanation of their behavior that undercuts the case for thinking that they have a belief in a reason for their actions. While in Johnny's case the attribution of belief that there was some good in the action did crucially depend on the Guise of the Good Thesis, it was also supported by these circumstantial, largely negative facts: the availability of a plausible belief to ascribe to Johnny, and the absence of an alternative explanation of his action.[15] So, while I rely on the Thesis in my understanding of Johnny's case, that reliance conforms to the general principle that belief is not attributed on the strength of a single indicator alone. The new types of cases are therefore different. They are real exceptions to the Thesis.

All of this notwithstanding, there is a strong case for not taking Jane's and Rachel's actions as damaging counterexamples. They are clearly exceptional, as the causes of their actions are inimical to the normal exercise of our powers of agency. Some may even challenge whether it is appropriate to call such actions intentional. I think that such doubts are unwarranted,[16] but that does not matter. We can allow that such doubts are natural, for the cases are ones in which normal powers of agency are temporarily reduced, and become partially ineffective.[17] That is why even though Jane and Rachel acted intentionally, and their actions do not conform to the Guise of the Good, they do not refute the Thesis.

That means that explanations and theses in the theory of action need not aspire to be exceptionless. I would go further and say that they should not aspire to be exceptionless, and if they are exceptionless that is a worrying sign, a sign that they miss important features of the situation. The examples under discussion bring out that being intentional can be a matter of degree. Actions are characterized as intentional by a variety of criteria, several of which can be realized to various degrees, making it appropriate to speak of degrees of intentionality. There are cases of which one should say: Yes, up to a point, or in a certain respect it was intentional, but in others less so. In some respects Jane and Rachel acted intentionally, but in others they did not. That is why their examples do not refute the Guise of the Good. That is a thesis about intentional actions, and if it is true of all fully intentional actions; and if one can explain the exceptions by showing that the facts that establish that the Thesis does not apply to them also account for the fact that they are examples of diminished intentionality, then they lose their force as counterexamples.

This burden is easily discharged in the case of Jane and Rachel: Their purpose, their goal of performing these actions, is, as it were, imposed on them from the outside, by a hypnotist or by a pathological condition, and that both stops them from conforming to the Guise of the Good, and makes their actions less than completely their own, and therefore intentional only in some respects.

In another place I discussed expressive actions along similar lines.[18] I argued that they do not conform to the Thesis precisely because of ways in which they involve loosened control over the actions, which means that while they are intentional there are respects in which they display diminished intentionality. How about the other counterexamples we noticed, those of idle actions like stroking one's hair? I noted the instinctive reaction that they are insignificant kinds of action. There are two ways in which they are marginal or insignificant. First, they are performed when our attention is elsewhere. That, as in other cases, affects their intentionality: In most cases they are actions we routinely perform, and therefore we can perform them without attending to them. But it does not matter to us if they fail, or change their character. Our fingers may slide out of their routine rhythm. The action may be interrupted, and we may still not notice, nor would the agent mind that the action failed, or got transformed from, say, stroking one's hair to gently flattening it. Second, typically these exceptions are relatively simple actions, consisting predominantly of routines of bodily movement. They do not include actions such as giving a party, campaigning in an election, or writing a novel.[19]

The second point shows that these actions are of marginal importance. The first point shows them to be, while intentional, of reduced intentionality. The fact that we do not fully attend to them shows that. It follows from this that the action is unlikely to be one of securing a result that goes beyond the disposition of one's own body. When one kicks a ball or turns on the tap one needs to attend to what one is doing, and one cannot attend to kicking a ball or turning on a tap without believing that there is a point in doing so. Again, these cases are exceptions because they are marginal cases of intentionality, not displaying all the features of intentional actions.

The revised Guise of the Good Thesis has other exceptions. Because I am unable to classify them exhaustively, I will mention only one other kind of exception:

Nibbling after blood:[20] An accident causing horrible injuries and mutilations has just happened outside Jamie's window. The sight will disgust him, and he knows that. There is nothing he can do to help the injured. Yet he is powerfully drawn to the window, and is looking, feeling disgusted, and physically ill, at the sight.[21] There is no doubt that he went to the window intentionally, and is intentionally looking at the injured

1. independent intention = for belief that action has value
125

people outside. I will return in the next section to the question of whether Jamie has a reason to behave as he does. The crucial point is that he does not think he has such a reason, and yet his behavior is intentional, and does not fall into any of the categories of exceptions so far examined. It should not be assimilated to the case of kleptomania. Jamie's case is meant to be one in which the agent is naturally motivated to act, but can resist. Jamie cannot help but feel drawn to look at the scene but he can suppress the urge, and stay away from the window. His situation is rather like that of someone who has a sweet tooth, and having had lots of chocolate already, is taking another piece, even though he knows that he will feel nauseated. weakness of will?

Jamie is another exception to the Thesis, and his case cannot be explained away in the way the others were. It is not a case of diminished or marginal intentionality. Yet I doubt that it can undermine the Thesis. It is possible that Jamie believes that he has no reason for his action because he is conceptually confused about reasons. For example, had he thought that one has reason to satisfy urges, like the urge to look at a gruesome scene (or the urge to have one too many pieces of chocolate), then he would have believed that he has reason to act as he does. Moreover, it seems plausible that if Jamie is mistaken about thinking that he, and people generally, do not have reasons to satisfy urges of these kinds, his mistake is a conceptual mistake, due to an incomplete, and somewhat mistaken understanding of the concept of a reason for action.

Whether all these suppositions are true depends to a considerable degree on whether there is, in fact, a reason to satisfy such urges. I will return to that issue in the next section. For the moment what remains is to explain why exceptions that are due to a conceptual confusion do not undermine the Thesis. Whether or not Jamie's is an apt illustration, the general point is that conceptual truths about the way people use concepts are bound to have exceptions when people misuse concepts. That is, given that the ability to use concepts involves the ability to misuse them, theses about concepts cannot be refuted by examples of their misuse.

4. REASONS AND VALUE

It is time to examine the third leg of the Thesis, namely that reasons for action consist of the fact that the action has some value. I will now assume that (1") is correct, that is, that actions performed with an independent intention are performed for reasons, as those are seen by the agents, that is, I will assume that independent intentions involve belief that there is a reason for the intended action. The question under consideration is whether reasons for action are that the actions have some value. If they are then (1") implies that barring conceptual ignorance or mistakes, actions performed with an independent intention are performed in the belief that the action has some value. 1. actions performed with

independent intention are performed for reason

The argument for this view will proceed in two stages, and be followed by an examination of some objections. The first stage concerns the character of reasons belief in which is necessary for action with independent intentions. Such actions, actions done for a purpose as we can also describe them, are actions that were done by people who had a view of their situation, and in light of that view found some reason to perform the action (so much is established once (1") is acknowledged). The reason must be something that makes the action one to perform, one that it would be good to perform, and that means that it must be something that renders the action desirable, namely a fact that shows some good in the action. In brief, the reason the agent thought he had must be something that shows that the agent knew what he was doing, and not only that he felt, and witnessed himself being, propelled toward acting by some psychological condition. There must be something that he believed to be true of the action and that he took to make the action attractive. There must be something that made him decide to act because what he took to be the reason seemed to him to make the action worthwhile. To take it to be worthwhile in the required sense, the agent's attitude to the reason for which he acts must be capable of sustaining certain counterfactuals: Had the agent been aware (or had he thought that he was aware) of undesirable features of the action he would have formed a view on whether the features that provide, as he believes, a reason for the action still make it the action to perform in spite of its undesirable aspects.[22] Such a view, and that is another conceptual observation, consists in some judgment on the relative importance of the good and bad features of the action.

Setiya did more than anyone else in recent times to challenge the Thesis. He thinks that intentional actions are taken for reasons but not in the belief that there is something good about the action. We need to address objections to the Guise of the Good advanced by him and others. But there are aspects of his view that reinforce my belief that the Thesis is right. In particular, he underlines the fact that agents who act intentionally know what they are doing and why:

It is sufficient to be acting for a reason that one meets the demand for an explanation of what one is doing and why. One need not also believe that the reasons for which one is acting are reasons to act in that way.[23]

Setiya recognizes the difference between reasons explanatory of an action and a normative reason for the action. Explanatory reasons of actions are facts that explain the actions. The following are three such reasons, possibly all truly explaining the same intentional action:

Jill did it because she was jealous of Jim.
Jill did it because she felt a sudden rage; a sudden rush of blood to her head made her do it.
Jill did it in order to inherit Jim's wealth, as she knew that she would after Jim's death.

[handwritten annotations in top margin: "independent intentions = reason for", "1. talks about the type of reason", "beliefs necessary) for independent intention"]

Only the last one explains the action by reference to a normative reason. Setiya insists, and is surely right, that whenever one acts intentionally
one believes in some explanation of one's action. He is also right to insist
that the explanation need not incline us, the spectators, to believe that the
action was justified. Any and all of the above explanations can be available
to the agent and none of them inclines me to believe that the action was
justified. It is also right that because they are explanations of intentional
actions they point to factors that (metaphorically speaking) pushed or
pulled the agents toward the actions. But while there can be a number of
(compatible but distinct) explanations of every intentional action, there
must be, for every action performed with an independent intention, at
least one explanation that meets an additional condition: It must explain
why the agent decided to perform the action, rather than resist the pull
toward it. Of the three examples, only the last, only the explanation via a
normative reason, does that. Depending on the circumstances the other
explanations may be more revealing of the action, or they may constitute
the more illuminating parts of a more comprehensive explanation that
includes all three as elements. But only the third, killing to inherit, even
establishes that the action was intentional (jealousy and a sudden rush
of blood to the head, together or separately, may explain loss of control
leading to accidental killing).

Setiya's account lacks the resources to distinguish between the first two
explanations and the third one. Doing that is essential for an account of
independent intentions. And, the suggestion is, what marks actions done
with independent intentions is that they are ones that their agents believe
to have some value in them, and thus the agents have available to them
explanations by reference to what they take to be normative reasons,
namely explanations purporting to show that there is some good in the
action.[24]

The second stage of the argument is required to counter one alternative understanding of actions for a purpose, and of normative reasons.
According to it the argument thus far shows only that in acting for a purpose one believes that some feature of the action constitutes a normative
reason for it. It does not follow that the agent believes that there is some
good in the action (thus rejecting the tail end of the previous paragraph).

If, however, a fact cannot be a reason for an action unless it establishes
that the action possesses some value, then in believing that there is a reason for an action one believes that the action has some value, unless one
is mistaken or confused about the concepts of a reason, or of having value.
So to deny that to act for a purpose involves acting in the belief that the
action has some value one has to deny that to be a reason a fact must
establish that the action for which it is a reason has some value. How
would the argument proceed? Imagine the following conversation:

Jumping: Abe: Why did you jump?—Ben: It was the only way I could save
my life. Abe: I can see that but is there any good in that?

[handwritten annotations in right margin: "involves believing most have value", "that acts for a reason for a reason that leans on", "denying that acts value = claims ... in its value"]

[handwritten annotation at bottom: "2. shows that there's good in action"]

Or, imagine a different conversation:

Job: Ben: Why should I go to the interview?—Abe: It will get you the job.—Ben: Why is that a reason to go to the interview?—Abe: Because if you have a job you will earn a living and will not starve.—Ben: I can see that, but is there any good in not starving?

The last question in each exchange appears out of place, and redundant. The suggestion is that reasons can be just ordinary, that is, nonnormative facts. What is special about them is that they stand in a normative relation to an action, being a reason for it. To say of them that they establish that the action has some value is superfluous. It does not contribute to the fact that the reason is a reason. Therefore, acting for a reason need not involve belief that there is some good in the action. It is enough if it involves belief that one has reason to perform the action.

This view, I will argue, ignores rather than replies to what the first stage of the argument established. To examine this claim I will focus on Ben and his Jump, and consider it in light of two further hypothetical situations:

Torture (and death): If Ben would be saving his life by jumping, he would be immediately seized by people who would first subject him to severe torture and then kill him.
Betrayal: Suppose that to save his life Ben has to reveal the whereabouts of a document that will inform the evil regime of the identity of his colleagues in the opposition, who will be tortured and killed.

Let us assume that Ben rightly thinks that were he in Torture he would have no reason to jump, and that had he been in Betrayal he would have had a reason to betray (that is, to save his life), but a stronger reason not to do so. It seems reasonable to assume that in Jump Ben not only believed that jumping is the only way to save his life but also that in the circumstances of the case that it would save his life is a reason to jump, that is, that he is not in a situation like Torture, and that belief was relevant to his action, as he would not have performed it had he believed that his situation is one in which he has no reason to save his life. Similarly, we can assume that he believed that the situation is not similar to Betrayal, that is, that it is not one in which while he has a reason to jump it is defeated by other considerations. The suggestion is not of course that Ben considers and rules out the possibility that he is in many specific situations where he would have no reason to save his life, or would have defeating reasons. Rather, the suggestion is that he entertains a general belief that he has an undefeated reason to save his life.

The first stage of the argument above showed that in order to have that belief, Ben needs to have and use certain conceptual capacities. Broadly speaking, he must be able to judge that certain situations constitute reasons and others do not, and that sometimes more than one reason bears on the cases for and against performing an action. It was further argued that we individuate reasons by the good they do, the good that actions instantiate. An action that saves the life of Abe, and protects some beautiful picture from destruction, is one that we have two mutually reinforcing

facts # action good

reasons to perform. They are two because
tinct good-making properties. For the purp
can accept that reasons are or can be ordi
will save your life. That does nothing to
reasons are individuated by the good that c
therefore that mastery of the concept of
standing of the notion of value. Therefore,
action motivated and guided by belief that
belief that there is some good in the actio

As we saw earlier, this argument does n
independent intentions are undertaken wi
lishes that (a) given the direct conceptual
value one is justified in attributing a belief that there is value in an action on
the basis of a belief that there is reason for it, so long as there is no evidence
that the agent does not have such a belief; (b) evidence that the agent does
not believe that there is value in the action in spite of there being a reason for
it establishes some conceptual confusion on the part of the agent; and (c)
given that action with an independent intention involves belief in there being
a reason for the action, any serious conceptual confusion about the nature of
reasons means that the action is intentional in some deviant way only.

Let it be accepted that the facts that constitute a reason for an action
also establish that there is some good in it. The rejection of the Guise of
the Good now comes to rest on an additional contention: that the action
has some value is not a reason for it. Stating that it has some good is nothing but another way of stating that there is a reason for it. For necessarily
'There is some good in Φing' is true if and only if there is a reason to Φ. It
now seems that rejecting the third part of the Guise of the Good (that
reasons for action are such reasons by being facts that establish that the
action has some value) depends on accepting some version of what is
known as "buck-passing."

Some of the reasons why "buck-passing" accounts of the good are false
have been explained elsewhere,[25] and the matter cannot be fully examined here. In rejecting the view I will say no more than that the good of
inheriting, surviving, getting a job, having friends, etc. does not depend on
there being a reason to bring them about. We can establish their value
without raising the question of whether there is reason to bring them
about, and if we conclude that there is reason to bring them about that is
because they are valuable. Hence, on cursory examination buck-passing
fails to grasp the nature of value. But without it the alternative to the
third leg of the Thesis fails.

5. SOME OBJECTIONS CONSIDERED

That concludes my two-step argument for the Thesis. Can it be sustained
against the objections it faces? One of them has to do with value inversion,

that sometimes people sincerely take themselves to be
value, choosing actions because they are evil, bad, or worth-
ing so with open eyes. Such cases hold many fascinations for
st as well as many horrors for those at the receiving end. I have
ed them elsewhere,[26] where I explained that another reason for
y theses in theory of action not being exceptionless is the ability to
eviate from any norm, including those of meaning and rationality. Not all
deviations are possible, but (given that determination of our beliefs, intentions, emotions, and so on is governed by multiple criteria) much is possible. I will not return to that discussion here. There are other objections:

One objection has to do with cases where agents do believe in normative reasons for their actions, but in ones that do not establish any
value in the action (for example, that it was undertaken to preserve
racial purity).

Second, there are those alien cultures whose normative reasons seem
to be entirely unrelated to anything we can make sense of.

Third, there are familiar cases in which the agent's judgment that there
was no value in the action or that there was no reason for it is hard to
dismiss as a case of being mistaken about his own beliefs. Jamie's case
above belongs here.

The first of the objections requires us to revisit some of the ground
already covered. Think of Jill who kills her uncle to inherit his fortune. We
can assume that she will deny that there is any value in her action, and
dismiss this as irrelevant because she is likely to be applying a different
concept of value, perhaps one in which only moral values are values. But
why impute to her a belief whose articulation requires a concept she does
not have? Because she takes the fact that as a consequence of the killing
she will inherit from her uncle as a fact that explains her action, in the
required way, that is by being a feature of the killing that determines her
to kill, not merely one that makes her kill. It guides her deliberation and
is subject to rational constraints.

This shows that inheriting is a rational factor in her mind, that it does
not explain her action in the way that the influence of alcohol might. And
as a rational consideration militating for the action it is capable of being
seen to be in competition with still further considerations. For example,
the fact, should she learn of it, that if she kills her uncle she will sleep no
more will give her pause, and may or may not lead her to desist.

Jill furnished us with the outline of an argument of why it is right to
attribute belief in value to a person who explains his action in nonnormative terms and declines to apply normative concepts to it. But it was an
easy case, because it makes sense to think that she has the belief we attribute to her at least in as much as the feature of the action she points to
(inheriting from her uncle) has value (even though not one justifying
killing anyone). Now suppose that you see Brian punching and kicking a
person in the street. You ask him why and he says: 'He is a bloody foreigner.' 'But what reason do you have to beat him up?' 'That is the reason:

He is a foreigner.' 'Why is that a reason?' 'It just is.' End of conversation, and end of Brian's own thoughts about the subject.

Here there is no value at all in the action. What can justify attributing to Brian belief in the value of his action in this case? In spite of this difference, in all essentials Brian's case is like Jill's. He regards the fact that his victim is a foreigner as a normative reason. He too recognizes other reasons, and can reason which of them, if any, prevails when they conflict. Patient inquiry will show the contours of his beliefs, and disclose what normative concepts are apt to describe his views, and they will be concepts that show what, in his eyes, is good in this or that action.

It still remains unclear how the Guise of the Good can be reconciled with the possibility of mistakes. There is no difficulty if the mistakes are purely factual. The claim that Jill kills her uncle because (let us assume) she thinks that she will have a better life if she inherits from her uncle is consistent with her being mistaken about the prospect of inheriting. Maybe her uncle changed his will the week before, etc. There is no difficulty in reconciling such mistakes with the Thesis. But is it consistent with normative mistakes? Imagine someone who explains that this person deserves better treatment than that because he belongs to a superior race so that his interests count for more than the interests of members of inferior races, or that sex with people of inferior races is wrong because it dilutes the purity of the race, and so on. If he shares our concept of the good, and believes that racial purity is good, then that is his mistake. But assume that, as in our previous examples, our racist does not have our philosophical concept of the good. He does not admit to a belief that preserving purity is of value. In fact, preserving racial purity has no value. What grounds do we have to attribute to him a belief that neither he nor we admit to?

The answer depends on our racist's grounds for his racism. He may believe that racial mixing leads to strife, or that it causes members of both races to fail to excel in the use of racially specific talents that he believes them to have. Such reasoning shows that he takes racial purity to be instrumental to genuine values such as the avoidance of strife, or the development of one's talents. He is wrong about the relationship between the ideals of purity, harmony, and fulfillment of one's potential. But given that he subsumes the mistaken value under real ideals or values it is plain that he believes that his racist actions have some value.

A difficulty exists only when the agents under discussion do not defend their belief in their false values by reference to any genuine values. They take them to be ultimate considerations, which cannot be justified by reference to any others. But even in such cases there may be direct evidence that these agents take their reasons, however misguidedly, to show that there is some value in their actions. For example, they are likely to recognize the relevance of questions of consistency, logical or factual, between their alleged consideration and others, which are genuine values. They may, of course, believe that their reasons are consistent with those values. And it may be impossible to convince them otherwise. That is neither here nor there. In acknowledging the relevance of the issue to decisions about what to do, or to whether their reasons are sustainable, they show that they treat their reasons as facts that contribute to the value of actions.

What if the agents are indifferent to the relations of their racial reasons to genuine values? They may have some priority rules, avoiding the need for reasoning about the relative case for one or another consideration. This scenario is even clearer when we turn to the second of the classes of cases I listed above, the case of thoroughly alien cultures. In the nature of things there are no examples to give. We imagine a culture where the concepts used in stating reasons for action are alien to us, and have no equivalents among our normative and value concepts. Possibly such a culture is not possible, at least not among humans. Be that as it may, the general argument given earlier, namely that independent intentions are formed for believed reasons, and that reasons relate to value, applies. The alien culture is not a counterexample. To be that we need to understand it. All we can say is that it is a culture of concept-using people, who can act intentionally. That, given the general argument for the Guise of the Good, is enough to establish that the Thesis applies to them, and our ignorance prevents us from finding anything to challenge or undermine the conclusion.

There will be the inevitable charge that in claiming that the Thesis applies to alien cultures we distort their meanings, and impose on them 'our' concepts, which are not suited as tools for understanding their culture. But the charge is unwarranted. No claim to understand alien cultures was made. The concepts used in the Guise of the Good are "our" concepts, and there is no pretense that they are not. Nor are they used to interpret aliens' worldview, or their ways of justifying actions. Only two claims about the alien cultures are made: One is that the people there use concepts (or it would not be a culture) and that sometimes they act with independent intentions. The Thesis is true of them for no other reason than that it states part of what is involved in having independent intentions, and in acting intentionally.

Finally, we have to address the third kind of objection, illustrated by the nibbling after blood type cases. Jamie, you will remember, intentionally goes to the window to look at the gruesome sight that makes him sick. He thinks that looking at it has only disvalue, and he should not act as he does. How can we say that in spite of this he really believes that there is value in his action (or for that matter that there is a normative reason for it)? The answer is in the details of the case. One misguided objection to the Thesis points out that sometimes we act in pursuit of desires that arose in us neither by deliberation nor in response to recognition of the value of their satisfaction. Hunger, thirst, and sexual desires are examples. In many such cases we recognize the value of satisfying such desires once they arise, thereby recognizing that there are reasons (not always undefeated) for satisfying them. These cases are therefore not counterexamples. The value of satisfying such desires is sometimes the value of having the desire and satisfying it. Food and sex are among the good things in life and they are better if we have them when we desire them. Even with food and sex the desire for them does not always come when it would be good to have them. Sometimes the only value in satisfying the desires is to get rid of them.

In his own eyes Jamie's case is rather like that. He thinks that there is nothing intrinsically good in looking at gruesome sights whether or not that is done in response to an urge to do so. That is what he is telling us when he denies belief in the value of the action. But he could have resisted the urge, and he did not. He decided to go to the window and look at the sight. That shows that he takes it that there is some value in his action. It will relieve him of the tension of wondering what things are like, wanting to see them, regretting not having done so. It will probably also give him some satisfaction, some pleasure, which he does not understand and probably does not want to understand. He looks out in order to rid himself of the urge and the tension it produces, and probably also in order to get that pleasure.

Perhaps, you will say, but that does not establish that he believes that there is some value in his action, given that he denies having the belief in its value. I think that his denial shows that he disapproves of his own action even while he is so acting. But that is typical of cases of *akrasia*, and Jamie's is one of them. In acting with an intention to see the gory sight he is acting in the belief that there is some good in so doing. But his disapproval of his own action leads him to be less than completely honest with himself. He is reluctant to admit to the satisfaction he derives, and confines himself to referring to the nausea he feels. His emphatic disapproval overpowers any recognition of the value of relieving his urge, which he does not want to acknowledge as a benefit, even though he knows that it is.

we act at GoG even when we do not know it

6. CONCLUDING REMARKS

Velleman complained that the Guise of the Good takes people to be square and bland. I suggested that it applies not only to larger than life fanatics like Stalin, whose reasons we can understand, but also to people who defy comprehension. Moulay Ismail was supposed to have said: "My subjects are like rats in a basket. And if I do not keep shaking the basket, they will gnaw their way through."[27] By all accounts he behaved accordingly. I doubt that Moulay Ismail was square or bland. Those who read the quotation as simply expressing concern for his continued rule underestimate him by ignoring the attitude to other people that it expresses. I do not think that I can understand many of his actions. Of course, we have learned to expect the worst of people. We may be shocked by stories of his conduct, but are not surprised. Something like that is what we expect to happen from time to time. That does not establish that we understand his reasons. Yet we have reason to think that the Guise of the Good was true of him, for even though much of his brutality was spontaneous, his actions were commonly informed by independent intentions.

Of course, the Thesis that I was defending is neither the one that Velleman or Setiya and other critics objected to, nor the one that others upheld. The question arises whether the modified Thesis retains the philosophical interest and the promise that the criticized Thesis held. In particular, can it still be seen as providing a key to the understanding of rational agency by explaining the nature of intentions? A brief survey of the modifications made and of one or two other points put in the course of argument suggests an affirmative answer.

The revised Thesis presupposes a distinction between embedded and independent intentions. It does not claim to apply to embedded intentions except inasmuch as they depend on and their content is determined by independent intentions. Hence it applies only indirectly (if at all) to derived embedded intentions, and it does not apply to intentional actions not governed by independent intentions. Even regarding independent intentions it allows for exceptions, provided they can be explained as deviations from the norm, either by being cases of less than complete intentionality or as anomic inversions of the norm. Finally, I emphasized that the Thesis attributes to agents belief that the action has some value-endowing property and that they recognize it as value-endowing. They need not be able to express that belief in words, and they certainly need not have the more general belief that their reason for the action is that it has some value (rather than that it has the specific value they take it to have).

This last clarification is vital to make the Thesis plausible. It would be absurd to assume that intentional actions presuppose possession of abstract concepts, nor does the purpose of the Thesis require it to assume that. This clarification does not undermine the claim of the Thesis to express a central element of intentional action. The other modifications and clarifications are not ad hoc. They arise out of the general nature of theses about concept-employing attitudes and actions. They apply to the full or mature form of the attitude, allowing exceptions in other cases, so long as the fact that the case is an exception explains why the case is less than paradigmatic of full intention, and allows for the possibility of people playing with the norms, twisting them in a variety of ways, a phenomenon very familiar from creative ways of using language, which achieve an effect by deviating from the norms (of meaning or grammar, etc.).

So the revised version of the Thesis retains its role in the explanation of action and of intentionality. From its earliest origins, whatever version of the Guise of the Good was viewed with favor was the keystone keeping in place and bridging the theory of value, the theory of normativity and rationality and the understanding of intentional action. Its success in fulfilling this key role makes the version here defended a variant of the traditional Thesis, serving the same role in establishing the interconnections of those wider theories.

Notes

This chapter benefited from discussions with Kieran Setiya, Niko Kolodny, Geoff Sayre-McCord, and from helpful comments on an earlier draft by David Enoch.

1. Which is borrowed from Aquinas *Summa Theologica* 1a2ae, 8, 1: What is willed is always willed '*sub ratione boni*.'

2. D. Velleman, "The Guise of the Good," (1992) reprinted in *The Possibility of Practical Reason* (New York: Oxford University Press, 2002), p. 99.

3. Meaning: that there is some good in the action is the reason for it.

4. Ibid.

5. In *Engaging Reason* (Oxford: Oxford University Press, 2000) I argued against the view of desires that is required for the correlation between them and intentions assumed by Velleman.

6. I discussed the explanatory role of normative reasons in "Reasons: Normative and Explanatory," *New Essays on the Explanation of Action*, ed. C. Sandis (London: Palgrave/McMillan, 2008) and will not return to these matters here.

7. I will not consider the conditions under which animals that do not possess concepts act intentionally, or have intentions, as I believe that those differ radically from the conditions under which animals possessing concepts act intentionally and have intentions.

8. It is important for the analogy that 'My brother is a bachelor' and 'My brother is unmarried' are distinct beliefs, just as intending to Φ and believing that there is some good in Φing are distinct mental states or attitudes.

9. It would be different if one were to say not that Johnny believes that there is some good in his action, but that he was thinking that at the time.

10. G.E.M Anscombe, *Intention* (Oxford: Basil Blackwell, 1957); Kieran Setiya, *Reasons without Rationalism* (Princeton, N.J.: Princeton University Press, 2007), p. 24.

11. Compare Augustine's desire to steal the pears that, he said, he 'loved only for the theft's sake' and 'Doing this pleased us all the more because it was forbidden. . . . I was being gratuitously wanton, having no inducement to evil but the evil itself' (Augustine, *Confessions*, trans. Albert C. Outler [Philadelphia: Westminster, 1955], book II, ch. viii, sec 16).

12. The claim in the text is a generalization of a claim often made regarding instrumental rationality, namely, that if you think that you have reason to pursue a goal you really have a reason to pursue the means to the goal. Several authors argued against this view: Broome, Wallace, Korsgaard. For my argument against this view, see "The Myth of Instrumental Rationality." *Journal of Ethics & Social Philosophy*, http://www.jesp.org/, 2005 volume 1, issue 1.

13. To be distinguished from sequences of bodily movements that may constitute one action (for example, lifting one's arm) but are not distinct actions in themselves.

14. Is it the case that they have conditional beliefs: that one should say 'went' when that is required to express one's thought in the way that one started to express it, etc.? Any attempt to pursue this thought runs into complications that expose the implausibility of the suggestion. We simply know how to use the language, etc. No specific beliefs of this kind are involved. At the same time we may interrupt, divert, or abort the sequence if we suddenly become aware that it requires an action that there is a clear and undefeated reason to avoid— intentional actions and semiautomatic action sequences are controlled by subliminal monitoring of their progress, both in getting to their goal, and in not involving undesirable actions.

15. More needs to be said: First, the mistake I attributed to Johnny is slight. It results from an incomplete mastery of the concepts of reason or the good. It is rather like the mistake of philosophers who reject the Guise of the Good. Second, it may be denied that classifying an act as a case of kleptomania provides an explanation. Kleptomania is a poorly understood condition. But we know enough about it to rule out some explanations, including the attribution of normal independent intentions. We know, for example, that kleptomaniacs often steal objects they have no need for and that they are eager to get rid of once the episode is over.

16. To see that, it is instructive to compare these cases with H. Frankfurt's description of what he regards as acting under coercion (H. Frankfurt, "Coercion and Moral Responsibility" in *The Importance of What We Care About*. Cambridge: Cambridge University Press, 1988), p. 80. It does not matter that his character-ization of coerced action is unduly narrow. His coerced actions are cases of people whose will is overpowered by the coercing action or circumstances, and they cannot help but do what they are doing. They act intentionally, but their actions are unlike what is normally understood as coerced action, which is action for a (perceived) reason to remove the threat. Frankfurt's coerced person does what is necessary to avoid the threat, but not for a reason. He has lost normal control over his power of agency. I think that in this case it is even clearer that the Frankfurt-coerced person is acting intentionally, but there is little reason to distinguish him from Jane and Rachel.

17. Only partially ineffective, for they act, controlling their conduct as they would had they decided to act not under the influences that make them act in the given circumstances.

18. J. Raz, *Engaging Reason*, pp. 36–44. One can also question whether expressive actions can be governed by independent intentions at all. I will not consider this question.

19. There are complications and further distinctions. For example, I can find myself operating an ATM without having noticed what I was doing. But in that case, while my movements may be intentional, I did not intentionally withdraw money from my account.

20. I am indebted to Ulrike Heuer for this example. My name for it derives from E.M.Forster: 'Of the many things Lucy was noticing to-day, not the least remarkable was this: the ghoulish fashion in which respectable people will nibble after blood' (*A Room With a View*, London: Edward Arnold, 1908, Chapter Five.

21. Cf. '"But," I said, "I once heard a story which I believe, that Leontius the son of Aglaion, on his way up from the Piraeus under the outer side of the

northern wall, becoming aware of dead bodies that lay at the place of public execution at the same time felt a desire to see them and a repugnance and aversion, and that for a time he resisted and veiled his head, but overpowered in despite of all by his desire, with wide staring eyes he rushed up to the corpses and cried, 'There, ye wretches, take your fill of the fine spectacle!'" (Plato, *Republic* IV: 439e).

22. Though, as we must always remember, he might have acted for what he took to be the lesser reason.

23. Kieran Setiya, *Reasons without Rationalism*, p. 12.

24. It is not clear whether Setiya's own view (that necessarily when acting rationally one acts under the Guise of the Good, but irrational agents do not always do so) is inconsistent with the Thesis here defended. Irrational actions are by their nature deviations from the norm, and if those who do not conform to the Thesis are irrational (in part) because of their failure to act under the Guise of the Good, then, as explained above, while their actions are exceptions to the Thesis they are not damaging counterexamples.

25. E.g., U. Heuer, "Explaining Reasons: Where Does the Buck Stop? *Journal of Ethics & Social Philosophy*, http://www.jesp.org/, 2006, volume 1, issue. 3.

26. "Agency, Reason and the Good," *Engaging Reason*, pp. 31–34.

27. Sultan Moulay Ismail was the founding father of the Moroccan royal Alawite dynasty. For our purposes it does not matter whether the attribution is true. It is enough that people can believe it to be true.

I. Every intentional action aims at object that is in some way: value

II. 2 kinds of intentional actions, but only one kind aims at GoG: independent actions

III. [crossed out] How then, can all intentional action aim [crossed out] there can be counterexamples

III. Weaker revised thesis faces counter examples
— they are just exceptions to GoG

IV Revised: actions performed with Independent Intention = performed because of belief that action has value. 2 steps:

1.

7

The Form of the Will

Sebastian Rödl

I shall seek to expound the meaning of the proposition *Doing something intentionally is representing doing it as good*, or, *Acting intentionally in a certain way is representing acting in this way as good*. It will transpire that this proposition unfolds the concept of a distinctive power to act: the will.

I. INTRODUCTION

1. *Good* Signifies a Form of Predication

Let us consider the logical form of our proposition. First, the values of the variable *doing such-and-such*, or *acting in such-and-such a way*, are action *forms:* drinking a glass of milk, peeling an apple, honoring one's parents. An action form is something general, a unity of an indefinite manifold. The representation of an action form is a representation of something general, a general representation, a concept. So, if doing something intentionally is representing doing it as good, then doing something intentionally *is applying a concept*.

Next, *good*, in our proposition, may appear to be an adjective, predicatively employed, and said of the action. Then representing as good would be judging that something is something: the action good. But then our proposition would be false. For it says that acting *is* representing as good; and acting is not judging. So perhaps representing as good is not judging that something is something.

It may help to think of an analogous proposition, namely, *Judging something is representing it as true*. Here, too, it may seem that *true* is an adjective, used predicatively, and said of the thing judged. But only for a moment. For it is obvious that that cannot be right. It entails that judging something is judging something else, namely, that the thing judged is true. And judging something cannot be judging something else. Frege concluded that the concept *true* relates to judgment in a different way from that in which any other concept does so. He suggested that *true* is not part of a predicate and does not contribute to the content of

138

a representation, but signifies its form, a form of predication, *the form that is judging*. Perhaps this is how it is in our case, as well. Representing doing something as good is applying a concept, an action form concept. It may be that *good signifies the manner in which this concept is applied*. Then *good* is not part of a predicate and does not contribute to the content of a representation. Instead, it signifies its form, a form of predication, a form of applying a concept, *the form that is acting intentionally*. This is the idea I aim to develop in this chapter.

2. *Good* Signifies the Formal Object of the Will

I described a conception of the logical character of the concept *true* suggested by Frege, and am proposing that the concept *good* has the same logical character, relating to action as *true* relates to judgment. That account of *true* does not originate with Frege, and the parallel account of *good* is not my invention. It is an ancient thought that the true is the formal object of the intellect, and the good the formal object of the will. That the true is the formal object of the intellect means that *true* signifies the form of an object of the intellect, that is, the character that an object of the intellect exhibits insofar as it is an object of the intellect. The intellect is the power of judgment, and its object is something represented in judgment. So *true* characterizes the object of the intellect solely with regard to its being represented in the manner of representing that is judging. Analogously, that the good is the formal object of the will means that *good* signifies the form of an object of the will, that is, the character that an object of the will exhibits as an object of the will. The will is the power to act intentionally, and its object is something represented in acting. So *good* characterizes the object of the will solely with regard to its being represented in the manner of representing that is acting intentionally.

If *good* and *true* signify a form of predication of an act of the will and the intellect or, equivalently, the formal object of the will and the intellect, then this explains the philosophical interest of these concepts. If they signified properties, it would be obscure why they should be a topic of philosophy. (Thinking that they signify properties, one will find these to be very special properties—a sign that one is on a path to nonsense.) According to the account I am suggesting *good* and *true* are a priori concepts by which the will and the intellect represent their object purely, according to the form that it bears as an object of the will and the intellect. Thus these concepts are original acts of the will and intellect, in which they represent their own nature, constituting themselves as self-conscious powers.

3. An Account of the Concept *Good* Is an Account of the Will

It is a principle of Aristotle's psychology that there is an a priori unity of a power of the soul and its object, wherefore one inquiry is of the power and its object. In our case, one inquiry is of the intellect, or judgment, and the true, and one inquiry is of the will, or intentional action, and the good. Following this principle, we are departing from a usual manner of discussing our proposition. It is usually assumed that it speaks of a judgment of value that predicates goodness of an action. It is taken to be clear (or to be clarified elsewhere) what a value judgment is and what it is to think something good. Then it is found that intentional action bears no essential relation to that. But we cannot exclude that the primary application of the concept *good* is to action and that the primary manner of applying the concept *good* to action is the one our proposition describes. Then we have no prior understanding of what it is to think something good in the light of which we could assess the truth of our proposition. Rather, our proposition is the source of that understanding. We shall leave it open whether all use of the concept *good* depends on the one of which our proposition speaks. In any case, if in our proposition *good* signifies a form of predication, the form that is acting intentionally, then that use of *good* can only be elucidated by reflecting on the nature of intentional action.

Thus there is a sense in which expounding the meaning of our proposition is to establish its truth. Independently of our proposition we know neither what it is to represent an action as good in the relevant way nor what it is to act intentionally. Our proposition identifies a certain manner of representing an action, namely as good, which is acting in a certain way, namely intentionally. If we can give an account of a form of representation that is representing as good and is acting, that account will supply a concept of goodness and a concept of acting intentionally that make our proposition true. Moreover, as this is how we arrive at these concepts, we shall be assured of their philosophical dignity. For, as we noted above, they are, so understood, a priori concepts through which the will, the power to act intentionally, represents its own nature.

We first consider the proposition analogous to the one that is our topic, namely, *Judging something is representing it as true* (II). Then we describe the form of predication that the concept *good* signifies, the form that is acting intentionally (III to V).

II. JUDGMENT AND THE TRUE

4. Judgment as Synthesis

Doing something intentionally is representing it as good appears to be analogous to *Judging something is representing it as true*. I am suggesting that the analogy is this: *Good* and *true* signify the form of an object, of the will and the intellect, respectively. They signify a form of predication, the form of an act of the will and the form of an act of the intellect, respectively. So let us consider the nexus of judgment and the true. If the analogy holds, the same nexus joins action and the good. I shall not aim to establish that the true is the formal object of the intellect. I only want to say something about what it means.

We can take our departure from the thought that *It is true* is a sentence variable, a prosentence.[1] What distinguishes the values of a given variable is their matter; what they share is a form. Thus Wittgenstein says that a variable signifies a formal concept, the concept of a form, namely, of the form that the values of the variable as its values exhibit.[2] *It is true*, a sentence variable, signifies the general form of what is said with a sentence.

Frege says as much when he remarks that *It is true* signifies what the declarative sentence form signifies.[3] A sentence is composed of words. It is not a heap, but a unity of words. The form of a declarative sentence, the declarative sentence form, is the unity of its words. What holds for the sentence and its words holds for what is said with them: What is said with a sentence is a unity, namely a unity of what its words signify. This unity is not signified by any of the words of the sentence, but by their unity, the sentence form. Frege says, *true* signifies that: what otherwise is signified not by a word, but by a unity of words, or the sentence form.

An elementary sentence joins a name and a concept word. The unity of what is said with such a sentence is the unity of the sense of a name and the sense of a concept word; this is the unity of an elementary thought. When we say a thought is a unity of elements, we are saying something that she who thinks the thought knows. She who thinks a thought knows its articulation, and knows it not in a separate act, but in thinking the thought. Therefore, we cannot distinguish the thought's being articulated from the thinking subject's knowing it to be articulated. We cannot distinguish its parts' being together from their being held together by her who is thinking it. This can be expressed by saying that thinking is synthesis and that this synthesis is the unity of the thought.[4] The synthesis is predication: It is joining the sense of a name and the sense of a concept word in such a way as to bring the object signified by the name under the concept signified by the concept word.[5]

We said *true* signifies the form of what is said with a sentence, the form of a thought. The form of a thought is its unity, the manner in which one conjoins its parts in thinking the thought. So, *true* signifies the unity of representations in a thought and thus the object of thinking as such. It signifies the form of the object, the formal object, of thought. As the intellect is a power to think, the true is the formal object of the intellect.

5. Force and Content

The proposition above—the one that is analogous to the one that is our topic in this essay—was slightly different. We said *judging* something was representing it as true and that the true was the formal object of *judgment*. According to Frege, we must distinguish, in a judgment, grasping a thought and acknowledging it as true. Every judgment is an act of thinking a thought, but not every act of thinking a thought is a judgment. One may suppose that such-and-such is true, thinking a thought without acknowledging it as true. It follows that the true is the formal object not specifically of judgment, but of an act of thinking common to judgment and, say, assumption and supposition.

If this were an essay on judgment, I would argue that this is wrong. As it is not, I confine myself to explicating what someone would think who thought it was wrong. He would think: We cannot comprehend judgment as composed of force and content as independent elements. For, we cannot comprehend the unity of the content independently of the force of judgment. *The force* of judgment *is the unity of its content.*

According to the Fregean doctrine, the act of acknowledging the thought as true is external to the unity of the thought acknowledged as true. Kant holds the opposite view. He holds that the force of judgment is the unity of its content. A judgment, Kant says, is a synthesis of representations according to the objective unity of apperception. The objective unity of apperception is the unity of representations in virtue of which they are represented as united in the object.[6] This unity, and so the act of judgment, carries generality and necessity: Representations joined according to the objective unity of apperception have not come together in the subject per accidens; they must be together. Equivalently, they belong together in every subject, or generally. So Kant says: The synthesis is the judgment. The force of judgment is the unity of the thing judged.

I said that *true* signifies the form of what is said with a declarative sentence. And according to Frege, this is the form of a thought, which is a content to which various forces may attach. The unity of such a content is provided from elsewhere; the source of its unity is not any of the forces that may join it. By contrast, according to Kant, there is not, on the one hand, the form of a content and, on the other hand, the force attaching to a content of this form. The force is the form. The force of judgment is that manner of holding together representations by which they constitute a content of judgment. The Kantian doctrine can be expressed by saying that the true is the formal object specifically of judgment.

I shall not defend this doctrine here. I expounded it because I want to put forth a parallel doctrine of the will and its object. An argument for the claim that the force of judgment is the unity of its content would, first and negatively, establish that it is not possible to understand the force of judgment if it is external to its content. Second, and positively, it would give a different account of the relation of judgment to, say, assumption and supposition, and of the unity of these acts. It is true that they have something in common and fall under a genus. But species and genus need not be related in such a way that the species is defined by the genus and a specific difference. What unites the species need not be an element contained in all of them (the content) to which another element, which is different in different species, is added (the force). It may be that the genus is defined by one of its species and the other species by reference to this, first and central, species. The unity of the species would then reside in the various relations other species bear to the primary species. (Such is, according to Aristotle, the unity of what is.)

III. THE WILL AS PRACTICAL REASON

6. Two Marks of Our Form of Predication: Productive and Necessary

Kant says there is a kind of synthesis that is judging. It is the unity of an object of judgment. The declarative sentence variable *It is true* signifies this unity. It signifies the formal object of the intellect, the power of judgment. I am suggesting that, analogously, there is a manner of applying a concept that is an act of the will. It is the unity of an object of the will. *Good*, in our proposition, signifies this unity. It signifies the formal object of the will, the power to act intentionally. Our proposition says about the relevant manner of applying a concept: Applying an action form concept in this way is acting, and it is representing so acting as good. That is, an act of the will is productive and conceives of itself as necessary.

Applying an action form concept in an act of the will is acting in such a way as to realize this concept. Applying the concept, here, is instantiating it. This defines the will in contrast to judgment. The form of judgment is the objective unity of apperception: a unity of representations in virtue of which they relate to an object. The form of the will, too, is the manner in which it relates to an object. However, its way of relating to an object differs from that of the intellect. The act of applying a concept, when it is an act of the intellect, does not account for the existence of the object that is known through the concept. Therefore the object must be given to the subject, and the intellect relates to an object in virtue of the subject's being affected by the object. An act of the will, by contrast, is an act of applying a concept in such a way as to instantiate it. Thus, here, the act of applying the concept is sufficient for the existence of that which is known through the concept. Therefore an act of the will does not receive its object through sensory affection. It relates to its object by being productive of it. Using "thought" as a term for any kind of conceptual representation, we can say that the will is a power of productive thought.[7]

In this formal character of our form of predication another is contained: A productive thought is a first-person thought and productive predication is self-predication. A first-person thought, by nominal definition, is such that, not per accidens, but in virtue of the manner of thinking it, the subject thinking it is she of whom she thinks. Or, it is a case of applying a concept such that, in virtue of the manner of applying the concept, she who applies it is she to whom she applies it. If the identity of the thinking subject with the subject of whom she thinks were not internal to the manner of thinking the thought, then the subject would not know that it was herself ("herself," here, being a first-person pronoun) of whom she was thinking just by thinking the thought. She would know this only in a further act of the mind, an identity judgment "I am the one of whom I am thinking." Now a productive predication of a concept satisfies this nominal definition of self-predication. For applying a concept productively is exemplifying it, and this is a character of the manner in which the concept is applied and, hence, something she who applies it understands not in a further act of the mind, but in applying the concept. As she applies the concept in this way, she represents herself, her who applies the concept, as exemplifying it. She self-applies the concept: She who applies the concept is she whom she represents as exemplifying it not per accidens, but in virtue of the way in which she applies the concept. The will, as a power to act, is a power to self-predicate action form concepts.

An act of the will is a productive and therefore a first-person thought. But this is not all. Our proposition says that doing something intentionally is representing it as good to do or as something one ought to do. *Good* and *ought* signify a kind of necessity. So an act of the will conceives of itself as necessary. It shares this character with judgment. Therefore, like a judgment, an act of the will is the kind of act to be the conclusion of an inference.

Inferring something from given premises is not just thinking it because one holds to the premises. It is thinking it on account of one's recognition that the premises provide sufficient grounds for thinking it. This recognition is not (cannot be) a further premise. Rather, it is the consciousness of the unity of the premises and the conclusion, which is constitutive of this unity as the unity of an inference.[8] So the conclusion contains a consciousness of itself as resting on the premises and as necessary on that account, and this consciousness is not part of its content, but is its form as the conclusion of an inference.[9] Therefore an act can be the conclusion of an inference only if it is such as to contain a consciousness of its own necessity; and an act that contains an understanding of itself as necessary is such as to be the conclusion of an inference. *Ought* and *good*, being concepts of necessity, designate the form of an act that may be the conclusion of an inference. As that inference concludes in an act of the will, it is a practical inference.

Our proposition describes the form of an act of the will as follows: It is a productive representation conceiving of itself as necessary. Reason is the power of inference, the power to represent the kind of necessity just described. So according to our proposition acts of the will are not only acts of productive thought, but acts of reason, which is productive, or practical, in those acts. The will is practical reason, says our proposition. If we are to understand it, we must see how the power of practical inference (practical reason) is a power to act (the will).

7. Practical Inference and the Causality of the Will

Doing something intentionally is representing doing it as good. This describes the form of an act of the will. It says that an act of the will applies a concept in such a way as to act (it is productive) and represents so acting as good (it contains a consciousness of its own necessity). Now the will would not be a distinctive power to act, and acting intentionally would not be a distinctive manner of acting, if an act of the will were a productive representation that also happened to conceive of itself as necessary. The will is a distinctive power to act only if its consciousness of necessity is the form of its productivity. That the will is practical reason must mean that its causality is constituted by practical reasoning. This is how Kant explains it.

> Ein jedes Ding der Natur wirkt nach Gesetzen. Nur ein vernünftiges Wesen hat das Vermögen, nach der Vorstellung der Gesetze, d. i. nach Prinzipien, zu handeln, oder einen Willen. Da zur Ableitung der Handlungen von Gesetzen Vernunft erfodert wird, so ist der Wille nichts anderes, als praktische Vernunft. (*Grundlegung zur Metaphysik der Sitten*, 412)

Kant defines the will as a power to act according to the representation of laws. We shall see that this is exactly right. But it will be helpful to be less specific at first. A law is something general, something that actions according to the law exemplify. So let us say, more generally, that the will is a power to act according to general representations, or concepts. As those concepts are instantiated in acting, they are action form concepts. Now Kant says this power is nothing other than practical reason because reason is required for the derivation of actions from action forms. This shows that the will is nothing other than practical reason if and only if acting according to the representation of an action form is nothing other than deriving the action from this form. Acting according to an action form concept (an act of the will) is deriving the action from the represented action form (an act of reason). So an act of the will is productive in this way: Its subject derives actions from the predicated action form, that is, reasons practically from the form to actions realizing it. An act of the will is the cause of action through practical reasoning.[10] In order to develop the meaning of our proposition, we must describe the structure of practical reasoning in such a way as to show how it constitutes a consciousness of its conclusion as necessary. And we must explain how that structure is the causality of the will so that its consciousness of necessity is the form of its productivity. We shall do the former in the next section, the latter in section V.

IV. PRACTICAL REASONING

8. Its Conclusion

The conclusion of a practical inference is a productive representation. This is what makes the inference *practical*. As the conclusion of an *inference*, the representation is conscious of itself as necessary. *Good* and *ought* express that consciousness.[11] Thus, "I should do *A*," "I ought to do *A*" can express a conclusion of practical reasoning, as can "It is good to do *A*."[12]

As productive, the conclusion of a practical inference is a first-person thought. *Ought* and *good*, signifying its form, signify its first-person character. Therefore, expressing the conclusion of a practical inference, "I ought to do *A*" is not equivalent to "It ought to be the case that . . . [I, do

$A] \ldots$," and "It is good to do A" not to "It would be good if it were the case that $\ldots$ $[I, do A] \ldots$." (The brackets indicate that the proposition contains the first-person concept and the concept *do A* and perhaps further material, leaving it open how these materials are conjoined.) A sentential operator does not affect the form of predication of the sentence to which it is applied. Hence, a subject that represents a state of affairs as necessary is not, in virtue of representing it in this way, identical with a subject that figures in that state of affairs. If the first person figures in the articulation of the relevant state of affairs, then this is incidental to that state's being represented as something that ought to be. Within the scope of "It ought to be the case that . . ." or "It would be good if it were the case that . . ." I refer to myself as other.[13] It follows that the necessity that these sentential operators express is not the necessity of a productive representation, and thus not the necessity the consciousness of which is the formal character of the conclusion of a *practical* inference. Perhaps "It would be good if it were the case that . . ." expresses a judgment of value. "It is good to do A" does not; it expresses an act of the will.

Reasoning practically is determining what to do or how to act by deriving it from something general. What is derived is specific in relation to that from which it is derived. Reasoning practically is specifying the general. For a reason I shall give in section V, I call the general item from which an action is derived an end. There are two kinds of general item from which an action may be derived, two kinds of end. Corresponding to them are two forms of deriving the specific from the general.

9. Finite End

The first kind of end is signified by a verb that is predicated under the contrast of perfective and progressive aspect, the contrast of being under way and being complete. An example is "getting the camera": It is something one may be doing ("He is getting the camera") or may have done ("He has got the camera"). Such an end conforms to Aristotle's definition of "kinesis." A kinesis may be said to be a finite end because it comes to a limit: I want to get the camera only as long as I have not got it. Once I have got it, my desire to get it dies. Having got the camera, I may want to get it again (having dropped it, perhaps), but this will be pursuing a different end.

Reasoning practically, I derive from a finite end what is preparatory for, or a part of, it. (It may be, or turn out to be, an improper part; that is, having done what I derived from the end, I may find that I need to do no more.) In my example, thinking that my camera is upstairs, I derive going upstairs as a part of getting the camera. "My camera is upstairs. So let me go upstairs," I think. From a given finite end, a potentially infinite number of actions can be derived as preparatory for, or parts of, it. A finite end does not limit the number of actions that may be derived from it in the manner described. In this way, notwithstanding its finitude, a finite end is a unity of a potentially infinite number of actions derived from it. As the idea of the general is the idea of such a unity, a finite end is general in relation to the actions derived from it. Deriving an action from a finite end is a manner of specifying something general.

Thinking that the camera is upstairs and wanting to get it play distinct roles in my inference. Getting the camera is the general item from which I derive going upstairs as to be done. I derive it recognizing the logical nexus of going upstairs and getting the camera: The former specifies the latter. It specifies it in the manner in which something specifies a finite end: It is a part of getting the camera. My recognition of this nexus is my knowledge that the camera is upstairs as this knowledge is put to the service of my end of getting the camera. I shall call the representation of the end the first premise of a practical inference. And the thought that mediates first premise and conclusion, revealing the object of the latter to specify the general item given by the former, I call the second premise.

Reasoning practically, I derive from something general something that is specific in relation to it, which, so deriving it, I represent as to be done, or as good to do. It follows that not only the conclusion of a practical inference, but its first premise, as well, represents something as to be done or as good to do. That going upstairs is a part of getting the camera can show that I should go upstairs only if I should fetch the camera. If indeed I conclude that I should go upstairs because this is a way to fetch my camera, then this shows that I represent getting the camera as good to do.

The first premise and the conclusion of a practical inference share the same form. Indeed, this form is in the first instance exhibited by the first premise and only on that account, and in this sense derivatively, by the conclusion. Both the conclusion and the first premise of a practical inference are acts of the will. By contrast, the second premise, which conjoins those acts of the will, is not an act of the will, but an act of the intellect. Thus we can call the first premise practical, and the second theoretical.

As the conclusion of a practical inference bears the same form as its first premise, it may be the first premise of another practical inference. There can be a series of practical inferences that interlock in such a way that the conclusion of one is the practical premise of the next. Such a series is the self-specification of the will (of which, alas, it is only capable with the help of the intellect).[14] Of any act of the will occurring in such a series, we can call the ultimate practical premise of the series its *principle*. According what I just said, the principle of an act of the will is an act of the will.

10. Infinite End

The first kind of end we considered was signified by a verb predicated under the contrast of perfective and progressive aspect. A second kind of end is signified by a verb the predication of which does not exhibit a contrast of aspect, but represents the act as always already complete. Such an end conforms to Aristotle's definition of energeia. Examples are: living healthy, honoring one's parents, and being true to one's word. In the representation of these ends there is no opposition of progressive and perfective aspect: as I am living healthy, I have lived healthy; as I am honoring my parents, I have honored them; as I am being true to my word, I have been true to my word. Hence, these ends do not come to a limit. It is not that, at some time, I am done with living healthy, or honoring my parents, or being true to my word. My wanting to live healthy does not expire. I may give up on it, and so my wanting to live healthy may come to an end; I may no longer want that. But that it comes to this is not internal to its logical character. Therefore we may call such an end an infinite end.

When I said that, reasoning practically, I derive what to do or how to act, I was, using these variables, *doing something* and *acting in a certain way*, looking forward to the distinction of finite and infinite ends, kinesis and energeia. It is natural to hear *doing something* as standing for verbs designating a kinesis, defined by a terminus, a result, an outcome, which is reached when the thing is done. The variable *acting in a certain way* does not suggest a terminus; it is natural to hear it as standing for verbs that designate an energeia. I want to live healthy; I want to honor my parents; I want to be true to my word. Here I do not want to produce a result that then would be the limit of my end. I want to act in a certain manner. When I derive an action from such an end, I determine what to do, not with a view to doing something else, but with a view to acting in a certain way.

This is a different form of specification from the one pertaining to finite ends, corresponding to the different form of generality of an infinite end. The action is not preparatory for, or a part of, the end. It cannot be, as the idea of lacking completion does not apply to infinite ends. Rather, the action *exemplifies* the manner of acting from which it is derived. Thinking that I have promised Frederik to help paint his apartment, I derive going over to his apartment at the designated time. "I should go over because I promised to help," I may think. In fact, this form of words leaves open the logical character of the end; it may still be that the fact that I promised to help Frederik reveals helping him to serve a finite end I am pursuing: I may have a scheme in which my act of fidelity is an element, or perhaps I want to be well regarded by Frederik with a view to unspecific advantages. Then "I am helping Frederik because I promised to do it" is formally like "I am going upstairs because my camera is upstairs."[15] But it may be different. I may think that the fact that I promised Frederik shows that I should go over, by revealing going over—not to be a part of a finite end, but—to exemplify an infinite end: being true to my word.

I described the roles of thinking the camera is upstairs and wanting to get it in practical reasoning. Wanting to be true to my word plays the role that wanting to get the camera played there, and thinking that I promised plays the role that there was played by thinking that the camera is upstairs. Being true to my word is the general item from which I derive going over. I derive it recognizing the logical nexus of going over to being true to my word: The former specifies the latter. It specifies it in the manner in which something specifies an infinite end: Going over, I give an example of acting in such a way as to be true to my word. My recognition of this logical nexus is my knowledge that I have promised as it is put to the service of my end of being true to my word.

Again, the general item from which I derive the action is represented in the same way as the action I derive from it: It is represented as a way in which to act, or else, as a way acting in which is acting well. That going over to Frederik is what it takes to be true to my word only shows that I should go over if one should be true to one's word, or else, if being true to one's word is acting well. And if indeed I think I should go over on the ground that I must do so in order to be true to my word, then I represent being true to one's word as a way in which to act, or as a way acting in which is acting well.

In a series of practical inferences, the predication of a kinesis verb can be derived from the predication of a kinesis verb (as when I reason from getting the camera to going upstairs). And the predication of an energeia verb can be derived from the predication of an energeia verb. (I may reason from being just to being true to my word.) But whereas the predication of a kinesis verb can be derived from the predication of an energeia verb (in my example I reason from being true to my word to helping paint an apartment), the converse is not possible. For something temporally unlimited cannot be subsumed under something temporally limited.

11. Principle and Outcome of Action

Kant defines the will as the power to act according to the representation of laws. Now I said (in section 7) seemingly more generally that it is a power to act according to concepts. Then I distinguished two kinds of such concepts, kinesis concepts and energeia concepts. The application of a kinesis concept is not a representation of a law, for a law sets no temporal limit to its applicability, whereas there is a temporal limit to the manifold united in a kinesis. By contrast, the application of an energeia concept is a representation of a law; a law according to which one acts is a manner of acting. Now the power to act according to energeia concepts includes the power to act according to kinesis concepts as the latter are needed to specify the former. Therefore, my description of the will as a power to act according to concepts differs from Kant's only in that it does not rule out that a will may be confined to kinesis concepts. However, as we shall see now, there is no such thing as a will that applies only kinesis concepts. There is no such thing because an act of the will is conscious of itself as necessary. The greater generality of our definition is spurious, and Kant's definition is more precise.[16]

A power to act only according to kinesis concepts is exercised in thoughts of the form "It is good to do A," "doing A" being a kinesis verb. However, such a thought necessarily rests on another thought of goodness.

For, a kinesis is such as to bring itself to an end. And it is not intelligible that something is in itself good insofar as it brings itself to an end. Something good cannot be such as to go out of existence. For what is represented in an act of the will is represented as possible through this act, and insofar as an act of the will, being a representation of something as good, contains a consciousness of itself as necessary, its object is conceived as existing, if it does exist, necessarily. But something that is such as to go out of existence denies itself necessary existence. A kinesis can be thought good only in relation to something it specifies and for the sake of which it is. A principle of an act of the will (the last practical premise in the relevant series of practical inferences) cannot be the self-predication of a kinesis verb.

This may seem to be too quick. Surely a kinesis cannot be considered good in itself, one might say. But it is wrong to conclude that it is considered good only in relation to its principle. Instead, it may be considered good in relation to its outcome.[17] Now it is certainly possible to think it would be good if p were the case and on that account do something with a view to bringing it about. In familiar cases, thinking it good if p were the case is relating its being the case to an end—doing something or acting in a certain way—as necessary for, facilitating, or in some other way serving this end. Then the goodness of achieving the outcome derives from the goodness of the action that the outcome serves; the outcome mediates a nexus of action and action. This explains what, in those cases, it means that an outcome is good. It explains it by hanging this use of "good" on its use as a mark of the form of the will. However, the objection requires that there be such a thing as thinking it would be good if p were the case, where thinking this is not relating its being the case to an action as serving it. Thus it supposes that there is an application of *good* to states of affairs that stands on its own feet. Furthermore, although this use of *good* is not to depend on its application to action, the latter must be able to depend on it: A thought that it would be good if p were the case must be capable of being the ground of an act of the will, a thought that it is good to do something as a result of one's having done which it will be the case that p. Unless the idea of a good state of affairs is related to willing in this way, it is irrelevant to an account of the will, and anyway empty. So, whereas I said a last premise of practical reasoning is the representation of a law, the practical application of an energeia concept, the objection holds that a last premise may represent an outcome, a state of affairs, as good.[18]

However, the fact that it would be good if p were the case need not speak in favor of thinking it good to bring it about. Even if it would be good if p, it may be that I must not bring it about. Perhaps it is someone else's office, or duty, or privilege to bring it about, or perhaps its goodness depends on its not being brought about by anyone. This may seem to show that we must include in the outcome not only what in a strict sense is the result of the act, but furthermore the fact that I am producing or have produced it. The thought from which I derive an act of the will is not "It would be good if *p*," but "It would be good if . . . [I, see to it that *p*] . . . ." However, I cannot reason from this premise to "It is good to see to it that *p*" or "I should see to it that *p*." For while "It would be good if . . . [I see to it that *p*] . . ." is not originally a first-person thought, "It is good to see to it that *p*" is. And without further premises, an originally first-person thought cannot be derived from a thought that is not origi- nally first personal.[19] Adapting an example from Anselm W. Müller,[20] we can bring this out by turning to the second person. "You must drink this glass of water" addresses a demand to you: In virtue of its form, it pre- sents itself as capable of determining your will. By contrast, "It must be the case that you drink this glass of water" refers to you and to the glass in the same manner; it no more addresses a demand to you than it does so to the glass. There is no way to derive a demand from it without rely- ing on a demand already in place.

An act of the will *in virtue of its form* is productive and therefore first personal. The alleged thought that it would be good if *p* were the case is not. This remains so no matter what is plucked into the content of "*p*." Hence, this alleged thought never provides a self-standing basis for a thought about what is good to do.[21] This shows that there is no self-standing use of *good* in application to states of affairs. An illusion of intelligibility arises when we unwittingly give the relevant phrase a sense that we do under- stand: relating a state of affairs to a given end. It is easy to fall prey to this illusion. It is well-nigh impossible not to fall prey to it when one does not even notice the difference between the use of *good* or *ought* as indicating a form of predication (which is productive and therefore first personal) and as a sentential operator.[22]

My aim in this essay is to elucidate the concept *good* as signifying the form of an act of the will. I say nothing about its content, which is given by a true ultimate practical premise of practical reasoning. But my reflections place formal constraints on its content. First, it can only be an energeia. Second, this energeia must be internal to the will in the sense that representing it as good must constitute the will as the will that it is, so that the idea of a further act of the will on which it may be based is empty and no question arises as to why it is good to act in this way. For an ultimate act of the will—a principle of the will— understands itself as such, and that is, as not depending on any other.[23] Kant argues that only the representation of the form of a law of the will satisfies this condition. Once it is recognized that whether it is good to do something cannot, ultimately, rest on the goodness of the outcome of one's having done it, it may well appear that Kant's view is the only viable one. However, Kant is not alone in rejecting the notion that the goodness of a will resides in its consequences. Aristotle, St. Thomas, and Hegel, for example, do so as well, as does anyone writing in their tradi- tion. The conception of the will and practical reason developed here is common to them all.

V. ACTING ACCORDING TO A REPRESENTATION

12. The Unity of Causality and Recognition of Accord

The will is a distinctive power to act only if the order described in the preceding section, in which one act of the will depends on another in such a way as to contain a consciousness of its own necessity, is nothing other than the causality of the will. I shall now seek to show that this is so.

Practical reasoning is the causality of the will if acting according to the representation of an end is deriving an action from this end. Thus we must consider what it is to act according to a representation. When someone is acting according to a representation, then the representation causes her action. Explaining why she is doing what she is doing, or why she is acting in the way that she is, we refer to this representation: She who is doing A according to her representation of doing B is doing A because she wants to do B. And she who is doing A according to her representation of a certain manner of acting, is doing A because she wants to act in this manner. However, this does not suffice. Someone's wanting to do something may cause all manner of movement on her part, which is not on that account a case of acting according to the representation of doing that. For example, someone may be falling ill because he wants to lose weight in this way: He has been wanting to lose weight for a long time, nothing he tried worked, at last his anxiety gives rise to somatic symptoms. As he is falling ill, he is not acting according to his representation of losing weight. It seems obvious what is missing: If he is to act according to his representation, he must recognize that his action accords with the represented end. He must subsume his action under the end as a part of or as exemplifying it. In order for someone to act according to the representation of an end, there must be not only a causal nexus of the representation and the action. Moreover, the subject must be conscious of the logical nexus, the accord of the action with the end. However this, again, does not suffice. We can embellish our example and add that our man recognizes that he will lose weight if he falls ill and welcomes his illness on that ground. We do not therewith represent him as acting according to his representation in falling ill.

That our two conditions on action according to a representation—the causal nexus of representation and action and the subject's consciousness of the logical nexus of action and represented end—are not jointly sufficient may appear to oblige us to search for further conditions. However, it is not that we lack and must seek to identify further conditions; rather, we lack and must seek to articulate the *unity* of those that we have.[24] In our example, causality and recognition have come together *per accidens*. The explanation "He is falling ill because he wants to lose weight" leaves open whether he recognizes that falling ill will further his end of losing weight. His recognizing this is *an independent reality* from the one that the explanation records. "He is falling ill because he wants to lose weight" represents one reality; "He thinks he should fall ill in order to lose weight" represents another. Consider by contrast her who is going upstairs because she wants to get the camera. We may be able to concoct a story in which someone is going upstairs because she wants to get her camera, in such a way that the causal nexus exists independently of her recognition of the logical nexus. Absent such a story, we understand the explanation to depict the subject to act according to her representation of getting the camera. And if it so depicts her, then it is true only if she is aware that going upstairs is a way to get the camera. Here, "She thinks she should go upstairs in order to get her camera," representing her as deriving going upstairs from her end of getting the camera, and "She is going upstairs because she wants to get the camera," explaining her going upstairs by her representation of getting the camera, record *the same reality*. Her deriving the action from the end is an act of *practical* reason as it constitutes the causality of her representation of the end. Practical deriving, deriving an action, is acting.

It may be objected that we failed to observe a distinction made in section 8. Our sad man does not think "I should fall ill" or "It would be good to fall ill." Rather, he thinks "It should be the case that . . . [I fall ill] . . ." or "It would be good if . . . [I fall ill] . . . ." By contrast, our photographer thinks, not "It should be the case that . . . [I go upstairs] . . .," but "I should go upstairs." This is correct and is a way to make my point. "I should go upstairs" differs from "It should be the case that . . . [I go upstairs] . . ." in that it bears the form of a conclusion of practical reasoning. A representation of necessity is not external to, but constitutes the causality of an act of the will only if it bears that form.

The concept of acting according to a representation signifies a special kind of causality: the causality of a representation constituted by the subject's deriving the action from the represented end. The subject's recognition of the accord of the action with the representation that is its cause is not added to an independently constituted causality; it is *the form of the causality*. Practical reason is not a term of causal relations of a kind that also characterize the movements of nonrational or even inanimate substances. Practical reason is a causality, which therefore is characteristic of movements of the rational subject.

13. A Representation That Possesses This Kind of Causality Is Productive

Kant says that acting according to the representation of an end is deriving the action from the represented end. Deriving something from something general is an act of reason. It is an act of practical reason when deriving the action is acting; and deriving the action is acting when it is the causality of the representation from whose object the action is derived. For when someone acts according to a representation, then "She is doing *A* because . . .," explaining the action by the representation, represents the same reality as "She thinks *A* is to be done because . . .," depicting her as deriving the action from the represented end.

A subject acts according to a representation if the representation causes her action in such a way that her deriving the action from the represented end constitutes the causal nexus of representation and action. An act of the will is a representation that exhibits this causality: It causes actions derived from it in such a way that the causal nexus is the subject's deriving the action. It follows that such a representation relates to its object as productive of it. If I want to get the camera, and am acting according to this representation (perhaps going upstairs), then it will be true that *I am getting the camera*, doing what I do. And if I want to be true to my word, and act according to this principle (perhaps going over to Frederik), then it will be true that *I am true to my word*, acting as I do. In general, if someone is doing *A* because she wants to do *B*, and the causality of her act of will is constituted by her deriving doing *A* from her end of doing *B*, then she is, in fact, and not per accidens, doing *B*. Not per accidens, for it is not per accidens, but a character of the causality that what the representation causes is its object. In this way, an act of the will is the cause of the existence of its object.

I spoke of the object of a representation according to which its subject acts as an end. I can now justify this way of speaking. An end is, as Kant says, the object of a concept insofar as the latter is regarded as the cause (the real ground of the possibility) of the former.[25] Now, when a subject acts according to a concept (if the action form concept causes the action by way of the subject's deriving the action from the represented action form), then she is instantiating the concept. Hence, a concept according to which its subject acts is the concept of an end.

14. A Metaphysical Dogma

The proposition *Doing something intentionally is representing it as good* describes the form of an act of the will. It describes it as a power of productive representations that contain a consciousness of their necessity, and thus as a power of representations whose causality in respect of their object is constituted by reasoning. Now it is a widespread dogma that causality is the same everywhere, governing the movements of inanimate substances as well as the actions of subjects of reason. This dogma makes our proposition incomprehensible, for it puts the concept of the will, which the proposition articulates, out of reach.

The concept of causality is a category; it represents a unity, the unity of something and the sufficient ground of its existence. It is not inconceivable that this category should admit of different specifications, that there should be different forms in which one thing may be the sufficient ground of another. Nor is it inconceivable that metaphysical distinctions between inanimate, sentient, and rational substances should signify differences in the form of causality to which changes and movements of those substances are subject, and that so should distinctions of corresponding kinds of movement, animal locomotion, say, and rational or intentional action.

It is remarkable, then, that many appear to think it reasonable not to consider this possibility, but to proceed on the assumption that the concept of causality that is part of the concept of intentional action is one that is equally applicable outside the sphere of action. They then seek the nature of intentional action not in a form of causality, but in special causes. This sets off a dialectic that has sustained and is sustaining philosophical production in the field. We shall follow it a few steps.

We considered someone who wants to lose weight, which desire makes him fall ill. He does, we imagined, recognize that he will lose weight in consequence of falling ill. Still, we reasoned, he does not act according to his desire because his recognition of the logical nexus of the action and his end is external to the causal nexus of the desire and the action. The desire causes the action in such a way that it remains an accident that the subject of the action so caused is aware of its accord with the object of his desire. It seems, then, that the subject's awareness of the logical nexus must not lie idly alongside the causal nexus, but must in some way inform it. Now if a causal nexus cannot be an act of reason, then the subject's recognition can figure in the causal explanation of her action only as a further cause. Thus we arrive at the idea that an action is caused by a desire and a belief.

But just as a desire, so can a desire and a belief cause all manner of movement on the part of the subject, who is not on that account acting according to the desire. In our example, it is not implausible that the man's recognition that falling ill would further his end of losing weight joins with his desire to lose weight in weighing him down until he is falling ill. It is not enough that a belief and a desire cause an action, even if belief, desire, and action are logically related in such a way that the belief reveals the action to further the desired end. Rather, the subject must recognize this relation. And not only this: Her recognition must enter into the causal account of the action, lest the belief and the desire cause the action in a way that leaves it an accident that the action so caused is known by its subject to accord with the end she desires, in which case she would not be acting according to her desire. Christine Korsgaard writes:

> Neither the joint causal efficacy of the belief and the desire, nor the existence of an appropriate conceptual connection, nor the bare conjunction of these two facts, enables us to judge that a person acts rationally. For the person to act rationally, she must be motivated by her own recognition of the appropriate conceptual connection between her belief and her desire. We may say that she herself must combine the belief and the desire in the right way. A person acts rationally, then, only when her action is the expression of her own mental activity. ("The Normativity of Instrumental Reason," in G. Cullity et al. (eds.), *Ethical and Practical Reason*. Oxford: Oxford University Press, 1997, 215–54, here 221)

This seems exactly right, but we must seek to explain what it means that the action *expresses* the subject's recognition, or, equivalently, what it means that the subject is *motivated* by her recognition. It is natural to think that what motivates an action causes it. But Korsgaard cannot mean that we must include the subject's recognition among the causes of her action. Korsgaard must intend the word "motivate" to signify a special kind of causality, which can only be the one I described.[26]

Davidson makes a suggestion that anticipates Korsgaard's appeal to "mental activity":

> Beliefs and desires that would rationalize an action if they caused it in the right way—through a course of practical reasoning, as we might try saying—may cause it in other ways. ("Freedom to Act," in *Essays on Actions and Events*, 63–82, here p. 79)

When Davidson says, "we might try saying," he means that saying it would be useless. And so it is as long as causality is thought to be uniform across rational and nonrational substances and their movements. Davidson speaks of the way in which belief and desire cause the action and thus may seem to distinguish *what* causes the action from *how* it causes it, the cause from the causality. However, for him, specifying the way in which x causes y is specifying a causal chain that links x and y, a chain whose members are joined by the one and uniform nexus of causality.

> An agent might have attitudes and beliefs that would rationalize an action, and they might cause him to perform it, and yet because of some anomaly in the causal chain, the action would not be intentional in the expected sense. ("Intending," in *Essays on Actions and Events*, 83–102, here 87)

If this is how we distinguish saying what causes something and how it causes it, namely as specifying a cause and specifying intermediary members of a causal chain that link it to its effect, then saying that the desire causes the action through a course of practical reasoning is representing that course of practical reasoning as a member of the causal chain. Davidson is right to insinuate that saying this is useless.

It is possible to follow the dialectic further. But it is not necessary, for its principle is transparent. We see it if we attend to a structural analogy that it bears to the regress into which Achill is led in his attempts to answer the tortoise.[27] A regress arises when we try to represent a unity of elements as a further element. There, the relevant unity is that of premises and conclusion, which Achill seeks to represent as a further premise. Here, it is the unity of a cause and what it causes, the unity of a causal nexus, the causality. The subject's derivation of the action from the representation *is* this unity; it constitutes the causal nexus. This is why all attempts to represent it as a further cause come to grief.

15. The Reality of the Concept of the Will Unfolded in Our Proposition

Doing something intentionally is representing doing it as good describes the form of an act of the will, articulating the concept of a power to act that is proper to the subject of reason as it is an application of reason, which, so applied, is practical. It may be granted that, so interpreted, our proposition is impeccable, but does not express knowledge, for the power it describes has no reality. However, no one can fail to know that the will is a reality. For, thinking "I should do that," "That is good to do," he is an example of its reality.[28]

Notes

1. Cf. Dorothy Grover, Joseph Camp, Nuel Belnap, "A Prosentential Theory of Truth," *Philosophical Studies* 27 (1975): S73–S125; Robert Brandom, *Making It Explicit*, Cambridge, Mass.: Harvard University Press, 1994, 285–98.

2. Ludwig Wittgenstein, *Tractatus*. Frankfurt: Suhrkamp, 1984, 4.1271.

3. Gottlob Frege, "Der Gedanke," in *Logische Untersuchungen*, Günther Patzig (ed.). Göttingen: Vandenhoeck, 2003, 41: "In der Form des Behauptungssatzes sprechen wir die Anerkennung der Wahrheit aus. Wir brauchen dazu das Wort "wahr" nicht. Und selbst, wenn wir es gebrauchen, liegt die eigentlich behauptende Kraft nicht in ihm, sondern in der Form des Behauptungssatzes, und wo diese ihre behauptende Kraft verliert, kann auch das Wort "wahr" sie nicht wieder herstellen."

4. This idea is misunderstood when it is thought to mean that a synthesis produces the thought. But thinking is no act of production. A product is separable from the act of producing it. It is there when the act of producing it has come to completion and is past. When I am placing the blue cube on top of the red cube, then, as long as I am doing this, the blue cube is not yet on top of the red cube. When finally the blue cube is on top of the red cube, as I have placed it there and am no longer placing it there. I was placing it there, but this is past, and now I am done. Conjoining the parts of a thought in thinking it is not like this. It is not that I am thinking, am putting the parts together, and then, as I have thought, have put the parts together, there is a thought, which I am no longer thinking, as my thinking, my putting together, is completed and past. Thinking does not admit of the contrast of progressive and perfective aspect, of being doing something and having done it. If thinking is synthesis, then this holds of its synthesis: There is no contrast of being conjoining and having conjoined the elements of a thought. Therefore, it does not matter whether we say that the synthesis is the source of the unity of the thought or that the synthesis is the unity of the thought. There is no difference.

5. It would be a distraction to pursue the matter here, but I do not think that Frege can deny any of this.

6. Immanuel Kant, *Kritik der reinen Vernunft. Werkausgabe Band III*, W. Weischedel (ed.). Frankfurt: Suhrkamp, 1968, §19.

7. My account may appear to be close to, but in fact is completely different from, a view David Velleman criticizes in "The Guise of the Good" (in *The Possibility of Practical Reason*. Oxford: Oxford University Press, 2000, 99–122), that desiring something is regarding it as good in the sense that the direction of fit of desire can be articulated by saying that desiring something is regarding it—not as being true, but—as to be made true. This represents desire as a force attaching to the same kind of content to which the force of judgment may

attach. And this makes it impossible to think of *good* as signifying the form of the object of desire.

8. The terms "reasoning" or "inference," practical or theoretical, do not primarily signify mental processes, but a form of dependence among acts of the mind, the one described above. Cf. Matthew Boyle, *Making Up One's Mind*, unpublished manuscript.

9. This shows what is right about the notion that the conclusion of practical reasoning "I ought to do *A*" means as much as "There is sufficient reason to do *A*." This is misleading insofar as it appears to specify the content of the conclusion of a practical inference, whereas, in fact, it articulates its form. The concept of a reason is a formal concept; it describes to what it applies with regard to its role in reasoning. A reason for acting is something from which one may reason to an action; it is something that may serve as a premise of a practical inference. Hence, saying that practical reasoning concludes in the thought that there is sufficient reason to do *A* is saying that the conclusion of a practical inference represents itself as a conclusion of sound reasoning. And this is right.

10. It has been noticed that our proposition describes the causality of the will as constituted by practical reasoning. But one cannot comprehend this idea if one thinks one independently understands causality and practical reason, and sets out to ascertain whether they come together in intentional action. As our proposition describes a unity that informs the elements it unifies, one will find it muddled approaching it with ideas of reason and causality not developed from it. Ever since Anscombe ridiculed accounts of practical reasoning that represent it to be like mince pie reasoning—about a special topic, as opposed to a special manner of reasoning—there has been sympathy for the aim of giving a formal description of practical reasoning that justifies calling it practical. But few people have had qualms over treating action explanation as mince pie explanation: representing special causes, as opposed to a special kind of causality. However, "action" in "action explanation" determines "explanation" in the manner in which "practical" determines "reasoning" in "practical reasoning": It signifies not the content of the explanation, but its form. Indeed, an account of practical reasoning that justifies calling it practical is an account of a causality that justifies calling its terms acts of the will.

11. Kant describes the relation of imperatives and thoughts of what is good to do as follows: "[Imperatives] say that to do or to omit something would be good, but they say it to a will that does not always do something just because it is represented to it that it would be good to do that thing" (*Grundlegung zur Metaphysik der Sitten*, Akademieausgabe 4, 413). The difference between *good* and *ought* does not lie in the act of mind they express, which in both cases is an act of the will. Rather, expressing its act by an imperative, a will acknowledges its liability to be affected by something other than reason. It is liable, on account of such affection, to hold to wanting to do something against its knowledge of what is good to do. Even then, the subject's representation of something as good to do is an act of the will. Otherwise there would in such a case be no conflict within the will, and that is, there would be no conflict. For there is no conflict between any act of the intellect, no matter what its content is, and an act of the will.

12. In ordinary language, all kinds of phrases are used to express acts of the will, and our phrases may on occasion express a different kind of act. This is

irrelevant. We are not interested in words, but in a form of representation. To this end, we stipulate that certain words shall express representations of this form.

13. John Broome uses the formula "I ought that such-and-such is the case" ("Normative Requirements," *Ratio* 12 (1999): 398–419). I do not know what this means. Broome frequently writes "I ought to see to it that such-and-such is the case," and this is intelligible, for it bears the form "I ought to do *A*": It says that I ought to do something the result of my having done which will be that such-and-such is the case. But Broome says that "I ought to see to it that such-and-such is the case" does not give the meaning of "I ought that such-and-such is the case," but is a manner of writing it that avoids its grammatical awkwardness. This leaves us without any idea of what "I ought that such-and-such is the case" might mean. I surmise that Broome is led to a meaningless form of words because he seeks to signify the productive character of the representation, which requires the first person. This yields an empty expression because a productive representation is the self-application of an action form concept, not a statement reporting that one bears a certain relation to a proposition.

14. In this lies the finitude of the will as it indicates its dependence on material conditions that are not its own deed. Cf. G. W. F. Hegel, "Die Idee des Guten," in *Wissenschaft der Logik*. Frankfurt: Suhrkamp, 1986.

15. Cf. Michael Thompson, *Life and Action*, Cambridge, Mass.: Harvard University Press, 2009, 93–96.

16. In his book *The Form of Practical Knowledge* (Cambridge, Mass.: Harvard University Press, 2009), to which the present essay owes a tremendous debt, Stephen Engstrom isolates from the will a power that he calls the power of practical thought, whose acts are productive and therefore first personal, but do not contain a conception of themselves as necessary. It follows that they are not acts of a power of practical inference, and indeed, Engstrom, although he credits practical thought with instrumental rationality, never speaks of practical thought as engaged in instrumental reasoning. Conversely, that in us the conception of something as a means to an end can take on the form of an inference and thus of a representation of taking the means as necessary reveals that we possess a will, and not just the power of practical thought.

17. The objection could be formulated as one against my use of the term "end." I distinguished two kinds of ends; both are actions, falling into the category of either kinesis or energeia. I argued that in the primary instance an end is an energeia and that derivatively, as specifying such an end, a kinesis may be an end. But it may be said that, properly speaking, not the action is the end, but its outcome.

18. If we define consequentialism as the thesis that the primary use of *good* is its application to states of affairs in "It is good that *p* is the case" or "It would be good if *p* were the case," and that its application to action in "It is good to do *A*" rests on that one, then the objection is an expression of consequentialism.

19. Cannot I reason from "He should do *A*," "I am him" to "I should do *A*" (for example, "The person who is responsible for *X* should do *A*," "I am responsible for *X*," to "I should do *A*")? Yes. But in this case, "I am him" shows me that I can derive that I should do *A* from the same general practical premise from which I derived that he should do *A*. And then neither "He should do *A*" nor, therefore,

"I am him" enters as a premise. The general practical premise will be an original first-person thought.

20. *Praktisches Folgern und Selbstgestaltung nach Aristoteles*, Freiburg: Karl Alber, 1982, p. 301.

21. David Velleman represents our proposition as saying: "[Someone] acts intentionally only when he acts out of a desire for some anticipated outcome; and in desiring that outcome, he must regard it as having some value" ("The Guise of the Good," 99). But the concept *good* used in our proposition does not signify a character of an outcome of action, the manner in which an action form concept is applied in an act of the will, which may be expressed by saying "It is good to do such-and-such," or "It is good to act in such-and-such a way."

22. There is an objective use of *good* and related concepts in the description of living beings. However, the same logical difference obtains there: "This bush needs water" is not the same as "It needs to be the case that this bush has water." Thus, the illusory notion that there are objectively good states of affairs receives no succor from this logical character of the living.

23. In this ultimate act of the will, the contrast of power and act collapses: This ultimate act of the will is the will. This shows the will to be self-constituting.

24. If this is right, then it is not possible to define acting according to a representation in terms intelligible independently of what they define. As conditions of acting according to a representation, both the causality and the subject's recognition of the logical nexus of its terms are of a special kind, the kind being defined by their unity, which unity is acting according to a representation.

25. Immanuel Kant, *Kritik der Urteilskraft, Werkausgabe Band X*, W. Weischedel (ed.). Frankfurt: Suhrkamp, 1968, §10.

26. Although I do not fully comprehend her exposition of it, it seems plain that in Korsgaard's "Acting for Reasons" (in *The Constitution of Agency*. Oxford: Oxford University Press, 2008, 207–29), which sets out to explain what it is for something to motivate an action, and how motivation relates to causation, Korsgaard defends a position that is very similar to, if not identical with, the one I have sought to lay out.

27. I am grateful to Kelly Dean Jolly for pointing this out to me.

28. Someone who did not possess the will could not have the concept of the will. In this way our possession of the concept of the will attests to its reality in us. (Andrea Kern, in *Quellen des Wissens* [Frankfurt: Suhrkamp, 2006] argues that the same holds of the power of knowledge and its concept.)

8

Goodness and Desire

Matthew Boyle & Douglas Lavin

> *It is always the object of desire which produces movement, but this is either the good or the apparent good.*
> —Aristotle, *De Anima*, III.10 (433a28–29)

1. INTRODUCTION

Aristotle famously held that all desiring is directed toward some actual or apparent good, and a long train of celebrated philosophers have agreed with him, from Aquinas and Kant to Anscombe and Davidson. Philosophers writing in this tradition have tended to find Aristotle's proposition not merely correct but obvious, so obvious that the Scholastics codified it in a dictum: *quidquid appetitur, appetitur sub specie boni*, "whatever is desired is desired under the guise of the good." The last few decades, however, have seen a vigorous attack on this guise of the good thesis. The Aristotelian doctrine has been dismissed as not merely wrong but naive, reflecting a picture of the human heart that is either hopelessly innocent or deliberately one-sided.[1] What accounts for this transformation? How could what seemed plain to so many come to seem so patently false?

Contemporary critics of the guise of the good thesis often support their rejection of it by citing putative counterexamples: cases in which people fail to desire what they regard as good (*accidie*), desire most what they do not think best (*akrasia*), or even desire what they do not regard as good at all, as when one person feels a purely malicious or spiteful urge to lash out at another. Milton's Satan, when he resolves "Evil be thou my good," expresses a perversity that is extreme in its degree, but the kind of impulse he feels is hardly unknown to us: We are all familiar with the chasms that can open between what we want and what we take to be good or valuable. Gary Watson provides a vivid sketch of this parting of ways:

> The cases in which one in no way values what one desires are perhaps rare, but surely they exist. Consider the case of a woman who has a sudden urge to

drown her bawling child in the bath; or the case of a squash player who, while suffering an ignominious defeat, desires to smash his opponent in the face with the racquet. It is just false that the mother values her child's being drowned or that the player values the injury and suffering of his opponent. But they desire these things nonetheless. They desire them in spite of themselves.[2]

Pointing to such cases, critics of the guise of the good thesis ask: How can it be true that desire is directed toward the good if sometimes it palpably isn't?

It seems doubtful, however, that attention to such cases by itself accounts for the contemporary turn against the guise of the good thesis. For whatever philosophers writing in the Aristotelian tradition meant by saying that we desire under the guise of the good, they were hardly unaware that people can want what they take to be wicked or worthless: They themselves emphasized such cases. What seemed to them obvious was not that perverse desires are impossible, but that they must be understood in a certain way: as involving a kind of mutiny of some of our motivational faculties, a mutiny that results in an object's being put forward as desirable by one faculty even as others deny its desirability. Contemporary critics of the guise of the good thesis, by contrast, do not feel pressure to interpret cases of perverse desire in this way: They do not see why *desiring* something need involve any tendency, however partial, to regard it as *desirable*. To understand the basis of the recent turn against the guise of the good thesis, we must understand the reasons for this change.

Why might it seem that desiring something must involve some tendency to see that thing as desirable? The intuitive reason seems to be this: A person who wants something can, in general, be asked *why* he wants it, and then he is expected to answer, not by giving some sort of psycho-history of his own desire, but rather by offering another sort of account—one that describes what we call his "reasons" for wanting the thing in question, the considerations he takes to "speak in favor" of pursuing that object.[3] The guise of the good thesis is, in effect, a claim about what sort of thing a reason is: namely, that it is a consideration that bears on what is good about what is wanted. Contemporary opposition to the thesis is bound up with a rejection of this claim. Thus many contemporary philosophers of action insist on a deep distinction between *justifying reasons*, which speak to the goodness of an object or course of action, and *explanatory reasons*, which speak to the question why, in fact, an agent was motivated to do a certain thing. If an agent can answer the question of why he wants to do something, then, on this view, he will be giving an explanatory reason, and while this *may* bear on what is good about the thing he wants, there is no obvious reason why it *must*.

This suggests that the real source of the turn against the guise of the good thesis lies in a shift in the understanding of reasons-explanation. The Aristotelian tradition sees such explanation as a particularly sophisticated form of *teleological* explanation, one that represents us as drawn, not simply toward ends that are, in fact, good, but toward goods that act on us in virtue of our representing them as such. Contemporary philosophers, by contrast, are nearly unanimous in their unwillingness to countenance an unreduced appeal to teleology. The fundamental explanation of action, they assume, must advert to some precedent psychological state of the subject, a state that is the efficient cause of certain bodily movements, and whose causal role in producing these movements can be specified without appeal to teleological notions.[4] It may be that our desires tend to move us toward things that are good for us; indeed, this tendency may figure in an evolutionary explanation of why *Homo sapiens* typically desire what they do. But even if it is a fact that our desires *tend* to move us toward what is beneficial to us, it is hard to see, from this standpoint, why they *must* do so, and still harder to see why they must *represent* their objects as good. For why shouldn't desires for things that the subject does not evaluate as good be capable of playing the same sort of causal role in producing behavior as desires that rest on such an evaluation? The characteristic explanatory role of desire seems to be one topic; the relation, if any, of desire to a sense of justification, another. It may be true that an agent can normally give his reason for acting in the sense of: the desire that explains his acting; but to infer that an agent must normally take himself to have a reason for acting in the sense of a justification for doing what he does—this, it seems, is to equivocate between two different senses of "reason for acting." As Kieran Setiya remarks in an important recent discussion:

> [W]e need a causal-psychological account of taking-as-one's-reason, not an account that appeals to what is seen as good. When an agent acts on a reason, he takes it *as* a reason, but that means he takes it as *his* reason, not that he takes it to be a *good* reason on which to act.[5]

Our aim is to challenge the assumptions that make such a distinction seem necessary, and thus make the Aristotelian doctrine about the relation between goodness and desire seem puzzling. We shall argue that the primary source of contemporary opposition to the guise of the good thesis lies in a certain set of views about action and its explanation, views that form the core of the standard "causal theory of action." But, we shall suggest, these views imply substantive and questionable commitments about the shape an account of intentional action must take; and once these commitments are questioned, the guise of the good thesis reemerges, not as an isolated and dubious claim about what motivates people to act, but as a proposition belonging to an attractive and coherent account of *what action is*.

On the Aristotelian view, what underlies the fact that rational agents must desire under the guise of the good is a general point about the explanation of any *self*-movement or self-change, a point that applies, in different forms, to the explanation of behavior in nonrational animals, and even to the explanation of the nutrition, growth, and reproduction of nonsentient living things. What these various kinds of explanation have in common is that they all have a teleological structure; and it is characteristic of the Aristotelian tradition to claim that, quite generally, this sort of structure applies only to a subject that is the bearer of a certain sort of *form*, a form that constitutes a standard of goodness for the subject in question, but that is equally implicated in any explanation of what the subject itself does. The special feature of the application of this explanatory structure to rational creatures is that such creatures belong to a kind in which this connection between action and goodness becomes self-conscious: They are creatures whose action is expressive of and explained by a self-conception that implicitly involves a *conception* of their own form. This, it will emerge, is why rational self-movers must desire under the guise of the good.

Our project in what follows will be to fill out this Aristotelian view of action, and, we hope, to present it in such a way that it appears to be, not merely a set of strange and antiquated ideas about how the world works, but rather a serious and defensible attempt to understand what action is. Our main aim in doing this is simply to bring out what is at stake in the acceptance or rejection of the guise of the good thesis. Many discussions of the thesis treat it as meriting attention simply because it has a certain historical authority and also, perhaps, a certain intuitive appeal. If we are right, its real interest lies in its connection with an approach to action that stands opposed in fundamental ways to the approach that dominates contemporary action theory. We can hardly hope to make a conclusive case for this alternative approach here, but we hope at least to make clear what it is and why it might have a powerful appeal. We will make this case by first presenting a challenge to the causal-psychologistic approach typically presupposed by critics of the guise of the good thesis (§3), and then sketching the outlines of an alternative, one that takes its departure from a general thought about the connection between self-movement and the form or nature of a thing (§4), and that represents the guise of the good thesis as the upshot of this general thought when it is applied to rational creatures (§5). To clear the way for this enterprise, however, it will help first to make a few points about how to understand the thesis and how to assess it (§2).

2. THE MEANING OF THE THESIS AND HOW TO ASSESS IT

Before deciding whether the guise of the good thesis is true, we must first consider what it means, and already here we face difficulties. Aristotle himself formulates the thesis in various ways: sometimes as a claim about the object of desire, sometimes as a claim about the aim of every "action or pursuit."[6] On which formula should we focus? Moreover, what should count as the "object" of a desire, or the "aim" of an action? If I want to eat an apple, for instance, is the object of my desire *an apple*, or *eating an apple*, or perhaps *my eating an apple*? Does the guise of the good thesis apply to all of these sorts of "objects," or only to certain ones? Finally, what does it mean to say that the object of desire or the aim of action must present itself to the agent "under the guise of the good"? Does it mean that the agent must *believe* that the object is good, or that there is something good about it, or that it would be good if . . . ? Or is the relevant attitude something altogether other than belief?

We will say something about each of these questions in due course. For the moment, our purpose is simply to point them out, in order to forestall a too-hasty assessment of the thesis. Many discussions of the thesis, both by its defenders and by its critics, proceed by marshaling intuitions about cases. But if the meaning of the thesis itself is not obvious, neither can we treat it as obvious at the outset what sorts of cases would speak for or against it. Indeed, the idea that the thesis admits of a direct assessment by reference to examples rests on a dubious assumption about the kind of claim that is at issue.

To see this, it will help to consider a case in point. As we mentioned earlier, much of the debate surrounding the guise of the good thesis focuses on certain sorts of apparent counterexamples: for instance, cases in which an agent does something, or desires to do it, out of sheer spite or malice. Discussing such cases, Michael Stocker observes that

> [w]hen we feel furious, hurt, envious, jealous, threatened, frustrated, abandoned, endangered, rejected, and so on, what we often seek is precisely the harm or destruction of someone, and not always the "offending party": "If I can't have her, no one will." "So, you are leaving me after all I have done for you. Well then, take that." "You stole her from me, now it's my turn to get even." "The whole day has gone so badly, I might as well complete it by ruining the little I did accomplish." . . . Given such moods and circumstances, harming another can be the proper and direct object of attraction. (1979, p. 748)

Each of these lines of imagined dialogue vividly evokes a sort of situation in which a person wants to cause harm, and Stocker persuasively argues that the harm caused is not necessarily regarded as itself something good, or as tending to produce some further consequence that is good. But does this disprove the claim that the object of desire is always wanted under the guise of the good? The answer depends crucially on what should count as the object of desire. Stocker assumes that "the object of desire," in the sense relevant to the guise of the good thesis, must be some end *achieved* by acting—someone's being harmed, or some further consequence resulting from someone's being harmed—rather than the desired action itself: my "getting even," in one way or another, for some perceived wrong done to me. If the latter is the object of desire, then the idea that the relevant desires represent their objects as good is no less plausible than the claim that to regard something as an act of "evening the score" is to regard it as good in at least one respect.[7]

Our purpose for the moment is not to give a detailed defense of this approach to Stocker's cases, but simply to bring out how supposed counterexamples to the guise of the good thesis can raise questions of interpretation whose resolution is no simpler than, and indeed closely intertwined with, the assessment of the thesis itself. As the literature on such cases amply illustrates, there is typically room for controversy about how to describe any given class of examples—about what to call the object of an agent's desire, how to characterize his attraction to it, and, consequently, whether to regard the cases as genuine counterexamples. The fact that such controversies break out is not just a reflection of philosophers' limitless appetite for dispute; it reflects the fact that the concepts employed in describing the examples are the very concepts whose proper employment the guise of the good thesis seeks to characterize. To suppose that the thesis admits of direct refutation by counterexample must presumably involve supposing that it asserts a necessary connection between two concepts—desiring and regarding-as-good—each of whose principles of application are clear enough. For if this were not assumed, how could we be confident in any given instance that the case we were considering was a clear-cut case of desiring that was clearly not a case of regarding-as-good? But the guise of the good thesis is surely intended as a contribution to the clarification of each of these concepts: It aims to say something about what each is. This does not imply that the thesis is correct in what it says, but it does suggest that the thesis must be assessed, not simply by appeal to cases, but by a systematic investigation of the importance of the concepts it links—of the role, if any, that each should play in a sound theory of action, and of the role of our power of reason in giving rise to action. In the absence of such an investigation, what we will be tallying will be, at best, people's intuitions about when to use the English words "desire" and "good," and we will lack any principled basis for deciding which intuitions to trust.

We have been making these points with reference to authors who attempt to refute the guise of the good thesis by counterexample, but related criticisms apply to authors who attempt to defend the thesis by appealing to intuitions about what desiring is. According to T. M. Scanlon, for instance, the idea of a mere disposition to act, where such a disposition lacks any evaluative component, "does not in fact fit very well with what we ordinarily mean by desire" since "desiring something involves having a tendency to see something good or desirable about it."[8] To support this contention, Scanlon cites Warren Quinn's well-known example of a man who finds himself with an unaccountable impulse to turn on every radio he sees: Such dispositions may be conceivable, but, Scanlon observes, their presence seems not to rationalize the actions they induce, and we are not inclined to call them "desires," or anyway not desires of the ordinary kind. There must be, Scanlon concludes, some connection between desire and positive evaluation, or at least between desire and the tendency to think that there is a "justifying reason" to pursue the desired object.

But even if this conclusion is sound, as we believe it is, we should want to be able to support it, not just by provoking intuitions about what desire *is*, but by arguing that this is what desire *must be*. After all, when we say that what we ordinarily mean by "desire" is a state that involves a tendency to regard the desired object as good, this is presumably not supposed to be merely a claim about what, as it happens, English-speakers are willing to call "desire": It is supposed to characterize a real, integral phenomenon that we pick out using this term. Moreover, the claim is presumably not that, as a matter of observed fact, there is a lawlike relation between two distinct kinds of psychological state, desiring and regarding-as-good. If the claim that desiring something involves having a tendency to see it as good were intended as this sort of empirical claim, then introspection and armchair reflection ought to give way to experiments and controlled studies. But this is clearly not the sort of validation that most advocates of the guise of the good thesis take it to require. The thesis is meant to state some sort of *necessary* truth about desire, something knowable on the basis of philosophical reflection rather than by observation and experiment. If this is the character of the thesis, however, it seems that it should be supported by principled argument, not just by intuitions about cases.

Defenders of the guise of the good thesis should also aim to give a principled defense of the thesis for another reason. For, however persuaded we are of the truth of the thesis, we will not really know, in the absence of a systematic investigation of the concepts it employs, what the thesis means. Our intuitive notion of "regarding as good" collects together diverse modes of consideration: A thing can be regarded as good, seemingly, in being regarded as enjoyable, conducive to health or well-being, profitable to oneself, just or fair, required by duty, expressive of friendship or kindness, etc. What is the principle that governs the inclusion of items on this list? Lacking such a principle, we will not be in a position to make well-grounded judgments about whether any given class of desires should or should not count as involving a presentation of something as good. But only an investigation of the systematic importance of the concepts of a good and of regarding something as good could supply us with such a principle.

Our project in what follows will be to mount a defense of the guise of the good thesis that brings out why the thesis *matters* by showing its place in a systematic account of the role of reason in action. We shall be arguing, in effect, that to understand what it is to desire something, in the sense that is relevant to the explanation of intentional action, we must understand desiring as bound together with representing-as-good; and we will be defending this claim, not as an observation about how we use the word "desire" or as an empirical law of human psychology, but as a necessary truth about a concept of central theoretical importance. But this need not commit us to denying that people sometimes desire things that in their considered opinion have nothing good about them. What we will deny is that it is possible to say what sort of thing such perverse desires are perverse cases *of* without appealing to the idea of a capacity to represent as good. This connection, we shall argue, is what anchors our understanding of the very concept of desire as it applies to rational creatures.

3. THE CAUSAL THEORY OF ACTION AND THE OBJECT OF DESIRE

To make a case for these connections, it is first necessary to contest a view about action and its explanation that is presupposed in much contemporary work in action theory. We believe that it is fundamentally this view, rather than the appeal of particular counterexamples, that underlies most contemporary opposition to the guise of the good thesis. In this section, we first sketch the view in question and then raise a difficulty for it. The view derives much of its appeal from its apparent inevitability. In pointing out a challenge it faces, we hope to show that it embodies a quite specific and questionable view about the shape a philosophical account of action must take.

The Problem of Action and the Causal Theory

To introduce the standard approach, and to bring out what can make it seem inevitable, it is useful to recall a common way of framing the question that a philosophical theory of action must answer. As David Velleman observes, philosophers of action tend to introduce their topic by quoting "a bit of Wittgensteinian arithmetic": "What is left over if I subtract the fact that my arm goes up from the fact that I raise my arm?"[9] Whatever Wittgenstein himself thought of the matter, contemporary philosophers who quote him typically assume that there should be a solution to this equation: a bodily intentional action should turn out to consist of a not-intrinsically-intentional bodily movement occurring in a context where certain further facts obtain. This much seems inevitable: For if I intentionally raise my arm, then certainly my arm rises; but not every arm-rising is an intentional arm-raising; so it seems that an intentional arm-raising must be an arm-rising about which certain further facts are true. And if this is right, then it seems that the task of the philosophy of action must be to specify which further facts are relevant.

Once this framework is in place, however, two points about the content of this specification will seem evident: first, that the facts in question must include facts about the *causes* of the relevant bodily movement; and second, that these causes must involve *mental states* of or *mental events* occurring in the acting subject. These assumptions constitute the framework within which the standard "causal theory of action" is elaborated. A bodily intentional action, it is held, consists in (1) a bodily movement (2) caused in some "right way" by (3) mental states or events of certain specific sorts. Different authors give different accounts of the sorts of mental states or events that are relevant, and there is debate over how to characterize the causal relation that must connect these with the resulting movement, but this general structure is common ground for most mainstream action theory.

Now, it is no surprise that the guise of the good thesis should look unmotivated to philosophers who conceive of action in this way. The whole point of the causal theory is to make the notion of an intentional action intelligible by showing that it just amounts to a bodily movement of an unproblematic sort with certain specific causal antecedents. If that is what an intentional action is, however, then the requirement that a representation of something as good should figure among these antecedents looks like a superfluous constraint on the mechanism. No doubt the agent who acts intentionally must act with the intent of doing something, and so a representation of *what he intends to do* must presumably figure among the causes of the movements he makes; but there is no obvious reason why the guidance of movement by such a representation need involve the presence of a *further* representation of that doing, or something achieved by that doing, as good. Any such constraint would seem to be a merely stipulative restriction on what we will count as "an intentional action," not a requirement that flows from the sheer idea of movement guided by thought, at least not if the causal theorist is right about what the guidance of movement by thought amounts to.

There might seem to be the possibility of motivating the guise of the good thesis by arguing that an agent's representation of what he intends to do must itself involve a representation of that action as good. For it is tempting to suppose that a conative attitude like wanting or intending must represent a certain action as *to be done*, and then to infer that this must involve representing it as *good* to do (or as something that ought to be done). But the causal theorist's analysis of the situation will not support this reading of the phrase "to be done." Insofar as it is right to say that an agent who wants or intends to do something must represent a certain action as "to be done," all this need mean, according to the causal theorist, is that he represents it as what will transpire if his want or intention is fulfilled. To say that such attitudes represent their objects as "to be done," that is, is simply to mark something about the "direction of fit" of these attitudes: They represent a certain state of affairs, not as already obtaining, but as what shall come to obtain if the relevant attitude is satisfied. But it is not obvious why this must entail any positive evaluation of the state of affairs in question: To suppose that it must is to confuse a "to be done" whose modal counterpart is "shall" with a "to be done" whose modal counterpart is "should."[10] In the context of the causal theorist's general understanding of what action is, then, the idea that conative attitudes must represent their objects as good will seems to be merely an additional restriction on the content of these attitudes, and one without evident motivation.

A defense of the guise of the good thesis, then, must begin by questioning the acceptability of the causal theorist's story about what action is. That is our aim in the remainder of this section: We shall argue that the causal theorist's project of explaining what it is for a bodily movement to be an intentional action by appeal to its psychological causes faces a basic difficulty, since the basic sort of psychological cause that such a theory must posit, a desire *to do something*, can itself be explained only by appeal to the notion of intentional action. It will emerge that the object of a desire to do is characterized by a distinctive kind of teleological organization, an organization that the causal theory cannot explain but must rather presuppose. It will be through seeking to understand this organization that we will, in the end, arrive at a rationale for the guise of the good thesis.

The Immediate Object of Desire

To bring out the difficulty facing the causal theory, it is necessary to consider more carefully what sorts of representations must figure among the causes of a bodily movement if that movement is to constitute an intentional action. There is considerable controversy among causal theorists about exactly what sorts of mental items must play a role here: whether all that is needed is a desire to achieve some end and a belief about how to attain it, or whether there must be further causal factors in play—intentions, plans, self-referential beliefs about the causes of my movements, etc. The difficulty we wish to raise, however, concerns a minimal commitment that any plausible version of the causal theory must make, namely the commitment that the causal antecedents of my intentionally doing A must include a desire *to do* A. It is hard to see how this could be denied: No doubt a person will often be moved to do A by further aims that are served *by* his doing A, but if he does A, and does so intentionally, then it seems that *one* thing that must move him is some motivating representation of doing A itself. Otherwise, whatever movements he makes will not themselves by guided by thought in the way that the adverb "intentionally" demands: They may be movements that are caused by a representation of some further end, but they will not themselves be realizations of any aim of the agent.

We have called this motivating representation a desire (and we will follow the usual practice of speaking indifferently of what the agent "desires" and what he "wants"), but for our purposes here, little hangs on this designation. All that is necessary is that the attitude in question should be a representation of what is to be done that plays a causal role in bringing the agent to do that very thing. We refer to this representation as a "desire" in deference to a long tradition of using this term to name the condition that produces animate movement,[11] but if some theorist wishes to insist that the attitude that moves us to act must be something else, we need not quarrel with this: The points we will make turn wholly on the *object* of the relevant attitude, the thing that we normally express with the infinitive phrase "to do A." The question we wish to press is whether the causal theorist is entitled to take attitudes toward this sort of object for granted in stating his theory; and if he is not, how his theory might do without them.

It is a striking fact about standard expositions of the causal theory that they tend to insist on rewriting desire-ascriptions that we would colloquially express by saying

(1) *S* wants to do *A*.

by transforming what follows "wants" into a proposition, as in

(2) *S* wants that *S* does *A*.[12]

This insistence on treating desire as taking a propositional object is of course not new to the causal theory: The idea that desire is a "propositional attitude" goes back at least to Russell.[13] But this view of desire has a special attraction in the context of the causal theorist's project: It helps to hold in place the idea that the satisfaction-conditions of desire do not raise any special problems over and above those raised by propositional attitudes in general. What is it for a desire to be satisfied? It is, causal theorists characteristically answer, simply for the condition it sets on the world to have come true, for a certain fact to have come to obtain. If desire can be treated in this way, as having for its object what Michael Smith calls a "way the world could be,"[14] then the idea that desire represents its object as *to be done*, whereas belief represents its object as *the case*, is to be explained, not by appeal to a distinction between two fundamentally different sorts of representational content, but rather by reference to the different causal relations in which representational states with the same sort of content normally or properly stand. And this is how causal theorists characteristically explain the distinction. Smith provides a helpfully explicit statement of this idea:

> [T]he difference between beliefs and desires in terms of direction of fit comes down to a difference between the counterfactual dependence of a belief and a desire that *p* on a perception that *not p*: roughly, a belief that *p* is a state that tends to go out of existence in the presence of a perception that *not p*, whereas a desire that *p* is a state that tends to endure, disposing the subject to bring it about that *p*.[15]

Other causal theorists would explain the "direction of fit" of desire somewhat differently, but the general approach pursued here seems to be crucial to the theory: for it is crucial to the theory that what it is for an agent to perform an intentional action should be explicable in terms of concepts independent of the concept of intentional action itself. In particular, a causal theorist must suppose, on pain of circularity, that the concept of desire (or whatever representational state is supposed to guide action) need not itself be explained by appeal to the concept of intentional action. But then the *object* of desire must presumably be some outcome of an unproblematic kind, some recognizable state of affairs, and the fact that this outcome is achieved *through intentional action* must be explained in terms of a certain special sort of causal process having contributed to its coming about. The assumption that "to be doneness" can be factored out of the object of desire, so to speak, and represented as part of the way in which the attitude in question relates to its object, as part of its "direction of fit," is thus crucial to the project. For if this were not possible—if the kind of desire that gives rise to action were itself explicable only as a desire to act intentionally in a certain way—then the explanatory program of the causal theory would be compromised. We would not be able to say what an intentional action is by appeal to the idea of a not-intrinsically-intentional bodily movement plus certain psychological causes operating in the right way, for the nature of the relevant psychological causes could not be explained without appeal to the notion of intentional action itself.

The idea that the object of desire is a certain state of affairs or proposition, the nature of whose obtaining can be treated as unproblematic, is thus a crucial prop to the causal theory. But what is the state of affairs toward which a desire of form (1) is directed? On the face of it, such desires do not appear to take a propositional object: What follows the attitude verb is not a whole proposition but merely a certain sort of verbal predicate, and one that appears in a curiously infinitival form. And although grammar may permit us to transform this object (awkwardly) into apparently propositional structures like the one in (2), problems begin to arise as soon as we ask when the condition that S *does A* counts as fulfilled.[16] For what condition on the world is set by the freestanding English sentence "S does A"? When does this "state of affairs" obtain? At any given time, a particular action will be either still underway, in which case we describe it in the progressive, "S is A-ing," or already complete, in which case we describe it in the perfect, "S has A-ed."[17] By using a verb in the infinitive to express what is wanted, desire-ascriptions of form (1) escape the problem of specifying which of these alternatives is in question; but we cannot construct a complete proposition setting a definite truth-condition without making a choice.[18] Should we, then, say that the propositional correlate of (3) is

(3) S wants that S will have A-ed?

This seems wrong inasmuch as it does not capture the desire *to bring the relevant state of affairs about* that is a part of (1). Would my desire to go to the store count as fulfilled if I were blown there by a powerful wind or miraculously transported there by God? The relevant want might lapse, of course, if my only reason for wanting to go to the store was that I wanted to have got there. Still, it seems that my original want would not have been *fulfilled* unless my having arrived was my own doing. But on the other hand, (1) certainly does not merely amount to

(4) S wants that S is A-ing

for this would be compatible with S's being indifferent about whether he actually completes the relevant action.

Nor, again, does it help to conjoin the two propositions to form

(5) S wants that S is A-ing and S will have A-ed

for the want involved in (1) is not just to have been in two unrelated states, but to have arrived in the end state in virtue of having done all of the A-ing that was required to A. But if we opt for something like

(6) S wants that S is A-ing as much as necessary in order that S will have A-ed

then it seems that such understanding as we have of the contained proposition here depends on our knowing that (6) is supposed to be equivalent to (1). For how much A-ing is necessary? Not much if I am blown by a wind, but that is plainly not what is intended: the point is that I should do enough of it to satisfy the want *to do A*—where this means, presumably to effect the condition of my having done A through a process of intentional action.

This is a long-winded way of bringing out something about the object of a desire to do A that is perhaps obvious, but that presentations of the causal theory tend to ignore: namely, that the object wanted is not some final state of affairs that might be brought about either intentionally or non-intentionally, but rather an object that "exists" only insofar as a certain intentional action has been carried through to its completion. This makes difficulties for any attempt to explain such wanting in the causal theorist's way, by appeal to the generic notion of representation of a "way the world could be" and the generic idea of a causal tendency. For to want *to do A* is not merely to want to be in some terminal state. It is, as we have seen, not to want to be in any mere state, but rather to want what is essentially a goal-directed course of action: "enough A-ing to have A-ed," as we were led to put it. And equally, to want to do A is not merely to want that the relevant course of action should occur just anyhow. It is, as we have seen, to want to be oneself the source of the relevant action: to want it to be *one's own doing*. When I want to do A, in short, the content of my want is of a form such that the world can only come to conform to that content insofar as it not only comes *to be* a certain way, but does so as the outcome of a goal-directed process guided by the agent. Indeed, even this way of putting the matter leaves the outcome and the process too external to one another: To represent my doing A is to represent, as it were, a kind of state of affairs whose obtaining *is* my having intentionally caused it to be.[19]

These observations do not constitute an objection to just any philosopher who asserts that an intentional action is a bodily movement with certain psychological causes, but they do present difficulties for philosophers who put forward this proposition in a reductive spirit, as a step toward an analysis of the concept of intentional action in terms of concepts better understood—philosophers who seek, by means of this connection, to give a substantive answer to Wittgenstein's question.[20] For they show that the relevant psychological causes must include representations whose nature can be explained only by appeal to the notion of intentional action itself: representations that represent their object as "to be done" in a sense that must mean precisely "to be done intentionally."[21] But if we cannot hope to give an account of wanting to do A that is independent of the idea of intentional action, then neither can we hope to give a reductive account of intentional action as a matter of movement caused in the right way by such wantings. An account of what it is to want to do *A* must rather presuppose an account of action, an account of the kind of event (*S*'s doing *A*) whose coming to be is the subject's intentionally causing it to be.[22]

4. ACTION, FORM, AND GOODNESS

We can hardly claim to have shown that causal theorists have no room for maneuver in responding to this difficulty, but we hope at least to have brought out a significant commitment that such theorists must undertake: They are committed to treating the sort of object at which an agent primarily aims, a *doing of A*, not as an unproblematic given, but as something itself requiring analysis. If the foregoing considerations are sound, constructing an account of action that eliminates reference to this sort of object is more difficult than is commonly supposed. The ease with which we pass from "my raising my arm" to "my arm's rising" can encourage us to think that we can hang onto the sort of thing whose coming to exist would satisfy an agent's aim while subtracting its intentionality; but in fact, as we have seen, the sort of object that an agent primarily aims to realize is precisely this: an action consisting of phases ordered intentionally toward a certain end (his having *A*-ed). No doubt it is true that, where such an object has come to exist, it will be possible to describe the movements that have occurred in terms that do not imply that an intention has been realized therein. But it does not follow that it must be possible to give an account of what it consists in for an intentional action to have occurred employing only such terms; and indeed, we have seen at least *prima facie* reason to suppose that this is *not* possible.

The importance of this result, for our purposes, is that it forces us to face anew the question of what intentional action is. The upshot of the last section is that we cannot explain the nature of this sort of event or process—an agent's intentionally doing *A*—by appeal to the idea of some unproblematic kind of happening with certain specific psychological causes. Rather, we must explain the nature of the relevant psychological causes by appeal to their directedness toward precisely this sort of process or event. But this simply returns us to the question of how to characterize the sort of process or event in question. The schema "*S* is (intentionally) doing *A*" marks the object of our interest, but invoking it does not by itself clarify how expressions of this form function, or what sort of conceptual surrounding they need to get a grip.

Our aim in the remainder of this essay is to argue for a broadly Aristotelian view of the required surrounding: a view on which the general notion of a goal-directed action is explained by linking it with the idea of the *form* of the subject that acts, and the more specific notion of an intentional action must be explained by linking it with the idea of a form that essentially involves the capacity for self-consciousness. This amounts to a fundamentally different sort of approach to understanding action from the sort pursued by causal theorists: The aim is not to specify conditions under which some not-intrinsically-intentional process amounts to an intentional action, but rather to explain intentional action as an irreducibly distinctive *type* of process, one that is to be characterized by bringing out the specific implications involved in positing a process of this kind, and by clarifying what *other* sorts of propositions must also be true of something that can be the subject of such processes. The guise of the good thesis will turn out to be a commitment that follows from this Aristotelian approach to saying what action is.

To bring out the attractions of this approach, it will be useful first to reflect on how to characterize the wider genus of which intentional action is a species. Contemporary discussions of the guise of the good thesis often treat it as an isolated claim about rational, intentional action. If that were right, the thesis would look implausible from the start. For clearly not all action is rational action. Animals and infants lack the powers distinctive of a rational agent: They cannot deliberate about reasons, form prior intentions, or reflect self-consciously on what they are doing. But although they are not *rational* agents, it would be perverse to deny that they are agents in some sense: not just the passive subjects of various events and processes, but the active source of certain happenings in which they are involved. When the dog *runs excitedly to the door* or the infant child *turns toward the sound of its mother's voice*, these are clearly self-originated, goal-directed actions of a sort. If they are actions, however, and if "action" here does not mean something utterly different from what it means in the rational case, then it seems that an account of rational action should conform to a shape that applies, at least in its general outlines, to the nonrational case as well. But if nonrational action can be accounted for without any reference to the notion of goodness, why must reference to this notion suddenly appear in the rational case?

This line of thought suggests that a principled defense of the guise of the good thesis should begin with a defense of a more basic principle, one that posits a connection between goodness and action-in-general. And this, in fact, is how we will argue for the thesis: by showing that it is the product of (i) a general point about the connection between the idea of action and the idea of the good of a thing; and (ii) a special point about the shape this connection takes in the rational case. Briefly, the thought is this: The most general idea of an *action* is the idea of a movement or change that in some sense comes "from the subject," rather than merely being the result of forces acting on the subject "from without." But this distinction between *self*-movement or *self*-change, on the one hand, and movement or change whose cause is external, on the other, must be drawn against the background of an idea of form which brings with it a standard of goodness. This connection holds for action in general, but in the rational case it takes a particular shape. For to be a rational creature means just this: to live by *thought*, which is to say by the employment of concepts. Hence the shape that the general connection between action and goodness takes in a rational creature will be one that involves thought: Rational action is a kind of movement that has its source in a subject's power to bring things under the concept *good*. The remaining pages attempt to fill in the picture just sketched. The rest of this section discusses the first part of the argument: the general connection between self-movement and goodness. The next section discusses the special form this connection takes in the rational case.

CHARACTERIZING SELF-MOVEMENT

There is broad agreement among contemporary philosophers of action that autonomous, rational action is not just an isolated topic, but one species of a wider genus that also includes more primitive forms of goal-directed activity. But how can we define the wider category? What *is* "goal-directed activity," and how is it distinguished from other kinds of worldly happening?

It will not do simply to say that a goal-directed activity is anything that can fill the "*A*" position in the schema

(7) *S* is doing *A*.

It is true that such propositions in general describe the here and now by relating it to a possible future situation: to assert a proposition of form (7) is to posit an outcome toward which *S* is tending, namely, its having done *A*. And by the same token, to assert (7) is to leave logical space for the possibility of failure: It can be true that *S* was doing *A* but never did *A*. But not every instance of this schema is goal-directed in the interesting sense. The bare schema "*S* is doing *A*" admits such substitutions as "The tree is falling over," "The smoke is rising to the ceiling," "The tidal wave is rushing toward the shore"; and these are clearly not instances of genuinely goal-directed activity. To count as genuinely goal-directed, one wants to say, a movement or change must in some sense *come from* the subject, and must be *for the sake of* the end. This, indeed, is a traditional way of defining an agent: agents are self-movers, things that themselves pursue ends. But when does a movement count as a self-movement, or as done for the sake of an end?

Having rejected the sort of approach that seeks to specify when a movement counts as an intentional action by appeal to its psychological causes, and having in any case widened our focus from intentional action in particular to goal-directed activity generally, we must seek a characterization of self-movement that does not appeal to specific causes, but rather identifies self-movement as a distinctive *type* of event or process. We must, that is, identify a kind of event-description that is as such a description of a movement by a subject for the sake of an end, a type of proposition of form (7) from which we can correctly infer *S is doing A goal-directedly*. But what role does the proposition *S is doing A* have to be playing in order for this adverbial attachment to be appropriate?

We can make progress on this question by observing that the truth of some but not all progressive propositions can be explained by adverting to further, more embracing progressive propositions with the same subject. Thus we can offer such explanations as

> Why is the plant budding?
> —Because it is growing a new leaf.
> Why is the cat crouching there waiting?
> —Because it is stalking a bird.
> Why is he mixing eggs and flour?
> —Because he's baking a cake.

But of course we do not suppose that we can explain the rain's falling to the earth by the fact that it is watering the plants, or indeed by reference to any larger purpose belonging to the rain. To suppose that we *could* explain the rain's falling in this way would be to take, as they say, an animistic view of nature. And nor will we suppose that the rain's falling to the earth itself explains the lesser phases in which this process consists: To suppose that the rain is falling past the treetops because it is falling to the earth would be equally animistic. These observations are clues to the solution of our problem: They suggest that a subject S is capable of the kind of goal-directed activity of which inanimate nature is incapable just if it is a potential subject of explanations of the form

> (8) S is doing A^* because S is doing A

where, intuitively, doing A^* is a way or means or part of doing A. We can call such propositions *judgments of individual teleology*, for they explain a lesser activity in which an individual subject is engaged by linking it to a more-encompassing activity in which that same subject is engaged, and thereby represent the accomplishment of the more-encompassing activity as a sort of *end* whose pursuit can explain things done in the service of it.[23]

This observation suggests a way of stating a condition under which a progressive proposition of form (7) ascribes goal-directed activity to its subject: It does so just if it can figure on the right-hand side of a proposition of form (8): that is, if it can figure as the explainer of a less embracing progressive with the same subject.[24] A proposition that can play this role represents its subject as engaged in a process that can explain its own realization, a process that can be the cause of its own coming to be, in whatever sense of cause is implied by the "because" in such explanations. And it seems that for *any* temporally extended process of A-ing, if the process is goal-directed, there will be some true explanation of this form in which the process figures. For if the process of A-ing is temporally extended, there will be moments at which S is A-ing but it is not yet true that S has A-ed—moments at which the process is underway but not yet complete. But if there is no part or phase of this process, A^*, which is occurring at some such moment and which can be explained in a judgment of form (8), then it seems that there can be no basis for saying that the accumulation of parts or phases toward the completion of the larger process, S's having A-ed, is goal-directed: The aim of the whole played no role in the realization of the parts. So it seems that, at least for temporally extended processes of doing *A*, it is a necessary and sufficient condition for their being goal-directed activities that they should be capable of figuring in true explanations of form (8).[25]

An indication that this characterization of goal-directedness is on the right track is that it gives a clear interpretation to the intuitive ideas that a goal-directed movement must (i) come from the subject; and (ii) be made for the sake of the end. For on the one hand, we have identified a kind of explanation that says why a subject is up to one thing by adverting to something else that same subject is up to, rather than by tracing the subject's activity to the influence of some other thing. And on the other hand, this kind of explanation says why the subject is up to something by saying what further end the subject's doing that thing would serve. Moreover, our characterization seems to be extensionally correct. For, in the first place, judgments that ascribe intentional actions meet our criterion: My intentionally doing one thing can explain my intentionally doing another thing. But our criterion is also satisfied by other kinds of progressive judgments: As the previous examples indicate, this general form of explanation can apply to nonrational animals and indeed to plants. Its application marks the feature of living things we are tracking when we say that what goes on with them is subject to teleological explanation.

Our criterion thus captures what is right in the idea that the sphere of the goal-directed is wider than the sphere of the intentional. At the same time, it leaves us with an agenda of problems: to explain, in an equally abstract way, what distinguishes the category of goal-directed progressives that ascribe, not merely the kind of purposiveness that we find in plant life, but the more determinate kind that we find among *animate* creatures, ones that can act in response to the promptings of sensation and appetite; and again, to explain what distinguishes within the latter category the further subcategory of animate goal-directed progressives that ascribe rational, intentional action.

Action and Form

For the moment, however, our aim is not to take up these special problems but to make a general point about the conditions under which any judgment implying goal-directedness gets a grip. The general point is this: Judgments ascribing goal-directed self-movement or self-change only have application to things to which a certain kind of *form* is attributable, a form that, in turn, makes room for a notion of what is *good* for things of that kind.

We will try to give a principled account of the connection between goal-directedness and form in a moment, but first let us simply observe that, for many such judgments, the point is obviously true. If we begin by considering, not rational action, but the more rudimentary kinds of goal-directed self-change or self-movement characteristic of plants and animals, it is plain enough that recognizing them involves bringing to bear a conception of the nature of the kind in question. In recognizing that a certain plant is, e.g., budding, as opposed to, say, developing a cancer, we are relating what is going on with it to a more general conception of how things go in the life of that kind of plant. In recognizing a cat as pursuing a mouse or as fleeing in response to a loud noise, we regard processes in which it is presently engaged as organized by general aims that belong to it as a cat. In these sorts of instances, at least, the general idea of processes in which a certain individual figures as an agent pursuing a goal seems to get a grip only against a certain sort of background: only inasmuch as the individual in question is regarded as an instance of a certain kind of thing, a kind with a certain characteristic form or nature, a kind to which certain ends and activities belong as such.

It is one of Aristotle's characteristic thoughts that ascriptions of self-movement or self-change to individuals presuppose such a background: for he holds that, in general, the topics of movement and change are to be understood against the background of the natures of things, where a nature is a "principle of motion and change," so that movements and changes that do not come about by chance are understood as the realizations of potentialities belonging to the natures of things that move and change; and he holds that the possibility of *self*-movement and *self*-change must be understood against the background of the special sort of form or nature that he calls a "soul."[26] This Aristotelian thought is the inspiration for our account, but our aim here is not to do Aristotle exegesis, but to show why the thought might be attractive in its own right. If ascriptions of self-movement to individuals presuppose a conception of the forms that those individuals bear, why is this so? In the remainder of this section, we will sketch an account of this connection. Our argument will be less than decisive at several points, but it should at least clarify why, given certain general views about the role of kinds in explaining the activities of individuals, the idea of a connection between self-movement, form, and goodness will seem compelling.

The first step is to note the striking and remarkable way in which ascriptions of goal-directed activity link a subject's present to a certain future condition toward which it is tending. It is not merely that, if S is doing A goal-directedly, and if nothing interferes, then it will eventually be true that S did A: that much is also true of "The smoke is rising to the ceiling." What is distinctive of goal-directed progressives is their implication that aspects of S's present activity are happening *because* they tend toward this future situation (S's having done A). Now, that should sound strange: How can a situation that does not yet exist explain a situation that does exist? A standard sort of objection to teleological explanation is that it would require some sort of "backward causation" or "pull from the future," and that such notions are unintelligible. But if we are convinced that progressive propositions that imply goal-directedness are sometimes true—and it is hard to see how we could even begin to think about living things and their activities without taking this for granted—then our task must be to understand what it can be about a subject that allows such propositions to be true of it. What can it be about an individual here and now in virtue of which its present activity is explained by an as-yet-unrealized end toward which it is tending?

We can begin to see how this might be made intelligible by noting that goal-directed progressives characterize a subject here and now by relating it, not necessarily to *the actual* future, but rather to *its own* future—to a possible outcome that would count as something the subject itself effected, rather than something that merely happened to it. Part of the point here is not special to goal-directed progressives in particular: in general, a progressive proposition of the form

(7) S is doing A

is not necessarily falsified because the relevant future state of affairs (S's having done A) does not come to obtain; it is falsified only if this was not the state toward which S was tending, the state that would have come to obtain had nothing interfered with its activity. In this sense, any progressive proposition of form (7) relates its subject, not to the actual future whatever it may be, but rather to a possible future that would count as the subject's own. Now, the crucial Aristotelian thought is that the distinction between a future that counts as the subject's own and one that does not must be drawn against the background of a conception of *what the subject is* and of what belongs to being that kind of thing—that is, of the form it bears and the nature of things that bear this form. This claim may initially sound dark and metaphysical, but we can bring it down to earth by restating it as a point about the relation between truths of the form we have been considering and truths of certain other characteristic shapes. The thought, in effect, is that where there are truths of the form (7), there must also be true *judgments of form-attribution* of the form

(9) S is an F

and true *form-characterizing judgments* of the form

(10) Fs do α (in conditions C)

where the description of the activity characteristic of the kind, α, need not in general be identical to the description that characterizes what the individual is doing (A), although in the simplest sort of case it might be. In the more general case, doing A will be some specific form or manifestation of α-ing, as rolling down this hill is a specific manifestation of rolling (*S is rolling down this hill; S is a bronze sphere; Bronze spheres roll [when on uneven ground]*). The relation that must obtain between A and some corresponding α would not be easy to specify, but in any case the Aristotelian thought is: There must be one.

Propositions of form (10) are general judgments about Fs, but they are stated without a quantifier, and are meant to state what are intuitively truths about the nature of Fs, truths that hold "if nothing interferes" or "other things equal" in the sense that they hold, not necessarily without exception, but rather in such a way that an F's doing α in conditions C is to be expected, while an F's *not* doing α in conditions C calls for special explanation.[27] If propositions of forms (7), (9), and (10) hold, and if A-ing is a form or manifestation of α-ing, then it is intelligible how it could already be true to say of S that it is headed toward the condition of having A-ed, and will reach that condition if nothing interferes. A subject can be *tending* toward a certain result, in the manner of (7), even though that result may not actually come about, precisely because a subject can have certain general *tendencies*, where describing a tendency is describing not how things *will* come out in any given instance but how things *do* come out if nothing interferes. But, the Aristotelian thought goes, general tendencies belong to individuals only inasmuch as those individuals bear some general form: for the very idea of a tendency is the idea of what happens "if nothing interferes," and the distinction between interference and noninterference would have no application to an individual thing if there were not some basis for distinguishing between those episodes in its existence that manifest the sort of thing it is and those that do not. The case where nothing interferes is the case where a thing manifests its own nature, the traits that characterize the sort of thing it is. So in committing ourselves to the distinction between interference and noninterference, we commit ourselves to regarding individuals as bearers of forms, and the forms themselves as characterized by general principles of movement and change, principles that are explanatory, other things equal, of the activities of the individual bearers of the forms in question.

The connections described so far hold not just for individuals who can be the subject of goal-directed progressives, but for any individual who can be the subject of progressive judgments of the form S *is doing A:* This attribution of a process-in-progress is possible only against the background of various general tendencies, and such tendencies can belong to an individual only in virtue of its being a certain kind of thing, the bearer of some general form. The special problem about goal-directed progressives was their implication that the outcome toward which S tends in doing A is in some sense what explains the parts or phases in which the realization of this tendency consists. The problem of understanding how goal-directed progressives can be true is thus the problem of understanding, not just how a certain future can be a subject's own, but how it can be so in a way that explains the subject's present activity.

Now, if the general problem about how a certain future can be a subject's own is solved by noting that subjects of change belong to kinds characterized by general tendencies to change, we should expect this special problem to be solved by noting that subjects capable of goal-directed activity belong to kinds of a special sort, kinds characterized by tendencies with a distinctive structure. Indeed, the general shape of the required structure follows from the very statement of the problem. How can the outcome toward which S is tending explain the occurrence of the process that proceeds toward it, and explain it in such a way that the whole process is intelligible as a case of self-movement or self-change, a process "coming from the subject" in the intuitive sense that we are seeking to explicate? Well, in the first place, the tendencies that characterize the kind to which S belongs must be tendencies toward some definite outcome or final condition, not merely tendencies that have no intrinsic limit, like the tendency of fire to spread or of iron to rust. They must, as we can put it, be tendencies toward a definite *end*. Furthermore, they must be tendencies whose being set in motion is in some sense due to the subject itself. They must, in other words, be tendencies of a special sort, which we can call *powers*, to mark the fact that the normal cause of their coming to operate (or, as we can say, to *act*) is not just some alien force acting on the subject, but a cause whose operation itself expresses the subject's nature.[28]

What this might mean, more concretely, is that the cause that summons a power to act does not depend on conditions whose holding is simply an accident given the nature of the kind of thing in question. That its powers are brought to act must be something for which the kind by its nature provides: If a given power's acting depends on its being in condition C, then the kind must have further powers that tend to secure that C holds—as always, if nothing interferes. And conversely: If P is a power of a kind K, then the acts of P must themselves be explanatory (other things equal) of Ks being in a condition in which various of their other powers operate. This is what secures that the end toward which an act tends is explanatory of the processes that contribute to its own realization: for, by contributing to the existence of the kind of thing whose nature it is to realize that sort of end, the achievement of that end is, in a sense, *the explanation of itself*—not through some occult form of backward causation, but by being an effect whose coming to be contributes to the very conditions that make its own coming to be no accident. In short, on this broadly Aristotelian view, a subject that is capable of goal-directed activity must belong to a kind characterized by powers that form a sort of self-sustaining system. For it is against this background that the idea of a subject capable of moving or changing *itself* becomes intelligible: Acts of self-movement or self-change are understood as movements or changes that are explicable by reference to such powers, and the goal-directedness of such acts consists in the fact that their tending toward a certain end is no accident given the general nature of the kind of subject that undergoes them.

This description of the structure of powers that characterizes a kind capable of goal-directed activity is highly abstract, but it should become more tangible if we reflect on how aptly it describes the sort of order we find in living things. Any given kind of living thing is characterized by a manifold of powers directed toward various ends, powers that constitute a sort of self-maintaining system: one such that the realization of any one of its ends supplies the condition for the realization of various others, and these in turn of others, in such a way that the kind "makes itself exist," so to speak. This self-maintenance occurs at two levels: first, individuals of the kind in question maintain their own existence through such processes as nourishing themselves, defending themselves from threats, healing from injuries, etc.; and second, the kind itself maintains its existence through reproductive processes in which members of the kind make others like themselves. For any given kind of living thing, we can describe powers that it has that subserve each of these two sorts of self-maintenance, powers whose various acts contribute to fulfilling the conditions in which life of that kind can continue. And it is characteristic of these powers that they not only contribute variously to the maintenance of the kind of living thing in question, but thereby contribute to the maintenance of themselves and one another in sound order: By seeking out and consuming nourishing food, a creature makes it possible for its injuries to heal; by healing its injuries, it makes it possible to seek out and consume nourishing food, etc. Indeed, this reciprocal interdependence extends to all of the essential powers of a living thing, for precisely insofar as they are essential, they are each needed to contribute to the maintenance of the system of which they are powers, but equally they each depend on all the other powers to operate in a way that maintains that system, and thus makes each power possible.[29]

The foregoing has been a highly programmatic attempt to characterize the background that must be in place if there is to be room for the ascription of goal-directed activity to individuals. Our proposals are obviously disputable at many points. Our purpose has merely been to sketch an approach, one that we hope looks recognizably Aristotelian, and that contrasts in important respects with the sort of approach pursued by contemporary causal theorists. Whereas the causal theorist's approach to characterizing action is reductive, this approach might be called holistic: It aims, not to replace talk of intentional processes (or teleological processes more generally) with something less mysterious, but to dispel the air of mystery in a different way, by showing how ascriptions of the relevant processes have a place within an intelligible system of types of proposition—a kind of system that we cannot easily do without if we hope to make sense of living things at all. If we are right that progressive propositions about individuals presuppose general truths of form (10), and that goal-directed progressives, in particular, can apply where such truths characterize a certain sort of self-maintaining system of powers, then some such system must be the background against which goal-directed progressives can be true of individuals at all.

Form and Goodness

Our aim was not only to bring out a connection between goal-directed activity and the presence of a certain sort of form but also to bring out a connection between this sort of form and the application of the concept *good*. We can now finally turn to this latter connection.

It is not a new suggestion that what it is for S to be good depends on what kind of thing S is. Peter Geach famously suggested that "good" is a "logically attributive adjective" that has sense only in relation to some substantial kind, and that can vary in sense depending on which kind is in question; and a number of other authors have argued that at least certain uses of evaluative language in application to the states and activities of individuals presuppose judgments about the kinds to which they belong and the natures of those kinds.[30] Thus a rosebush is said to be doing poorly if it does not bud and flower in the season proper to rosebushes, and a human being's tooth development is said to be defective if he does not come to have the normal thirty-two adult teeth. The evident aptness of such evaluations, as far as they go, suggests that at least *some* sorts of evaluations are kind-relative. But it certainly seems a long and dubious way from here to the topic of intentional action; and lacking a principled account of *why* the kind to which individuals belong should constitute a standard for the deeds of those individuals, it is easy to doubt whether a kind-relative notion of goodness has any bearing on the deliberation of a rational agent.

We will consider how these issues bear on the deliberation of a rational agent in the next section. Before turning to that topic, however, we need to say something general about why, if being a goal-directed agent presupposes being the bearer of a form in the sense described above, such forms should equally constitute evaluative standards for the acts of the agents who bear them. The answer will be, in a way, disappointingly quick. It is that this is something we have already conceded in all but name in assigning the notion of form the place we have given it in our account. To represent an individual as the bearer of a form, in the sense we have been specifying, is to represent that individual as a sort of thing that as such pursues certain ends, ends that stand, when things are going well, in a sort of balance or equilibrium, a balance on which the existence of such things depends. To the extent that such a thing achieves those ends, it succeeds in pursuits that belong to it as such. And by the same token, to the extent that it fails, it fails in pursuits that belong to it as such. Inasmuch as the form in question is essential to individuals that bear it, these pursuits belong inalienably to those individuals: They cannot cease to be pursuers of these ends without ceasing to be. And inasmuch as their particular doings are to be understood as acts of powers directed toward certain general ends, these ends will be the measures of those acts, in the way that any act is a success or failure in virtue of its fulfilling or not fulfilling its end. That attributing a form to a thing, in this sense, involves attributing to it something that is a standard or measure of its activity, a standard relative to which it may be acting well or poorly, is thus a truism, not a controversial addition to what has already been said.

A certain standard of goodness for a thing follows inevitably from its belonging to a kind characterized by a functionally organized system of powers: This, we suppose, is the crux of Aristotle's famous "function argument."[31] If the objection to this is that it illegitimately infers an "ought" from an "is," we are not sure that we understand the charge. The sort of "saying what a thing is" that is at issue here is: ascribing to it a certain form, where a form is something that as such involves directedness toward certain ends. If the question is supposed to be why the thing at issue ought to pursue those ends, we ask: From what standpoint is this question posed? If the thing in question genuinely is a bearer of such-and-such a form, then it *is* a pursuer of such-and-such ends, and essentially so. *It* can no more renounce these ends than it can cease to be itself. But if the objection is that there can be no such thing as a "form" in the sense that would validate these claims, then we would want to dispute this, though to confront the various challenges to this notion would be too large a task to take on here. We hope the foregoing discussion suggests, at any rate, that the costs of giving up this notion would be significant. For it suggests that the notion belongs, not simply to some strange pre-modern metaphysical outlook, but to a characterization of the underlying structure of forms of thought and speech that we all constantly employ, and whose soundness few philosophers seriously question. If the Aristotelian standpoint on goal-directed activity is right, then to regard something as a goal-directed agent is necessarily to regard it as the bearer of a certain form, and thus as directed toward a certain system of goods, goods the pursuit of which orients, more or less remotely, its various particular doings.

5. GOODNESS AND REASON

But what does all this have to do with the claim that we must act under the *guise* of the good? How do the points we have made about the connection between self-movement and goodness underwrite a connection between intentional action and the *representation* of something as good? The connection, we shall suggest, turns on a point about the special form that this connection takes in a creature capable of *reasoning* about how to act.

Human beings are rational creatures; our capacity for action is a rational capacity. What does this mean? Thomas Aquinas explains the point as follows:

> The will is a rational appetite. Now every appetite is only of something good. The reason of this is that the appetite is nothing else than an inclination of a person desirous of a thing towards that thing. Now every inclination is to something like and suitable to the thing inclined. . . . But it must be noted that, since every inclination results from a form, the natural appetite results from a form existing in the nature of things, while the sensitive appetite, as also the intellective or rational appetite, which we call the will, follows from an apprehended form. Therefore, just as the natural appetite tends to good existing in a thing; so the animal or voluntary appetite tends to a good which is apprehended. Consequently, in order that the will tend to anything, it is requisite, not that this be good in very truth, but that it be apprehended as good.[32]

This passage is useful for our purposes because it argues for the guise of the good thesis in just the way that we have been seeking to argue for it: by deriving it from a more general thought about the connection between goodness and the inclination to do something, together with a thought about the special character of this connection in the rational case. The focus of this last section will be on this connection between the thought that we possess a faculty of *rational* inclination and the claim that we pursue the *apprehended* or *apparent* good.

KINDS OF INCLINATION

Aquinas says that whereas the "natural appetite" of nonsentient agents like plants results from "a form existing in the nature of things," and tends toward a good that exists in them *simpliciter,* both the "sensitive appetite" of nonrational animals and the "rational appetite" of human beings follow, in different ways, from an "apprehended form" and tend toward "a good which is apprehended." His point can be expressed as follows. A plant just belongs to a certain living kind, a kind that has a particular way of inhabiting its environment, taking in nourishment, making possible its own growth and reproduction, and so on. In representing a certain plant as engaged in some teleologically structured process (growing a new leaf, taking in nourishment from the soil, etc.), we see what is happening with it as oriented toward obtaining something suitable to that kind of plant. We thus represent the prospect of obtaining the relevant good as in a certain way already active in what the plant is doing here and now, even though the good in question has yet to be obtained: The plant's present activity is already informed by its natural tendency, as a plant of such-and-such a kind, to pursue certain goods. Or speaking in Aquinas's way: The form of the relevant good already exists in the plant's nature, as something toward which it is naturally inclined.

A nonrational animal too acts in fulfillment of various teleologically oriented inclinations, but it stands in a different kind of relationship to these inclinations in virtue of having the powers of sensation and appetite. It does not just inhabit an environment; it can perceive its environment and react to it. It does not just take in nourishment; it can seek it out. Generally, animals do not just *have* inclinations to pursue certain goods as a part of their nature; their nature involves their *apprehending* particular things that are good for them (which is not to say: apprehending *that particular things are good for them*) and pursuing those apprehended things. So those things toward which an animal is inclined—the forms that its inclinations seek to realize—are not just fixed by its nature but are present to it in virtue of particular perceptible things having made an impression on it. In this sense, its way of life essentially involves apprehension: It pursues apprehended forms.

A rational creature is different again. Such a creature does not merely have certain purposes that it naturally pursues, as a plant does, and it does not merely feel appetites for perceived goods, as a nonrational animal does. A rational creature is one that apprehends its environment and its good in a still more profound sense: It is a creature that brings its representations under general concepts, and this means that it can not only acquire particular representations of the world through perception but think in the abstract about what is true, and also that it can not merely have particular desires but reflect on how to attain particular goods, on how to combine various sorts of goods in a life well-lived, and on the notion of *a good* as such. With these powers, moreover, comes the capacity for a distinctive kind of self-movement, one that involves the ability to think about what to pursue and how to obtain it. The fact that rational creatures do not merely have certain things that are goods for them, or merely desire things that are, in fact, good—the fact that they can reflect on the concept of a good life—is an aspect of their practical self-consciousness.[33]

The life of a rational creature is thus profoundly different from the life of a nonrational creature, but, if Aquinas is right, this difference does not disrupt the general connection between self-movement and goodness. Rather, it transforms the kind of good that is in question, and makes an individual creature's relationship to its own good correspondingly more complex. For, taking the second point first, a rational creature's self-movement is mediated by *thoughts* about, and in the favorable case by knowledge of, its own good: Its capacity for action is a capacity to pursue what it *takes* to be good. And by the same token, the life of a rational creature will be one that essentially involves exercise of the power of reason, and will imply the existence of goods of a specifically rational kind (e.g., contemplation, friendship, justice). The concept *good* to which a rational creature attains will be the concept of what is good in the life of that kind of rational creature, and this will not be merely determined by its "nature," if this means something independent of its reason. It would be a mistake to suppose that a rational creature is merely a creature that has certain naturally given inclinations and is capable of thinking about how to put them into practice. That is not the sort of nature a rational creature has: Its nature is to live a specific sort of rational life, and its good will involve whatever features life by reason must involve.

The Rational Apprehension of Goodness

To substantiate this standpoint on rational agency in detail would require another essay, but the basic points follow from the considerations of §4, together with the thought that a rational agent is one that determines how it acts by thinking about how to act. For to say that a rational agent is one whose thinking about how to act determines how it acts is to say that it is an agent whose doing A depends on its capacity to reflect on the question "What shall I do?" in such a way that its acceptance of the answer "A" can constitute its setting to do A.[34] At a minimum, this will involve the power to consider the relation of means to ends: A rational agent will be one who, if he is intentionally doing A, and if he recognizes that doing A^* is means of doing A, can thereby come to do A^* because he is doing A.

In short, a rational agent will be one whose thinking can make true propositions of the form

(8) S is doing A^* because S is doing A.

This is the kind of proposition that was the focus of our discussion in §4, the kind on which our characterization of goal-directed movement hinged. But observe that, when applied to rational agents, propositions of form (8) take a special turn: They require for their truth that the subject should *know* the relevant explanation to be true. A subject who does not know that he is doing A is not doing A *intentionally*, and a subject who does not know that he is doing A^* because he is doing A is not doing A^* *with the intention* of doing A.

Now, if a rational agent is one whose self-movement is subject to explanations that are essentially known to their subject, what follows about the way in which such an agent must think of his own actions and of what explains them? Well, if we are right that, in general, truths of form (8) presuppose general truths about the kind to which the subject belongs, truths that carry implications about what is good for things of that kind, then a rational agent, in knowing what it is doing and why, will *know* truths with such presuppositions.[35] Moreover, his knowledge of such truths will not be merely an observer's knowledge: His taking such facts to hold will, as we have seen, be essential to their holding. This implies that, on pain of regress, his grounds for believing that he is doing A^* because he is doing A cannot be grounds for believing that this fact *already* obtains—for until he takes the relevant fact to obtain, it does not. He must, if he is to be rational in making such a judgment, have another kind of ground: a ground for believing that, in accepting a certain justification for doing A^*, he will be making it the case that he is doing A^*. But what kind of grounds could these be? There is at least this constraint on them: They must be grounds that are potentially such as to warrant a judgment of the relevant kind; and we have argued that the relevant kind of judgment is one that presupposes facts about what is good for bearers of his sort of form. But then, if the considerations of the preceding section are correct, it follows that a rational agent's grounds for making a judgment of form (8) must be grounds that bear some relation to general sorts of aims belonging to creatures of the form that he bears.

This conclusion obviously needs further explanation, and we will elaborate on it in a moment; but first let us note how well it coheres with some familiar facts about how we know what we want and what we are doing. We noted in §1 that a person who wants something can in general be asked *why* he wants it, and then he is expected to answer, not by describing how, as a matter of past history, his want arose, but rather by explaining what, here and now, speaks in favor of pursuing the aim in question. Similar points apply, *mutatis mutandis*, to an agent's knowledge of why he is doing what he is doing: If S is doing A intentionally, then S is expected to be able to say why he is doing it by giving the reasons he takes to speak in favor of doing A. Moreover, as G. E. M. Anscombe observed in a famous discussion of practical reasoning, explanations of this sort have a characteristic structure: Where there is a substantive answer to the question "Why are you doing A?" (or "Why do you want to do A?"), a full statement of this answer terminates in some "desirability characterization" that represents what is sought as desirable or *good* in some intelligible respect (pleasant, appropriate, conducive to health, beneficial to a friend, required by fairness, satisfying of some intelligible life-ambition, . . .).[36] The agent may be wrong in supposing that the desired object would really *be* good in the relevant respect. Indeed, an agent may do something although, in his considered judgment, it is not a good thing to do at all. But even in this sort of case, if the agent has acted intentionally, we expect him to be able to explain what he did by saying what it was that seemed *prima facie* attractive about it, what form of good it at least appeared to promise. And, as Anscombe remarks, "the good (perhaps falsely) conceived by the agent must *really* be one of the many forms of good" (1963, §40).

At least as a characterization of the presumptively normal case, these Anscombean descriptions seem evidently true: A rational agent is normally assumed to be in a position to explain his own doings and wantings-to-do, and the kind of explanation that is called for here is one that relates the doing in question to something that might intelligibly be taken to be some form of good. But why *should* the primary explanation of what an agent wants or is doing be one that he can himself supply, and why should it take this particular shape? Our account of the conditions under which a rational agent can know himself to be the subject of a fact of form

(8) S is doing A^* because S is doing A

suggests answers to these questions. For we have observed, first, that a rational agent's grounds for such a judgment must be grounds for believing that in so judging he is *constituting* the explanatory relation at issue; and we have argued, second, that his grounds for so judging must ultimately advert to the way in which the present goal-directed activity serves some general sort of aim belonging to creatures of his form. The first point speaks to the first question: He must be able to give the explanation because this is a sort of explanatory relation that holds only insofar as the subject takes it to hold. The second point speaks to the second question: The explanation must terminate in a desirability characterization because what is articulated in such a characterization is precisely an account of the general aim that this case of goal-directed activity instances, and this is the sort of ground that any truth of form (8) must ultimately have.

An Excessively Idealized Picture?

The preceding paragraphs are an attempt to give some content to the Thomistic-Aristotelian idea of a hierarchy of different kinds of life, distinguished by different sorts of relation to form, but united by an abstract structure that connects the ascription of self-movement to individuals with the recognition of them as belonging to kinds that supply norms for their activities. This picture of a "ladder of nature," with nonrational animals occupying one rung and rational animals occupying another, higher rung, is often dismissed as reflecting a discredited worldview, one that is incompatible with Darwinian biology and with a more general commitment to naturalism. It would be impossible for us to address this general misgiving here. We can only ask the reader to consider whether our claims that the recognition of self-movement brings with it a certain kind of explanatory framework, and that the recognition of rational self-movement involves the application of a distinctive version of that framework, need stand in tension with a naturalistic understanding of the evolutionary background and material basis of vital processes. Our own view is that, if the standpoint articulated here is in tension with anything, it is only with certain philosophically contentious interpretations of what naturalism must involve.

Having tabled this broad misgiving, however, there is a more specific concern that we can address. This is the concern that our account of rational agency is excessively *idealized*. This concern can take two forms. First, our account of a rational creature's relationship to its own good may seem to demand too much intellectual sophistication, more than actual human beings typically possess. Second, even if it is granted that rational creatures must be capable of conceiving of their own good, the claim that intentional action in general reflects a subject's taking what he is pursuing to be good may seem to imply a naive or pious view of what moves us to act. We address these objections together because, although they take issue with different aspects of our conception of rational agency, we believe they are both rooted in a failure to grasp the logical character of the guise of the good thesis. Answering the objections will give us an opportunity to clarify this character.

Consider first the charge that the account demands too much intellectual sophistication on the part of rational creatures. Can't children and unreflective adults possess the capacity to act for reasons even though they never have reflected on the general concept *good*? Of course they can; but to focus on the question of whether rational creatures in general must make explicit use of this concept is to miss our point. To see this, compare this charge of intellectualism with a similar charge that might be brought against the claim that rational creatures must believe under the guise of the true. Here too it is natural to object that only a quite sophisticated reasoner gives thought to the concept *true*. But the point of saying that rational believers must believe under the guise of the true is not to insist that all their beliefs take the form "p is true," but rather to point out something about the manner in which they must consider any belief of the form "p." A rational believer is one who can reflect on his grounds for holding any given belief, one who can put to himself the question of whether p and why. "Truth" names, so to speak, the dimension in which answers to the question of whether p add up: A consideration is relevant only if it speaks to whether p is true, and a creature that is not capable of distinguishing relevant from irrelevant answers to this question is not yet capable of reflecting on its grounds for belief. Thus any rational creature must at least implicitly possess the idea of truth: Its capacity for reflection involves a capacity to bring the standard of truth to bear, even if it has never reflected on this standard as such or mastered a term that designates it. It may not have the predicate "is true" in its vocabulary, but the standard that this predicate designates provides the structure of its reflection. Moreover, even an unreflective rational subject who believes a proposition accepts it *as true* in a plain enough sense: Such a subject has the power to reflect on what he believes, and if, on reflection, he does not take the relevant proposition to be true, he will, in so judging, have changed his belief about it.

Similarly, the point of saying that rational agents must act under the guise of the good is not to insist that their practical reasoning must arrive at conclusions of the form "Doing A would be good," but rather to point out something about the manner in which they must consider the question of whether to do A. Just as a rational believer is one who can reflect on his grounds for belief by putting to himself the question "Why p?" so a rational agent is one that can reflect on his grounds for action by putting to himself the question "What speaks in favor of doing A?" Just as "truth" names the standard we apply in answering the former question, so "goodness" names the standard for answers to the latter: It specifies the topic on which a consideration must bear in order even to be a candidate answer to the question. And although there may be rational creatures that have not reflected on this topic as such or learned a term that designates it, still any such creature must grasp this topic at least implicitly, for it must recognize what *kind* of answer the question "What speaks in favor of doing A?" calls for, on pain of not being a rational agent at all. If this is right, then the intentional actions of a rational agent express his regarding those actions *as good* in a plain enough sense: for such an agent has the power to reflect on how to act, and if on reflection he does not accept that a given way of acting has at least something good about it, he will in so doing have changed his mind about whether to do it.

But isn't this account of the motivation of intentional action too pious? Don't we sometimes intentionally do things that we judge to be wicked or worthless? No doubt we do, but care must be taken in interpreting this fact. It is sometimes suggested that the capacity for rational reflection effects a radical separation between an individual subject's thinking about what to do and any general facts about what kind of creature that subject is and what is good for such creatures.[37] On this view, the power to reflect on the question "What should I do?" is the power precisely to *transcend* any allegiance to the goods of one's kind—not, as we maintain, the power to relate to those goods in a way mediated by the capacity for self-consciousness. This conception of reason as the power to transcend any merely automatic allegiance to a certain list of goods does, of course, contain an important truth; namely, that a rational creature is one that can ask itself, with regard to any given putative good, "Why should I care about that?" In acknowledging this truth, however, we should not forget how one goes about answering this sort of question. Suppose the putative good in question is, say, justice to one's fellow human beings, and suppose that some agent seeks to call the authenticity of this good into question: What sorts of considerations might figure in his critique? Well, he might, for instance, condemn justice as Thrasymachus and Callicles do, by arguing that the life of a just person is cowardly and slavish. But notice that in doing so he would be condemning one putative good by appealing to others—in this instance, the goods of a courageous and free existence. And surely some such appeal would occur in any intelligible answer to this sort of question. A rational subject can call the value of any given good into question, but such questioning must, if it is to be intelligible as reasoning at all, appeal to other goods whose value is not in question.

Even an agent who does something he takes to be wicked or worthless can normally say why he did it, at least in the sense that he can say what feature of the action was *prima facie* appealing to him. Moreover, the action's at least *seeming* attractive to him in the relevant respect is precisely what explains his performing it, in spite of his reservations. If this is right, then such examples do not show the guise of the good thesis to be false. Indeed, they rather tend to confirm it. For, as Aquinas notes in the passage quoted at the beginning of this section, the presence of reason in us is exactly what makes room for willings that do not tend toward things that are good "in very truth": Once we are equipped with the thought that rational action involves an exercise of the power to judge things good, we are in a position to recognize that there can be appetites that the subject does not judge or believe to be good at all. Such appetites would be akin to perceptual appearances: they would be *appearings-good*, just as perceptual appearances are appearings-true. They would present themselves as *prima facie* grounds for choice, just as perceptual appearances present themselves as *prima facie* grounds for judgment. But just as a subject can disbelieve the testimony of his senses even as the appearances persist (e.g., I can disbelieve that the stick in the water glass is really bent although it continues to look bent), so a subject can disapprove of the urgings of his appetites even as these urgings persist (e.g., I can think that lust is encouraging me to do something bad, although the impulse to do it remains as strong as ever). The objects of such appetites are not believed good, but the appetites themselves continue to represent those objects as good in a perfectly intelligible sense: They present their objects as having features that make them *prima facie* desirable, even if we doubt that something with those features would really be desirable.[38]

We thus arrive at the traditional view that when a person intentionally does something he judges to be wicked or worthless, this reflects a kind of mutiny of some of his motivational faculties, a mutiny that involves the action's being put forward as desirable by appetite or passion, even as reason denies its desirability. This sort of mutiny is certainly possible, but what is not possible is that it be the normal case. For a subject possesses the power of practical reason only if his reflection on what to do is in general determinative of what he actually does do, and we have seen that a rational subject's reflection on what to do must be at least implicitly sensitive to his judgments about what would be good to do. Hence a rational agent must in general judge his actions to have something genuinely good about them; and even in the cases where he does not, this will be because he is subject to an appearance of goodness that engages his power to act in conscious pursuit of ends, even as it overpowers his judgment about what is really good.

CONCLUSION

The thesis we have been defending is abstract. This bears emphasizing because it brings out how many questions of substantive moral philosophy are left open by our conclusions. We have concluded that a rational agent must act under the guise of the good in the sense that he must in general pursue ends in virtue of taking there to be something good about those ends. We have granted that his recognition of this standard of goodness may be merely implicit, and we have said about the relevant standard only that it must reflect more general facts about the kind to which the agent belongs. We have not said anything about the content of this standard, not even whether the propositions that characterize it depend merely on abstract facts about what it is to be a rational being (this would be a kind of Kantian view), or on more determinate facts about what it is to be a *human* rational being (this, we believe, would be closer to Aristotle's view). In any event, to investigate the content of our concept *good* would require a different kind of reflection from the one in which we have been engaged: We have merely been investigating the *form* of this concept, and the kind of role it must play in our practical thought. But this investigation suffices to answer philosophers who would deny that this concept has any role to play in our wanting and willing.

Our project has been to make a case for the Aristotelian doctrine that rational agents must desire under the guise of the good; but we hope that even readers who are not convinced by this case will now possess a clearer view of the context into which the guise of the good thesis fits. Most contemporary opponents of the thesis discuss it in isolation from broader issues about teleological explanation and the relation between an individual creature and its kind. Our aims have been, first, to show how the thesis fits into this larger framework, and second, to suggest that the framework itself is not just some antiquated worldview that we can brush aside, but a perceptive analysis of forms of thought that are essential to our everyday understanding of ourselves. If the thesis turns out to articulate a commitment involved in the application of these forms of thought, then it cannot be lightly dismissed, for we can no more brush aside these forms than we can brush aside our capacity for choice itself.

Notes

For comments and suggestions, we are very grateful to Rachel Cohen, Wolfram Gobsch, Matthias Haase, Richard Moran, Jessica Moss, Arthur Ripstein, Sebastian Rödl, Amélie Rorty, Tamar Schapiro, Kieran Setiya, Martin Stone, Gisela Striker, Sergio Tenenbaum, and to audiences at the universities of Basel, Colgate, Leipzig, and Toronto.

1. A representative expression of this new standpoint occurs near the beginning of Michael Stocker's "Desiring the Bad" (1979). According to Stocker,

> it is hardly unfair, if unfair at all, to suggest that the philosophical view is overwhelmingly that the good or only the good attracts. At least, this is how I am forced to interpret so many philosophers. This affords me no pleasure, since that view . . . is clearly and simply false. (p. 740)

For similar assessments, see J. David Velleman, "The Guise of the Good" (2000a), esp. pp. 118–19; and Kieran Setiya, "Explaining Action" (2003), esp. p. 353.

2. Gary Watson, "Free Agency" (1982), p. 101.

3. For a *prima facie* justification of the guise of the good thesis by appeal to these sorts of observations, see, for instance, Joseph Raz, "On the Guise of the Good" (this volume).

4. This is not to say that contemporary authors are unwilling to speak of a person acting *in order to achieve a certain goal* or *because he had a certain aim*. Most authors admit that these are genuine explanations, and that they may be called "teleological" inasmuch as they relate the agent's action to an end. What they do not admit is that the goodness, or represented goodness, of the end plays an essential role in the explanation: On their view, to say that an action is explained by a certain end is really to say that it is explained by a certain precedent psychological state of the agent (his wanting to achieve that end) whose efficacy does not depend on its tendency to move the agent toward things that are good for him. This view of action-explanation accords well with the widespread view that, in general, superficially teleological forms of explanation should, in principle, be reducible to explanations of other kinds. As John Hawthorne and Daniel Nolan observe in a recent article on teleological explanation:

> [W]hen contemporary philosophers and biologists tell stories about . . . natural teleology they tend to proceed as if there is a different underlying explanation: superficial teleology gives way to an underlying reality that is not fundamentally teleological at all. This is so even in the case of mental activity. Teleology gives way to mental representations that play efficient causal roles (which in turn may enjoy deeper explanations that proceed via categories that are not mentalistic at all). ("What Would Teleological Causation Be?" [2006], p. 266)

5. "Explaining Action" (2003), p. 380. Compare also J. David Velleman's contention, in an influential paper on the guise of the good thesis, that

> even if desiring something consists in regarding the thing as good in a sense synony-mous with "to be brought about," it isn't an attempt at getting right whether the thing really is to be brought about, and so it doesn't amount to a judgment on the thing's goodness. ("The Guise of the Good" [2000a], p. 117)

6. For the former sort of formulation, see the passage from *De Anima* quoted in the epigraph above. For the latter formulation, see *Nicomachean Ethics*, I.1.

7. Admittedly, in some of Stocker's examples, the party with whom the agent seeks to "get even" is not a party who could reasonably be regarded as having given offense. Indeed, in some cases, it is not a person at all, but a thing (the world, the day) on which the agent acts out a fantasy of revenge. These sorts of knowingly unreasonable or fantastical actions raise interesting prob-lems for action theory, but they do not interfere with the point that, inasmuch as the action is wanted as a way (however unreasonable or fanciful) of getting even, it is wanted under an aspect of the good. Such desires, even the irratio-nal ones, seem to be primitive manifestations of the desire for justice, and surely this sort of desire cannot be assumed *not* to be a desire for a certain form of good.

This is not to deny that there can be desires to harm that are not retributive, perhaps desires that are purely sadistic. For *these* sorts of desires, however, it would be much less plausible to claim that the agent can simply want to do harm without wanting thereby to achieve some further end (getting pleasure, exercising power over others, etc.).

8. T. M. Scanlon, *What We Owe to Each Other* (1999), p. 38.

9. Velleman 2000b, p. 1. Compare Wittgenstein, *Philosophical Investigations* (1972): §621.

10. This, in effect, is the diagnosis of the appeal of the guise of the good thesis suggested in Velleman 2000a—although stating it this way glosses over certain complexities in Velleman's account.

11. See, e.g., the quotation from Aristotle that appears as our epigraph.

12. The assumption is often not made explicit, though it comes out in the widespread use of a schematic "p" to represent the object of desire. One author who gives explicit attention to the point is Alvin Goldman:

> My analysis of intentional action will make use of a certain species of wanting—viz., wanting to do certain acts. Such wants are not essentially different from other wants, like wanting to possess certain objects. Wanting an automobile consists (roughly) in feeling favorably toward the prospect of owning an automobile. Wanting to take a walk consists (roughly) in feeling favorably toward the prospect of one's taking a walk. (1970, pp. 49–50)

Notice how, in the last sentence of this remark, wanting *to take a walk* becomes wanting *one's taking a walk*, which includes a subject term. Since Goldman elsewhere uses "p" as his schema for the object of desire, he presumably intends that the complex noun phrase "one's taking a walk" be transformable, in turn, into a proposition.

13. See Bertrand Russell, *An Inquiry into Meaning and Truth:* "We pass next to the analysis of 'propositional attitudes,' i.e., believing, desiring, doubting, etc., that so-and-so is the case" (1992, p. 21).

14. Cp. Smith 2004, p. 165.

15. Smith 1987, pp. 53–54.

16. In offering (2) as the proposition-directed counterpart of (1), we are following a widespread practice, but actually we feel unsure exactly what English grammar requires in the propositional complement here. Perhaps it should be in the subjunctive, as in

(2') *S* wants that *S* do *A*.

But whatever form of the verb "to do" appears linking "*S*" and "*A*," the question will remain: When does this supposed "state of affairs" obtain?

17. Or in the simple past: "*S A*-ed." In either the perfect or the simple past, the verb phrase expresses *perfective aspect:* It represents the event in question as completed rather than underway. For convenience, we will focus on the contrast between the progressive and the perfect, but it is really this contrast between forms that express imperfective aspect and forms that express perfective aspect that is crucial to our argument. For further discussion of this distinction and its relation to English verb forms, see Comrie, *Aspect* (1976).

18. It would not help to suggest that the agent wants that there be a certain event, as in

(2') S wants that $(\exists e)(e$ is a doing of A & e is by S).

For when "is" there such an event? Does this require the truth of "*S* is doing *A*," or "*S* did *A*," or what? Each answer would set off a chain of difficulties similar to the one we describe below.

19. Certain sophisticated versions of the causal theory attempt to capture something like this point by making the content of the motivating want or intention self-referential: by stipulating, e.g., that I do *A* intentionally only if I am moved to do *A* by a desire that *this very desire* should be the cause of my doing *A* (compare Harman 1976; Searle 1983, ch. 3; Velleman 1989; Setiya 2003). We believe that this sort of maneuver would fall prey to a version of the difficulty we have raised, since the phrase "doing *A*" remains in the content clause, and this sort of content is one to which the causal theorist is not entitled to appeal. Our aim here, however, is simply to show how the presence of this phrase makes a difficulty for the most straightforward and natural version of the causal theory. More complicated versions of the theory make the difficulty harder to detect, but we believe that they do not ultimately eliminate it.

20. Some philosophers who would regard themselves as advocates of a causal theory of action do not have this ambition: Donald Davidson (1980b, 1980c) and Jennifer Hornsby (1980, 1995), for instance, argue that the intentional actions must have certain psychological causes, but do not aim for a reductive account of intentional action in these terms. What we have been saying does not constitute an objection to such views, though we believe that the kind of investigation of action we go on to propose in the following sections does, if it is sound, raise questions about the sort of theorizing about action that these authors undertake. For the present, however, our interest is in the kind of causal theory that aims at reduction. For it is the assumption that *this* sort of causal

theory is possible that supports the widespread conviction that *doing something intentionally* is not a special and irreducible kind of event or process, but an event or process of some more generic kind with certain special causes. This is the conviction we ultimately aim to challenge.

21. Difficulties would also arise, we believe, if we investigated the notion of *cause* on which such an account must rely. It is widely recognized that not just any sort of causal relation will do: The cause must operate "in the right way." Davidson famously doubted whether there could be a noncircular account of what "the right way" must be (1980b, p. 79). Contemporary causal theorists tend to suppose that Davidson was wrong about this. The foregoing considerations are an attempt to show, from a different angle, why he was right to doubt the possibility of reduction.

22. For a more systematic argument for this conclusion, to which the present discussion is much indebted, see Michael Thompson, *Life and Action* (2008), part 2.

23. There may be explanations that fit the grammatical pattern of (8) but that do not imply a teleological relationship between the lesser process and the greater one: for instance, "The dryer is shaking because it is running its spin-cycle." If this is a genuine explanation, however, it seems intuitively clear that it is an explanation of a different kind from the kind offered when a proposition of form (8) is used to mark a teleological connection: the dryer's shaking is not, intuitively speaking, a way or means or part of its completing its spin cycle. One test of whether an explanation of form (8) is genuinely teleological is whether it can be transposed into an explicitly teleological form, as in:

(8') S is doing A^* in order to do A.

This will be possible at least in the case of animate teleology: There may be reservations about making the transposition in the case of plants. But even there, it seems that such an explicitly teleological description should apply, if not at the level of the individual plant, then at least at the level of the kind to which it belongs:

(8") Ks do A^* in order to do A. (They grow leaves in order to absorb sunlight, roots to take up water, and nutrients from the soil, etc.)

A fuller treatment of these topics would need to investigate the special features of the explanatory structure that exists when a proposition of form (8) is used in the way that we intuitively recognize as teleological. We do not attempt this here, however; our aim is just to sketch a general approach and bring out some of its attractions.

24. Compare the characterization suggested at Thompson 2008, p. 112.

25. The consequences of this point for the understanding of intentional action are explored in greater depth in Lavin, "Must There Be Basic Action?"

26. For the idea of nature as a principle of movement and change, see *Physics*, II–III, and for the connection between nature and form, see, especially, *Physics* II.1 and II.7. For the idea of the soul as the form of a living thing, see *De Anima* II, in particular II.4 for the idea of the soul as the cause of specifically vital movement and change. See also the discussions of the general connection between nature and teleological (or final) explanation in *Physics* II.8, and of the connection between teleological understanding and the soul in *Parts of Animals* I.1.

27. Such judgments are characteristically expressed using sentences of the
type linguists call "generics." For an overview of the characteristic significance of
such sentences and the problems they raise, see the introduction to Carlson and
Pelletier 1995. For illuminating discussion of the relevance of generic propositions to the understanding of teleology in living things, see Moravcsik 1994 and
Thompson 2008, part 1. The more general Aristotelian thought that, to make
sense of the notion of an individual substance undergoing motion or change, we
must see that substance as belonging to a certain substantial kind characterized
by various general ways of moving and changing has been defended in a contemporary context in Wiggins 2001, chapter 3.

28. Once again, it will plainly be a complicated matter to say how an
instance of goal-directedly A-ing must be related to the general description of
what a given power is a power to do (α) if the A-ing is to instance or belong to
α-ing. Indeed, the potential complexity involved here will presumably increase
with each step up the "ladder of nature": from plants, to nonrational animals, to
rational animals. In the vegetative case, what any individual plant can be said to
do goal-directedly will probably cleave pretty closely to what it belongs to the
general powers of things of that kind to do. Already in the case of nonrational
animals, however, the presence of the power of perception (to say nothing of
capacities for learning, adaptation, etc.) will introduce possibilities of goal-directed
activity that have no direct counterpart in the kind: for, e.g., in virtue of being able
to perceive a certain mouse, an individual cat can get into the act of *hunting that
mouse*. Whatever powers of cat-kind this activity instances will certainly not be
powers to do *that:* They will presumably involve only a power to *hunt mice* or
possibly just to *hunt things* that meet certain general parameters. And the distance
between any general description of the power exercised and the appropriate
descriptions of the action undertaken will receive another and much more
radical multiplication in a rational creature, for an individual rational creature
will be in a position to determine the *how* and the *wherefore* of its action in all
sorts of ways that are not anticipated in the powers belonging to its kind.
Nevertheless, if the Aristotelian view is right, representing a rational creature as
engaged in intentional action will involve representing what it is doing as in *some*
way connected with the operation of powers characteristic of its kind. We say
more to develop and defend this view about rational creatures in the next
section. For further discussion, see Boyle, "Rational Animals and Rational
Powers."

29. The resulting system thus constitutes the kind of unity that Kant called a
"natural purpose," which is "the cause and effect of itself." Compare Kant,
Critique of Judgment (1987), part 2, §§64–65.

30. See P. T. Geach 1956 and Anscombe 1958, and for more recent represen-
tatives of this "Aristotelian naturalist" tradition, Foot 2002 and Thompson 2008,
part 1.

31. See *Nicomachean Ethics* I.7.

32. *Summa Theologica*, IAIIae.q8.a1.

33. If this seems a dark suggestion, compare it with Kant's well-known claim
that the imperative "ought" expresses "the relation of an objective law of reason
to a will that is not necessarily determined by this law because of its subjective
constitution" (*Groundwork*, Ak. IV:413). Kant's claim suggests a way of looking

at the significance of normative language more generally: namely, as expressing the idea of a distinction, and the possibility of an accord, between how something is actually and how it is in the nature of that thing to be (a distinction, as Kant would put it, between how the thing is actually and the "law" that governs it). To think of the objective laws of something's constitution in this way is to think of them as specifying its good. And if this is right, then a creature that can think about what it ought to do and what is good for it would be thinking in terms that presuppose a conception of *its own* constitution. Such thinking expresses not just awareness of myself as an individual, but an at-least-implicit idea of what *kind of thing* I am: for when I think of how I ought to be, I am thinking in a way that must measure how I actually am against some general standard, a law I am under, or nature I bear, in virtue of the kind of thing I am.

34. This is not to suggest that, whenever an agent intentionally does one thing with a view to doing another, this must be the product of prior deliberation about this course of action: The claim that intentional action must always be the product of prior deliberation is both factually untrue and subject to difficulties of principle. But this is not our claim: We hold that the capacity for intentional action requires a *capacity* for reflection on the question "Why do *A*?" Only some intentional actions are the result of actual prior reflection on this question, but even in the case of actions that are not the result of prior reflection, the relevance of the capacity for such reflection is evident in the fact that an agent is *able* to say what he is doing and why if the question arises.

35. Note that we are not claiming that, in general, if I know that *p*, and *p* presupposes *q*, then I know that *q*. That an agent who knows a truth of form (8) about himself must have views about what good would be served by his so acting will follow only given further considerations that we explain below.

36. Anscombe 1963, §37. See also §§38–40 for further elaboration of the point.

37. For this sort of view, see, for instance, John McDowell, "Two Sorts of Naturalism" (1995).

38. For development of the idea that appetites can be understood as appearings-good, and the use of this idea in replying to supposed counterexamples to the guise of the good thesis, see Sergio Tenenbaum, *Appearances of the Good* (2007).

References

Anscombe, G. E. M. 1958. "Modern Moral Philosophy." *Philosophy* 33, no. 124, pp. 1–19.

———. 1963. *Intention.* 2nd ed. Oxford: Basil Blackwell.

Aquinas, Thomas. 1948. *Summa Theologica.* 3 Vols. Trans. Fathers of the English Dominican Province. New York: Benziger Brothers.

Aristotle. 1984a. *The Complete Works of Aristotle.* 2 Vols. Edited by Jonathan Barnes. Princeton, N.J.: Princeton University Press.

———. 1984b. *De Anima.* In *The Complete Works of Aristotle.* 2 Vols. Edited by Jonathan Barnes. Princeton, N.J.: Princeton University Press.

———. 1984c. *Metaphysics.* In *The Complete Works of Aristotle.* 2 Vols. Edited by Jonathan Barnes. Princeton, N.J.: Princeton University Press.

———. 1984d. *Nicomachean Ethics.* In *The Complete Works of Aristotle.* 2 Vols. Edited by Jonathan Barnes. Princeton, N.J.: Princeton University Press.

———. 1984e. *Parts of Animals*. In *The Complete Works of Aristotle*. 2 Vols. Edited by Jonathan Barnes. Princeton, N.J.: Princeton University Press.

———. 1984f. *Physics*. In *The Complete Works of Aristotle*. 2 Vols. Edited by Jonathan Barnes. Princeton, N.J.: Princeton University Press.

Boyle, Matthew. "Rational Animals and Rational Powers." Unpublished ms.

Carlson, Gregory N., and Francis Jeffry Pelletier, eds. 1995. *The Generic Book*. Chicago: University of Chicago Press.

Comrie, Bernard. 1976. *Aspect*. Cambridge: Cambridge University Press.

Davidson, Donald. 1980a. *Essays on Actions and Events*. Oxford: Oxford University Press.

———. 1980b. "Freedom to Act." In Davidson, *Essays on Actions and Events*. Oxford: Oxford University Press.

———. 1980c. "Mental Events." In Davidson, *Essays on Actions and Events*. Oxford: Oxford University Press.

Foot, Philippa. 2002. *Natural Goodness*. Oxford: Oxford University Press.

Geach, P. T. 1956. "Good and Evil." *Analysis* 17, no. 2, pp. 33–42.

Goldman, Alvin I. 1970. *A Theory of Human Action*. Princeton, N.J.: Princeton University Press.

Harman, Gilbert. 1976. "Practical Reasoning." *The Review of Metaphysics* 29, no. 3, pp. 431–63.

Hawthorne, John, and Daniel Nolan. 2006. "What Would Teleological Causation Be?" In John Hawthorne, *Metaphysical Essays*. Oxford: Oxford University Press.

Hornsby, Jennifer. 1980. *Actions*. London: Routledge.

———. 1995. "Agency and Causal Explanation." In John Heil and Alfred Mele, eds., *Mental Causation*. Oxford: Oxford University Press.

Kant, Immanuel. 1987. *Critique of Judgment*. Translated by Werner J. Pluhar. Indianapolis: Hackett.

———. 1993. *Grounding for the Metaphysics of Morals*. Translated by James W. Ellington. Indianapolis: Hackett.

Lavin, Douglas. "Must There Be Basic Action?" Unpublished ms.

McDowell, John. 1995. "Two Sorts of Naturalism." In *Virtues and Reasons: Philippa Foot and Moral Theory: Essays in Honour of Philippa Foot*, eds. Hursthouse, Lawrence, and Quinn. Oxford: Clarendon; New York: Oxford University Press, 1995, pp. 149–79.

Moravcsik, Julius. 1994. "Essences, Powers, and Generic Propositions." In *Unity, Identity, and Explanation in Aristotle's Metaphysics*, ed. T. Scaltsas, D. Charles, and M. L. Gill. Oxford: Oxford University Press.

Raz, Joseph. Forthcoming. "On the Guise of the Good." This volume.

Russell, Bertrand. 1992. *An Inquiry into Meaning and Truth*. London: Routledge.

Scanlon, T. M. 1999. *What We Owe to Each Other*. Cambridge, Mass.: Harvard University Press.

Searle, John R. 1983. *Intentionality*. Cambridge: Cambridge University Press.

Setiya, Kieran. 2003. "Explaining Action." *Philosophical Review* 112 (3), pp. 339–93.

Smith, Michael. 1987. "The Humean Theory of Motivation." *Mind* 96 (381), pp. 36–61.

———. 2004. "The Structure of Orthonomy." In *Agency and Action*, ed. John Hyman and Helen Steward. Cambridge: Cambridge University Press.

Stocker, Michael. 1979. "Desiring the Bad: An Essay in Moral Psychology." *Journal of Philosophy* 76 (12), pp. 738–53.

Tenenbaum, Sergio. 2007. *Appearances of the Good*. Cambridge: Cambridge University Press.

Thompson, Michael. 2008. *Life and Action*. Cambridge, Mass.: Harvard University Press.

Velleman, J. David. 1989. *Practical Reflection*. Princeton, N.J.: Princeton University Press.

————. 2000a. "The Guise of the Good." In *The Possibility of Practical Reason*. Oxford: Oxford University Press.

————. 2000b. "Introduction." In *The Possibility of Practical Reason*. Oxford: Oxford University Press.

————. 2000c. *The Possibility of Practical Reason*. Oxford: Oxford University Press.

Watson, Gary. 1982. "Free Agency." *Journal of Philosophy* 72 (April), pp. 205–20.

Wiggins, David. 2001. *Sameness and Substance Renewed*. Cambridge: Cambridge University Press.

Wittgenstein, Ludwig. 1972. *Philosophical Investigations*. Translated by G. E. M. Anscombe. Cambridge: Cambridge University Press.

9

Good and Good For

Sergio Tenenbaum

1. INTRODUCTION

One of the most famous arguments in Rawls's *Theory of Justice* is the argument against utilitarianism. According to Rawls, by redistributing utility without any concern about who the "bearers" of utility will be, utilitarianism fails to respect the distinction among persons. As Rawls puts it:

> This [classical utilitarianism's] view of social cooperation is the consequence of extending to society the principle of choice for one man, and then, to make this extension work, conflates all persons into one through the imaginative acts of the impartial sympathetic spectator. Utilitarianism does not take seriously the distinction between persons.[1]

The principle of choice for individuals allows a person to sacrifice what is good for him at one time for the sake of what will be better for him overall; in Rawls's estimation, the utilitarian illicitly generalizes from that principle to the conclusion that one can also unproblematically sacrifice what is good for one person for the sake of what is overall better. This idea that there seems to be something wrong with the way that utilitarianism moves from intrapersonal to interpersonal trade-offs has been widely discussed and often endorsed. The idea that one cannot think about interpersonal redistribution of goods or utility simply on the model of intrapersonal redistribution of goods or utility without further argument now enjoys the status of a default position.[2] However, it is worth noting that Rawls's argument seems to depend on a duality between something like "good" and "good for," and despite the abiding influence of Rawls's argument, the relation between "good" and "good for" in the context of this argument has not received any adequate account, or so I will argue. This is particularly important for someone who is tempted by the guise of the good thesis. If the characteristic claim of the guise of the good thesis, or what I call "the scholastic view,"[3] is that desires, and perhaps other practical attitudes, represent their objects as good, then the existence of these two evaluative notions make the scholastic view ambiguous. Are the objects of desire conceived as good *simpliciter* or as good for the agent? In the absence of a proper justification for one of these options, it's not clear why we should accept *any* version of the scholastic view.

In light of these concerns, I have a particular interest in the notions of "good" and "good for." Notions such as well-being and welfare are put to work for various philosophical jobs, and I doubt that there is one univocal sense of "well-being" and "good for" that is employed in all these debates. However, I am interested in these two notions only insofar as they are two candidates for being the formal end of practical reason and action,[4] for being what an agent necessarily aims at when he or she acts or reasons practically, and thus the conditions of adequacy to which I'll hold an account of these notions are not the same that inform many theories of well-being.

Arguably, there are important historical precedents for the view that each of these notions is the one that plays this role in practical reasoning and action. According to some interpretations of Aristotle, *eudaimonia*, the end of all actions, is better understood as something that is good *for the agent*. On the other hand, Kant certainly holds that the good *simpliciter* is the object of rational volition; in fact, in Kant's view, the good is nothing but that which is necessarily the object of every rational agent's faculty of desire.[5] No doubt that there are many other evaluative notions, but no other seems to be a serious candidate to be the formal end of practical reason. No one would claim, for instance, that all action and all practical reasoning aims at the beautiful or the aesthetically good. However, the overall nature of both "good" and "good for" places each of them as a natural candidate for exactly this role.[6]

This chapter will argue that "good" is primary and "good for" should be understood as some way in which certain things persistently *appear* to be good to certain agents. In the course of arguing for my view, I try to show that the various explicit and implicit accounts of the distinction in the philosophical literature do a poor job of accounting for important intuitions about the distinction, but here again the importance of these intuitions should be gauged in accordance to whether they generate a notion that can be a plausible candidate for being the formal end of practical reason.

In order to get a better grip on the notions of "good" and "good for" as I understand them, it is worth examining how Rawls's argument seems[7] to be relying on such a distinction. This (putative) dependence can be better appreciated if we look at what happens when a distribution is fair. Suppose that a fair distribution would force Bill to sacrifice some of his income for the benefit of the worse off. Let us assume that there are no further complications; we accept that this is the just outcome, and that all things considered, this is what ought to happen. Now it would be natural to say that it is good that the money be redistributed, and insofar as Bill has a well-developed sense of justice, is fully informed, etc., he will agree with this judgment, and, one hopes, be willing to accept that the income be redistributed. However, Bill must also experience the whole transaction as a sacrifice. After all, it was the whole point of the argument from the separateness of persons that Bill cannot, or at least need not, treat trade-offs with other agents in the same way that he would treat trade-offs among different time slices of his self. In particular, he cannot, or need not, think that his loss was fully compensated by the gain made by someone else in the same way that one is fully compensated when one makes a sacrifice at a certain point in one's life so that one can benefit from a greater gain at a later point. Or, as one would ordinarily put it, the redistribution is good but not good for Bill; what is good and what is good for someone are capable of diverging. So it seems that there is a very natural path from Rawls's classic argument to the conclusion that there are two independent overall evaluative perspectives captured, respectively, by the notions of good and good for. Of course, none of these remarks are supposed to help establish Rawls's conclusion, or, for that matter, any other definitive conclusion. They only aim to show a quick route to the intuitive plausibility of the view that "good" and "good for," suitably understood, mark two relatively independent evaluative perspectives. In fact, it is worth looking at what was said by someone who recently argued against the existence of these two independent evaluative notions:

> Why should we not just promote all agents' valuable activity, without worrying about anyone's well-being? Of course, there'll be trade-offs to be made between different people's valuable activity, as there are trade-offs to be made between different valuable activities in our lives. . . . The same values are involved in these interpersonal trade-offs as in the intra-personal ones. We can make the trade-offs without thinking of well-being, so why not do so?[8]

This is exactly the kind of analogy that Rawls thought to be illicit in *A Theory of Justice*.

The first section of the chapter tries to present more specific intuitions that seem to require that "good" and "good for" be capable of constituting diverging overall evaluative perspectives, while also presenting some intuitive reasons to think that these notions are importantly related. This section ends by trying to express more precisely the difficulty in accounting for all these intuitions. The next section argues that a number of seemingly promising ways of accounting for the relation between "good" and "good for" face serious problems. In the last two sections, I offer an alternative suggestion of how to understand the relation between these notions, a suggestion that promises to do better than the accounts discussed in the third section while remaining compatible with various substantive views on the nature of well-being. I should point out that these issues deserve much more attention than I can give them here. This chapter should be seen only as a sketch of a problem and a solution; its cogency depends on the availability of a more detailed account of the view proposed here.[9]

2. THE INTUITIONS AND THE PROBLEM

The notion of "good for" has been identified in the literature with a notion of well-being. However, the notions that go under this heading are often trying to capture different concepts and often have different aims. Many philosophers developing the notion of well-being take it as a constraint that this notion will provide the material for moral or political theory construction. Although I'll look at similar constraints, my aim is not to try to see what notion of well-being can support this larger theoretical purpose, but to try to account for much simpler intuitions such as, for instance, the intuition that certain choices that we ought to make involve personal sacrifices; that sometimes people who behave badly do well for themselves; that sometimes I experience my duties as a constraint that I reasonably wish I could somehow avoid; etc. The conjecture of this chapter is that these are the intuitions that suggest that we have two evaluative perspectives, each of them constituting a plausible candidate for being the formal end of practical reason, so that if we can account for these intuitions while privileging one of these two notions, we have thereby shown that the privileged notion is the only serious candidate for being the formal end of practical reason.[10]

In all these cases, we seem to encounter two evaluative notions that are diverging; one that tells us what we ought to do, and the other that tells us that something else is desirable from a certain privileged perspective. Note, in contrast, for instance, Raz's understanding of the notion of well-being. Raz says that the concept of well-being "captures one crucial evaluation of a person's life; how good and successful is it from his point of view?"[11] This could be understood as compatible with the notion of "good for" I want to capture. However, when Raz considers the life of a person who "undergoes great deprivation in order to bring medical help to the victims of an epidemic," he argues that this person is still doing well in terms of well-being, since "his life is no less successful, rewarding, or accomplished."[12] It seems that Raz is right in saying that, in an important sense, the life of such a sacrificing individual is successful and accomplished, and I would venture to say that it is, in fact, a life of an agent who, as far as we can tell, chooses rightly. Moreover, such an agent must look back at his life and find that his life is or was a meaningful one. However, in many ways, not all is so great from the agent's point of view, and, more important for our purposes, ordinarily one would not consider sacrificing oneself this way to be something that is *good for* the individual. In fact, it seems that this is exactly what constitutes this agent as a *sacrificing* agent;[13] that is, we regard the choices of the agent as cases of sacrifice precisely because they are not good for the agent; they are the kind of losses for the agent that on Rawls's view are not compensated by other people's gains. These are the intuitions that lead us in the direction of a wedge between "good" and "good for." All these are pretty trivial intuitions, but, if I am right, they're enough to generate serious difficulties in understanding the relation between "good" and "good for," as I understand it.[14]

(a) Agents and Beneficiaries of Sacrifice

> Teresa gives up her chance of having a stellar career in the music industry, a career that would generate a lot of money and fame for her, so as to help the poor in the third world. She has now just finished rescuing many children who were trapped in a cave. The rescue effort caused her to fracture many bones, but since she can't get any medical treatment she needs to endure a great deal of pain.

Now there would be something obviously inappropriate if Teresa's friend Karol would say, as he sees her at this moment, "Hi Teresa, you are doing really well. Once again you succeeded in promoting something great. Your life is just great; in fact, it's hard to see how things could be going much better for you!" Of course, there is a sense in which Teresa's life *is* great, but there seems to be an obvious sense in which her great pain and deprivation is *not* great. Now, if the children she saves go on to have lives much like the life that Teresa forsook, *they* will have very good lives, even though, in some sense, none of them has promoted as much good as Teresa did. In fact, it seems intuitive to say that this is exactly what Teresa did that was so great: by sacrificing her chance to lead a life that is good for her, Teresa allows each of the children to lead a life that is good for him or her.

(b) Getting Away with Murder and Being Framed for It

This is adapted from the movie *Body Heat:*

> Matty murders her rich husband, but she is careful enough to frame Ned for it. Ned spends the rest of his life in a maximum-security jail. Matty moves to a tropical paradise, where she enjoys all the money she inherited from her husband as well as a successful career as a lawyer.

Here it would seem inappropriate, to say the least, for Matty's friend Dick to say: "Oh you poor Matty, things have gone awful for you. You made some poor choices in your life, and you failed to promote the good on various occasions," or to feel pity for Matty for being one of the constituents of a state of affairs that is intrinsically bad. Matty did something awful and, as we would say it, "she got away with it"; that is, she is now doing really well for herself despite having done something so awful.[15] In fact, it seems that one would be tempted to say that it's not fair that things *go so well for her*[16] after what she did. No doubt, for Ned life is awful, and things do go very badly for him. The fact that at least Matty is doing well can, if anything, only make things worse for him.

(3) WISH AND DUTY

Let us look at the following case:

> Marshall is about to talk to his grandmother on the phone. He hasn't had her over in a long time, so he thinks it is his duty to invite her to come for dinner sometime the following week. He takes family duties very seriously, even though he finds his grandmother extremely dull, and he does not particularly enjoy cooking. He'll call her and invite her, and if she accepts the invitation, he'll go ahead and make dinner for her and entertain her for that evening. However, Marshall dreads the thought of cooking for his grandmother and spending an evening with her. As he calls her, he wishes she'll decline his invitation.

It seems perfectly reasonable that Marshall should have these attitudes, and the obvious explanation is that although he thinks it would be good to have his grandmother over for dinner, it would not be good for him to spend an evening in this manner. It would make very little sense for an impartial observer to have the same conflicting attitudes as Marshall. The impartial observer would simply wish for whatever she thought would be best to happen.

(d) Inheritance

Let us look at the following case:

> Paris did not know that she had a very rich distant relative, a young man she had never met. She learned about his existence when he died without leaving a will and she turned out to be the nearest of kin, and the rightful inheritor of all his money.

Here it is perfectly appropriate for a friend to say (although it might be insensitive to put in these exact words): "I guess it's sad to hear that this guy died. But overall this is good news! You're so lucky; things have turned really well for you." Again the obvious explanation is that although the redistribution of the money could not possibly compensate for the badness of someone's death, it is still *good for Paris* that things turned out this way. Notice that it seems to make sense for Paris to wish that she would inherit money in this way, to see it as a desirable outcome, in a way that it would not make sense for an impartial observer who would regard this scenario, other things being equal, more or less as simply resulting in the net loss of one life. Similarly, it could not matter for an impartial observer, other things being equal, whether Paris or someone else inherits the money. In light of these cases, it seems that we can come up with the following desiderata for an account of the relation between "good" and "good for":

> (1) SACRIFICE—At least sometimes, when the agent chooses what is good *simpliciter*, she will be making a sacrifice. A sacrifice involves doing something that is in some way not good from the perspective of the agent.

(2) AGENT'S EMOTIONS AND ATTITUDES—The appropriateness of certain agents' emotions such as pride or shame depends on whether what the agent chose was good for him or not (that is, even if paying myself a large bonus is what is best *simpliciter*, I should not feel the same pride in doing it as I would feel if I accepted a pay cut because it was what I thought to be best *simpliciter*).

(3) DIVERGENCE OF ATTITUDES—In some cases the attitudes of impartial observers and the recipient of a benefit or a harm will, or ought to, diverge. While it might make sense for me to be glad that I, rather than a stranger, inherit some money, it makes no sense for an impartial observer to have the same attitude.

(4) TEMPTATION AND NORMATIVE CONFLICT—Cases in which "good for" and "good" diverge are typically cases in which the agent faces temptation and in which there is at least an apparent normative conflict.

Moreover an adequate account of these notions should be able to answer a host of questions. What should a rational agent do when she could either promote the good or what is good for her? Should she always choose one over the other? Should she weigh the two? And how should she feel with respect to the fact that she failed to promote what is good or what is good for her? Should it matter (to her) in any special way that she failed to promote what is good or good for her? What should the attitude of a third party be when someone chooses what is good for him rather than what is good *simpliciter* or vice versa? These are the kinds of questions that, ideally, an account of the relation between what is good and what is good for would be able to answer.

Before we move on, I should first note that, as we saw even in Teresa's case, although "good" and "good for" may potentially diverge, there are also strong intuitions that they are related. It seems that almost nothing, if anything at all, could count as good if it were not good for someone. Even if some people are convinced, for instance, that unobservable beauty is good, it would be hard to deny that many things are good because they are good for someone. As Mill suggests, a sacrifice is only good if it results in something that is good for someone.[17]

Now the most straightforward way of explaining the difference between "good" and "good for" would be to claim that there are two irreducible evaluative notions here, something like prudential value and moral value. Let us first distinguish between two ways of understanding these evaluative notions. The first one is purely descriptive: To say that something has a certain kind of value is just to attribute a certain kind of (natural or nonnatural) property to it. If the claim is that there are two such properties and one is not reducible to the other, this is all fine and good, except that it doesn't seem to get us what we wanted. First, it tells us nothing yet about why agents should *care* about whether what they promote is good or good for them. Making the distinction this way does not capture our intuitions about these notions, since it seems that, if not in all cases at least in typical cases, it matters to us, and it should matter to us, that something is good or good for us. Moreover, it does not tell us how to understand the seemingly incompatible demands that *the good* and *the good for someone* make on an agent. Finally, this way of making the distinction also tells us nothing about how the notions are *related*. No doubt a view that took these notions to be descriptive could try to add an account of the demands that these values make on us and of the relation between the values, but my point is only that, by itself, the strategy is incomplete. We'd need to add to this account a further account of the nature of these demands, and it is the plausibility of accounts of *that* kind that I am trying to examine.

In fact, the issues I want to examine can be brought into focus by considering a view that admirably answers a related question; namely, classical utilitarianism. Classical utilitarianism has a very elegant way of explaining "good" in terms of "good for." According to classical utilitarianism, one's greatest happiness is what is best for the agent (and the more happiness an agent enjoys, the better it is for her). One's happiness is understood as total pleasure minus total pain. The general good is the sum of the happiness of all agents; the greater the sum, the better the state of affairs. However, classical utilitarianism by itself does not say whether one should pursue one's own good or the general good, whether it should matter to an agent that she has to pursue one at the expense of the other, and if so, how it should matter, whether there are two competing notions of right corresponding to two competing evaluative notions, etc. But these are exactly the questions we will be interested in.[18]

More generally, we can put the issue in the following way. I will assume that evaluative notions are supposed to have normative implications. Now the question is how we are supposed to understand the normative implications. If they generate only *prima facie* or *pro tanto* reasons, then we can understand that sometimes one reason will override the other, and that, perhaps, the overridden reason might generate some regret. But we cannot understand, for instance, why it might be inappropriate to say to Teresa that her life is just great, or that she couldn't be doing much better. After all, the mere fact that there is *something* of *some* value that was not pursued can hardly give us a reason to think that someone's life is not going very well. And it's hard to see why we should not think that Matty does much worse than Teresa, since Matty presumably chose to act on a reason that was only a *prima facie* reason, whereas Teresa at least chose in accordance with what there was most reason to do. Although it is not clear how this suggestion would deal with cases (c) and (d), which do not center on choices, it is hard to see how it could serve as the basis of a satisfactory account. After all, it is not clear how these resources could explain the asymmetries in Marshall's and Paris's positions on the one hand, and the position of the impartial observers on the other hand, given that there's nothing in the distinction between *prima facie* and all-out reasons to distinguish their positions. For instance, one could say that it makes sense to regret that a lesser good was not promoted even when a greater good was, and we can feel some satisfaction in the obtaining of a lesser good even

when a greater good was not obtained. But this is very far from accounting what happens in *Inheritance*. After all, the impartial observer sees
nothing good in what happens; rather than observing a rich person and a
not-so-rich person, the impartial observer sees now a rich person and a
dead person. But this is surely not how Paris sees things.

More precisely, we can see the problem as arising from a conflict among
the following tenets:

(1) "X is good for A" and "X is good" express genuinely evaluative claims.
(2) In some cases, it is true that all things considered, X is good for A,
while it is true that all things considered Y is good, when X and Y are not
jointly realizable states of affairs.[19]
(3) Evaluative truths imply normative truths.

These three claims on their own are not mutually incompatible, and all
the parties to the debate in section 2 accept (1) through (3). To generate
a conflict we first need a much more specific version of (3):

(3a) Evaluative truths of the type "all things considered, X is good for A"
and also of the type "all things considered, X is good" imply rational
requirements of the kind "All things considered, A ought to bring about
X," when it is in A's power to bring about X.

And we need to add a clause with respect to the impossibility of true di-
lemmas of rationality:

(4) It is never true that all things considered we ought to bring about X
and Y when X and Y are not jointly realizable.

Obviously we cannot construct a parallel claim to (3a) for every single
kind of evaluative claim. What would all things considered be most beautiful, for instance, is not necessarily what we should bring about. This is
because aesthetic goods are what we can call a "merely contributory
good"; these goods merely contribute, or may contribute in certain conditions, to our estimation of the value of a state of affairs. Claims about
aesthetic goods are claims about a *kind* of good, not claims about *the*
good or what is good *overall*. If we can show that either "good" *sans
phrase* or "good for A" is a merely contributory good, or that one is just a
kind of good of the other type, then we have an easy route to deny the
truth of (3a) while staying clear of any contradiction. The most obvious
way of doing this is by employing a reductive approach; it is to try to
show that either to say that "X is good" *sans phrase* is just to say that X is
a contributory good for A of a certain kind K, or to try to show that to say
that "X is good for A" is just to say that X is a contributory good *sans
phrase* of a certain kind K. Indeed these are the two reductive approaches
we will consider below.[20]

Claim (4) is reasonably intuitive but it has been denied exactly
because of conflicts between impersonal and personal goods. Sidgwick
has famously suggested that reason could not settle between the demand

to pursue the greatest good and the demand to pursue the individual good; or in our words, the demand to pursue what is good and what is good for oneself.[21] Denying (4) would constitute what we might call "incommensurability approaches." Ideally, we would investigate the plausibility of particular approaches of this kind, but I'll leave them aside and simply assume that if we can come up with an alternative account, it would be better to come to the conclusion that there are not two incompatible, formal ends of practical reason.

As the astute reader has noticed, strictly speaking, (1), (2), (3a), and (4) do not generate a contradiction unless we also assume that some of the situations in which all-things-considered evaluative claims of the two kinds of conflict are cases in which the agent can bring about X or Y. This is, no doubt, a weak enough assumption, and it does us no harm to add it right here. However, even in cases in which the agent cannot bring about either X or Y, the conflict between the two all-things-considered evaluative judgments is still problematic. Whether things turn out for the best or not implies the appropriateness of various attitudes of rejoicing, regret, etc., or so I'll assume. Some of these implications might conflict with our ordinary attitudes toward outcomes in which what is good and what is good for X turn out to be different. When examining the plausibility of various options, we need to see not only if they prescribe the right actions but also whether they explain why we think that certain attitudes are appropriate. Indeed, some of the cases above are cases in which we might be puzzled about exactly how to explain a certain attitude, and my contention is that often it's harder for a theory to explain the appropriateness (or inappropriateness) of certain attitudes than to explain why a certain action is the one the agent ought to perform. Although I'll not try to spell out more precisely the conditions of adequacy with regard to these attitudes, I'll often examine whether a certain view matches our intuitive judgments about the appropriateness of certain attitudes. I would be remiss not to end the suspense here, and reveal from the outset that I'll try to show that it is not possible to account for these intuitions and desiderata by rejecting either (4) or (3a) on its own. The better account, I will argue, rejects (3a) *by rejecting* (1). I want to argue that "good for" is not a genuine evaluative notion; rather, it captures how the evaluative landscape *appears to be* to a certain agent.

3. REDUCTIVE APPROACHES

(A) Reduction to Good For

There are at least two kinds of approaches that are popular in the literature that can be broadly described as reduction of the "good" to "good for," a Humean and an Aristotelian one.[22] Let us start with the Humean approach. According to the Humean, our desires, projects, and, more generally, our "subjective motivational set" determine what is good for us, and we have only reason to pursue what is good for us. This easily explains what goes on in *Inheritance*. The outcome is obviously good for Paris, but not for her young rich relative. The Humean also allows, of course, that one's desires or projects might involve commitments to a broadly impersonal pursuit such as morality. One can at first think of morality as a system that prescribes or gives some kind of positive valence that we can term "morally good."[23] On its own, "morally good" is a purely descriptive term, and says nothing beyond the fact that a certain action is recommended by a certain system of rules. However, insofar as morality becomes an agent's project, or is somehow incorporated into the agent's motivational set, then such an agent has reason to pursue what morality recommends.[24] We can then describe scenarios (a) through (d) as cases in which what morality recommends conflicts with what would satisfy other members of the agent's motivational set. The conflict between "good" and "good for," on this view, is a conflict between different ends that an agent has.[25]

Humean theories of morality have been widely criticized, but my concern is much narrower. Some of the well-known problems with Humean theories affect their plausibility of providing a good understanding of the relation between "good" and "good for." So, for instance, many philosophers complain that Humeans make the reasons to be moral desire-dependent, and that this is a very counterintuitive understanding of the nature of moral reasons. So this view cannot capture the desire-independent nature of what is good. The Humean seems to thrive in explaining why Matty's life is good for her; after all, she got all that she wanted, she succeeded in all her projects, and no lack of information seems to have misled her in her understanding of what was good for her. What many ethicists think is rendered incomprehensible by the Humean view is how there was any kind of normative demand that would have required Matty to have refrained from behaving the way she did.[26]

However, even if we ignore these problems it is unclear that this way of conceiving the relation between *good* and *good for* will preserve the intuitions brought forth in (a) through (d). All that we need to see to make this point is that the theory cannot treat the difference between moral reasons and nonmoral reasons that are reasons for the agent, as anything but the difference between *prima facie* and all-out reasons. At best, the Humean can say that Teresa had to forego something that she had some reason to pursue in light of her stronger commitment to morality. But compare Teresa's situation with the situation of someone who realizes that he has better reasons on this occasion to pursue his own good than the good of others. Suppose, for instance, that Milton, unlike Teresa, comes to the conclusion that he should not suffer great pain to save children who are undergoing some kind of deprivation. It's not that Milton has no kind of commitment to morality; he is just like most of us. He is unwilling to sacrifice as much as Teresa for the sake of unknown children. Assuming that Teresa is not self-deceived, making any mistakes of deliberation, etc., the Humean has to regard Teresa's and Milton's situation as exactly the same with regard to the pursuit of their own good. Teresa is pursuing her own good to the same extent as Milton; it is just that the content of their own good is slightly different. And both are doing just as well for themselves. It is not just that the Humean view cannot explain why sacrifices are demanded from people who do not care enough about others to make them; the Humean view also fails to explain why it still counts as making a sacrifice when people *do* care. The Humean account makes Teresa's life, full of pain and deprivation, a life in which things are going well for her, and renders Teresa's friends' bizarre remarks mostly appropriate.[27]

The Aristotelian view does not make one's reasons dependent on one's desires but rather on a conception of human flourishing. Now an Aristotelian view could claim that anyone's flourishing is equally important from anyone's point of view, but this would not be a reduction of "good" to "good for";[28] if anything, it would be a reduction that would go the other way around. The Aristotelian view I would like to consider takes it to be the case that each person aims, or should aim, at his or her own flourishing.[29] Now this general Aristotelian view is compatible with many conceptions of flourishing and many views about the relation between one's flourishing and actions that we ordinarily classify as morally good. In particular, we can distinguish between two kinds of view; one that allows that pursuing what is morally good would undermine one's flourishing at least in certain occasions, and a conception that claims that the pursuit of one's flourishing is never incompatible with doing what is morally required, or what is morally best.

I'll first consider views of the latter kind, which I consider the most successful of all the views we'll discard. So, according to this sort of view, a human being cannot flourish unless she leads a virtuous life. However, I take it that under any plausible version of this view being virtuous does not suffice for flourishing; in some cases, the absence of what Aristotle calls "external goods" will prevent the virtuous agent from flourishing. So the Aristotelian view can do well in explaining Teresa's predicament: Being virtuous has required that she deprive herself from external goods and thus from the possibility of having a truly flourishing life. Thus her life, despite being virtuous, is not going well. The Aristotelian can say this, without having to concede that Teresa chose the wrong thing. For things might have been even worse, with regard to her flourishing, had she not helped the children. The Aristotelian view can similarly explain our intuitions in *Inheritance*. For the external goods transferred in this manner from the young relative to Paris now contribute to *her* flourishing.

I must say that even at this point the Aristotelian account already encounters some difficulties. Even if the Aristotelian understanding of *Inheritance* is fully adequate, it's not clear that this understanding of Teresa's predicament is so compelling. After all, if the Aristotelian view wants to claim that Teresa did what she had most reason to do (or that she chose her good, or some similar claim), he must say that Teresa did relatively well in terms of flourishing, better than if she had just ignored the plight of the children and returned home to safety, or just led a life that most of us lead. The Aristotelian can say that it would have been even better if Teresa had ended up not suffering pain and deprivation, but cannot, at this point, recover the intuition, that had Teresa chose not to undertake such enormous sacrifices, she would have chosen what would be better for her.[30]

The Aristotelian view seems also to have difficulties in accounting for *Wish and Duty*. It seems that either having dinner with his grandmother contributes to Marshall's flourishing, in which case, he should make the promise and wish she could come, or it does not contribute to his flourishing, in which case, Marshall should not invite her. Aristotelians have tried to explain similar phenomena by trying to make an argument roughly along the following lines.[31] Certain dispositions, such as loyalty, are essential for the agent's flourishing. But having this disposition requires that the agent act in accordance with the disposition even when the disposition leads us to perform actions that do not contribute to our flourishing. One cannot flourish unless one is a loyal friend, but once one is a loyal friend, one will be ready to sacrifice oneself even when such a sacrifice would curtail one's flourishing. And perhaps the same strategy will help us account for Teresa's plight; her commitment to the cause of humanity might have been essential for her flourishing, but now living up to this commitment will be harmful to her flourishing.

I cannot give a full examination of the plausibility of this view. I will here mostly register my reasons for being skeptical that this move will help the Aristotelian much. In particular, I can't see how this move can be made without making the Aristotelian view into what Parfit calls a "self-effacing" view. The loyal friend cannot recognize both that being loyal to one's friend on this occasion is in all things considered detrimental to her flourishing, and that her flourishing is her "ultimate end," and yet reasonably conclude that she should be loyal to her friend in this occasion.[32] But to explain our intuitions in terms of a self-effacing theory is basically to postulate an error theory. It's hard to see how it is true on this view that Teresa ought to help the children (or that Teresa should judge that helping the children is overall good on this occasion), or that Marshall ought to make this promise to his grandmother. These seem to be just beneficial illusions; one would need to deny that these very plausible claims are, strictly speaking, true.

(B) Good For *to* Good

What about trying the other way around? What about saying that there is only "good" and that "good for" should be reduced to good? The central idea of this view is that various things are good, and that all agents have reasons to pursue these goods, but that "good for" should be understood in terms of this more general notion of "good." Now there are various ways one could try to reduce "good for" to "good." As we'll see, the view I favor can also be classified as a reductive view of this sort. But in this section, I'll be concerned mostly with attempts to reduce "good for" to "good" in which "good for" is a kind of good. In other words, the reduction that I now have in mind always takes the form:

(Red) X is good for A if and only if X is good and p.

or

(Red*) X is good for A if and only if X is good and X is F.

I'll only look at one possible substitute for the second conjunct proposed originally by Moore, and more recently by Regan.[33] According to this view, "X is good for A" should be understood as "X is good and X occurs in the life of A"; I'll call this view the "Moorean view."

The Moorean view can only be plausible if combined with a view that all the relevant goods are good experiences. Otherwise, it's hard to see how it could match what we ordinarily take to be good for someone. Let us assume that instances of beautiful singing, rather than experiences of listening to beautiful singing, are themselves good. I have a beautiful voice, but I am also deaf and it hurts my throat when I try to sing. Now, if for any reason, I end up singing, the instance of good singing would occur in my life, but it would be rather counterintuitive to think that my singing is something that is good for me. However, even if one thought that other things were good, one could still claim that only experiential goods that occur within the agent's life constitute what is good for the agent. There is a lot that this view can account for at a certain level of explanation. We can say that what's wrong with Matty, from the point of view of an impartial spectator, is that she gets undeserved goods in her life, and undeserved goods call for resentment rather than pity. We can say that Teresa sacrifices herself because she brings about the most good by bringing a lot of pain to her life. The money will result in more goods occurring in Paris's life, and Marshall's life will be spared the pain of boredom if his grandmother releases him from his obligations.

But there is immediately something dissatisfying about this account. After all, given that all we add by saying that the good occurs in the life of the agent it is that we give it a certain location in the agent's mental life, the fact that something is good for the agent makes no extra normative claim on the agent. So there is no reason why, on this view, it should matter more to the agent that a good occurs in his life than that it occurs in the southwest corner of San Antonio. Now the Moorean might object that whether or not it *should* matter to the agent, it *does* matter to the agent. Even if "good for" makes no *normative* claim on us, the fact that X is good for A should lead us to expect that A cares for it. Although this move may explain, for instance, why Paris's friend might be happy for her, it still leaves quite a bit unexplained. For instance, why, on this view, are

Teresa's actions a sacrifice? It is not true that Teresa cares more for the goods in her life than for the goods in the lives of the children; the fact that she chose to sacrifice herself for their good is clear evidence that she cares more for their good. But in this case there is nothing that the Moorean can offer to restore our sense that things are not going well for her in order to explain the impression that Karol's remarks are wholly inappropriate.

Of course, the Moorean can say that as much as Teresa is interested in sparing the children from pain, she also cares about the good in her life. But this, first, does not explain why the fact that she is in pain should be any different for her than the fact that many other children cannot be saved by her actions (especially given that, again, Teresa is the sort of person who obviously does care for other children). Moreover, not all can be perfect. Although her actions brought about some bad things, they obviously brought about much more good. Karol's remark that Teresa's life is great might be off the mark on this view, but overall when someone thinks that things are going badly for Teresa they cannot be using any overall evaluative claim. There is no reason for Teresa to, say, turn to God and complain "Why me?" Overall, she must think that things have turned out really well from the point of view of all that matters and should matter to her, and thus from all the relevant points of view.

It is similarly difficult for the Moorean to explain Marshall's position. After all, Marshall does care enough about doing nice things for his grandmother that this is what he'll do if she doesn't stop him. In assuming that it is good that Marshall entertains his grandmother this way, we also assume that this is what Marshall should care about overall. So why does it make sense for him to wish that she would turn down the invitation? Again the Moorean, one can insist that although Marshall *has no reason* to wish for his grandmother to turn down the invitation, he does so wish. But here the Moorean appeals to an irrational and unexplained psychological fact to account for something that seems quite reasonable. Perhaps Marshall could be a more loving grandson, such that he would fully enjoy cooking for his grandmother and entertaining her. It might even be better if he were a more loving grandson. But given that he isn't, his attitudes seem perfectly reasonable.

I find the Moorean view most problematic when we try to understand questions of desert. We want to say that Matty doesn't deserve to end up doing so well; if anyone deserves this kind of life it is Teresa, not Matty. One way to make sense of the idea that she does not deserve her life is to say that things should not be so good for someone who is so evil. You only deserve things to go well for you if you are a good person. But if "good for" just marks the location at which a certain good occurs, why should it matter whether it occurs in the life of someone who did evil or if it occurs in the life of someone who did good? If, as Regan suggests, we should "just promote all agents' valuable activity, without worrying about anyone's well-being," why should it matter that valuable activity happened to be in the life of an evil person? Why should it be any different from promoting valuable activities on Sunset Boulevard, given that Sunset Boulevard was the location of so much that was evil? To be sure, the Moorean can say that it is just a fact that there is value in good things occurring in the lives of good people and disvalue in them occurring in the lives of bad people. I have nothing in general against having such primitives in one's theory. However, it is a strike against one's view when one must make into a primitive something that seemed to have an obvious explanation.

We can put matters in an admittedly unfair and oversimplifying, but I think helpful, manner. Reducing the *good* to the *good for* makes moral actions a matter of self-indulgence, and thus fails to leave room for understanding what one gives up when one makes a sacrifice, as well as the possibility of normative *demands* to make genuine sacrifices. Reducing the *good for* to the *good* alienates the agent from his life in such a way that one cannot understand how there could even be any such thing as genuine sacrifice and genuine rewards, let alone genuine demands to make sacrifices or to offer rewards to those (and only those) who deserve them.

4. THE APPEARANCE VIEW

I want to suggest a different way of understanding the distinction between *good* and *good for*. It is a reductive account in the sense that we end up with only one kind of evaluative dimension. However, it is not an account that reduces "*good*" to "*good for* and *p*" or vice versa. In fact, I think that the problem with the approaches surveyed is that it took each case in which we want to say that "X is good" or "X is good for A" as a genuine instance of value, and the question then was whether one kind of value could be reduced to the other, or if they were two disparate, incommensurable kinds of values.[34] Rather, my view is that the difference is not between kinds of value, but a difference in perspectives. "Good for" marks the things that will seem good from the perspective of the agent, and "good" marks what is, in fact, good.

In order to lay out this proposal more clearly, it is worth starting with a traditional view about the relation between desiring and the good that I call "the scholastic view." According to the scholastic view, to desire X is to conceive X to be good, and to be averse to X is to conceive X to be bad. Now many philosophers think that not all desires are for the good,[35] and, although this is less discussed, I take it that the same philosophers would think that not all aversions are for the bad. I do think that the scholastic view is true in full generality,[36] but my argument will not depend on this strong claim. All that we need is that in many cases desiring goes together (causally or conceptually) with conceiving something as good, and that in many cases being averse goes together (causally or conceptually) with conceiving something as bad. But perhaps more important to the view I will defend is that "conceiving to be good" or "conceiving to be bad" does

not imply "judging it to be good" or "judging it to be bad." "Conceiving" is
to be understood in terms of appearance: something that inclines us or
tempts us to judge in a certain manner, something that is a *prima facie*
(though not necessarily *pro tanto*) reason to judge, but that we sometimes
can recognize as being illusory.

We can distinguish three kinds of illusory appearances. Some kind of
illusory appearances just go away once we realize they're just an illusion.
Suppose as I am hiking I stop and notice something that seems to me to
be a sleeping wild animal. I focus my attention and I realize that it's just
a rock formation. Once I can see what is in front of me as a rock formation, it is likely that it no longer appears to me to be a sleeping animal. I'll
call such illusions non-recalcitrant. Not all perceptual illusions are non-
recalcitrant. The well-known Müller-Lyer illusion is not like that. If I see
lines drawn in this manner, they'll continue to appear to me to be of different sizes even when I know that they are not. These kinds of illusion
are recalcitrant. However, even though the illusion is recalcitrant, it often
does not affect belief formation. Even if the lines still appear to be of different sizes, I have no problem in these situations sticking to the belief
that I form once I measure the lines with a ruler; my knowledge is after
this point completely stable. I'll call this kind of illusion a benign recalcitrant illusion.

One might think that in the theoretical realm at least, all recalcitrant
illusions are benign. However, it is not so clear that this is true. Take, for
instance, a non-perceptual appearance. Many people are susceptible to
the illusion that some kinds of "jinxing" are possible. So one might think
that boasting about how one will win the next race will have some influence on the outcome of the race, or that being overconfident about
one's chances that one's poem will be selected by the prize committee
will diminish the probability of this happening. Often one is fully convinced that this is just a superstition, but one still might find it hard to
shake off its influence in belief formation. I have no doubts that jinxing
is not causally efficacious, and yet, when someone tells me about how
my favorite team is likely to win the World Cup, I still feel compelled
to issue cautionary remarks, and point out things that may prevent this
desirable outcome.[37] Illusions that still influence one's beliefs even
when we know that they are illusions can be called "malignant recalcitrant illusions." Now if we accept that desires and aversions are at least
sometimes appearances in the practical realm, we can think that they
also may constitute illusions of all three kinds. My general view is that
something counts as good for the agent or bad for the agent if it appears
to the agent that a certain object is good or bad in a certain stable manner. One kind of stability is the kind that is generated by practical
knowledge; in this case, X appears good to the agent, because the agent
correctly judges it to be good in a stable manner.[38] Cases of practical
knowledge of this kind are cases in which what is good and what is good
for the agent do not come apart.

But another kind of stability is generated by the existence of a recalcitrant illusion, especially the existence of a malignant recalcitrant illusion. These are cases in which what appears good to the agent is not good, or cases in which what appears to be bad for the agent is not bad, but the illusion does not go away even if one knows that the desires and aversions in question are not accurate conceptions of value. These are cases of divergence between what is good and what is good for the agent. The divergence is not between two kinds of values, but between an objective and a subjective perspective on value.

Let us start by looking at a simple comparison. Let us look at two cases in which I think that something bad must happen for a greater good.

(i) Staying Fit

Paula has made a New Year's resolution to run every day. Paula thinks that staying fit is not only instrumentally good but also intrinsically good. However, Paula now realizes that she has an unexpected opportunity to climb the corporate ladder. But to take advantage of this opportunity, she needs to work long hours, and given her other commitments, she won't be able to keep her running schedule. Paula is very ambitious, and she knows that this is a unique opportunity. Given these considerations, she decides it's better to give up on her New Year's resolution.

(ii) Anesthesia

Jerzy needs to have a certain dental procedure, and he lives in a country where one has to pay a very high price for anesthesia. Jerzy comes to the conclusion that the best thing is to endure the pain so that he can use the money to help his ailing wife.

When Paula wakes up in the morning to go to her job, she might regret, to some extent, not being able to run to stay fit. She recognizes this as a valuable activity. But it would certainly not be far-fetched to think that this regret in no way threatens the stability of her judgment that, all things considered, or overall,[39] it's better to advance in her job. There's no serious temptation for her of going running, or any real chance that Paula will wake up one day, and just go running instead of showing up for her job.[40] We can say in this case that there is no recalcitrant illusion, or at least no malignant illusion, associated with Paula's desire to run every morning. The same is not true in Jerzy's case. Certainly the pain gives rise to temptation, and it's hard to rule out the possibility that if he can change his mind during the procedure, he would. Even if Jerzy is fully convinced that the money is better spent in helping his wife, it'll take a great deal of effort for him to stick to his decision because *it constantly appears to him that suffering the pain is worse*—or so I'll contend. It is common to think that a victim of torture breaks down by saying, or thinking, something like: "I'll do anything if the pain will just stop." My contention is that the victim of torture is at this point under an inescapable illusion (or is nearly so) that nothing is worse than the pain.

But what is true in the torture case is true more generally; when we are focused on pain, especially intense pain, other evils will pale in comparison, and the good of pain relief will appear to be particularly great. Now even if the torture victim does not confess, it is still true that given the nature of pain, it'll keep appearing to him that very little is worse than the pain, even if he can keep coming back to his view that it is better not to cooperate with the torturer. The fate of the person being tortured is similar to someone who knows she is under massive perceptual illusions. As, say, illusions of her friends coming in and saying hurtful things to her would assail her, she would have to make an immense effort not to be taken by the illusion. She might, by dint of this effort, never act badly, or feel hurt by what her illusory friends say, but it would constantly appear to her that they were in front of her, and it would be plausible to describe her even as momentarily forming false beliefs that she would keep correcting. Similar things, *mutatis mutandis,* can be said about pleasure.

If one accepts this view about how pain affects our evaluative point of view, we can put forward the following hypothesis, which I'll call "the appearance view" with regard to what makes the case that X is good for A:

> (GOOD FOR) X is good for A if and only if X contributes in a persistent way to making it appear to A that the actual state of affairs is better (more good) than it would appear to A if X did not obtain.
>   (BAD FOR) X is bad for A if and only if X contributes in a persistent way to making it appear to A that the actual state of affairs is worse than it would appear to A if X did not obtain.

There are obvious questions about how to understand the counterfactuals in these definitions, but I will assume that just as we have an intuitive understanding about whether it would have been better or worse if certain events had or had not occurred, we can also have an intuitive sense of whether it would make things appear better or worse for the agent if certain things had or had not happened.[41] And as we'll see, we might want to modify each definition so that we restrict the range of appearances to genuinely practical appearances.

It seems that the appearance view has no trouble explaining the fact that the notions of good and good for are related. After all, one is just a subjective conception of the other. However, although this shows that the notions are related, it does not seem to show that they are related in the right way. After all, this does not explain how what is good for each agent is a *constituent of* what is good. Any reasonable theory of the good *sans phrase* would take what is good for an agent to be of tremendous importance; for some theories, it is all that could possibly be good. It seems that, if anything, the fact that something merely appears to someone to be good would be of no importance whatsoever.

But this is incorrect. First, and most obviously, sometimes things appear just as they are, so the fact that something appears to be good is obviously not incompatible with its being good. Of course, this is unlikely to lay to rest those who think that what is good for the agent is a constituent of what is good, but it is important to notice that this account does not claim that "good for" refers to a set of nonveridical illusions in the life of an agent. However, the appearance view also does not preclude that what is good for an agent is a constituent of what is good. Let us call a state in which it appears to the subject of the state that **p** an "appearance state"; we will be mostly concerned with states in which it appears to the agent that something is good or bad, or as I will call them, "evaluative appearance states." Now describing a state as an appearance state does not necessarily describe all that it is relevant to evaluating this state. For instance, a state in which it appears to me that I am going to fall to my death could also be a thrilling experience. Pain, if I am correct, is a state in which it appears to the subject of pain that overall the state of affairs is bad, and it can also constitute a malignant recalcitrant illusion; even when one judges that it is worth undergoing some pain for a greater good, the pain might threaten the stability of the overall judgment that one ought to endure the pain. But, of course, one can accept this understanding of pain and yet think that the existence of pain typically makes a state of affairs worse than it would otherwise be. In particular, the following popular theories are immediately committed to the relevance of states in which things appear for the agent in a certain way:

(i) Endorsement Theories

Theories that claim that it is a necessary condition of certain states being valuable that a certain agent judges it to be valuable will be theories that accept that appearance states are, if not valuable in themselves, at least conditions of value. The same goes for a theory that takes an appearance state to be a constituent, or a condition of something being a constituent of the good if it accepts any of the following: The value of certain states of affairs depends on whether an agent approves of it; or the value of the state of affairs depends on the agent endorsing its desirability; or the value depends on the agent having the appropriate desire for the state of affairs; or an end is only valuable or worthy of being pursued if it is reflectively endorsed, or properly incorporated into a maxim, etc. After all, approving something involves judging it to be good, and thus, approving something is an evaluative appearance state. The same goes for endorsing. Not everyone accepts that every case of desiring is one in which something appears to be good for the agent; however, it is hard to deny that many of them are, and, in particular, it is plausible to assume that only desires in which their objects appear to be good in some way to the agent can be determinants of whether something is or is not a constituent of the good.

(ii) Theories in Which Pleasure and the Absence of Pain Are Important Goods

Given the above understanding of pain, and a similar understanding of pleasure, both pains and pleasures are evaluative appearance states. So any view that accepts that these are important constituents of the good will accept that evaluative appearance states are important constituents of the good.

(iii) Kantian Theory

Here is a coarse sketch of such a view: Suppose one thinks that the objects of one's inclinations are putatively good, but in order to be, in fact, good, it is necessary and sufficient that they also conform to certain conditions. Such a view would also take evaluative appearance states to be constitutive of the good, albeit in a more complex way.

It is worth mentioning that in not all of these cases does it turn out that something is good *because* it is good for the agent. Especially in (ii), it would be more precise to say that what makes something good is also what makes it good for the agent. However, this does not seem to be a problematic implication; our intuitions do not so clearly favor one option over the other. But it is also important to note that the fact that the appearance view is compatible with all these views enables it to have, or at least to borrow, an advantage over the Moorean view. The Moorean view has troubles explaining why so much of what is good is also good for someone; the appearance view, on the other hand, can simply piggyback on whatever explanations such other theories offer for their account of the good.

(A) Teresa and Matty Reconsidered

The best way to test further the plausibility of the appearance view is to see how it deals with each example. Let us start with Teresa. Teresa does bring about much good to the world. But she does by causing herself to suffer a great deal of pain. The consequence of this fact is that she can do it only by having this state of affairs constantly appearing to her to be bad. Things are not great for her in the sense that no matter how convinced she is that she did the best possible thing, it keeps appearing to her that what she did was bad. One might compare Teresa's predicament with, say, a mother who can only save her son by then suffering from constant illusions that he is dead. No matter how much the mother cares for her son, this is obviously not an enviable position, since it keeps *appearing* to the mother that the son is dead. Given that her pain constitutes a malignant recalcitrant illusion, from Teresa's point of view things are not as good as one might have thought they would be simply because from her point of view things keep appearing to be bad.

It is true that on this view, the fact that Teresa judges that her choice was correct will make it the case that things are better for her than if she were a selfish person whose same suffering accidentally helped the children in the same way. After all, the fact that she judges it to be good must contribute to things not appearing as bad to her, or at least not in the same way, as if she did not think it was good to help the children. But I do not find this consequence counterintuitive; the fact that Teresa accomplished something that she finds important must indeed contribute to things not being as bad for her as they would otherwise be.

Similar things can be said about Matty. Given Matty's evaluative views, she is now in the position that things appear good to her; she is in a special kind of fool's paradise. The state of affairs is one that stably appears to Matty to be good. As for Ned, who was framed for the murder, the state of affairs will appear to him even worse than it actually is. It is worth considering in more detail Matty's situation. Our attitudes to someone in more traditional versions of fool's paradise tend to be ambiguous. Whether it is better to know or not that one's spouse has had an affair is a primary example of an unsettled bar controversy. On the other hand, almost no one doubts that it would be particularly cruel to point out to a dying mathematician a major fallacy in the "proof" she thought had been the greatest achievement of her career. We might pity the betrayed spouse or the dying mathematician, but we certainly pity them mostly for having a disloyal spouse and for not having succeeded in finding the proof. It is difficult in the case of the betrayed spouse to say whether we should pity him more or less for not knowing that the affair happened. But in the case of the dying mathematician we would pity her even more if she were to learn that her proof was fallacious. At any rate, we must note that the kind of mistake that leaves you in a fool's paradise is not always necessarily the subject of pity. And although we do not want to exchange our position with the person who is in a fool's paradise (after all, we know that that state of affairs would be, in fact, worse), there is something obviously enviable about a fool's paradise. And this is similar to our attitude toward Matty. Although there is something clearly enviable about Matty's situation, the morally good agent would not want to be in her place. But it seems hard to accept that there is no significant difference between Matty's case and the case of the betrayed spouse or the dying mathematician, and it would be hard to accept that our attitudes need to be the same in all these cases.

The source of the difference must be that Matty's illusions are not theoretical but evaluative. Matty's views of the nonevaluative world are perfectly accurate. The illusion in Matty's case (just as in Teresa's case for this matter) lies in her evaluative attitudes, not in her theoretical attitudes. And since practical mistakes are more blameworthy than theoretical mistakes,[42] it might be inappropriate to feel pity for Matty even if it turned out to be true that it was appropriate to feel pity for the betrayed spouse or the dying mathematician solely on account of their mistake.

But Matty's case might also be different from the betrayed spouse and the dying mathematician for more profound reasons. For we can think that evaluative appearances and theoretical appearances make different contributions to what is good for an agent. So far we have presented the appearance view as not discriminating between things appearing good or bad in virtue of the evaluations of the agent and things appearing to be good and bad in virtue of the agent's beliefs. But an appearance view that makes *good for* and *bad for* only relative to evaluative appearances will be able to distinguish between Matty's case and the case of any fool in more traditional versions of a fool's paradise.

One could argue that what is good for an agent is determined solely by evaluative appearances; we judge how good or bad various states of affairs are for the agent by examining how good or bad they would appear to the agent if she were to know how the world actually is. We could justify such a view by arguing that what we're interested in is how the agent responds to the actual facts; how what's the case would affect how things appear to him as good or bad. Such a view, however, could not do justice to the case of the dying mathematician, and it would judge that it is indifferent to someone's good whether they know or fail to know that, for instance, their beloved daughter is still alive. More plausibly, one could argue that evaluative appearances and theoretical appearances contribute in different ways to what counts as good for the agent; but of course the plausibility of such a view depends on whether we can explain more precisely how each appearance contributes to an agent's good.

We can think about our judgment of how things are going for the agent as an imaginative exercise. As we imagine how things are going for her we form two sets of appearances: how good or bad things appear to the agent, and how good or bad things would appear to the agent if she were to learn what we know. Suppose someone erroneously thinks that he has won the Nobel Prize. If we imagine the truth revealed to the false Nobel Prize winner, he'll be no doubt saddened by it. But if he's like most of us, he'll also not just think "Oh, at least it was fun while it lasted." The revelation of the truth would "spoil" how he perceives the past; the celebrations will now appear completely inappropriate and silly, the gloating shameful, and the sense of superiority misplaced. The memories of this time are more likely to be experienced with shame than with joy. It will be very different from, say, someone who had an extremely fun birthday party on the wrong date. Finding out the mistake later would probably do very little to retrospectively spoil the fun.[43] But things are even more complicated if we think about a father who erroneously think that his daughter is dead; this situation is not parallel to the case of our fake Nobel Prize winner. If the father were to find out that his daughter was alive, he would not look back at the way he felt as inappropriate or would feel any kind of retrospective joy for it; grief and sadness are appropriate not only when one's loved ones are in fact in distress but also if we believe that they are in this situation, or even when we just suspect that they are.

A more satisfactory view would say the following: We count not only how good or bad a state of affairs appears to the agent now but also how it would appear if the truth were to be revealed to the agent, including how the past would retrospectively appear to the agent once the truth was revealed. Although this is the view I favor, I must confess our conception of what's good for someone becomes somewhat messy and ambivalent at this point. We, or many of us, seem sometimes tempted by the thought that ignorance is bliss, especially in situations in which we want to spare someone the truth. A fully satisfactory account of "good for" would try to accommodate or explain away these intuitions more precisely. But for our purposes what matters is that any such refinement would be a matter of refining how different appearances make a contribution to what is good for the agent; but my aim here is just to argue for the claim that the referents of "good for" and "good" stand to each other as appearance to reality.

Before we move on, it should be noted that the appearance view gives a more satisfying explanation of moral desert than the Moorean view does. It seems quite compelling to think that it is unfair that the price of bringing about some good is that things will appear bad to you. And it seems in general unfair that things will appear bad exactly for someone who brought about much good. On the hand that everything will appear to be good from the point of view of someone who brought about so much that is bad seems equally unfair. Of course, the latter is true only if one was culpable in bringing about bad things. And one might think that the appearance view makes Matty innocent, since it makes Matty just mistaken about an evaluative fact. It is worth noting that this kind of ignorance is what Aristotle calls "ignorance of the universal." And although I cannot argue here the plausibility of the view that ignorance of the universal is blameworthy, it is at least a respectable view in the thorny landscape of philosophical views about moral responsibility.

(B) Marshall and Paris Reconsidered

Obviously Paris's receiving the inheritance will bring many changes to Paris's evaluative appearance states. Not only will it change much that is recalcitrant in making things appear good or bad for Paris, but also Paris, with the money, can promote what *she* takes to be good. Now Marshall's case is a bit more complicated. Marshall recognizes that it is best to invite his grandmother, but he faces the prospect of boredom and painful cooking, which will recalcitrantly make things appear bad to him (or it will at least make having his grandmother over for dinner appear worse than not having her over). But it also seems safe to assume that the prospect of pain is itself something that is inherently unpleasant; that is, the prospect of pain is not just a representation of a future state in which it will appear to the agent that things are bad, but a representation of a future state that also *now* appears to be bad—in many cases, a representation of a future state that appears even worse than it actually is. But if this is the case, we can understand that Marshall's wish is the offspring of this recalcitrant illusion; from his point of view, he cannot but experience the prospect of his grandmother not coming with relief, since given the nature of his evaluative appearance states, it can't but stop appearing to him that it would be better if it were not to happen.

5. CONCLUSION: SOME COMPLICATIONS

I have said at the beginning that I am here only sketching a view that needs to be further developed to be fully persuasive. I want to briefly point out a couple of important complications that a more detailed treatment of the issue would have to address; I do not claim that these are the only ones.

As many philosophers have noted, the relationship between my good and the good of others is similar to the relationship between my immediate good and my future good. My immediate good can be the source of temptation; when I go to the dentist I experience it as a sacrifice for my later good. And yet, here the Moorean view might seem perfectly adequate: Something is an immediate good if and only if it is a good and it would be brought about in the immediate future. Is this a problem for my view? I think that, if anything, the opposite is true. Even if we grant this modified "Moorean" that this is a correct description of the immediate good, it does not explain why we are tempted to pursue what is immediately good for us even when a greater good lies ahead in the future. In order to explain this fact, we need to invoke a similar structure of recalcitrant appearances; the immediate good is the source of temptation exactly because it keeps appearing as better to us than what lies ahead. In fact, George Ainslie's groundbreaking work on hyperbolic discounting of future goods can be understood as explaining the nature of the illusion in question, an illusion structurally similar to familiar perceptual illusions.[44] Of course, we would still need to sort out how different appearances contribute only to what counts as what is immediately good and to what counts as good for the agent in a more general manner, and, again, this issue deserves more attention than I can spare here. But the basic idea is that we would want to exclude from our more general notion of the *good for* any recalcitrant appearances that simply reflect a temporal bias.

We might also suspect that the distinction between *good* and *good for* obscures the different ways in which we respond to the goods of different people. Let us take one aspect of how we relate differently to what is good and what is good for someone, an aspect that I have emphasized at different points here: We experience the promotion of the good as a sacrifice and the promotion of what is good for us as a temptation. We can now ask how the good of a loved one figures in our experience in relation to what is good and what is good for us. No matter how much I love someone, there will be (at least possibly) cases in which I ought to forego promoting my own good so as to promote his good. Moreover there'll also be cases in which I ought to forego promoting the good of my loved ones in order to promote the good. When we look at these cases, we do find that we can easily assimilate my concern for the good of my loved ones to the concern I have for my own good or for the good in general. A dramatic case of the former would be a father who is being tortured by terrorists who want to know the whereabouts of his daughter. I take it that in this case we would think that the father must be *tempted* to give in, and if he doesn't give in, we'll admire the kind of sacrifice he performed for his daughter's sake. So this would lead us to assimilate the good of someone's loved ones to something that contributes to what is good, but not to what is good for him. On the other hand, suppose Francis can somehow illicitly influence a job search for a job that his daughter Sofia very much wants, a job search that would otherwise certainly favor Martin, who is much more qualified for the job. In both cases, we can assume Francis knows that what is good, and what he ought to do overall, is not to help his daughter. In these cases, it seems that for Francis the relation between Sofia's good and the good in general is similar to the relation between his own good and the good. Choosing rightly will be something that he'll experience as a sacrifice, and he'll be tempted to pursue Sofia's good, rather that what is simply good. Here Sofia's good seems to play the same role in Francis's life as his own good.[45] These two cases seem to suggest that the good of our loved ones does not function exactly as a part of our own good, or as just one kind of a good *sans phrase*, but it seems to somehow squeeze between the two.

Of course, so far all that these two cases seem to show is that sometimes the good of a loved one is a constituent of our own good, and sometimes it isn't, a rather trivial result. However, matters are not so simple, when we look at cases of multiple conflicts. Suppose Frank is a repentant mafioso now trying to be an honest and law-abiding citizen. However, his former buddies think that he owes them a lot of money, much more money than Frank has right now. If Frank does not pay the money to his buddies, they will do horrible things to him. Frank suddenly remembers where he hid some money stolen from Bing that had not been previously found. The money is enough to pay off the Mafia, but could also be used to send his drug-addicted daughter Nancy to a very expensive, but also very effective, rehab facility. Frank judges, let us assume correctly, that what he should do is to return the money to Bing. But when he thinks about his beloved Nancy, and how this money could turn her life around, Frank fears that he'll succumb to the temptation of using the money for this end. Frank knows that if the money was rightfully his, he should spend it this way, even if this would lead him to great suffering. He certainly thinks that if he's going to fail to give the money back to Bing, it would be better to use the money for Nancy's sake than to use it to save his skin. But he is really scared of his old buddies, and he's afraid that if they'll show up at the door, he'll be too weak to resist the temptation to give them the money.

It seems here that in the *very same scenario*, in relation to Francis's own good, the pursuit of Nancy's good is a sacrifice, and its effective pursuit requires that Francis overcome the temptation of the pursuit of his own good, but, in relation to what is good, the pursuit of Nancy's good is a temptation, a temptation Frank thinks he should resist in order to pursue what he thinks is good. In this case of multiple conflicts, it does not seem that the good for one's loved ones can be assimilated completely to a constituent of either one's own good or the good *sans phrase*. It seems instead to also occupy an intermediary position between the two. And to make things worse, it is not hard to imagine how the good of a good friend will stand as an intermediary between the good of one's daughter and one's own good, and the good of one's spouse, one's close relatives, one's distant friends, etc. might occupy any place in between one's own good and the good. Needless to say, there is no reason to stop here at three distinctive evaluative rankings; we can easily imagine the goods of various friends and relations occupying various intermediate positions.

The problem of how to understand our relation to the good of our loved ones is a difficult one, and insofar as it presents a problem for, or a gap in, my view, it also presents a problem for (or a gap in) all other views. However, I think the view put forward here is in a good position to allow for the existence of intermediaries between what is good and what is good for someone. After all, how recalcitrant an appearance is can be not only a matter of degree but can also vary from situation to situation. Thus the good of my loved one might give rise to recalcitrant appearances only in the presence or absence of other evaluative appearances. These facts about evaluative appearances can at least provide us with the basic materials to carve up an intermediate notion; however, a final assessment of the suitability of these materials will require a more detailed account than I can provide here.

I have claimed that my view is compatible with various substantive accounts of well-being, but the reader might have noted that at least one major account seems to be left aside; namely, objective lists. Although, strictly speaking, it is compatible with my view that the items in the list would be such as to generate recalcitrant appearances, this wouldn't be a particularly plausible position. However, objective list views do not aim to answer the desiderata I presented above, so I think it is fair to suggest that they are not trying to understand the same concept. In my understanding of the conceptual landscape, these are actually theories about what is, in fact, good *simpliciter*, but theories that claim that what is, in fact, good *simpliciter* is agent-relative. Here again, more remains to be said, but I hope to have taken at least one important step in giving an account of the notion of good for that does not leave us with competing candidates to be the formal end of practical reason.

Notes

A version of this chapter was presented at the Workshop on Desire and Good in Toronto in May 2007. I would like to thank all participants for their questions and comments. I would also like to thank for their comments on earlier versions of this paper, Ruth Chang, Bennett Helm, Tom Hurka, David Merli, Jennifer Nagel, Rob Shaver, Wayne Sumner, and Katja Vogt.

1. John Rawls. 1971. *A Theory of Justice*. Cambridge, Mass.: Belknap Press of Harvard University Press.

2. Some accounts of personal identity (nearly) collapse the distinction between interpersonal and intrapersonal redistribution, and obviously not everyone is convinced by Rawls's view that it is illicit to generalize from the intrapersonal to the interpersonal case as it will be clear below. However, Rawls is clearly tapping on an important intuition about redistribution.

3. See Sergio Tenenbaum. 2007. *Appearances of the Good: An Essay on the Nature of Practical Reason*. Cambridge: Cambridge University Press.

4. For a more detailed explanation of what I mean by the "formal end of practical reason and action," see *Appearances of the Good*. For brevity's sake, from now on, I'll simply refer to the "formal end of practical reason."

5. Immanuel Kant. 1997. *Critique of Practical Reason*. New York: Cambridge University Press.

6. I come back to this point later.

7. "Seems" is appropriate here, since Rawls's argument is certainly suggestive, but vague enough that one would not want to commit oneself to be advancing the only possible interpretation of the argument.

8. Donald H. Regan. 2004. "Why Am I My Brother's Keeper?" In Donald Wallace, ed. 2004. *Reason and Value: Themes from the Moral Philosophy of Joseph Raz*, xxx–xx. Oxford: Clarendon. Pp. 202–30.

9. The last section discusses some of the complications that need to be addressed.

10. Assuming, of course, there are no further candidates for such a role.

11. Joseph Raz, *Morality of Freedom*, (Oxford: Oxford University Press, 1986), p. 289.

12. Ibid., p. 296.

13. See M. Overvold. 1980. "Self-Interest and Self-Sacrifice," *Canadian Journal of Philosophy* 10:105–18, on the claim that an appropriate notion of what is good for the agent needs to make sense of cases of sacrifices as cases in which the agent chooses something that is not good for her.

14. For obvious reasons I'll from now on omit the qualification "as I understand it."

15. Stephen Darwall defines "well-being" in terms of what someone who cares for the agent would rationally want for the agent for the agent's own sake. Darwall's account comes closest in the literature to the one I am putting forward here, but it is not clear what we should say about what we would desire for the agent's own sake in cases of immoral actions. Darwall explicitly uses cases of sacrifice to argue against certain views of well-being. He rightly points out that

many desire accounts are unable to account for the fact that an agent might desire, and even rationally desire, to sacrifice herself for the sake of an other and should not lead us to conclude that the sacrifice is good for the agent. But by the same token, it also would seem wrong to say that sacrificing herself would be good for the agent in cases in which the agent is morally *required* to sacrifice herself. At the same time I find it hard to say that it would be rational to want for someone's sake that they perform an immoral action; at least, a quite plausible view about the rationality of morality would rule out this possibility. Of course, one could insist that even if it would be *irrational* to want that she does not sacrifice herself in these cases, it is rational to want that she does not sacrifice herself *for her sake*. But I find it hard to make sense of this idea, unless "well-being" is explicating "for her sake" rather than the other way around.

16. At this point I am only claiming that this is at a first glance an intuitive view. Many philosophers have denied that in such situations things are going well for her; Plato, for instance, famously claims that the tyrant harms himself.

17. It is not exactly what he says, but it is obviously implied by J. S. Mill. 1979. *Utilitarianism* (G. Sher, ed.). Indianapolis: Hackett.

18. It is worth noting that I am not saying that the utilitarian cannot add to his view a specific account of the relation between good and good for of the kind that I am suggesting. In fact, the account I propose in section 4 is compatible with utilitarianism.

19. I am ignoring grammatical issues of whether we should say "X is good" or "X would be good" for not-yet-realized states of affairs for the sake of simplicity.

20. I should point out that when considering these views, I am not claiming that they were put forth with the aim of answering the questions I am posing here.

21. Henry Sidgwick. 1981. *The Methods of Ethics*. Indianapolis: Hackett.

22. I am of course not claiming that these views are explicitly offered as attempts to address the problems I have raised.

23. This approach is compatible with thinking that the subject matter of morality cannot be described simply in terms of the pursuit of the greatest good. This is the view defended by Foot, within a broad Humean framework, in "Utilitarianism and the Virtues," *Mind*, 94, 196–209.However, since this does not make much difference to my argument, I will use it as a simplifying assumption that every action that morality recommends gets classified as "morally good."

24. For classic formulations of views along these lines, see B. Williams, "Internal and External Reasons" in his *Moral Luck* (New York: Cambridge University Press, 1982) and Philippa Foot, "Morality as a System of Hypothetical Imperatives" in her *Virtues and Vices and Other Essays in Moral Philosophy* (New York: Oxford University Press) pp. 157–74.

25. Or perhaps in case (b) between an end that Matty has and an end that *other* agents have, since it's not clear that Matty is in any way committed to morality.

26. See, for instance, Christine M. Korsgaard. 1997. "The Normativity of Instrumental Reason." In Garrett Cullity and Berys Gaut, eds. *Ethics and Practical Reason*. Oxford: Oxford University Press.

27. Overvold makes a similar point. See Overvold. "Self-Interest and Self-Sacrifice."

28. I don't really know of anyone who defends exactly such a view. Richard Kraut, however, does think that "in saying that our ultimate end should be happiness, Aristotle must be taken to mean that ultimately we are and should be aiming at *someone's* happiness, whether our own' or another's (Richard Kraut, *Aristotle on the Human Good*, (Princeton: Princeton University Press, 1989), p. 145).

29. See, for instance, Rosalind Hursthouse. 1999. *On Virtue Ethics*. Oxford: Oxford University Press.

30. We'll see below, when discussing *Wish and Duty*, a possible way around the objection for the Aristotelian.

31. See P. Foot. 2002. "Moral Beliefs." In P. Foot. 2002. *Virtues and Vices and Other Essays in Moral Philosophy*. New York: Oxford University Press.

32. McDowell makes a similar point in J. McDowell. 1996. "Two Sorts of Naturalism." In *Mind, Value, and Reality*. Cambridge, Mass.: Harvard University Press.

33. G. E. Moore. 1993. *Principia Ethica*, rev. ed. New York: Cambridge University Press; Regan. "Why Am I My Brother's Keeper?" 202–30.

34. This might seem not quite true for the Humean approach.

35. Michael Stocker. 1979. "Desiring the Bad: An Essay in Moral Psychology," *Journal of Philosophy* 76:738–53; J. David Velleman. 1992. "The Guise of the Good," *Nous* 26:3–26.

36. See Sergio Tenenbaum. *Appearances of the Good*.

37. For fascinating cases of recalcitrant illusions in the realm of theoretical reason regarding our beliefs about motion, see M. Kozhevnikov, and M. Hegarty. 2001. "Impetus Beliefs as Default Heuristics: Dissociation between Explicit and Implicit Knowledge about Motion," *Psychonomic Bulletin and Review* 8:439–53.

38. I am using "judging to be good" and "judging it to be bad" in a way that should be neutral between thinking that the attitude in question is an (evaluative) belief, or thinking that it is a different kind of all-out attitude peculiar to the practical realm. See, on this issue, Tenenbaum. *Appearances of the Good*.

39. Davidson famously distinguishes between "all things considered" and "all-out" judgments in Donald Davidson. 1980. "How Is Weakness of the Will Possible?" In Donald Davidson, ed. 1980. *Essays on Actions and Events*. Oxford: Clarendon.

40. I'll assume that at least some cases of *akrasia* involve a temporary reversal of one's all-out evaluative judgment. Although my view can be presented and argued for independently of this assumption, it does simplify matters a great deal to make it.

41. One must also make sure that one does not run afoul of the conditional fallacy, etc. But I'll not get into these complications here.

42. Of course, in light of difficulties justifying treating these mistakes differently, one might argue that we should hold agents that make these different kinds of mistakes to be equally blameworthy. But this position would also require a revision of our attitudes; all that I argue is that I can explain why

these attitudes are warranted, *assuming* that our ordinary views about blameworthiness and related matters are also justified.

43. Of course someone could have the same attitude of finding out that he didn't win the Nobel Prize that most people would have if they found out that they celebrated their birthdays on the wrong date. But I think in this case our views about how he's doing when he falsely believes would also change; after all, the Nobel Prize is, for this person, just an excuse to have a party.

44. G. Ainslie. 2001. *Breakdown of Will*. Cambridge: Cambridge University Press. Ainslie does not endorse this understanding of hyperbolic discounting as a form of illusion, though he does explicitly compare it with perceptual illusions.

45. I take it that some such phenomenon is what leads Cocking and Kennett to suggest that friendships can be morally dangerous. See D. Cocking, and J. Kennett. 2000. "Friendship and Moral Danger," *The Journal of Philosophy* 97: 278–96. Even if they are wrong that a good friend would help her friend to hide a body (see B. Helm. 2009. *Stanford Encyclopedia of Philosophy*. S.v. "Friendship."), a good friend would be *tempted* to help.

References

Ainslie, G. (2001). *Breakdown of will*. New York: Cambridge University Press.

Cocking, D., & Kennett, J. (2000). Friendship and moral danger. *The Journal of Philosophy, 97*, 278–296.

Davidson, D. (1980). How is Weakness of the Will Possible? In D. Davidson (Ed.), *Essays on actions and events* (pp. 21–42). Oxford: Clarendon Press.

Foot, P. (1985). Utilitarianism and the virtues. *Mind, 94*, 196–209.

Foot, P. (2002a). "Moral Belief" in her *Virtues and vices and other essays in moral philosophy:* Oxford University Press.

Foot, P. (2002b)"Morality as a System of Hypothetical Imperatives" in her *Virtues and Vices and Other Essays in Moral Philosophy* (New York: Oxford University Press) pp. 157–174

Helm, B. (2005). Friendship. *Stanford Encyclopedia of Philosophy*.

Hursthouse, R. (1999). *On virtue ethics:* Oxford University Press.

Kant, I. (1997). *Critique of practical reason* (M. J. Gregor, Trans.). New York: Cambridge University Press.

Korsgaard, C. M. (1997). The Normativity of Instrumental Reason. In G. Cullity & B. Gaut (Eds.), *Ethics and Practical Reason* (pp. 215–254). New York: Clarendon Press.

Kozhevnikov, M., & Hegarty, M. (2001). Impetus beliefs as default heuristics: Dissociation between explicit and implicit knowledge about motion. *Psychonomic Bulletin and Review, 8*(3), 439–453.

Kraut, *Aristotle on the Human Good*, (Princeton: Princeton University Press, 1989).

McDowell, J. (1996). Two sorts of naturalism, *Mind, value, and reality* (pp. 167–197). Cambridge, Mass.: Harvard University Press.

Mill, J. (1979). *Utilitarianism (G. Sher, Ed.)*. Indianapolis: Hackett Publishing Co.

Moore, G. E. (1993). *Principia Ethica (Revised Edition)*. New York: Cambridge Univ Pr.

Overvold, M. (1980). Self-Interest and Self-Sacrifice. *Canadian Journal of Philosophy, X*(1), 105–118.

Rawls, J. (1971). *A theory of justice*. Cambridge, Mass.: Belknap Press of Harvard University Press.

Raz, J. (1986). *The morality of freedom:* Oxford Univ. Press.

Regan, D. H. (2004). Why Am I My Brother's Keeper? In R. J. Wallace (Ed.), *Reason and Value: Themes from the Moral Philosophy of Joseph Raz* (202–230). Oxford: Clarendon Press.

Sidgwick, H. (1981). *The Methods of Ethics*. Indianapolis: Hackett.

Stocker, M. (1979). Desiring the Bad: an Essay in Moral Psychology. *Journal of Philosophy, 76*, 738–753.

Tenenbaum, S. (2007). *Appearances of the good: an essay on the nature of practical reason*. New York, Cambridge: Cambridge University Press.

Velleman, J. D. (1992). The Guise of the Good. *Nous, 26*(1), 3–26.

Williams, B. (1982) "Internal and External Reasons" in his *Moral Luck* (New York: Cambridge University Press.

10

Aspects, Guises, Species, and Knowing Something to Be Good

Philip Clark

Occasionally we catch philosophers agreeing, if not on answers then at least on what questions matter. At present, nearly anyone working in ethics will tell you we need to understand practical reasoning. And nearly anyone interested in practical reason will tell you we need to know whether one can pursue something without seeing it as good. I want to ask, of this latter question, whether it really does matter philosophically. I don't doubt that we need to understand how value is related to desire, reasons, deliberation, character, choice, action, and so on. But I am worried that the tendency to square off over the guise of the good is a distraction. Accordingly, I begin by considering why the relation between pursuit and value is philosophically interesting. Then I argue that if I am right about why it is interesting, we don't need to settle whether it is possible to pursue things without seeing them under the aspect of the good. Instead we should note that guises of the good are one thing and the guise-of-the-good thesis is another. The former may matter even if the latter does not.

As I see it, what makes guises of the good interesting is that they promise to yield a viable epistemology of value. Anscombe is the modern oracle. Channeling Aristotle, Aquinas, and Wittgenstein, and repelled by the moral philosophy of her time, she outlines an escape plan for those who would like to understand how we negotiate the so-called fact value gap. The rough idea is that if you want to see how the world can guide evaluative thought you need to look at a particular kind of thought that is neither value judgment per se nor evaluatively neutral factual belief. In this kind of thought, one looks at what a person is pursuing and tries to make sense of the pursuit in terms of the point the agent sees in it.

Suppose, for example, that you notice me spray painting my shoe. You ask why I am doing that, and I reply that this way my left shoe will weigh a little more than my right. You ask why I want the left shoe to weigh a little more. Now suppose I just look at you blankly and say, "That's it." I seem not to understand your puzzlement. You grasp for straws. "Is this some sort of performance art, on the theme of asymmetry?" "No." "Is someone going to weigh your shoes as part of some game?" "No. Why do you ask?" Anscombe's thought is that anyone who understands what the question is must be at least dimly aware that we have not reached an answer. There are, she thinks, answers that could close off this line of questioning, and part of understanding the question "Why?" is having some grip on the difference between answers that can be stopping points and answers that cannot. Perhaps I say, "Well, I have this inner ear problem and the paint helps me keep my balance." There is still plenty to be puzzled about here. One might wonder how I could believe such a small adjustment will affect my balance. But we have reached a turning point in the sequence of "Why?" questions. If you profess puzzlement about why I want to keep my balance, it will be you and not I who has become difficult to interpret. It will be my turn to try and figure you out.

Crucially, Anscombe is an objectivist about the distinction between answers that can be the end of the story and answers that cannot. If someone says, "Oh *now* I get it, he's making the left shoe a bit heavier than the right," and acts as if no further elaboration need be available, we will have to consider whether she is being sarcastic, perhaps, or whether she is just not trying to understand the overall pursuit. In the end we may be forced to conclude that she is as much in the dark as anyone else. So on Anscombe's view, success in this sort of understanding is a world-guided affair. The extent to which one can succeed depends, in part, on whether the behavior falls under the right sort of description.

It is not my purpose here to defend Anscombe's remarks, at least not to the death. I am just considering why the guise-of-the-good thesis is interesting, and I am using Anscombe to get at that. Still, it may help to consider a couple of worries one might have.

One worry is that the notions of intelligibility and understanding in play here come down to familiarity. True, some descriptions are stopping points and others are not, but maybe the difference is just that some descriptions make the behavior familiar to the questioner and others do not. Adding weight to left shoes is not an activity with which most of us are familiar, whereas keeping our balance is, and that's all there is to the difference in intelligibility. This makes intelligibility less objective than Anscombe thinks it is. Different people will be familiar with different things, so the answers that can be stopping points will vary from person to person.

I do not think we can rest, though, with this reduction to familiarity. Imagine a person who habitually interprets other people's emotions as being about him. When people are obviously annoyed, for instance, he systematically assumes they are annoyed with him. He has no idea why he does this. It makes no sense to him. In therapy, though, he talks with others who do the same thing. They've been there. They know what it's like. That is, they know what it's like to do this thing that they cannot understand. If understanding came down to familiarity, they would understand it. But they don't. Similar remarks apply to procrastination. Some delaying makes sense, but a lot does not, and yet many of us are intimately familiar with the kind that does not.

A second worry is that any baffling example can be redescribed in a way that makes it intelligible. Faced, for instance, with Raz's claim that "I cannot choose to have coffee because I love Sophocles,"[1] the philosopher goes to work. What if I believe Sophocles used coffee to heighten his creative powers? Can't I then choose to have coffee as a kind of tribute, perhaps as part of a ceremony marking the date of his death? So I can too choose to drink coffee because I love Sophocles!

This sort of response misses the point. One might even say it makes Anscombe's point. Raz aside, Anscombe will agree that this sort of redescription is often, perhaps always, possible. Her point is that in crafting the new example, one deploys one's knowledge of what sorts of descriptions make for intelligibility and what sorts do not. One does not invent just any old redescription. Rather, one cleverly exploits the sort of description that can make sense of the choice. Philosophers do this without reflecting on what they are doing. Anscombe just wants to suggest that by reflecting on the knowledge that we deploy in crafting these examples, we can begin to understand how the world guides our thought about value.

To pick up the story, then, we need to get value in here somewhere. As I said, the rough idea is that success in the kind of understanding that dispels Anscombe's question "Why?" occupies a position beyond evaluatively innocent factual description, but short of value judgment per se. By value judgment per se I mean the act of judging, of something, that it is good. And by judging of something that it is good I mean judging that it is actually desirable. To judge of something that it is actually desirable is not necessarily to judge that it is to be pursued, all things considered. Having decided that the swerve control feature in an automobile is actually desirable I may, upon learning that only the V6 has that feature, abandon my plan to get the swerve control feature. I go right on thinking the swerve control feature is actually desirable. But I judge that, all things considered, it's better to go with the four cylinder vehicle. It's just that you can't have everything that's actually desirable.

In contrast with judging of things that they are good, however, we also judge of certain kinds of things that they are good kinds of things. I am not sure this will seem like much of a contrast, but I want to suggest that it is. Claims about what sorts of things are good sorts of things are quite unambitious, in comparison with claims about what is good. Note, for instance, that one can hold that pleasure is a good sort of thing without holding that all pleasures are good. This is as easy as holding that a cat is a four-legged kind of thing without holding that all cats have four legs. It seems to me simply true that a cat is a four-legged kind of thing. But to say this is not to say of anything that it has four legs. Likewise it seems to me simply true that pleasure is a good sort of thing. But again, to say this is not to say of anything that it is good.

This is not the place to hash out precisely what we *are* saying, when we say a cat is a four-legged kind of thing. What matters is this: In saying this thing about cats we do not rule out the possibility of, say, three-legged cats. But we do rule out the possibility of three-legged cats of a certain sort. If we discovered groups of cats with three legs, we could, under some circumstances, find ourselves having to rethink whether a cat is a four-legged kind of thing. The situation could resemble that of a researcher who comes upon some flying squirrels, and is thereby forced to revise her earlier view that a squirrel is a flightless sort of thing. So at least some claims of the form "An F is a G sort of thing," do have some content. Roughly, they say every F is such that either it is G or a certain range of conditions obtains. Thus, for example, "A cat is a four-legged kind of thing" says every cat is such that either it has four legs, or it has lost one or more legs, or it had a birth defect, or some practical joker bred some three-legged cats, or . . ., where not just anything belongs on this list. If the cat's romping around on its three legs gets to look too much like the flying squirrel's gliding around on its extra skin, complete with a wider population of interbreeding three-legged cats, then the cat too will start to look like a counterexample.

Applying our analysis of "An F is a G sort of thing" to value, now, we get:

"An F is a good sort of thing" says every F is such that either it is good or . . ., where not just anything belongs on the list.

Thus, for example, "A pleasure is a good sort of thing" says every pleasure is such that either it is good or a certain range of conditions obtains. This leaves room, though, for the idea that the pleasures of the torturer (or the child who likes offering to share his cookie and then dashing the hopes of his classmates by giving them tiny crumbs) are not good. Whether a pleasure is good may depend on what the pleasure is taken in. The " . . ." part of the analysis covers the relevant conditions.

The analysis connects the idea of a good sort of thing with the idea of a thing's being good. How does Anscombe use this connection to explain our knowledge that things are good? The idea is that unless the conditions mentioned in the " . . ." clause do obtain, a thing's belonging to a good sort suffices as a ground for knowledge that it is good. In Anscombe's terms, a thing's being F, where an F is a good sort of thing, is "brute relative to" that thing's being good.[2] Let's suppose, for instance, that the satisfaction of a need is a good sort of thing. This means that barring conditions in the relevant range, a thing's being a satisfaction of a need is adequate to ground knowledge that it is good. The inference does not always go through. For instance, the fact that something satisfies the Hells Angels' need for an image makeover does not show that it is good. Nevertheless, the fact that something satisfies your choir's need for more tenors may suffice as a ground for knowledge that it is good.

Now I think we have the materials to sketch the Anscombian epistemology of value. Suppose it occurs to me that I'm spending a lot of time running to the third floor to use my computer. It would be convenient, I think, to have a computer on the first floor. How do I know it would be convenient? I know it on the basis of factual circumstances of the sort just mentioned; this way I can check my e-mail without having to run upstairs. These facts are "brute relative to" the conclusion that it would be convenient to have a computer downstairs. They may not entail that it is convenient, but they can still ground knowledge. Having ascertained that it would be convenient to have a computer on the first floor, I use my knowledge that convenience is a good sort of thing. How do I know convenience is a good sort of thing? I know it through my grasp of the Anscombian question "Why?" To understand that question, recall, is to understand what sorts of answers can be stopping points and what cannot. Convenience is the sort of thing that can be a stopping point. If you pretend to be baffled by my desire to have convenient access to something I use all the time, you are the one who will need to elaborate. This is how we know that convenience is a good sort of thing.

But of course we still have not arrived at knowledge that this instance of the convenient is good. Not all instances of the convenient are good. These days children have convenient access to pornography. A domestic dispute may escalate because a weapon happens to be lying around. Here Anscombe will say that although the fact that a thing is convenient does not entail that it is good, it is brute relative to that conclusion. In other words, it is going to show that the thing is good unless something stops it, and only certain sorts of things can stop it. In the story of me and my e-mail, there appears to be nothing to stop it. Hence, having a computer on the first floor is not only convenient, it is actually desirable; that is, good.[3]

Needless to say, convenience is but one example. To generate more examples of good sorts of things, we just think about what sorts of things can terminate a series of "Why?" questions. Here is a short list of examples. I've used adjectives, but one can add "the," as in "the convenient."

Interesting
Bold
A musing
Organized
Accurate
Comfortable
Accomplished
Tidy
Pure
Free
Strong
Tasty
Safe
Intelligible
Peaceful
Productive

Each of these has instances that are not good, I think. Yet each picks out a good sort of thing. Roadside carnage is interesting, even fascinating, particularly if the victims are human. Some dead baby jokes are funny; we've all struggled not to laugh at sick humor. Antifreeze is tasty, and lethal, to dogs. Voldemort is a highly accomplished wizard, a great wizard, in fact, but this instance of the great is terrible, not good. A tidied-up crime scene is often not a good instance of the tidy. Counterexamples like these can make the list seem philosophically uninteresting. Anscombe is almost unique, at least in our time, in suggesting that our capacity to construct such a list is what makes evaluative knowledge possible.

What makes evaluative knowledge possible, on the Anscombian view, is the same thing that makes most any knowledge possible. To know whether something is a snake, say, or whether something is frozen, you have to understand the question at hand. You have to know what is being asked in asking whether this thing is a snake, or whether that thing is frozen. Moreover, knowing what is being asked means knowing what sorts of considerations count for and against different answers. You need to know the relevance, for example, of whether the thing walks or slithers, or what heat would do to it. And then you use this grasp of what counts as evidence to infer, from what you already know about the thing, that it is or is not a snake, is or is not frozen, and so on. Likewise, understanding a question like "Would it be a good idea to get the brakes checked?" means knowing what sorts of things would count for and against different answers to that question. And this, in turn, means knowing what is and is not a good sort of thing. Our grasp of what does and does not belong on the list of stopping points for a series of "Why?" questions is thus vital to our capacity to know of something that it is good. But what goes on the list is an objective matter. It is available to anyone who understands what is requested in asking "Why?"

Philosophers familiar with the term "thick concept," a well-worn term of art in recent ethics, may be inclined to see the above as a list of thick concepts. But being a thick concept is not enough to get something on the list. Something can count as a thick concept even if the value judgment associated with it is false. "Unchaste" counts as a thick concept even if the evaluation it presupposes is not true. But to earn a place on Anscombe's list, an entry must actually be a good sort of thing. Again, Anscombe's objectivism is showing here. But it is a modest kind of objectivism, because the claim that something is a good kind of thing is not too ambitious. The modest objectivism does have garishly objectivist implications, though, when coupled with the idea that "good sort" is brute relative to "good."

A second difference between thick concepts and good sorts of things is that the evaluations that figure in thick concepts generally rest on some presumed connection with items on our list. Chastity takes us to items like the pure and the clean, for instance, as opposed to the impure, the spoiled, and the filthy. This is what makes it possible to think critically about the concept. One can consider whether the behaviors that count as chaste are instances of the pure and the clean at all, and whether they are desirable instances, especially in view of other items on the list, like the free, the pleasant, and the bold.

Let's go back, now, to the project of this chapter. The project was first to consider what makes guises of the good interesting, and then to suggest that in view of why they are interesting, we don't need to settle whether one can pursue a thing without seeing it as good. So far we are not even done explaining why the guise of the good is interesting. I have only provided a review, or maybe a sympathetic reconstruction, of Anscombe on how we know the good. The notion of an aspect, guise, or species of the good has not yet appeared.

Or has it?

I think it has, under the guise—if I may use that word—of a good sort of thing. When philosophers say things like "Everything wanted is wanted under the aspect of the good," what they are trying to say, I think, is that everything wanted is wanted under one or another description "F," such that the F is a good sort of thing. To want something under a description, moreover, is for that description to lie at the end of a sequence of answers to "Why?" questions. Thus, for example, a computer on the first floor is something you want under the description "convenient" if the reason why you want it winds up in an appeal to the convenience of it. And if the reason does wind up there, that suffices to qualify you as wanting the thing under the aspect, guise, or species of the good. It suffices because the convenient is a good sort of thing.

Notice that on this view it is misleading to speak of the guise of the good as if there were just one. If a guise of the good is just a good sort of thing then there are as many guises, aspects, or species of the good as there are items on the list of stopping points.[4]

Now at last we can say why guises of the good are interesting. They are interesting for the same reason that good sorts of things are interesting. And good sorts of things are interesting because by noticing that they exist, that they lie between pure fact and value judgment per se, and that we grasp them through our understanding of the question "Why?" we can understand how we know what is good. This is more than any non-cognitivist or non-naturalist can give us, and it spans the gap without reducing value to fact, so we really ought to be riveted by guises of the good.

Now let's turn to the traditional dispute about the guise of the good. This is a dispute about a class of claims linking pursuit to the perception of value. The class includes the following:

i) Everything wanted is wanted under the aspect of the good
ii) In acting intentionally, one necessarily aims at something one sees as good
and iii) Nothing can count as a person's reason for acting unless it links the action to something the agent sees as good.

Do we need to know whether these claims are true? If these claims are just crazy, that seems worth knowing. And they will be crazy, if we take seeing something as good, or under the aspect of the good, as judging or believing the thing to be good.[5] Counterexamples abound, but we need look no farther than Satan, who wants to do evil, acts intentionally, has his reasons, and is under no illusion that the things he does are good. Indeed, the thought that his instances of corruption, pestilence, and ruination are good would take the fun out of it for him.

But my suggestion is that the reason philosophers reach for these curious words *aspect*, *guise*, and *species*, rather than just saying you can't pursue anything unless you think it is good, is that they are trying to say something else. They are trying to say that you can't pursue anything except under some description "F," such that the F is a good sort of thing, a thing belonging to the list begun above.[6] If that is what they are trying to say, then what they are saying is not crazy. We can easily imagine, for instance, that Satan's desires terminate in good sorts of things, without imagining that he thinks the things he wants are good. This is just what Anscombe does imagine:

> 'Evil be thou my good' is often thought to be senseless in some way. Now all that concerns us here is that 'What's the good of it?' is something that can be asked until a desirability characterization has been reached and made intelligible. If then the answer to this question at some stage is 'The good of it is that it's bad,' this need not be unintelligible; one can go on to say 'And what is the good of its being bad?' to which the answer might be condemnation of good as impotent, slavish and inglorious. Then the good of making evil my good is my intact liberty in the unsubmissiveness of my will.[7]

David Velleman reads this as suggesting that Satan is moved by a thought of good. And he notes that this makes Satan look like a lover of the good, a "rather sappy Satan."[8] But I am suggesting that to read her more charitably we should take her to mean that Satan is moved, not by a thought that something is good, but by a thought of a good sort of thing. Her suggestion is that what qualifies Satan as seeing his bad acts under the aspect of some good is that he sees them as instances of the strong, the free, and the uncowed, as opposed to the impotent, the slavish, and the inglorious. He is right that his acts of corruption, pestilence, and ruination are instances of the strong, the free and the uncowed. And the strong, the free, and the uncowed really are good sorts of things. But what Satan knows as well as anyone is that his acts are not good instances of these sorts of things. They are bad instances of good sorts of things, just as a tidied up crime scene is a bad instance of the tidy. In fact, it is because he sees his deeds as bad that Satan sees them as instances of intact liberty in the unsubmissiveness of his will. Good acts are what God wants, so they amount to slavish submission. There is nothing sappy about Satan, so construed. He does not act from a thought of good, since he does not think his acts are good. Moreover, we can see why the thought that his deeds are good would take the fun out of it for him.

On a charitable reading, the disputed claims are not crazy. This is not to say they are true. But is there any urgency about this residual dispute? At least one author has chosen to set it aside. In an article called "Putting Rationality in Its Place," Warren Quinn argues, not that desires are necessarily for things-seen-as-good, but that if a desire is to "rationalize action" it must be for something seen as good. Inspired by similar examples from Anscombe and Foot, he deploys a thought experiment in which someone goes around turning on radios:

> Suppose I am in a strange functional state that disposes me to turn on radios that I see to be turned off. Given the perception that a radio in my vicinity is off, I try, all other things being equal, to get it turned on. Does this state rationalize my choices? Told nothing more than this, one may certainly doubt that it does. But in the case I am imagining, this is all there is to the state. I do not turn the radios on in order to hear music or get news. It is not that I have an inordinate appetite for entertainment or information. Indeed, I do not turn them on in order to *hear* anything.[9]

What is interesting about Quinn's approach is that he is "careful not to raise the question" whether the person in the example has a desire to turn on radios, or wants to turn on radios.[10] Quinn's attitude appears to be "Call it a desire if you want. Then my thesis is that among desires, the ones that rationalize are the ones that are connected with value in some way." The effect of this is to focus our attention on the kinds of things that can make sense of a pursuit, and to set aside questions about whether all pursuit is oriented to the good. In focusing attention on what can make sense of a pursuit, Quinn is directing us to the knowledge we have of what sorts of things can terminate a series of "Why?" questions. It is that knowledge, I claimed, that Anscombe wants to use to explain evaluative knowledge. So Quinn's handling of the issues takes us to what I said was interesting about guises of the good, while leaving aside the residual puzzle about whether everything pursued is pursued under the aspect of some good. It homes in on guises of the good while leaving the guise-of-the-good thesis aside.

Note also that Quinn does not say guises of the good are the only things that can make sense of a desire. As Michael Stocker points out, sometimes a desire is made intelligible not by the nature of its object but by the attitude or emotion from which it flows, as when we act from hatred or anger.[11] When that happens there may be nothing in the nature of what is wanted that makes sense of the desire. One may have to look behind the desire, so to speak, rather than in front of it. Such examples challenge the guise-of-the-good thesis. If Stocker is right, they are cases where what is wanted is not wanted under any guise of the good. But Stocker's examples do not challenge the idea that guises of the good are what make evaluative knowledge possible. The Anscombian position, as I see it, is that in order to understand how we know something is good we have to look in front of desire, at the thing wanted, and notice that some objects of desire make the wanting intelligible and others do not. We may not need guises of the good to understand a desire, but we do need them to understand the epistemology of value.

There will be those who want to defend the guise-of-the-good thesis against these and other counterexamples, and I am not out to deter them. But I suggest that we pause and ask what actually hangs on that dispute. Meanwhile we should be enthralled with guises of the good themselves, because they may well tell us how we know things are good.[12]

Notes

1. Raz, 1999: 8.

2. See Anscombe, 1981, especially page 28.

3. Here we exploit a difference between knowing values and knowing animals. Something's being a horse is a rather weak ground for thinking it has between thirty-six and forty-two teeth. Better to count. By contrast, its being convenient to have a computer downstairs can be quite a strong ground for believing it would be a good idea.

4. Anscombe (1976: 75) says "*Bonum est* multiplex: good is multiform," and goes on to speak of wanting a thing under the aspect of *some* good, rather than the aspect of *the* good.

5. See Stocker, 1979 and Setiya, 2007: 39–48 and 59–67.

6. Michael Stocker quotes Joseph Raz saying roughly this. See Stocker, 2008: 125.

7. Anscombe, 1976: 75.

8. Velleman, 2000: 119.

9. Quinn, 1993: 236.

10. Quinn, 1993: 246.

11. See Stocker, 2004 and 2008.

12. For their help with this chapter I thank Judith Baker, Andrew Furtado, Jessica Moss, Kieran Setiya, Wayne Sumner, Sergio Tenenbaum, and Jennifer Whiting.

References

Anscombe, G. E. M. (1976) *Intention*. Ithaca: Cornell University Press.

(1981) "On Brute Facts" and "Modern Moral Philosophy," in *Ethics, Religion, and Politics*. (The Collected Philosophical Papers of G. E. M. Anscombe; v. 3) Minneapolis: University of Minnesota Press, 22–42.

Quinn, Warren. (1993) "Putting Rationality in Its Place," in Philippa Foot ed., *Morality and Action*. Cambridge: Cambridge University Press, 228–255.

Raz, Joseph. (1999) "When We Are Ourselves: The Active and the Passive," in *Engaging Reason*. Oxford: Oxford University Press, 5–21.

Setiya, Kieran. (2007) *Reasons without Rationalism*. Princeton: Princeton University Press.

Stocker, Michael. (1979) "Desiring the Bad," *Journal of Philosophy* 79:738–753.

(2004) "Raz on the Intelligibility of Bad Acts," in R. Jay Wallace, Philip Pettit, Samuel Scheffler, and Michael Smith eds., *Reason and Value: Themes from the Moral Philosophy of Joseph Raz*. Oxford: Oxford University Press, 303–332.

(2008) "On the Intelligibility of Bad Acts," in D. K. Chan ed., *Moral Psychology Today: Essays on Values, Rational Choice and the Will*. Dordrecht: Springer Netherlands, 123–140.

Velleman, David. (2000) "The Guise of the Good," in *The Possibility of Practical Reason*. New York: Oxford University Press, 99–122.

Contributors

Rachel Barney is an associate professor and Canada Research Chair in Classical Philosophy at the University of Toronto. She is author of *Names and Nature in Plato's Cratylus* (2001), and various articles on Plato, Aristotle, Stoicism, Neoplatonism and the sophists.

Matthew Boyle is an assistant professor of philosophy at Harvard University. He has written on topics in philosophy of mind and moral psychology, and is presently completing a book on the nature and significance of self-consciousness.

Philip Clark is an associate professor of philosophy at the University of Toronto. He writes mainly on ethics, metaethics, and practical reason.

Matthew Evans is an assistant professor of philosophy at New York University. He is the author of several articles on Plato's ethics and philosophy of mind.

Douglas Lavin is an associate professor of philosophy at Harvard University. His main interests are in ethics and the philosophy of action.

Jessica Moss is a Fellow in Ancient Philosophy at Balliol College and lecturer of philosophy at Oxford. She is the author of several articles on moral psychology in Plato and Aristotle, and at work on a book on pleasure, perception, imagination, and desire in Aristotle.

Joseph Raz is the Thomas M. Macioce Professor of Law at Columbia Law School. He is the author of *Between Authority and Interpretation* (Oxford University Press, 2009), *The Practice of Value* (Oxford University Press, 2003), *Value, Respect and Attachment* (2002), *Engaging Reason* (Oxford University Press, 2000), and other works.

Sebastian Rödl is a professor of philosophy at the University of Basle. He is the author of *Self-Consciousness* (2007), and various articles on the philosophy of mind and the theory of action, as well as articles on Hegel and Kant.

Kieran Setiya is an associate professor of philosophy at the University of Pittsburgh. He works primarily on questions in ethics and action theory, and is the author of *Reasons without Rationalism* (2007).

Sergio Tenenbaum is an associate professor of philosophy at the University of Toronto. He is the author of *Appearances of the Good* (2007), and various articles on ethics, moral psychology, and Kant's ethics.

Index

Tappolet, C., 25 n. 2
Taylor, C.C.W., 25 n. 1, 28 n. 29, 80
    n. 35
teleological explanation, 194 n. 4 (*see
    also* action, teleological v. causal
    explanation of)
telos, 69–70
temptation, 208, 226–28
Tenenbaum, S., 5, 25 n. 2, 61 n. 42,
    105 n. 4, 108 n. 30, 199 n. 38,
    229 n. 3, 231 n. 36
thick concepts, 239
Thompson, M., 101–2, 103, 104, 106
    n. 7, 159 n. 15, 197 nn. 22&24,
    198 nn. 27&30
Thomson, J.J., 106 n. 12
true
    as formal object of the intellect,
        139, 140–41
truth, 190–91
Tuozzo, T., 80 n. 36

uncodifiability, 96
utilitarianism, 202

value judgment, 236
Velleman, J.D., 29 n. 37, 106 n. 6,
    111–14, 133–34, 135 n. 6, 160 n.
    21, 168, 194 n. 1, 195 n. 10, 196
    n. 19, 241
vice, 99–100

virtue, 34, 38, 95–98
Vlastos, G., 25 nn. 1&5, 28 n. 32, 41,
    58 nn. 19&25

Wallace, J., 135 n. 13
Wallace, R.J., 106 n. 8, 107 n. 21
Watson, G., 25 n. 2, 30 n. 46, 161–62
weakness claim, 7
Wedgwood, R., 108 n. 30
Weiss, R., 28 n. 26, 57 n. 11
welfare. *See* well-being
well-being, 203, 205, 228, 229–30
    n. 15
Whiting, J., 78 n. 22
Wiggins, D., 198 n. 27
will
    as defined by Kant, 145, 149
    as practical reason, 143–45,
        152–53
    causality of, 144–45, 152–53
    formal object of, 139
    weakness of (*see* akrasia)
Williams, B., 108 n. 31, 230 n. 24
Wilson, G., 107 n. 24
wish, 66
Wittgenstein, L., 141, 168, 173, 234,
    195 n. 9
Wolfsdorf, D., 25 n. 1
wrongdoing, 34, 35–36, 54

Zeyl, D.J., 25 n. 1